Michigan's
Lumbertowns

Great Lakes Books

*A complete listing of the books in this series
can be found online at http://wsupress.wayne.edu*

Philip P. Mason, Editor
*Department of History,
Wayne State University*

Dr. Charles K. Hyde, Editor
*Department of History,
Wayne State University*

Michigan's Lumbertowns

Lumbermen and Laborers in Saginaw,

Bay City, and Muskegon, 1870–1905

JEREMY W. KILAR

WAYNE STATE UNIVERSITY PRESS
DETROIT

ISBN-13: 978-0-8143-2073-0   ISBN-10: 0-8143-2073-2

**Library of Congress Cataloging-in-
Publication Data**

Kilar, Jeremy W.
    Michigan's lumbertowns : lumbermen
and laborers in Saginaw, Bay City, and
Muskegon, 1870–1905 / Jeremy W. Kilar.
       p.   cm. — (Great Lakes books)
    Includes bibliographical references.
    ISBN 0–8143–2072–4. —
    ISBN 0–8143–2073–2 (pbk.)
    1. Lumber trade—Michigan—History.
2. Michigan—Industries—History.
3. Saginaw (Mich.)—Economic
conditions. 4. Bay City (Mich.)—
Economic conditions. 5. Muskegon
(Mich.)—Economic conditions.
I. Title. II. Series.
HD9757.M5K54 1990
330.9774'46041—dc20   89–38826
                                 CIP

Portions of this book previously appeared in
somewhat altered form as Jeremy W. Kilar,
"Great Lakes Lumber Towns and Frontier Violence: A Comparative Study," *Journal of Forest
History* 32 (April 1987): 71–85; Jeremy W.
Kilar, "Black Pioneers in the Michigan Lumber
Industry," *Journal of Forest History* 24 (July
1980): 142–51; Jeremy W. Kilar, "Community
and Authority Response to the Saginaw Valley
Lumber Strike of 1885," *Journal of Forest History* 20 (April 1976): 67–79. The author grate-
fully acknowledges permission to reprint.

For my mother
Sophie M. Kilar
1915–1989

Contents

Illustrations and Maps

9

The last big drive of 1887
Muskegon Booming Company sorting grounds
George J. Tillotson's mill
Biedler Manufacturing Company
Lumber inspectors
Western Avenue, east from First Street
The Opera House
Muskegon's first fire department
Burned district, March 1887
Charles Hackley's house
Mill workers
Bridge Street boardinghouse
Carpenters and Joiners Union Local No. 100
Charles Hackley
Thomas Hume, December 26, 1917

Maps

Acknowledgments

Twenty years ago, when I first came to the Saginaw Valley, there were few visible reminders left of the once gigantic logging and lumber trade that existed along the Saginaw River. The discerning observer could still see rotting wharf posts and a few skeletons of sunken lumber barges in the muddy banks of the Saginaw, and the lumbermens' mansions remained, some restored to dignity and eminence along tree-shaded streets. The townspeople were largely unaware of their communities' once proud past. My study of Michigan's leading lumbertowns began when I became curious about the largely unexamined story of logging in the state's first and largest commercial lumbering area.

Michigan's Lumbertowns grew out of several preliminary articles published in the *Journal of Forest History* and is a revision of my doctoral dissertation presented at the University of Michigan. During these years of writing, many individuals and institutions inspired, encouraged, and contributed to my research. I am especially grateful to Robert F. Berkhofer, who encouraged me throughout the dissertation stages, influenced the shape of the manuscript, and championed the broad, interdisciplinary approach evidenced in the study. Likewise, Maris A. Vinovskis, Patrick C. West, and David L. Lewis were always supportive and suggested several useful changes in the revised manuscript.

This undertaking would not have been possible without the inspiration and encouragement of past mentors. William T. Bulger at Central Michigan University and Henry F. Vassel instilled in me years ago the foundations that enabled me to pursue this study.

Delta College gave me invaluable time and financial support to complete both the dissertation and book-length manuscript.

People at several historical societies helped with manuscript and photographic material. Barbara Martin of the Muskegon County Museum, Charles Hoover and Thomas F. Trombley of the Historical Society of Saginaw County, and Dawn Meisel, curator of collections at the Historical Museum of Bay County, all provided helpful direction to their photograph collections. Robert Fleming at Delta College helped with photographic reproductions, and Jennifer Lundahl gave considerable time to sketch the maps and illustrations used in the text. Judy Brow and Esther Berkan of Delta's library were always available to fulfill special requests.

I am most appreciative of the advice of my colleague, Fred W. Renker of the English department at Delta College, who read and edited the manuscript, and Laurel Brandt and Anne Adamus of Wayne State University Press, who gave many thoughtful suggestions throughout the revision process. I also owe a special thanks to Connie Cron, who did the thankless job of typing the first manuscript, and to Susan Richmond, who processed the final copies.

Special recognition must also be granted my wife, Mignon Weber-Kilar, and my children, Annalisa and Stephen, who say they have heard too many lumber stories and consequently suffered more than the author throughout this endeavor.

Introduction

Cities—or "urban regions"—thus constituted a kind of way-station between the old village society and modern American society, and, indeed, were a most important catalyst in the making of our contemporary national community. Though urban society was local in its origins, rapid growth and economic-cultural dominance over wide adjoining areas combined to transform the world we have lost to the world we now have.

—DAVID J. RUSSO, *Families and Communities*

Two out of every three pine trees that came crashing to the ground in Michigan's Lower Peninsula in the nineteenth century ended up in Saginaw, or Bay City, or Muskegon. By 1880 there were about 120 sawmills stretching along the Saginaw River and nearly 50 surrounding Muskegon Lake. If men were going to make fortunes cutting and selling pine, Saginaw, Bay City, and Muskegon were the places to begin. Energetic lumbermen hired thousands of mill hands, who worked twelve-hour shifts six days a week, operating the saws that chewed up the logs brought from the state's interior forests. The noisy mill towns became wide-open and wicked. To these towns—with their gaslights, saloons, and bawdy houses—the lumberman, the shanty boy, the mill man, and the immigrant laborer all came looking for excitement and success.

Michigan's Lumbertowns is a comparative study of three lumbertowns in the late nineteenth century. Community studies of this sort usually fall into two classifications: the city or town "biography"—often a narrative chronicling local events—and the case study—in which the author intends to compare and generalize with other communities. This book falls into both categories. Because historians have generally ignored the history of Michigan's leading lumber mill towns, this book may be seen as an urban biography that studies local events previously chronicled only by folklorists, journalists, and memorialists.[1] The foremost lumbertowns in Michigan evolved from the wilderness to become flourishing urban industrial centers. The story of how a complex socio-cultural and economic landscape emerged and transformed these lumbertowns requires careful recounting by the professional historian.

More important, the study of town and city success, failure, or merely continued existence is better understood if we know how a town compares with the experience of other towns and cities. That the once prosperous lumbertowns did not become ghost towns but instead, after decades of adjustment, reemerged as twentieth-century industrial cities emphasizes that all natural-resource towns in the nineteenth century had convulsive lives. Like a living organism, a city or town may experience different stages of maturity. Some towns—often those based on a limited natural resource—had relatively short lives; other towns survived, prospered, and grew to become metropolitan centers. Yet many towns or cities lived on, neither dying nor achieving great heights, yet continuing to provide a relatively decent standard of living for their residents. To varied degrees these places maintained a rugged durability that simply kept them going.

A few historians have written about settlements that became ghost towns, and many have written of cities that experienced rapid and phenomenal growth. Others have examined small New England towns that never grew, or larger inland communities that emerged as great cities or typical American towns. But little effort has been made to bridge the gap between success and failure—at least for the nineteenth century—and unfold the history of towns or cities that persevered amid recurrent economic predicaments. Although there are many places like Chicago or Denver or Cripple Creek or Silver City, there are also hundreds of places like Saginaw, Bay City, and Muskegon, familiar only to those who live in or near them.

The question is, Why did so many towns or cities fail to develop fully even with the best will at their command? David Russo points out that "neither town nor city historians provide an adequate answer to the question because neither group is sufficiently concerned about the other's community." Town biographies and urban histories are often written in isolation, yet what is significant and distinctive will stand out only if we place each community's past in a proper comparative perspective.[2] The three lumbertowns I have chosen are ideal for a comparative history explaining the durability of midsized industrial towns.

Saginaw, Bay City, and Muskegon had the qualities necessary for urban prosperity. They began in the 1830s as Midwest "booster" towns, attracting businessmen who created "paper cities" that were in turn sold in all-out competition. They had natural locational advantages: good harbors and major river thoroughfares into the forested interior. More important than geography, though, was a "break in transportation." "The greatest centers will be those where the physical transfer of goods (from one conveyance to another) is accomplished with a change in ownership."[3] In lumbertowns, logs were cut into boards and then shipped to distant markets. The transportation break encouraged the development of banks, exchanges, warehouses, and spin-off industries. Economic and locational advantages enabled Saginaw, Bay City, and Muskegon to become the three leading lumber ports in the state. Between 1870 and 1888 no other logging centers came close in output of lumber. The cities were not only alike in their importance but also shared a similar origin, geography, economy, and population (ranging from twenty-five thousand to forty-five thousand). They became core cities serving regional areas, yet each was far enough away from a large metropolitan center that its frontier nature was preserved for some time, and its economy could develop without overwhelming competition.

Kenneth Jackson and Stanley Schultz note that the "difference between prosperity and stagnation for a city frequently lay in its leaders and the degree to which they were willing to risk their resources in the struggle for economic empire." That is, the success or failure of a city "depended on its locational advantages *and on* the aggressiveness and foresight of its civic and business leaders."[4] This observation is critical in evaluating the abilities of lumbertowns to first prosper, and then continue to exist when natural resources gave out. Even more critical to examining lumbertowns or other Midwestern and Western natural resource towns was the issue of resident versus absentee leadership. As can be seen for Bay City, absentee ownership caused abdication of economic leadership when trees and lumber were no longer available. The aggressive business leaders essential to ensure a town's viability were often present only during short periods of rapid economic expansion. When natural resources were depleted, an entrepreneur often abandoned the town he helped establish and moved on to greener forests. Yet in Saginaw and Muskegon some lumbermen persisted, investing millions in these communities to help restore an economic base. When profits were so large in a business that simply required another migratory step westward, why were some businessmen willing to stick it out in towns whose futures looked so bleak?

Besides variations in the nature of each town's lumbermen-entrepreneurs, there is another critical point in determining successful urban status: ethnic composition. Bay City had large and persistent ethnic blocs that were internally more cohesive than those in Saginaw and Muskegon. This difference, coupled with entrepreneurship, may help explain why a community turned into a Saginaw or Muskegon or into a Bay City—that is, into cities of medium size experiencing reasonable growth, or into a town of broken dreams with unfulfilled and limited ambitions. People helped determine what type of community a lumbertown became, and the individual lumberman's perception of community often influenced his reinvestment decisions.

Divergent cultural traits developed during the heyday of the lumbering era adumbrated the economic future of leading lumbering centers. At the end of the nineteenth century, when there was nothing left to cut, the lumbertowns were thrown on their own resources. Reflecting their individual cultural identities, each lumbertown developed dissimilar efforts to sustain urban industrial status. Although all three communities managed to survive, each community interpreted progress differently. Saginaw recovered and more than doubled its lumber-era population. Muskegon, struggling against the greatest odds, reclaimed a remarkable semblance of prosperity. Bay City procrastinated, debated, and in the end adopted a form of nongrowth durability. An examination of these three towns before and during the postlumber era provides a vantage point from which to generalize about communities at large.

This book concentrates on the period when demand, technology, and capital came together and permitted the frontier mill towns to emerge as mechanized industrial islands in the wilderness. The "lumber era" for Saginaw, Bay City, and Muskegon began shortly after the Civil War and lasted one generation. Between 1870 and 1890 all the trees were cut; in the late nineteenth century declining natural-resource towns had to reassess local progress. By 1905 each community had economically and politically redirected itself into the twentieth century. Within this time frame the scope of the twin themes of entrepreneurship and ethnicity, several interrelated propositions will be investigated.

How did the urban impulse—the quest for "progress"—dominate the entrepreneurial motives of the lumbertowns' settlers? Despite locational advantages, it was by no means predestined, which capitalist or which city would become a leader in the lumber business. Focusing on the lumbertowns' beginnings, early chapters portray the entrepreneurs who founded and established the lumber industry in the three Michigan communities. The role of absentee owners and their effect on the economic and cultural milieu of the community is compared and contrasted with that of resident lumbermen.

Lumbertowns were multiethnic cities in which class affiliations were often subordinate to ethnic and occupational group attachments. Cultural divisions and behavioral differences between ethnic groups and between the three communities were wide, as evidenced by different family strategies regarding work, schooling, and home ownership, and by responses to the economic and political environment in each city. How did the various ethnic groups change or contribute to the stability of lumbertowns? Immigrant workers in each lumbertown are examined as ethnic status groups seeking a role in society, which either reinforced community bonds or alienated and ostracized cultural segments from the community.

For years, lumber historians have stated that the lumbertowns could easily match the cow towns and mining camps "blow for blow with action, mayhem, tragedy, violence, color, loneliness, songs and legends."[5] Prostitution, physical violence, and homicide characterized these frontier communities. Logging centers were much like cattle towns: both prospered in the same period; both had populations that were seasonal and transient; they catered to a free-spending laborer logger or cowboy who had just finished a seasonal drive; and both experienced mayhem and violence. How, then, do lumbertowns' experiences fit in the American frontier tradition? Did the lumbertowns make necessary adjustments to violence to preserve the lucrative business of the lumberjack?[6] Did the toleration of violence in any way affect the future social and economic development of individual lumbertowns?

This book examines the interaction of three communities' social, cultural, and economic institutions and assesses the effect on peoples' lives. Community experience defines the entrepreneurial character of the lumbertowns' sawdust barons as well as the character of the laboring mill men. This experience explains how the forces for progress induced changes that presaged the socioeconomic future of each lumbertown.

CHAPTER ONE

Lumbering and Lumbertowns

The Americans regard the forest as a symbol of the wilderness, and consequently of backwardness; so it is against the trees that they direct their onslaughts. In Europe trees are cut down to be used; in America, to be destroyed. The man who lives in the country spends half his life in fighting his natural enemy, the forest; he goes at it without respite. . . . The absence of trees is the sign of civilization, as their presence indicates barbarity.

—GUSTAVE DE BEAUMONT, Marie or, Slavery in the United States: A Novel of Jacksonian America

In 1831 Alexis de Tocqueville and Gustave de Beaumont sailed to the New World as young magistrates commissioned by the French government to study American prison reform. At first neither Tocqueville nor Beaumont envisioned traveling west to the Michigan Territory. However, having come this far, they were determined to experience the American wilderness—"an altogether savage region." They were told at Buffalo and Detroit that the "last inhabited place till the Pacific" in the country was the small settlement along the Saginaw River.[1] Unwilling to wait for a steamboat, the travelers trekked overland from Detroit along an overgrown military road to the Saginaw settlement. Tocqueville described the outpost as consisting of four or five log cabins: "Thirty persons, men, women, old people, and children at the time of our visit composed this little society, as yet scarcely formed—an opening seed thrown upon the desert, there to germinate."[2]

One would have to search far to find a more striking picture of the vast forests in their primitive magnificence than that etched by Tocqueville and Beaumont. South of Saginaw the travelers stopped to measure the circumference of a towering pine. They stood in awe before what was perhaps the finest pine forest in the Great Lakes states. Yet, within this grandeur, the American pioneer was intent

on removing every last tree. The forest was the settlers' chief obsta-
cle to survival and only when the trees were gone did they experience civilization. Couple this need to clear the land with the "self-
interest" of the parsimonious Puritan settlers that Tocqueville and
Beaumont found in central Michigan and soon some enterprising
person would discover that enormous profits could be made from
cutting the forest and selling the wood. Tocqueville and Beaumont's
two-week escape into the Michigan wilds not only provided invaluable imagery and commentary on the land in its primitive state but
also offered serious insight into the developing social and economic
landscape that soon would witness "the sons of civilization and industry breaking the silence of the Saginaw."[3]

LOCATING THE LUMBERTOWNS

The pine forest that so impressed Tocqueville and Beaumont was
destined to attract knowledgeable lumbermen and become the center of a great logging industry. Yet until the mid-1830s there was
little reason for anyone to get too excited about the pine trees in
Michigan. Eastern populations were still receiving their timber from
Maine, Pennsylvania, and upstate New York; and although Chicago
was beginning to grow, the Western states had not reached a point
where their lumber needs required imported timber. Pine remained a
"latent resource" until the demand and the technological ability
were developed to exploit it.[4]

The settlement of Michigan fortunately coincided with the
changing market for timber in both the East and West. Although
the Michigan Territory was opened to settlers in 1818, its population—which stood at 8,896 in 1820—grew slowly until the Erie Canal was opened in 1825. Still, by 1830 the territory had only 31,639
inhabitants. Not until the speculative land boom of the 1830s did
people begin to immigrate in numbers. When Michigan entered the
Union in 1837, its population was nearly 175,000.[5] Population
growth increased demands for building materials. By the mid-1830s a
few scattered sawmills were being built along the state's major
streams: the Saint Clair, Grand, Saginaw, and Muskegon rivers. Until about 1840 these sawmills were built to supply local markets.

It was the growing demand for Michigan pine in the Midwest,
though, that stirred the interest of the lumbermen-investors from
Maine and New York in Michigan pinelands. As Chicago grew and

the Midwestern prairies began to be settled, there developed an almost insatiable demand for building materials. After the Panic of 1837, Eastern buyers began purchasing timberlands in the Lower Peninsula.[6] Not until 1847, however, when the supply of timber in upstate New York was rapidly dwindling, did Michigan pine make a profitable entry into the Albany and Tonawanda lumber markets. By the end of the Civil War, both Eastern and Midwestern lumber centers depended on Michigan for pine boards.

The lumber industry in Michigan thus developed into two main geographical districts. The eastern district was the first to be extensively exploited and peaked in 1882. It comprised the cities along the Saginaw River, various production points along northern Lake Huron, a few scattered lumber mill towns in the Thumb area, and the eastern interior Lower Peninsula. The principal markets for this district were the lumberyards in Tonawanda, Buffalo, and Albany. Sailing vessels and lake steamers transported finished lumber to the yards where canal and rail connections gave access to Eastern markets.

The western, or Chicago, district was centered on the lumberyards throughout the Chicago and southern Lake Michigan area. Mill towns along the western shore of the Lower Peninsula—especially Muskegon, Manistee, Ludington, and Marinette-Menominee—the shore of Green Bay, and the Upper Peninsula sent timber to Chicago. The rail network radiating throughout the Midwest from Chicago enabled it to supply the vast, newly settled Plains states with lumber.[7] Chicago itself was a ravenous consumer of lumber especially after the 1871 fire.

Natural transport routes were the most important physical factors that affected the location of the lumber mill towns and distribution centers that made up these two districts. Michigan's location on the Great Lakes gave it an unrivaled water transport network. Timber could be stored and dried conveniently at port cities and shipped cheaply and quickly to major lumberyards in the East and West. The largest port cities—Saginaw, Bay City, and Muskegon—had safe harbors, extensive nearby waterways in which to store logs to continuously feed the sawmills, and easy access to the interior supply of Michigan pine.

Michigan's pine woods covered about two-thirds of the Lower Peninsula. The best pine was north of an east-west line from Bay City to Muskegon. In this midstate region, the forests were not exclusively pine but mixed softwoods and hardwoods. Yet there were belts of pine, like the one running for eighty miles along the Tittabawassee River; here was the best pine in the state. Full-grown pines reached 175 feet with diameters between 2 and 7 feet. A hearty tree, the white pine had unsurpassed building qualities. It had few knots and was clear, light, soft, and easily worked; it became the nation's basic building material.

Although the pine tree was the "green gold" that attracted the lumbermen to Michigan and the Great Lakes offered cheap transport to major markets, it was the natural river network in the interior that convinced the lumbermen that cutting and removing the ponderous pine could be profitable. Without the rivers the timber would be inaccessible. Streams and rivers became the main arteries of transporting logs to the mills. It was natural, therefore, that major sawmill towns would be built at the mouths of rivers. The size of a river's watershed along with its natural harbor greatly influenced the economic future of most lumbertowns.

The most important river system of the eastern half of the Lower Peninsula was the Saginaw. An unimposing, sluggish, and short stream of about twenty-five miles, the Saginaw River is fed by an impressive network of tributaries that extends for nearly nine hundred navigable miles and drains over six thousand square miles of land within the watershed.[8] Four main tributaries—the Cass, Flint, Shiawassee, and Tittabawassee—flow into the Saginaw within a few miles of one another just south of the city of Saginaw. The Tittabawassee, the longest and most important tributary, reaches 117 miles northward and is fed by the Pine, Chippewa, Tobacco, and Cedar rivers. In contrast to its rapidly moving feeder streams, the Saginaw is wide and slow moving; however, these characteristics made it ideal for storing logs and constructing mill sites along its banks.

The western side of the state is dominated by the Muskegon River, one of the longest and largest rivers in Michigan. Beginning at Higgins Lake in the north central part of the Lower Peninsula, the Muskegon winds for three hundred miles until it reaches Muskegon Lake, which in turn empties into Lake Michigan. The Muskegon River basin drains an area of 2,880 square miles. Muskegon Lake, like the Saginaw River, provided a safe harbor and a vast storage pond for logs coming down the river. It, too, was an ideal site for sawmills and settlement (see map 1).

At the mouths of these rivers, the lumberman-entrepreneur located his mill site to maximize profits. The founders of the lumber-

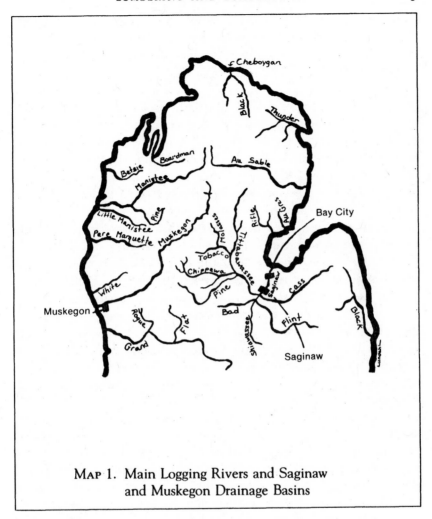

MAP 1. Main Logging Rivers and Saginaw
and Muskegon Drainage Basins

towns were singularly motivated in their actions to make money.
Equally significant, once the lumber industry developed, it was characterized by unrestricted competition. The insatiable demand, the
apparent endless availability of standing timber, undisciplined markets, and little collusion to limit production created an industry
with no effective internal price controls. Without effective price
controls, the lumbermen sought short run profits by maintaining
full-scale output and by limiting outlays or product costs. In short,
as Bruce Catton underscored, the lumbermen set the exploitative
pattern: "Take what there is, take all of it, and take it as fast as you

can, and let tomorrow's people handle tomorrow's problem."[9] Although these economic motives for early settlement eventually marked the lumbertowns culturally, cost efficiencies also determined the advent and location of lumbertowns.

Three types of costs related to location are generally postulated: procurement, processing, and distribution. Costs of procurement were the most expensive and most important in lumbering—getting the lumber to the processing points.[10] Sawmills, though, could not be located in the interior woods. Like agricultural products, timber was harvested over a large area. This required that heavy, ponderous sawmill machinery be located where timber could be drawn from a wide region. The location of the sawmills was due to the buoyancy of pine. Lumbermen took advantage of this characteristic by dumping logs into a river and letting them float downstream. River men cleared the streams and prodded the logs along until they reached the sawmills at the mouth of the river. This method of procurement was an extremely cheap means of transport. The mouths of rivers were natural breaks in transportation, and here arose the industry for milling logs into boards.[11]

Processing costs were those associated with transforming the logs into boards. Logging town location was important in determining processing costs. Timber was stored and kept afloat in holding ponds until it was moved inside the mills by conveyor belts. The larger the water storage facilities, the longer the mills could cut before their supply of logs ran out. Water power was not an important determinant because scrap from cutting supplied the fuel to power stream-driven sawmill equipment. Yet the grouping of several sawmills around a key processing point provided economies of scale. Services of small foundries, shipping facilities, and cooperative booming and market arrangements cut costs. However, costs could also increase as land prices went up and labor's demands became more expensive.

The lumbertowns were poorly located to maximize distribution costs. Ideally, cost economies could be effected by locating as near as possible to the areas of greatest consumption. Because this was not possible for the lumber industry, much of the lumber went rough sawn to the distribution centers in New York state or Chicago. Steamers and small sailing vessels were reasonable means of transporting the lumber to markets. Still, while freight rates often remained competitive, large, sometimes economically irrational variations were frequent. These practices prompted several large lumber operators to integrate their business vertically by purchasing their own ships and lumberyards at marketing centers.

Transportation costs likewise determined the characteristic seasonal pattern of the Great Lakes states lumber industry. The most demanding task, of the many involved in logging, was moving sixteen- to twenty-foot logs cut from the towering pine to where they were to be sawed into boards. Moving 300-pound logs necessitated innovative methods of transportation. Thus, most tree-cutting or logging operations took place during the winter. The easiest method of moving heavy timber was to drag it over frozen ground along specially iced tote roads or through the snow on sleds. Throughout most of Michigan's lumber period, woods work continued to be almost exclusively a winter operation. An adequate snowfall that began in November and stayed on the ground until late March or April was ideal. Substantial snow depths were needed to successfully float the logs downstream during the spring runoff. Once the logs were skidded from the woods, they were stored on river banking grounds or rollways or piled in natural or artificially created holding ponds. As soon as the river thawed in the spring, the loggers broke the timber away from the rollways and tumbled it into the rapidly moving river below. "River hogs" rode the logs downstream and kept the river free of jams and obstructions.

As the logging business grew in the 1850s, the number of firms driving logs, the volume of logs, and the need for constant river improvements complicated the driving process. As a result, "booming companies" evolved, and in 1855 they were empowered by the state legislature to control river traffic by driving, rafting, and sorting all logs on a particular river. The first booming company in Michigan was the Muskegon Lumbermen's Association organized in 1852. Charles Merrill ran a private company along the Saginaw and Tittabawassee rivers from 1856 until 1864. The volume of logs became so large that in 1864 a cooperative, the Tittabawassee Boom Company, was chartered. By the late 1860s the company had twelve miles of booming grounds or log storage pockets along the lower Tittabawassee, employed more than 500 men, and was the largest booming works in the world.[12]

The sawmills operated during the summer months. Usually they started up in May and depending on the supply of logs, ran through, at best, October. By then the logs were generally all cut and the men were laid off or returned to the woods to once again cut next year's supply. Most sawmills were alike in their basic appearance.

They were usually two-story structures built close to the river or lake. The furnaces, power plants, and machinery to drive the saws were usually located on the first floor. Cutting was done on the second floor. Logs pulled up from the mill pond were fed into circular saws or gang saws that ripped the logs lengthwise into one-inch boards. The rough boards were edged and planed and then stacked along the river's wharves to dry and await shipment to market.

Because the lumbering business was seasonal and exploitative, an unstable industry was created that affected individual mills and lumbertowns. As long as log transportation depended on the vagaries of the weather, lumbermen could not develop rational manufacturing and marketing strategies. A stable industry needed control over the volume of raw materials; however, because the supply of logs depended on climate, logging remained unregulated and highly competitive. Mild winters or little snowfall sometimes produced spring floods that carried away logs or brought so many to the mills that the markets became glutted. Throughout the Michigan lumber period, lumber production in Saginaw, Bay City, and Muskegon remained erratic.

Economic instability was also a result of the lumber industry's lack of concentration of ownership. Made up of thousands of independent mills, the industry was basically decentralized. As such it was particularly susceptible to the boom and bust cycles of the American economy and construction industry. Even the largest enterprises controlled only a fraction of output and could offer no effective monopolistic control. Trade associations were formed to fix prices, but the spread-out nature of the business, plus the differing weather patterns, made it impossible to fight price cutting.

Despite these market fluctuations, when times were good, lumbermen in Michigan made considerable personal fortunes. In the half-century before 1890, they had produced an estimated three billion dollars in wood products. This was more than twice the value of all the gold mined in California since 1848.[13] The big operator especially, well endowed by family and Eastern backing, could usually command enough capital to carry him through poor years. By the mid-1880s the advent of the logging railroad made it possible to get the logs out regardless of the winter weather. No longer was the industry guided by prices determined by unpredictable elements. Lumber production itself became more mechanized and a machinelike efficiency came to the frontier lumbertowns. Prosperity now seemed possible for everyone. However, just as the industry was becoming well organized, the trees ran out.

BEGINNINGS: 1830–1860

The Saginaws

Soon after Tocqueville's visit, settlers began to trickle into the Saginaw Valley. Still, getting to Saginaw was difficult. The military road built to the old fort never amounted to much. It was passable on foot and horseback, but overgrowth and fallen trees made wagon transport impossible. Steamboats from Detroit made periodic visits and carried a few settlers, household goods, and supplies.[14]

Growth of the Saginaw area reflected the rapid population increase in the state between 1832 and 1837 during the five years Michigan was negotiating statehood. Immigrants arrived so rapidly that the territory's population doubled. The military road to Saginaw was improved, and settlers followed northward the extension of the road.[15] By 1837 the state census recorded 920 people living in Saginaw County.

Land speculation influenced the rapid growth of the Saginaw basin as much as internal transport improvements. Jackson's war on the Bank of the United States led to the redistribution of federal money to state banks in 1833. This stimulated a proliferation of state and local banks. Inflation resulted and land prices rose quickly. Eastern speculators caught the fever and invested in new banks and paper town sites.

Settlement of the Saginaw Valley was spurred by these governmental policies. Land speculators moved into the Saginaw region and bought choice lands.[16] The best farmlands were purchased near town sites, roads, and anticipated railroad routes. Buyers of timber also moved in—although not yet in great numbers—to set aside future forestland. Records of the General Land Office indicate that most of the purchases in the land mania of 1836 seldom exceeded the minimum price of $1.25 per acre. Land records show that in 1835 there were 41 land buyers in Saginaw County; in 1836 the number jumped to 155. During the Panic of 1837 the number slipped to 88.[17]

Speculators also spearheaded town building. As they were purchasing choice agricultural lands, promoters concomitantly built

cities in the Saginaw Valley. In 1835 Samuel Dexter, who had originally purchased land around old Fort Saginaw in 1824, sold his
holdings—the paper town of "Saganaw City"—to Dr. Abel Millington of Ypsilanti for $11,000. The following year Norman Little pur-
chased Millington's holdings for $55,000. Little was one of the
farsighted men who like many other enterprisers in the speculative
era represented a combination of personal initiative and economic
privilege. Little's father, Dr. Charles Little, had journeyed to Saginaw in 1822. A companion of Dr. Little kept a journal of their trek
west and recorded that they had an "admiration of the appearance
of the Saginaw country," and that it was indeed "susceptible to settlement and cultivation." Little and his companions bought several
hundred acres of land on both sides of the Saginaw River and returned to New York with visions to develop the scrawny frontier
settlements.[18]

Although nothing became of Charles Little's original land holdings, Norman Little returned to Saginaw in 1835 determined to
build the city his father had dreamed about. Little stepped off the
steamboat *Governor Marcy* into a little knot of people who had come
to welcome the first steamboat ever seen on the Saginaw River. He
brought with him a few business friends from Detroit and letters of
credit from the New York financial firm of Mackie, Oakley and Jen-
nison. A small, rather tidy appearing man with well set eyes, graying
hair, and a cropped beard, Little radiated the experience of a promoter. Before he left New York he had flooded the East with advertisements describing the attractions of Saginaw. They boasted of an
anticipated deep water canal, running from Saginaw across the state
to Lake Michigan, that would someday make Saginaw a leading port
city. Little also carried a redrawn city map of Dexter's original plat,
now renamed "Saginaw City." The map depicted 408 developed
blocks.

Little personified in all ways the promoter who came west in the
1830s. In every lumbertown, the western promoter invariably began
his career as the agent of Eastern capitalists. They maintained this
eastern connection for the obvious reason that city building required significant capital. New towns depended on outside money for
canals, railroads, streets, and new construction. The Eastern financiers who backed men like Little came to know their towns and often established strong personal as well as financial ties with local
leadership.

Once ensconced in Saginaw, Little set out to expand and improve
his holdings. With imagination and leadership, he convinced the

newly moneyed state legislature to support the construction of a canal that would connect the Saginaw with the Grand River. Construction got under way in 1837 as soon as Little's firm became the
successful bidder on the project. Lots were sold and businesses
opened in the city. Saginaw prospered under Little. A contemporary
gazetteer aimed at enticing new settlers to the state described the
settlements in 1838:

> Here is a post office, a deputy collector's office, a banking associ-
> ation, a printing office, 2 dry goods stores, a hardware store, 2 ware-
> houses, a tannery, one steam saw mill in operation and another
> erecting, a druggist, a lawyer, and 2 physicians. There are owned here
> a steamboat, a sloop and a schooner. The village is very recent, hav-
> ing been commenced only three years since under the auspices of a
> company for its settlement, but it is remarkably flourishing. Many
> buildings were erected the past two seasons.[19]

From Tocqueville's thirty-one residents six years earlier, the city now
numbered four hundred.

The attractively printed map and flaming-red posters in New York
and Detroit convincingly advertised Saginaw City, but reality was a
bit disappointing to town visitors. The steam sawmill was ponderous
and slow. The bank, post office, and collectors offices were small
buildings. Scattered along the riverbank were small traders' shacks
and a large red building that housed the general hardware store. An
old log tavern was apart from the other buildings. A shoe shop and
two or three other residences with attached businesses were widely
scattered on the small bluff above the old military stockade. A few
early residents, among them Little, had what were described as
"very nice residences" in the southwest part of town.[20] From the
river, Saginaw City hardly looked like a town. It was a collection of
oddly shaped and constructed buildings arranged in a seemingly unplanned manner along a low bluff overlooking the waterway.

Little, though, continued to anticipate a flood of visitors and
speculators, and to house them he and his brother built the Webster
House, a hotel large enough to meet the needs of a city of ten thousand. Not only the grandest residence north of Detroit, it turned out
to be also the emptiest.

Little's dreams were shattered by the financial panic that began in
1837 and sent the nation and so many speculative towns, including
Saginaw City, into a five-year depression. The panic ended the wild
speculation that had energized so much of the Midwest. Saginaw
City changed from a bustling trading center to a farm village of a

few inhabitants.[21] The bank closed and the residents' paper money suddenly became worthless. Little's canal contract was canceled by the state. In 1841 Little and his associates were compelled to sell their remaining assets and land holdings in Saginaw City. Little returned east to find new financial backing; his brother, William, maintained a mercantile business in the city.

Throughout most of the 1840s Saginaw City languished. The population remained at about four hundred for the five depression years. In middecade German immigrants began to move into the county. The pioneer band of hardy, German Lutherans came from Franconia, Bavaria, to establish Indian missions and escape religious harassment. The Germans quickly established four agriculture settlements north, west, and south of Saginaw City. Other settlers began to again trek westward from the New England states. By 1850 the city had half a dozen stores, one sawmill, five carpenter shops, three blacksmiths, and three boat and shoe shops. There were also three hotels. The population had reached about nine hundred people.

It was also in the late forties that Norman Little returned from New York. His efforts to attract capital had been successful. Emphasizing the potential lumber resources in the valley and the apparent dwindling supplies in the East, Little secured the support of James Hoyt and Company, New York. Forming a partnership with James Hoyt and his son Jesse in 1848, Little returned to Saginaw City and tried to buy back the city he had established earlier. However, the price was too high; rebuffed he went across the river to the east bank. Here, where the land was low and swampy—the Indians and French traders had refused to encamp here—Little purchased from the Detroit Banking Company a large tract running more than a mile along the river and encompassing twenty-four hundred acres.[22]

The tract was quickly surveyed and platted. The "Hoyt Plat" was an unlikely spot for a city, but Little's decision to develop a new town coincided with the beginnings of the lumber boom. The original plat was surveyed and published in 1850. Laid out in the familiar grid pattern, Plank Road (Genesee Street) ran away from the river and connected with the old military road from Detroit. At the river Plank Road intersected with Water and Washington where twelve riverfront lots started the city. Here pine boards were laid on pilings for sidewalks. A resident could literally fish off the walkways in frequent times of high water.[23]

Little was certainly not one to undertake an investment of such magnitude and see his dreams wash away amid floods, swamps, and

low ground. Before the city was actually platted, the promoter secured a charter from the state legislature to build a plank road to
Flint along the route of the old military road. Little built a sawmill
to cut the planks, and in 1852, as the plat map was being published,
the toll road opened connecting East Saginaw, as the settlement
came to be called, with Flint. The new town enterprise soon flourished. Immigrants arriving overland had no river to ford, and soon
East Saginaw was growing faster than old Saginaw City. Little became president of the Genesee Plank Road Company and in 1853 he
established a regular stage run between his city and Flint.

Norman Little was not only a man of great foresight; he also remained an able promoter. Conscious of the latent wealth of the forests, he exploited this fact in eastern advertisements. His timing was
opportune. Eastern capital was available for investment in Michigan
pine, and there were jobs to be found. Jesse Hoyt soon followed Little to East Saginaw. Hoyt and Little were the mainstays behind East
Saginaw's success. In 1850 the U.S. Census reported that the settlement had about 536 people. By 1854 its population rivaled that of
Saginaw City. East Saginaw was incorporated as a village in 1855
and became a city in 1859. Saginaw City was incorporated as a city
two years earlier. Although Little built a fine new house on the east
side of the river, he had little time to see his city grow. Norman
Little drowned crossing the Saginaw River in 1859.

At the time of Little's death, a chronicler of East Saginaw's history recalled the city's physical appearance:

> There were foundaries and machine shops, blacksmiths, two grist
> mills making wheat flour, three churches, five doctors, and as now, a
> surplus of lawyers, one newspaper, the Enterprise, four schools, five
> volunteer fire companies, a band, a military company and five or six
> hotels. There had been some shipbuilding, and W. L. P. Little carried
> on extensive wholesale and retail businesses, and was also Receiver of
> the U.S. Land Office with Moses B. Hess as Register.[24]

Although Little anticipated a green gold rush, the lumber business
remained in its infancy. There were about twenty-three mills in the
Saginaw area by 1855, producing a hundred million board feet of
lumber a year. Although the figure looks large, by the mid-1880s
some large Saginaw River mills alone produced fifty million or more
a year.

It was also in the 1850s that the two fledgling communities developed a rivalry and animosity that was to last for decades. The

rivalry not only accelerated the intense town boosterism inaugurated by Little, but supplied these cities with a competitive drive that perhaps portended immediate as well as future economic success. By the end of its first decade East Saginaw's population had grown to 3,000. Across the river the population in Saginaw City reached 1,699 in 1860.[25] The town rivalry that emerged in the decade took the form of competition for populations through urban improvements. Little's initiative coupled with the Hoyt's money enabled East Saginaw to be more progressive. The east siders had the first cedar block paved streets, the first bridge across the river at Genesee Street, and the most extravagantly decorated hotel north of Detroit, the Bancroft House. Saginaw City tried to keep pace, but financial resources were fewer and the entrepreneurial drive lacked direction. For decades the older town was content to replicate the civic improvements begun in East Saginaw.

The first speculative reasons for founding Saginaw and East Saginaw established the entrepreneurial nature of both towns. Moreover, the speculation engaged in by Little and the Hoyts defied the classic image of the promoter who platted paper cities to bilk an unsuspecting public. They were speculators who purchased land at substantial risks—as seen by Little's failure in Saginaw City—and tried to improve the community and surrounding region to guarantee profits. They were also resident promoters. Unlike many eastern promoters who hired agents and invested in new lands from some distance, Little and the Hoyts at first took up residence in their community. They directed planning and growth and built communities in which they took more than a passing economic interest.[26] Initial speculative enthusiasm later gave way to entrepreneurial urban competition. Divisiveness and feuding did not stifle urban progress as both past and contemporary chroniclers of the city's history are prone to hypothesize. In fact, competition accelerated population growth and the construction of urban amenities. Speculation and urban rivalry established competitive entrepreneurial practices that later were to serve the Saginaws well at the end of the lumber era.[27]

The Saginaws especially became Western colonies into which Eastern financiers poured surplus capital. In doing so these investors used their financial acumen to make profits and to integrate the West into the national economy. Despite the distance and hazards of travel and communication, these men moved capital with relative ease. They employed local citizens and resident promoters like Little, built canals, banks, and generally changed dramatically the frontier

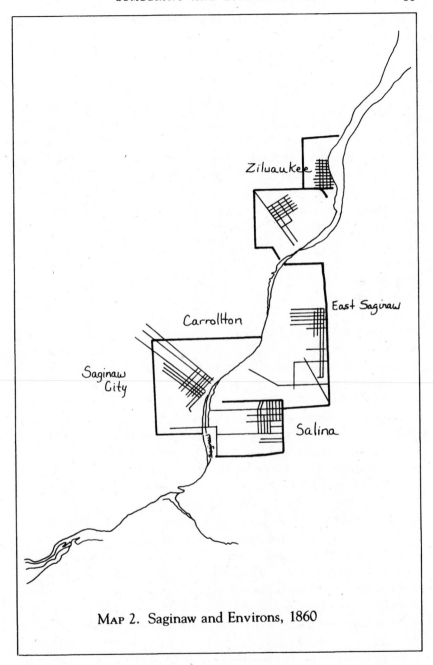

MAP 2. Saginaw and Environs, 1860

communities they helped start. Men like the Hoyts and Little were risk-takers who pushed urban development into the lumber era. The Saginaws were founded by town boosters who gave the communities a competitive economic framework that bolstered the towns' economies for decades.

Bay City

On July 27, 1831, Tocqueville and Beaumont intended to leave Saginaw and once again "penetrate the humid depths" for Detroit. However, their horses still had saddle sores from their earlier trek north and this persuaded them to stay another day. To pass the time the companions descended the Saginaw toward the mouth of the river to hunt. In doing so they passed through the vast prairies of grass that would someday become Bay City. The prairies were separated from Saginaw City by several miles of intermittent but large swamps, which geographically isolated Bay City from Saginaw for decades and encouraged separation and town rivalries that persist to this day.

Had Tocqueville and Beaumont trekked near the mouth of the Saginaw, they undoubtedly would have met Leon Tromble building his log cabin along the east side of the river in what is today downtown Bay City. Tromble came from Detroit in 1831 as a government agricultural agent to teach the Indians to farm. Under the provisions of the 1819 Treaty of Saginaw, the Chippewa—who had farmed the Saginaw Valley for centuries—requested that the white man reeducate them in the agrarian skills that had been lost during the fur trading era. Tromble was a remnant of that earlier era. He was first a fur trader and came to what was then known as Lower Saginaw to cultivate the fur trade, as well as potatoes for the Indians. He cleared half an acre of fertile ground on the prairies, planted a crop for the Indians and himself, built a one-room log house, and then returned to Detroit to get his family. Tromble instructed an Indian in cultivation and directed him to till the soil, watch his cabin, and harvest furs. Though furs were harvested, the crops were forgotten, and when Tromble returned he found the potato patch neglected. Neglected, that is, in the white man's vision of how a proper garden should be cultivated. Despite the weeds, the fertile soil yielded a supply of potatoes that fed the Trombles through the winter.

Leon Tromble did not remain long at Lower Saginaw. Despite offers by the Indians to trade their reservation lands along the river, Tromble refused to swap his horse for a section. Later he recalled: "Who would then have thought a city would one day stand where there was nothing but swamp, with long grass, in which a man could stand and be hid—where there was scarcely an opening in the woods around it, in which the wolves made plenty of howling."[28]

Tromble's comments may explain the slower rate of Lower Saginaw's development in contrast to Saginaw City. Besides the swamps, low ground, and thick prairie grass, Lower Saginaw did not have a convenient overland access trail. Moreover, all the land on the west side of the river at its mouth was part of a forty thousand-acre Chippewa reservation, and several choice sections on the east side were held by individual Indians who had secured them from Lewis Cass in the 1819 treaty. Early settlers like Tromble were sent as government agents to aid the Indians. Apparently, they were either honest enough not to dupe the Indians of their land, considered the land worthless (which was most likely), or were so unsure of Indian title that they made no efforts to establish speculative settlements.

Few settlers trickled into Lower Saginaw before statehood in 1837. In 1834 Benjamin Cushway, like Tromble a trader and government agent, built a log cabin and a blacksmith shop on the west bank of the river one mile south of Tromble's residence. Also in 1834 John B. Trudell, another fur trader turned fisherman, built a third log cabin just south of Tromble's. In the next year Joseph and Mader Tromble, nephews of Leon Tromble, arrived along the lower Saginaw River. The Tromble brothers are considered Bay City's first real settlers because they came with a definite idea of developing the region. They purchased a 312-acre tract along the river, about three miles south of Leon Tromble's cabin, and, in doing so, secured the first government land patent in the area. The Trombles also brought cattle with them and proceeded to construct a large frame house on high ground near the river to be used as a trading post and residence. The Center House, as it was soon to be called, was built of lumber brought from Detroit and served as the focal point for early land speculation and settlement of Lower Saginaw.[29]

The Trombles, Cushway, and Trudell were soon followed by the promoters. Albert Miller, recently appointed judge of probate in newly organized Saginaw County (1835), purchased land from the Trombles in 1836. In July of that year he hired a surveyor and laid out the city of Portsmouth. He then journeyed to Detroit and tried to sell lots and secure funds for city improvements. Apparently finding no interest, Miller sold part of his interest to other speculators, including Governor Stevens T. Mason, and formed the Portsmouth Company in early 1837.

A new treaty in 1837, when Michigan gained statehood, compelled the Indians to sell several of their reserve lands along the

Saginaw and consequently attracted a few more promoters. Miller, financially reassured, invested $5000 in "goods," bought a steam engine and sawmill equipment, and purchased for $2,500 a vessel to ship all of this to Portsmouth. While he trekked northward overland, the "unprincipled scamp" he had hired to sail his ship to Saginaw Bay stopped at Port Huron and settled in for the winter, living off the ship's provisions. Not until the spring could Miller find his ship, rescue his sawmill equipment, and build his sawmill.[30]

Back at Portsmouth, Miller redrew the town plan and filed a new plat map that, except for changes in street names, remains accurate today. The new village extended north and south and east and west for about thirteen blocks. The functional grid pattern was broken only by the river, a public square, and a wider street, or Broad Way, eight blocks from the river. Miller's town was platted out and lots offered for sale; however, before the judge could move to the new settlement the panic struck. The new mill at Portsmouth was closed and Miller "retired" to farm a small parcel north of Saginaw City.

While Miller was finishing his sawmill in 1837, James Fraser, a recent Scottish immigrant, formed the Saginaw Bay Company. He attracted several investors, again including Governor Mason, and purchased from the half-breed John Riley, most of the 640-acre reservation that Riley had been granted by the Treaty of Saginaw. Radiating from the area Leon Tromble had cleared several years earlier, town lots were surveyed and laid out by Fraser for the village of "Lower Saginaw." Fraser's town ran parallel to the river for about fourteen blocks and eastward into the interior about ten blocks. The Saginaw Bay Company, like Judge Miller with his sawmill, built several structures in 1838 to stimulate sales. A warehouse, a large dock, a square log blockhouse, and a small bank building were erected. However, the Lower Saginaw experiment was completed just in time to suffer the effects of the panic. With few lots sold, Fraser temporarily abandoned the project at Lower Saginaw. The blockhouse and warehouse were closed and the bank building sold to one of the local settlers.

Although the first promoters themselves did not fail completely, their efforts in Portsmouth and Lower Saginaw had to await further developments. In 1843 Fraser bought out the original investors and restructured the Saginaw Bay Company with the financial aid of James G. Birney and his brother-in-law, Daniel H. Fitzhugh and others. Birney, who ran for the presidency in 1844 while a resident of Bay City, directed changes in the original Lower Saginaw plat. Two public parks were now included, and in every other block two lots were set aside for churches. Religious groups would become sole owners of the property upon construction of a church on the lots. Birney, coming from New York by way of Ohio after an unsuccessful bid for the presidency in 1840 on the Liberty party ticket, was a social and moral activist. He moved to Lower Saginaw in the spring of 1842 and plunged into farming land on both sides of the Saginaw River. Having sold an inherited plantation, he had enough capital to purchase several large parcels and bring his Durham cattle north from Ohio. Birney managed the development of Lower Saginaw as a resident promoter and Fitzhugh remained in New York to sell lots and attract settlers to the river settlement. However, unlike Little and the Hoyts in Saginaw, developers in Bay City never matched their downriver neighbors in capital or promotional experience. Their entrepreneurial interest sometimes conflicted with their social and moral views.

Correspondence between Birney and Fitzhugh provides insight into town-building along the lower Saginaw. Birney deplored the treatment of the Indians and wrote that he "raised his voice against the inequity of making the Indians drunk and cheating them." His chastising brought resentment from some of the traders and slowed settlement of Lower Saginaw.[31] He also tried to instill some formal morality into the community by conducting regular religious services in his home. Birney's efforts at moral uplift may have been unusual for a town promoter, but they failed to attract the number of settlers that Little and Hoyt did with more pragmatic methods of town boosterism. Lower Saginaw developed slowly during the 1840s. By mid-decade, according to Birney, there were about 130 residents scattered along the lower Saginaw River. Birney did establish a school and several commercial buildings appeared. He worked hard to secure a post office for the settlement (1846); and in the winter of 1847–48 the first sawmill at Lower Saginaw was built along the river. Yet by the end of the decade Lower Saginaw and Portsmouth still resembled pioneer river-trading outposts and rural agricultural settlements. The villages were hemmed in by swamps and forests; there were no streets and the mud and water were at times ankle deep. Little urban development took place comparable to what was happening up theriver in the Saginaws.

By midcentury prospects for the growth of the settlement began to brighten. In the winter of 1847 lumberman Henry W. Sage came

from New York to Lower Saginaw to purchase timber for his yards in
Ithaca. While at Saginaw City, Sage and several companions took a
sleigh downriver with the intentions of purchasing land in Lower
Saginaw from Birney. However, Birney was too ill to even meet with
the visitors and they returned the next day without negotiating a
purchase. Nevertheless, Sage shipped to Ithaca the "first cargo of
clear lumber ever sent from the Saginaws" and noted the abundant
resources and ideal mill sites available.[32] Although Sage and his
partners did not purchase any land, their visit was really the first
effort of lumbermen who were also substantial capitalists to seriously
consider the area's exploitable timber resources.

Birney's ill health and apparent inability to attract settlers encouraged his brother-in-law to send his son, Daniel H. Fitzhugh, Jr., to
Lower Saginaw. Arriving with more capital, Fitzhugh tried to instill
new life into the barren settlement. He supervised the construction
of the new sawmill in Lower Saginaw and used the newly sawed
wood to build a "very pretentious dwelling along the river."[33]
Fitzhugh remained in Lower Saginaw for three years, but in 1851 the
sawmill was blown up killing the fireman and destroying the mill's
machinery. Daniel Fitzhugh returned east in that year to attend to
his father's real estate interests.

Although Fitzhugh experienced misfortune, his efforts at establishing Lower Saginaw as a sawmill center succeeded in attracting
several other entrepreneurs. Between 1850 and 1854 twelve new
mills were built in Lower Saginaw. Still, these were small and
crudely equipped sawmills. The price for milled lumber remained low
and shipping costs were high. Consumption was confined largely to
nearby hamlets and the populated areas of southern Michigan. Eastern woodlands had not been exhausted yet and the movement westward of the experienced and well-financed lumbermen from New
England would not come until the Civil War. Still, there were
enough speculators who did come. Some even built sawmills and
waited patiently for the anticipated lumbering boom.

Sawmill construction also brought workers and small-scale development to Lower Saginaw. A doctor and a lawyer arrived, the Fraser
House and Wolverton House hotels were built, and several boardinghouses were constructed near the sawmills. In 1857 Bay County
was organized and separated from Saginaw and Midland counties despite the persistent opposition of Saginaw merchants and politicians.
When the state legislature finally approved the county measure, its
legality was challenged all the way to the Michigan Supreme Court

where the act was upheld in 1858. The political and legal obstruc-
tionism that the Saginaw representatives employed to block Bay
County's establishment generated ill feelings between the two settlements that persisted for decades. Concomitantly with the granting of
county status, Birney drafted a resolution changing the name of
Lower Saginaw to Bay City.

In 1859 the village of Bay City incorporated and had a population
of seven hundred. There were about fourteen sawmills in and near
the city as the dawn of the lumber era was about to break. Fishing
was an important export industry to the bay village and employed as
many workers as lumbering. Little effort at agriculture was made and
residents continued to import foodstuffs from Saginaw or by schooner. Transport was entirely by water. There were still no roads coming into the city. The newly incorporated village expanded Fraser's
original plat by adding a mile of streets southward nearly reaching
the Portsmouth settlement. There was little growth eastward into
the forestland away from the river. The town plat, though, was a
linear scheme that remained largely imperceptible. In 1860 the population of 810 was scattered along nearly two miles of waterfront
characterized by floating fishing barges, drying nets, sawmills, millponds, drying lumber, several boardinghouses, twelve saloons, and
scattered businesses and homes. As one observer noted, "The physical beauty of the place was little improved."[34]

Across the river from Bay City and the village of Portsmouth entrepreneurs and ethnic settlers built three hamlets that would eventually become West Bay City. The oldest area of settlement on the
west side of the river was the village of Banks. Joseph Tromble, who
along with his brother had constructed the Center House at Portsmouth in 1836 and subsequently sold their property to Judge Miller,
later moved upriver about a mile and settled in what was to become
Banks. The village, built on low ground on a bend near the mouth
of the Saginaw River, was settled by French fishermen. Tromble surveyed and platted out Banks in a square three hundred acres in
1843, but, like Bay City, there was little growth until the 1850s. By
the end of the Civil War three sawmills that employed primarily
French mill men, several salt blocks, and fishing occupied the four
hundred or so residents.

The salt that could be extracted from the brine water beneath the
cities of the Saginaw Valley became the economic reason for the
founding of Salzburg. Scattered salt springs flowing from the banks
of Saginaw's tributaries were known to the Indians, and the state

had long been interested in tapping this vital resource.[35] Processing was neglected until 1859, when, through the efforts of Saginaw Valley representatives, the state legislature passed a bill that granted a bounty of ten cents a bushel on manufactured salt and a tax exemption for property used in salt production. The bounty and especially the tax exemptions prompted Dr. Daniel Fitzhugh, who had recently moved to Bay City, and James Fraser to plat a tract of land across the river from Bay City-Portsmouth.

Twenty years after founding Lower Saginaw together, Fitzhugh and Fraser, with the aid of James Birney's son, a state representative who got the salt bounty and tax exemption through the legislature, set out on another speculative venture. A rather small, triangular town site was platted and soon three salt-manufacturing establishments were built. Fitzhugh named the site after the Austrian resort and salt-mining city of Salzburg. Despite their initial optimism, in 1862 the state salt bounty was repealed. Yet Fitzhugh, who eventually became sole owner of the enterprise in Salzburg, established a manufacturing center and sold all the lots in the village. Salt manufacturing remained an important by-product operation of the sawmills. Scrap wood and sawdust were used to boil brine water and extract the salt residue. Salzburg, which eventually became part of West Bay City, attracted many German farmers and settlers from nearby Frankenlust and was soon characterized as a thoroughly German sawmill village.

Before he was to return to Bay City in the early sixties, Henry Sage had been purchasing pinelands throughout the state ever since his visit to the Saginaw Valley in 1847. By 1862 Canadian reserves could no longer supply his New York sawmills and lumberyards. It was time to move the operation west. Sage picked an ideal site directly across the river opposite downtown Bay City. The land was between the settlements at Salzburg and Banks and was known for its beautiful grove of oaks interspersed with tall pines. Sage seemed determined to buy the site from Dr. Fitzhugh and Birney's widow despite their apparent unwillingness to part with the land. He returned each year between 1860 and 1863 trying to negotiate a deal. Finally in 1863, with the aid of Fitzhugh's old partner, James Fraser, a purchase price of $21,000 for 116 acres was agreed upon.

Sage purchased the land in partnership with John McGraw of Poughkeepsie, New York. By the spring of 1864 construction began on a sawmill. When the mill was placed into operation a year later, it was reported to be the largest sawmill in the world. Perhaps these

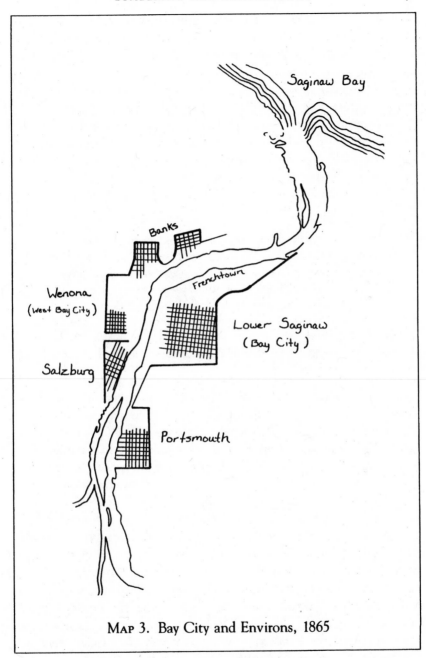

MAP 3. Bay City and Environs, 1865

claims were slight exaggerations but Sage did have a grand vision. His mill was certainly one of the largest along the Great Lakes as well as one of the most modern and efficient. Besides the mill, Sage

built a company store, a warehouse, a brick office building, a boardinghouse, a tenement apartment, and twenty-three individual dwellings. Wenona, as the settlement was originally called, was indeed at
its inception a company town. The 116 acres were platted into a
gridiron street network with 400- x 200-foot blocks, each block con-
taining sixteen lots, 50 x 100 feet. Each lot sold for about $200.

Wenona grew very rapidly. A well-planned and controlled environment coupled with the nearly one million in expenditures that
Sage and McGraw poured into the settlement, it attracted entrepreneurs and workers. Within two years there were seven hundred residents in Wenona. In 1868 the editor of the *Delisle Directory* wrote of
the settlement:

> The Village was scarcely a history apart from the mill. Like Topsy, in
> the song, it was raised—if not on corn, certainly on the sand which
> is there—its growth has been quite as astonishing. It has no oldest
> inhabitant, no old buildings, not an old association, nor an old land-
> mark. Famed as the Saginaw Valley is for raising cities, Wenona is yet
> a marvel in the eyes of the Saginawians; not even a *Sage* could have
> foretold that in the short space of four years a promising city would
> arise, containing twelve hundred inhabitants, and all the conve-
> niences of city life.[36]

The success of West Bay City (Salzburg, Banks, and Wenona) and
Bay City (Lower Saginaw and Portsmouth) gave evidence that both
the promoter and the investor were welcomed in the lower Saginaw
River region. However, unlike the risk-takers in East Saginaw, Birney, Fitzhugh, and others in Bay City were more conservative investors who struggled through difficult times to effect gradual economic
development. They hesitated to build a city and internal improvements in advance of the lumber era. Not until the lumber period
had arrived did the large expansionist investor-industrialists like
Sage and McGraw move into Bay City. These individuals built
nearby towns and established an economic framework for Bay City,
but as absentee investors they never developed an interest in their
community that could transcend their desire for profits. When
economic contraction occurred, which was inevitable in a natural
resource town, these eastern capitalists largely abandoned their investments. Economic dislocation and personal suffering were prolonged because Bay City was economically unprepared for the end of
the white pine era.

Muskegon

While the Saginaws were engaged in spirited struggles of competition and town rivalry characteristic of the speculative boom of the
late thirties, Muskegon remained an outpost community in the wilderness. Despite the Treaty of Washington in 1836 that surrendered
the western part of the territory, including Muskegon, to the soon-
to-be state, speculators did not discover the Muskegon River region.
The locality remained a fur-trading outpost, and its unhealthy climate—low lying, marshy ground around the lake, mosquitoes and
fleas—discouraged town promoters. Other prominent investors,
while promoting Grand Rapids forty-five miles southeast, ignored
these nearby lands because they considered them too far north of the
state's settled areas.[37] Thus speculative town building and promotion
never characterized Muskegon's settlement. Settlers came instead to
exploit the area's resources. First the furs and later the timber attracted people whose "intention was to make all the money possible
and retire to some large city to enjoy their wealth."[38]

The transition from one extractive, exploitative industry to another was nevertheless gradual. Explorers and fur traders camped
along Muskegon Lake time and again decades before the first efforts
at permanent settlement were made. During the War of 1812 agents
of the British Fur Company built log cabins at the southeastern edge
of the lake. Year by year a few additional pioneers established outposts. By the mid-1830s there were about six what might be called
permanent residents scattered along Muskegon Lake.

The experiences of one of these pioneers, Martin Ryerson, may
well represent the transition stages that characterized Muskegon's
early development. Ryerson, who was someday to become one of the
city's wealthiest residents, arrived in Muskegon by way of Detroit
from Paterson, New Jersey, in 1835. Still in his teens, Ryerson fell in
with an Ottawa Indian fur trader by the name of Trucky. Unable to
afford further travel fare, Ryerson was hired by Trucky as a cook on
one of his Grand River flatboats. Ryerson eventually traveled to
Muskegon and secured a fur-trading position with the American Fur
Company. At Muskegon Ryerson worked in the fur business but was
enough of a realist to anticipate the end of the fur trade. The Indians moved north after the 1836 treaty, and pelts were becoming
scarce. Ryerson took what profits he had accumulated in the fur
business and other odd jobs and bought a small sawmill. Unlike similar traders in Bay City or Saginaw, Ryerson saw no future in urban

speculation. He envisioned few long-range prospects on a lake that he described as shallow, congested with weeds and wild rice. The upper end near the Muskegon River was covered with dead timber killed by high waters. Ryerson took note of Muskegon because of its bad climate and mosquitoes and ague. It was not a place to settle permanently.

Newcomers to Muskegon, and there were few, were lured by information from early surveyors and fur traders regarding the potential value of the dense stands of pine along the lakeshore and riverbanks. Local historians consider Muskegon's founding to be the year the first sawmill was built along the lake in 1837. Benjamin H. Wheelock, an agent of the Muskegon Steam Mill Company, began to build the first sawmill in January 1837. The stockholders in the Steam Mill Company remained in Detroit and Ann Arbor. In August of that year, the Buffalo and Black Rock Company built a water-powered sawmill at the mouth of Bear Lake just north of Muskegon Lake. A third mill was added a year later; however, the Panic of 1837 and limited demand restricted production and forced the original mills to change ownership several times by the mid-1840s.

In these embryonic years, Muskegon comprised four primitive settlements clustered around trading posts and sawmills. Each hamlet (Bluffton, Lakeside, Muskegon, and North Muskegon) was separated from its nearest neighbor by a mile or more of timberland. Towering pines rising 150 feet effectively isolated the individual logging operations from one another. As logging operations progressed, a widening crescent of stumps gradually brought these tiny hamlets closer together.

The center of development of the early community was along the south shore of Muskegon Lake. Bluffton—a trading outpost at the mouth of the lake near Lake Michigan—Lakeside, and Muskegon were the three settlements most favored for topographical and geographical factors. Early settlers came from the south over primitive trails from Grand Rapids, and supplies and mail deliveries reached the south shore more quickly. The first post office was in Bluffton where the footpath from the south ended. Early lake schooners also found it easier and closer to land along the south shore. The mile-wide, swamp-covered flats at the moth of the Muskegon River at the east end of the lake made land access to the north side difficult.

Attracted by the natural resources, men like Martin Ryerson came early to exploit the area's timber. Optimistically, they built primitive sawmills before regional markets could absorb their output of lumber. Yet the combination of geographical factors—the Muskegon River stretching into the interior, a harbor that never freezes, and the seemingly endless pine forests—encouraged the pioneers to persist. Despite restricted markets and production, slow but significant growth took place in the Muskegon lumber industry in the first decade and a half after its founding. The number of mills increased from three in 1840 to ten by 1854. As the industry grew, new and better equipment expanded capacity at a rapid rate. In 1850 six mills produced 14,500,000 feet; four years later ten mills turned out 28,100,000 feet per year.

As the sawmilling business grew, the physical layout of the three mill settlements along the south shore shared similar appearances. Gathered close to each mill were usually a blacksmith shop, a stable, a lumberyard (to dry cut wood), a dock, a small general store, a boardinghouse, and a few scattered dwellings. The sawmill and drying docks were always at the end of the lake to facilitate the movement of logs and the transport of lumber. Behind the mill site were the varied residences. Small, drab, and unpainted, built amid a field of decaying stumps, the mill settlements were notably unattractive. The odor of fresh cut pine, mingled with the smoke that belched from the mills' engines and steam boilers, drifted over the roofs of the workers' homes. Usually several small, frame structures housed the married workers and their families, and one or two boardinghouses accommodated unmarried men. A total of twenty or thirty buildings made up each settlement.

The small populations and primitive existence along the lake was reflected in the lack of physical amenities available to the residents. Because no promoter was profiting from the sale of land or town lots, no effort was made to improve or refine the settlements. There was no bank, no public cemetery, no daily mail service, no church, no newspaper. Houses were built wherever convenient, with little or no thought of street patterns. Not until 1849 did Muskegon become the first hamlet to record a plat of anticipated streets. Until new demands for Muskegon's timber increased, clusters of crude buildings, surrounded by brush and pine stumps and a few sawmills were all that made up each community. Their combined populations did not exceed four hundred at any time before 1853.[39]

Muskegon remained an isolated community until market demands in the early 1850s changed its size and future prospects. As Chicago grew it became a prime consumer of Muskegon lumber. Easily accessible by schooner and steamship, Muskegon not only exported lumber but also imported merchandise, freight, and people on returning lumber steamers. The railroad network that spread into the prairies of Illinois and Iowa also became an artery to move lumber westward from the great Chicago wholesale yards.

Despite the growth of commerce, overland transportation to Muskegon remained difficult. In 1846 Martin Ryerson, who had expanded into the mercantile business, built a wagon road between Muskegon proper and Ravenna where it joined the road that had recently been opened to Grand Rapids. Yet Ryerson's road was poor, and in 1849 it took an entire day to travel by team a mere four miles.[40] The road was nothing much more than a track among stumps, sand, and mud. In 1851 the road was improved by the addition of planks, and a stage line began irregular operation over the track. By 1853 it took a day in good weather to drive the fifteen miles between Muskegon and Ravenna.

Other elements contributed to Muskegon's growth. A post office was established in 1848; several new sawmills were constructed in 1853; a school system was organized in 1849; and a bank was established in 1855. Logs began to be floated down the Muskegon River in the early fifties, and the milling business developed some early organization. The plat for Muskegon, developed in 1849, encouraged lot sales in that area. The early plat, though, added little to the aesthetics of the stump-strewn settlement. Right-angled roads intersected in the familiar grid pattern on a plat that measured about seven square blocks on each side. The area along the waterfront, where settlement first concentrated, remained unplatted. Lots within the initial plan sold for $45; by 1856 the price rose to $100.

After 1853, with the availability of new Western markets for lumber, Muskegon grew rapidly. Populations in the three hamlets increased from four hundred in 1853 to two thousand in 1857. Logs choked the Muskegon River and new sawmills were built to consume the flow. By 1857 there were sixteen mills in operation on the lake employing more than 550 men and cutting more than 100,000 feet of lumber each day. Sawmills began to encircle the lake by 1860. Although only a few mills dotted the north shore, the south shore was lined with mills, docks, and piles of drying lumber. The city's physical appearance, though, remained uninviting. Boardinghouses for unmarried workers were built near the mills and in residential areas. Houses were small, flimsy, and unpainted shacks of two or three rooms. Many of these were originally built by lumbermen and

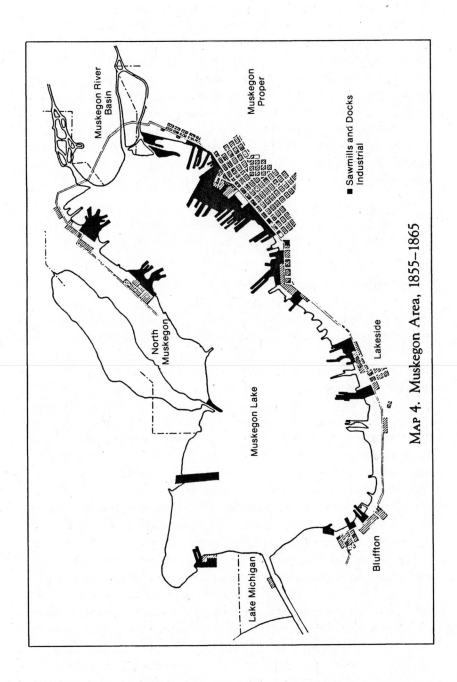

MAP 4. Muskegon Area, 1855–1865

leased to families. Residences were built on stump-filled lots. Sandy soil and little vegetation added to the drab appearance of the mill towns' residential areas. In the southwestern portion of the city a few better homes were constructed on a slight rise. Most of these, of course, belonged to men who had acquired some money in the early lumber days and had taken advantage of cheap construction costs to build large, comfortable residences.

By 1860 some settlers had arrived who were someday to be important in the shaping of Muskegon. Ambrosia Sanford, who married the Muskegon County sheriff, arrived in 1858. Her letters to her parents in New York described early Muskegon:

> I was much pleased with the looks of the village—it is not nearly as wild as I expected. There are many fine buildings, some quite fine dwellings. The village is spread over quite a tract situated on the south side of the lake.[41]

Other settlers may have been less pleased with the physical city, but they nevertheless viewed with considerable optimism the economic prospects offered by the bustling community. Charles H. Hackley worked his passage by schooner to Muskegon in 1856. Hackley, who was to become Muskegon's most generous benefactor, sailed from Kenosha, Wisconsin, with seven dollars in his pocket. By noon on the day of his arrival, Hackley secured a laboring job and in the following winter went into the woods for $30 a month as a logger. Other early settlers now diversified mercantile and trading ventures into lumbering. Martin Ryerson, who had built a large retail outlet, invested in two sawmill partnerships in 1857. George Ruddiman, an early settler, persuaded his brother, John, to move to Muskegon. Separately and in partnership they built up several large sawmills around the lake. There were auspicious opportunities for the insightful and ambitious entrepreneur in Muskegon during the fifties.

Eastern capitalists were less important in developing Muskegon. Frontiersmen and westerners—men of initiative and imagination—with some capital often took the lead in developing the Lake Michigan city. Emerging after the depression of the late 1830s and early 1840s, Muskegon's entrepreneurs avoided the economic setbacks that characterized Saginaw's and Bay City's early years. As a frontier boomtown, Muskegon attracted talent that believed in the virtues of the city. Some of these men like Ryerson and Hackley had the skill, enterpreneurial daring, and good fortune to sustain their and the town's economic goals.

The village of Muskegon, like its sister lumber cities Saginaw and
Bay City, continued to grow rapidly in the 1860s. The lumbering
business, although thrown into a slight disarray by the start of the
Civil War, experienced from 1862 on "eleven fat years."[42] During
these years lumbering evolved in all three representative communities from a small-scale, localized activity to a dominant regional industry. It changed from an operation that needed few laborers to one
that often required several hundred employees; it grew from an industry yielding small profits to one that rewarded the lumbermen-
entrepreneurs with substantial income; and it refocused from an
industry supplying local sales to one supplying great outside markets.
In those years, the lumbering hamlets also evolved from backwoods,
shanty towns to vigorous, industrial urban centers.

CHAPTER TWO

Lumbertown Enterprise

*For with all its handicaps, the lumber industry in Mich-
igan was basically an industry that grew great in a time
when it could hardly do anything else.*

—BRUCE CATTON, *Michigan: A History*

In the spring of 1878 woodsmen left the forest as they had every
spring. Those who were not hired on as river hogs, to drive the logs
down the swollen streams, threaded their way through the forests
over muddy tote roads and trails to isolated wayside railroad stations.
Here they purchased the infamous "ticket to hell." With a couple of
hundred dollars in their pockets the loggers headed for the great logging towns. They set out to take part in the annual orgy of drinking,
fighting, and whoring; and then, before all of their pay was squan-
dered, to secure a summer job in the sawmills or return to outlying
farms. The "Catacombs" of Bay City, "White Row" in East Saginaw,
and the "Sawdust Flats" of Muskegon—tangles of saloons and brothels—were the "hells" that the woodsmen sought. But the great lumber manufacturing plants that lined the rivers and lakes are what
kept the men in town. Men came here to celebrate, to survive until
next winter; some came to get rich.

Lumbering was the source of the entrepreneurial ethic. The lumber business spun an entrepreneurial matrix into which virtually all
other aspects of town life were interwoven. The foremost component
of the community economic base in the lumbertowns was the lumberman. Their capital sped up and shaped settlement and growth in
the Muskegon and Saginaw regions. After the Civil War the small
and crudely equipped sawmills that appeared during the antebellum
decade gave way in number and size to large-scale lumbering operations. Capitalist-lumberman from the East began to move into the
regions, and Saginaw and Muskegon lumber flooded eastern lumberyards and Chicago. The sawmill villages that became towns during

the Civil War developed into complex urban, industrial communities by the 1870s. For the moment predictions that it would take decades to cut all Michigan's pine brightened community prospects. Some lumbermen and many townspeople committed themselves permanently to these new industrial environments. While industrialists and entrepreneurs prospered, lumbertown enterprise—in fact, all aspects of local life—remained largely determined by the growth and development of the lumber trade.

TECHNOLOGY AND LUMBERTOWN GROWTH

While some truly spectacular profits could be made in the early days of lumbering, there were also many opportunities for going bankrupt. But the lore of lumbering and logging ignored the failures and like much of history concentrated on the phenomenal success stories. Although the vagaries of the weather and an uncontrolled market usually favored the large operator, enough little men sold out in time or became big operators that uncountable fortunes were made in the lumbering era. Saginaw, Muskegon, and Bay City, not surprisingly, had more than their share of these men of good fortune. Henry H. Sage, for example, an eastern entrepreneur who came into Bay City with substantial capital, multiplied his fortune through his mill and timber investments in Michigan.[1] Others like John McGraw, Ami Wright, and the Eddy brothers replicated Sage's entrepreneurial investment practices and success. Yet for every well-financed eastern lumberman, there were men like Charles Hackley who came to Muskegon with nothing and built substantial fortunes. It has been recorded that in one day, his best day in the lumbering business, Hackley made a profit of $365,000.[2] Starting off as laborers, men like Hackley who possessed some education and foresight could easily become land-lookers or bookkeepers. For them it was common to experience a meteoric rise to success.

For a small lumber manufacturing operation to get started the costs for site, physical plant, and machinery were substantial. The large operator frequently multiplied these costs by vertically integrating his operation to include timberlands, dams, docks, housing, and company stores. In the early years of lumbering before the end of the Civil War, most mills were built in sparsely populated areas where there was little competition and cheap land along the major tributaries. The amount of capital necessary to build a mill varied greatly depending on size and machinery. Before 1860 the average mill probably cost about $5,000 or $6,000. For example, John Drake and his brother came to Bay City in 1851 with $15,000 to "engage in the lumber business." Although they had little experience in lumbering, they purchased forty-four acres of land near West Bay City that included a mill, an engine and boiler, iron works, saws, and a siding machine for $1,400. Curtis Emerson bought an old mill near Saginaw for $6,000; although he soon spent another $10,000 on updating the machinery.[3]

Although the little man who was industrious, canny, and lucky could make it, there were more and more sawmills of very high capitalization. Especially during the expansion years of the late fifties and sixties, the fluctuating market favored the large operator. The repetitious economic pattern of nineteenth-century lumbering—scarcity and high prices, followed by glut and loss of income—favored the large operator. The lumberman-entrepreneur usually commanded enough capital to carry him through a bad year. Lumber mills not only increased in number but also in size during the 1860s (see table 1). For example, Ami Wright's mill in Saginaw City was producing about 15 million board feet annually in 1860. By 1870 expansion and new equipment increased production to 25 million annually. Large operators like Sage, McGraw, Ryerson, Hackley, Wright, and others aimed at turning out at least 25 million feet per year. These mills proved to be most efficient and capable of weathering the vagaries of fluctuating cycles.[4]

TABLE 1.

Number of Mills and Aggregate Capital Invested in Lumber Manufacturers for Selected Lumber Counties, 1860 and 1870

	1860			1870		
Place	–	Capital	Average for Industry	–	Capital	Average for Industry
Saginaw	28	$607,000	$21,678	64	$4,199,600	$65,618
Muskegon	27	635,150	23,524	56	2,810,900	50,194
Bay City	20	416,200	20,810	46	2,542,500	55,271

SOURCE: *Eighth Census of the United States, 1860, III, Manufacturers,* passim; *Ninth Census of the United States, 1870, III, Statistics of Wealth and Industry,* 679–83.

Although there may be some truth in Bruce Catton's observations that "the lumber industry in Michigan . . . grew great when it could hardly do anything else," the rapid expansion of the sixties and seventies was much more complex than merely the simple exploitation of an overabundant resource. Improved technology and transport made the large increases in production possible. New, sophisticated sawing machines in the sixties and the railroad in the next decade were used to increase production. Before the Civil War there were few improvements in primitive sawing techniques. Many mills continued to run the dangerous circular saw, which cut a wide, wasteful kerf and tended to split apart and fire off chunks of metal at the operator. The safer sash saw also continued to be used but was slow and cumbersome.[5] Finishing cut lumber was the slowest part of the operation and consequently lumber was often sold rough sawn.

Most technological innovations had to do with sawing. The gang saw was an adaptation of the sash saw. Multiple blades were added to a much larger frame, and by the late fifties one saw could cut two or three logs simultaneously into boards. "The gang saw became the monstrous giant of the mills." An improved circular saw was invented in 1860 that was made of steel and employed curved sockets for the teeth that prevented shattering. These newly designed blades were thinner and less wasteful, and they soon took a favored place in the mills along with the gang saw. Later the band saw improved on these sawing methods. By 1870 most of the medium and larger mills used muley, sash, circular, and gang saws in combination.[6]

Although sometimes premature experimentation delayed the introduction of new equipment, the lumbermen in the major lumber cities were usually quick to adopt new equipment and rationalize production. Many of the larger operators who moved into Michigan from New England had already adjusted to declining timber supplies and brought with them the new and efficient cutting methods. These early entrepreneurs also sought the most advantageous sawmill locations; and, early on, their choices often favored the Saginaw and Muskegon river regions. Solomon Johnson and his brother, who cofounded the city of Zilwaukee just north of Saginaw City, are believed to have installed one of the state's first gang saws in 1848, though their inexperience in installing the saw compelled them to abandon the new technology. Charles Merrill later brought the first successful gang saw to Saginaw in 1854. Merrill had used the gang

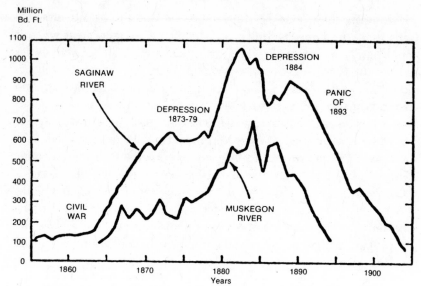

GRAPH 1. Lumber Cut by Saginaw and Muskegon Sawmills,
1855–1904

saw in Maine where the depleted supply of timber forced efficiency
in cutting. Likewise, the band saw was introduced into the state by
James McCormick of Bay City in 1858, although its slowness and
poor reliability postponed widespread acceptance for twenty years.
Nevertheless, improvements in mill machinery brought rapid increase in output per employee. In 1860 the mills commonly used one
employee for each one thousand feet cut per day; by 1876 one
man could cut two thousand feet; and by 1888, it was estimated
that one worker would cut three thousand feet.[7] All this makes it
clear why the Saginaw and Muskegon river cities came to be the
leading lumber centers in the state. Advantageous geographical locations brought men of capital and experience to these lumbering
regions. Capital and experience coupled with ambition and foresight
enabled the lumbermen-entrepreneurs of Saginaw, Bay City, and
Muskegon to build an industry that dominated the state's economy
for decades.

   The lumberman's emphasis in the mills on speed and greater efficiency led to a minor technological revolution that turned the struggling river mill towns into mechanized islands in a rapidly fading
wilderness. Sawmills that a generation earlier were small, primitive,
hand-operated affairs began to resemble the factories that characterized eastern industrial towns. In 1877 such an analogy struck a *New*

York Tribune correspondent traveling through Bay City. His description of John McGraw's mill was reprinted in the *Lumberman's
Gazette*.

> The mill of John McGraw and Company is at the upper end of Bay
> City. The firm owns 600 acres of land, and a third of their property is
> occupied by their saw mill, salt work, drying kilns, and other build-
> ings and storage places. The sawmill has a greater capacity than any
> other in this section, and is believed to be the largest in the world. It
> is rated at 40,000,000 feet of lumber for the season, but, if needed
> could be worked up to double that capacity. Over 350 men are em-
> ployed, and during the past six weeks over 200,000 feet of lumber
> have been cut every day. One day, when the mill was tested to its
> utmost capacity, 180,000 feet were cut in three hours, or at the rate
> of 675,000 feet for the day of 11 1/4 working hours.[8]

The mills not only attracted men who worked with machines but
they also attracted others who sought to improve the machinery that
they worked with. The climate in which industrialization and entrepreneurial expansion could take place had been created. The lumber
manufacturing era can truly be said to have started in the late
1860s. The lumbertowns became vigorous urban centers, and although peak production years with increased industrial development
and sophistication were a decade away, the economic patterns that
were to guide the fate of the three lumbertowns had become firmly
set. Any change that was to take place in the pattern of urban development was related directly or indirectly to the rise of lumbering.

Lumbering enterprise came to dominate most facets of economic
life in Saginaw, Bay City, and Muskegon by 1874 (see table 2). In
the early lumber era, little diversified manufacturing existed. Lumber
production during the early part of the era was primarily all rough-
sawn lumber. Diversification when it did take place was almost always within the scope of manufactured wood products. Besides
sawmills, shingle mills, planing and turning mills, the state census
industrial assessment in 1874 included stave and hoop factories and
barrel and woodenware factories as representative lumber manufacturing concerns.[9] As populations increased, entrepreneurs tried to
develop industries that would avoid the seasonal manufacturing
schedules of lumbering. Taking advantage of cheap fuel, raw materials, capital, and increased demands of the local market, lumbermen often built important subsidiary manufacturing establishments
near their sawmills. Still, important nonlumbering diversification
would have to wait further maturation of the settlements.

Table 2.
Employment in 1874

Place	Population	Persons Employed	Employed in Agriculture	Employed in Manufacturing	Employed in Lumber Manufacturing	Employed in All Other Manufacturing
Saginaw County[a]	48,087	14,087	2,837	3,675	2,606 (70.0)	1,035 (28.1)
Bay County[b]	24,832	7,615	727	3,204	2,563 (80.1)	628 (19.5)
Muskegon County	14,895	4,732	503	2,052	1,613 (80.0)	439 (20.0)
Michigan	1,334,031	358,280	164,029	59,346	27,807 (47.0)	29,775 (50.0)

[a]Combined populations of East Saginaw and Saginaw City.
[b]Combined populations of West Bay City and Bay City.
Figures in parentheses represent percentages of the total number employed in manufacturing.
Percentages for Bay City and Saginaw exclude flour milling manufacturers, 0.4 and 0.9, respectively.
SOURCE: Census of State of Michigan, 1874, pp. xxiv–xxv, lii–lx, 270–430.

SUBSIDIARY LUMBERING ENTERPRISES

Three major subsidiary enterprises profited lumbermen directly. One of these was salt processing. The state bounty of ten cents a bushel prompted several lumbermen to investigate the possibility of adding salt manufacturing to their sawmill operations in 1859.[10] Twenty-two men, including William Little and Jesse Hoyt, all residents of East Saginaw, invested $50,000 to establish the East Saginaw Salt Manufacturing Company. Because "none of them knew anything about the manufacture of salt," it took the company nearly a year to sink its first salt well. However, the report to their stockholders, published in the *Saginaw Courier* in February 1860, "struck the community like an electric shock." The "strength and purity" of the brine water coupled with the profits from an initial production of nearly eleven thousand barrels in six months prompted others to begin salt processing.[11]

Besides Fraser's, Fitzhugh's, and Birney's attempts at Salzburg, James McCormick and Judge Albert Miller sank salt wells in Portsmouth in 1860. By the end of the Civil War almost every sawmill owner along the Saginaw River had drilled a brine well and was producing salt as a by-product. Even though the state bounty was repealed in 1861, producing salt in lumber manufacturing became an inexpensive operation. Production merely required pumping and boiling away the brine water in large cast-iron kettles. As the brine water boiled, salt crystallized along the edges where it would be scraped and scooped from each kettle, then purified and packed in wooden barrels. Sawdust, scrap lumber, and later steam and solar-heating methods were used to evaporate the brine. Whatever method was used, costs were generally kept low.[12]

Induced by the successful salt operations at Saginaw, a few Muskegon lumbermen tried to replicate the lucrative sideline. In 1868, after it was reported that operators in Saginaw had exported 200,000 barrels, lumberman Gideon Trusdell hired an experienced salt producer from Syracuse, New York, and drilled a well on his mill property. Despite optimistic predictions and the discovery of a rich vein of brine, the amount of brine below the surface did not warrant investment in a salt-manufacturing plant. More wells were drilled in the 1870s, and as late as 1882 Martin Ryerson sank $10,000 into a well that went to twenty-one hundred feet. However, while oil was found in several wells—to the disappointment of the lumbermen— large quantities of brine were never found, and after Ryerson's expensive failure no new attempts to produce salt were made in Muskegon.

Although the manufacturing of salt in the Saginaw Valley was important as a lucrative sideline to lumbering, it became more significant as a subsidiary when the lumbermen were compelled to form cooperative associations to market salt. Throughout its history the lumber industry in Michigan was marked by its continuous inability to organize and control lumber production. However, unlike lumber production, out-state as well as local competition enabled lumbermen to form successful salt pools to eliminate competition from independent sellers. Competition was twofold: the many Saginaw Valley producers and the older, experienced producers of Onondaga and Syracuse, New York. The New York manufacturers lowered prices in the mid-1860s to control the Chicago market and force the valley producers out of business. The rapid decline in price prompted the drive toward combination along the Saginaw.[13]

An effort at association in 1866 was led by the manufacturers in East Saginaw. By 1868 the Saginaw Salt Company invited Bay City manufacturers to join and together they formed the Saginaw and Bay City Salt Company. This organization handled four-fifths of the salt shipped from the Saginaw Valley. It lasted until 1872, when increased demand persuaded several large producers to operate independently and sell at higher prices than the company offered. However, in 1876, after four years of rapidly increasing production, the Michigan Salt Association was organized and effectively regulated prices as well as controlled railroad shipping rates for salt in the valley. It regulated prices when necessary by restricting production and, when independents threatened prices, the association, as Sage stated, "put the knife to the jugular and bled all concerned till they were anxious for equitable arrangements."[14]

Salt manufacturing became a profitable enterprise. Sage estimated that his annual profits from salt production during the seventies ranged from $25,000 to $30,000.[15] Any panoramic view of the Saginaw River would disclose scores of narrow, four-story, derrick buildings along both sides towering above the brine wells. Outside the manufacturing of lumber and its associated occupations, salt manufacturing employed more workers than any other operation. In 1880 about one-quarter of all wage earners in the sawmills worked producing salt. There were forty-eight salt operations in the Saginaws and twenty-eight around Bay City. A pamphlet describing Bay City industries in 1883 stated that "fully one half of the salt of the United States . . . is made in the Saginaw Valley."[16]

A second enterprise, booming and boom companies, directly supported the lumber trade. The necessity of running logs by water produced a body of state statutes that defined and formulated the "laws of the waters." Michigan courts in the early 1850s adopted the so-called saw-log test of navigability. If a stream could float a log, it was a navigable, public waterway. Vessels, barges, and sawlogs had equal rights. The state legislature later gave powers of enforcement to county boards of supervisors, a privilege awarded the lumbermen. Their political and economic power in most logging counties provided the lumbermen with absolute rights to alter common waterways to ease log transportation.[17]

With access and movement eased, the lower reaches of the Muskegon River and the Saginaw tributaries soon became clogged with logs. To bring order to the confusion over which logs went to what sawmill, boom companies were formed. In 1855 the legislature granted individual boom companies exclusive rights to handle the log drive on certain rivers. A booming company could contract with owners to run their logs and also charge others, who were not contracted, for their logs that mingled with the drive. Under the new law the loose cooperatives that moved logs disappeared, and in 1855 Muskegon led the way in forming the first full-fledged booming company, the Muskegon Lumbermen's Association. A year later Charles Merrill built a boom south of Saginaw City and furnished services to Saginaw and Tittabawassee operators. These enterprises handled all the driving of logs down the rivers, improved the rivers throughout their length by damming and clearing, and sorted the logs at the mouth of the river according to each log mark. The loggers separated their stock on common river by stamping each log with a distinctive log mark. The boom companies assessed each owner a fee for each thousand feet of logs handled.

Further modifications to the Booming Act in 1864 empowered lumbermen to form cooperatives that effectively created booming monopolies. On the Muskegon River the association, which was losing money, was quickly absorbed by the new Muskegon Booming Company. Incorporated at $40,000, the new company attracted money from almost all the leading lumbermen in Muskegon. In its first year it rafted more than 90 million board feet of logs cut on the Muskegon River. Over on the Saginaw, Charles

Merrill sold his booming interest to the newly formed Tittabawassee Boom Company. Wellington Burt, Amasa Rust, and Merrill were prominent as directors of the company. Bay City lumbermen, although investors, never dominated the Tittabawassee company's board.[18]

Boom company operations soon expanded dramatically. With sizeable stock investments and the legal power to assess fees, the operators could undertake river improvements by building dams, sluiceways, and even changing the course of the tributary streams. At the sorting grounds along the Tittabawassee near Saginaw or on Muskegon Lake, booming became big business. The sheer magnitude of the task required large work crews and considerable investment. In one year the Tittabawassee and Muskegon booms rafted and delivered more than 600 million feet of logs.[19] This figure represents three million logs passing through the booming grounds in one season.[20] More logs—by board feet—were floated down the Tittabawassee in the nineteenth century than any other logging river. The Tittabawassee Booming Company vied for years with Weyerhaeuser's Beef Slough in Wisconsin for boasting honors as the largest boom works in the lake states and hence in the world.[21]

Rafting and sorting logs at the booms sometimes went on for seven months between mid-April and mid-November. As a lumbertown enterprise these activities became the largest sources of employment. In average years the work forces both in Saginaw and Muskegon easily numbered five hundred men. These numbers were exceeded in peak cutting years. Another two hundred men were employed on the drive and later to clear streams for the following year's run of logs. Because of the dangers involved in driving and booming, wages were often higher for boom men. These workers were often single, transient men—often French Canadians—who lived in boardinghouses along Muskegon Lake or, as in Saginaw, in rough-hewn shacks built intermittently along the nearly twelve miles of the Tittabawassee booming grounds. Higher wages and dependable employment extracted some loyalty from the workers toward the boom companies. These single, largely itinerant workers were also active participants in the carousing and brawling that characterized lumbertown nightlife.

Boom companies were also profitable enterprises. High dividend rates were paid to lumbermen-stockholders through years of operation. The records of the Tittabawassee Boom Company indicate that all during its existence, even in depressed years, the company gave generous returns.[22] The first dividend issued in 1866 amounted to fifty percent of the capital stock.[23]

A third enterprise that developed as a supplement to lumbering was the manufacturing of wood products. At first when a log was cut into boards, considerable cull lumber—boards rejected as poor quality—was left to be burned or cast into nearby rivers. In the 1860s, though, almost every sawmill began to manufacture usable products from scrap lumber. Laths for wall plaster were first cut from the cull timber. Later fence pickets, wooden boxes, and crates were also cull products that soon found ready markets. By the 1880s waste products from the mills went into the manufacture of hames, curtain rods, mop handles, baskets, and kindling wood.

Wooden barrels were in demand especially after the salt industry became profitable. In Saginaw and Bay City most of the sawmills that processed salt built cooperages. Hardwoods were brought in and cut into barrel staves. So successful did the barrel business become that the Saginaw Valley was shipping "shooks"—unassembled barrels—nationally in the 1880s. Longer staves than those used for barrels were also manufactured for making cisterns, water tanks, and hooped wooden pipes. By 1880 cooperages were the fifth largest source of employment in the Saginaw Valley.[24]

Several other wood-related products were also manufactured in the lumbertowns. Planks and cedar blocks for paving streets, sidewalks, and plank roads were manufactured. Shingle mills appeared where sizeable quantities of cedar shingles were cut to supply not only local markets but much of the Midwest. Woodenware works also were established early. These concerns produced washtubs, churns, pails, wooden bowls, and utensils. The Bousfield Woodenware Company in Bay City became the largest such factory in the world in the 1880s.

It is significant that in the later years of the lumber era many of the wood product firms were no longer using softwoods but cutting nearby hardwoods for their products. In doing so, the demand increased for finished wood. Previously, much of the pine was cut and sent to markets unfinished. But as demand increased, planing mills were built in the lumbertowns and turned out finished softwood that was used for doors, blinds, window frames, and household moldings. In time the same mills finished hardwood for woodwork, doors, benches, and carriages. Soon hardwood was being used for furniture, pianos, ice boxes, and toilet fixtures. In this manner, especially in Muskegon where more skilled immigrant craftsmen settled the lumber industry set the stage for the development of furniture manufacturing.

Other Lumbertown Enterprises

The sawmills, salt manufacturing, booming companies, and the woodenware business were all industries that were either directly or indirectly controlled by lumbermen. Yet there were several other manufacturing enterprises in the lumbertowns that ran independent of the lumbermen but were still, nevertheless, almost entirely dependent on the sawmill business for their livelihood. Shipbuilding, for example, began in the Saginaw Valley soon after the area became a sawmill center. The H. D. Braddock Company, lumber manufacturers in Bay City, built several large, three-masted schooners shortly before the Civil War. In Muskegon the booming company was the first enterprise to have a shipyard. Tugs and dredges that were needed to move logs around the lake were built near the booming grounds. The availability of cheap, accessible hardwood, plus good harbors, made both the Saginaw and Muskegon waterways ideal locations to build ships.

After the Civil War, as commerce on the Great Lakes grew rapidly, shipbuilding became a major industry especially along the Saginaw River. The state helped dredge the Saginaw River channel in the early seventies to allow larger vessels along the waterway. Several small firms continued to build wooden schooners and steam tugs to serve the lumber business. However, other more enterprising individuals built large ship-manufacturing operations. James Davidson opened a shipyard and dry dock in Wenona (West Bay City) in 1873, and Frank Wheeler followed in 1877. By the 1880s, during peak contract years, Wheeler's yard employed as many as fourteen hundred men. In the late eighties some of these yards began to manufacture steel boats instead of wooden sailing ships.[25]

Sawmills also created a ready market for special iron and steel products. An increasing demand for boilers and the need to repair sawmill machinery encouraged the early start of foundries. There were six or seven foundries in each of the lumbertowns employing a handful of workers. These shops manufactured saws, log loaders, pilers, lumber trimmers, marking hammers, engines, refuse burners, and saw frames for the mills and logging crews in the woods. The foundries were creative places. Each lumbertown had a foundry or two that invented new machinery to ease some stage of logging and lumbering. New equipment increased the efficiency of the mills and added technology that sped up the pace and profits of lumbering.

The machinery industry was also important because as it grew it became the basis for later, postlumber-era industrial diversification. Several individual firms were important from the long-range view. The Muskegon Iron Works founded by Alexander Rodgers grew to employ nearly seventy men in the 1880s. It remained a stable industry in Muskegon that lasted until after World War I. The Industrial Brownhoist Works in Bay City manufactured railroad equipment and sawmill and marine lifting machinery. After the lumber mills closed, Brownhoist grew to become the city's largest employer in the early twentieth century. Saginaw had several important foundry operations, probably the most important being the machine and boiler manufacturing firm of Henry and Edward Wickes. They became the primary manufacturers of the revolutionary gang saw in the 1870s.[26]

Varied enterprises that cannot be classed as either woodworking or metalworking plants also operated in the lumbertowns. Most of these were closely related to the lumbering business supplying equipment and foodstuffs. Many also simply developed as suppliers to the concentrated populations in the three towns. Food-producing plants served the local area but, more important, found ready markets in the logging camps and small interior towns. As early as 1855 the Michigan Agricultural Society reported:

> The 113 camps now in the woods will require, on an average, 14 barrels of flour and 12 barrels of pork each during the winter, making in all 1,682 barrels of flour, and 1,356 of pork. Each camp will also require, on an average, 3 bushels of corn or corn meal per day—225 bushels for 75 days—and for the whole 113 camps, a total of 8,475 bushels. Hay, say 15 tons per camps, or 1,685 tons in all.

This early assessment was based on an estimate of only eighteen hundred men in the woods. During the early seventies there were probably at least twenty thousand men in the interior camps of lower Michigan, and by the peak years, ten years later, this number doubled. To feed these men there were thirteen flour mills in Saginaw, where nearby agriculture was more developed, and about five grist mills in Bay City and one in Muskegon. At the Muskegon site, wheat was brought across Lake Michigan from Milwaukee.[27]

In Saginaw grist milling was an important light industry. Grains were purchased from nearby German farm settlements and ground into flour that brought substantial and stable incomes to several producers. German farmers provided grains, as well as markets, for brewery and malt plants in the Saginaws and Bay City. Nearby agriculture also enabled Saginaw to establish several small meat-packing concerns, soap manufacturers, and bakeries.

Knitting mills and clothing manufacturing establishments cut shirts, pants, gloves, and underwear for the workers in the camp. Cloth producers employed single women, wives, and daughters of sawmill workers. They were usually small concerns employing at most twenty to forty females and apparently provided "above average" working conditions.[28]

The loggers were also a ready market for other commodities. Several cigar shops cut, chopped, and rolled tobacco for local consumption. Harness, saddle, and leather firms supplied the harnesses that were indispensable to loggers before means other than horsepower were used to pull logs out of the woods. Tin and copperware shops supplied metal cooking utensils to the camps. Saginaw was also home to several printing firms and a few brickyards and tile yards, all producing primarily for local consumption.

In time, diversified manufacturers had developed to various degrees to supply the demands of local markets and settlements. New manufacturing establishments encouraged innovation and change to keep up with the demands of an entrepreneurial clientele that raced ahead to cut nearby timberland. East Saginaw and Saginaw City made the best beginnings in diversified manufacturing (table 3). The success of the Saginaws was based in part on nearby agriculture, competition between East Saginaw and Saginaw City, and the development of an early railroad network. Bay City and Muskegon relied heavily on lumbering and its subsidiary industries for their industrial base until late in the lumber era.

LUMBERTOWN SERVICE ENTERPRISES

Some enterprises directly attended the personnel of the lumber trade rather than the trade itself. These were not the lifeblood of the manufacturing cities, but nevertheless, commerce in wood did attract associated consumer and service industries.

The mill workers and shanty boys were a transient lot who populated a lumbertown between spring and October and November. Al-

TABLE 3.

Manufacturing Production of Lumber and Wood Products 1880

Manufactures	Saginaw County			Bay County			Muskegon		
	Number Established	Wage Earners	Value of Production $000	Number	Wage Earners	Value of Production $000	Number	Wage Earners	Value of Production $000
All Manufactures	428	5,429	9,313	151	3,401	8,100	301	4,264	7,312
Lumber, sawed	83	1,680	4,758	46	1,953	5,832	19	1,833	4,115
Lumber, planed	3	51	224	3	14	94	9	415	602
Sash, door, blinds	4	105	132	3	63	59			
Cooperage	22	115	140	14	83	107			
Woodenware	1	180	80	1	130	160			
Wood boxes	3	83	50						
Furniture	6	68	73			7	273	314	
Salt	48	652	965	28	531	936	5	105	178
Foundry, machine shops	17	235	406				3	8	20
Shipbuilding	11	253	415	9	327	341			
Handles, wood									
Files	1	14	20						
Agricultural implements									
Carriages, wagons	4	48	62				7	22	33
Upholstery	1	10	20						

Table 3. (Cont')

Manufactures	Saginaw County			Bay County			Muskegon		
	Number Established	Wage Earners	Value of Production $000	Number	Wage Earners	Value of Production $000	Number	Wage Earners	Value of Production $000
Tin, copperware	15	41	48				8	18	33
Saddlery, harness	10	30	63				3	8	13
Leather, all kinds	4	24	143						
Galvanizing	1	15	20						
Needles and pins									
Marble, stonework				1	15	20			
Paper									
Printing, publishing	7	70	48				4	59	45
Charcoal									
Brick and tile	10	146	51	4	21	81	11	205	280
Liquor, malt	7	33	124						
Bakery products	6	15	36				9	20	43
Coffee and spices	1	4	50				3	9	13
Soap and candles	1	7	25						
Tobacco products	10	68	62				15	64	69
Meat packing	2	13	210	2	8	105	3	10	255
Flour, gristmills	13	57	559	5	36	242	17	75	101
Clothing, men's	2	71	77				21	65	
Woolen goods									
Total, all enumerated manufactures	293	4,088	8,861	116	3,181	7,977	144	3,189	6,157

Source: U.S. Census Office, Tenth Census of the United States: 1880, vol 2, Manufactures (Washington: Government Printing Office, 1886), pp. 265–71.

though it is difficult to discern precisely how many passed through town each season, the number of mill men employed in the sawmills and other lumbering enterprises probably gives an idea of net in-migration. Certainly, then, there were between ten and fifteen thousand shanty boys, especially in the spring, who migrated into the cities along the Saginaw River alone. Half as many no doubt visited Muskegon. In the 1880s, as more industrial diversification took place, populations became larger and more stable. But throughout the period, Michigan's lumbertowns never successfully altered the seasonal nature of logging and sawing. However, the spectacular springtime influx of earlier years did slacken toward the end of the lumber period, and business enterprises, despite population stability, contracted.

Among the stores serving the transient market, general merchandise outlets were important enterprises. These very successful, popular merchants carried a general line of products combining clothes, groceries, and camp equipment to obtain local retail sales, as well as the wholesale logging camp trade. Every fall, camp foremen, cooks, and blacksmiths would equip their camp for the winter cutting season. Once the snows isolated the camps in mid-winter, resupply was difficult and expensive. Owners arrived before the fall encampment and often bought supplies in bulk and dispatched them to distant logging settlements. In the spring, after the long logging season, and in the fall before going into the woods, the mercantile shops did brisk business supplying clothing, dry goods, and boots and shoes to the transient shanty boys. Through the rest of the year these stores included enough miscellaneous merchandise to attract individual sawmill workers, community businesses, residents, and nearby farmers.

Though there were large mercantile establishments at each of the lumbertowns, Saginaw and Muskegon were in especially strategic positions for provisioning the logging camps. Near tributary streams that ran hundreds of miles into the interior, they were the first towns with easy access to shanty boys and logging camps. George and Edward Morley understood this when they moved to East Saginaw from Ohio in 1863. They bought into a hardware store as partners and within a few years purchased a handsome store on Water Street. Goods were loaded from a rear door onto scows and steam tugs to be poled or driven upriver to lumber camps. By 1881 Morley Brothers purchased from Jesse Hoyt a 240-foot lot along Washington Avenue in the business district of East Saginaw. Here they built the "second largest hardware and general merchandise store in the nation and a showplace for Saginaw." As early as 1860 Muskegon had six general merchandise stores supplying camps. The most imposing of these were the two firms owned by Martin Ryerson. Chauncy Davis competed with Ryerson; he owned a three-story structure that by 1857 was selling $75,000 worth of goods annually.[29]

Clothing followed general merchandise businesses as a lumbertown commercial product of importance. Loggers with $200 to $400 in accumulated wages accounted for much of the clothing market because after several days of carousing and brawling in their winter wares, their first major expense upon hitting town was a new set of clothes. Caulked boots were packed away, or more likely thrown into the river, and heavy wool mackinaws and flannel pants were left behind at the clothing store. The shanty boy emerged in a new, brightly patterned, red flannel shirt, new suspenders, pants, shoes or boots, and a felt hat. Throughout the era, newly, sometimes expensively, and often tastelessly garbed shanty boys paraded through town as part of the local color that struck the lumbertown visitor.

Jacob "Little Jake" Seligman, a German-born Jewish clothing merchant, for several years paid close attention to the lumbertown clothing trade. Seligman immigrated to the United States in 1859, and after several years as an apprentice tailor in New York, he moved to Detroit and went into the clothing business. By 1870 Seligman amassed some capital and decided to expand his business into Bay City and East Saginaw. Realizing the potential of the lumbering trade, he sold his Detroit store in 1874 and concentrated his interest in East Saginaw. Seligman made his presence felt quickly. Calling himself "King Clothier" or "King Banker," he bought large spaces in the local newspapers not only to advertise his business but also to keep himself in the news. Because he was one of the largest advertisers, the newspapers reported every move Seligman made. His downtown East Saginaw store was a prime location to tap the carousing and transient shanty boys. At the end of the spring drive, Seligman would hire a band and stage a parade through the streets of East Saginaw. From the back of the bandwagon he tossed out vests and promised that anyone who returned a vest to his store would get a free suit to match. Even though the vests were usually torn into several pieces by eager shanty boys, Seligman apparently kept his promise. He hired Indians, dressed them in bright, old military uniforms and sent them about town carrying "Little Jake" sandwich boards.[30]

Lumbertown business brought sizeable profits for Seligman. He himself "caught the fever" and invested in timberlands, became part owner of the Everett House Hotel, purchased and sold several business blocks, and owned the largest stable of horses in town. He also purchased the East Saginaw Railway when it was still a horse-drawn system. As sole owner he converted the carriages and laid steel track. In 1889 he converted the line to electricity. Much of Seligman's fortune grew from the private bank he operated in his clothing store. He would accept lumber company scrip or notes for merchandise or cash at a discount. Later he would redeem the scrip from the lumber companies for cash. When the lumber business began to fade, Seligman sold his store in 1893 and eventually moved to Detroit. In poor health he left Michigan and settled in Salida, Colorado. In 1911, unable to recover his health, he took his own life.[31]

Little Jake Seligman's achievements reaffirmed that the rough and tumble environment of the lumbertowns often permitted financial success regardless of origin or race. Many of the service trades that catered to the shanty boy such as barbering and restaurants were owned by or employed black pioneers. There were thirty-two black barbers in the Saginaws and twelve each in Bay City and Muskegon in the early seventies. Many of these black men made contributions to lumbertown enterprise. Saginaw barber James J. Campbell accumulated property valued at $2,300; Abram Reyno, another barber, accounted for $3,400. Benjamin Rochester and Stephen R. Buck, both barbers, listed personal worth at $5,200 and $2,000. Several self-employed black draymen acquired small personal fortunes. Beginning as teamsters for a lumberyard or sawmill, individual blacks were able to purchase wagons and achieve self-employment. Some like Daniel Fairfax of Bay City and Charles Peterson of Saginaw parlayed their investments in wagons into property wealth of more than $50,000 apiece. James H. Baker made a comfortable living as owner and operator of the New Crescent Lunch Counter and Ladies Dining Room—one of the few respectable eating establishments in raucous Bay City that boasted of having no bar.[32]

The lumbertowns also contained the usual complement of doctors, lawyers, realtors, druggists, and blacksmiths. Hotel and boardinghouse keepers, though, offered a service peculiarly necessary to the lumbertowns. The seasonal influx of transient shanty boys, single mill workers, visiting salesmen, businessmen, and high-rolling absentee lumbermen offered profits that encouraged the construction of all types of overnight facilities.

Hotels that served the well-heeled customer were built during the halcyon days of land speculation before the lumber boom. However, they probably reached their peak of extravagance when the Bancroft House was opened in East Saginaw in 1859. An expansive, four-story brick building, it accommodated two hundred guests at a time. A French chef was imported to cater to the lumber barons, leading merchants, and politicians who visited its sumptuous restaurants and banquet hall. It was out of place amid the mud streets and sluggish bayou area of early East Saginaw, but the lumbermen went first class in bringing civilization to the wilderness.

In time each lumbertown developed one or several ostentatious hotels, which became a center for parties and banquets. In Muskegon, the Occidental was the most conspicuous of that city's fourteen hotels in the early 1870s. After additions and modifications it emerged several years later as an imposing four-story brick structure. In Bay City, the Fraser House was a large, Italianate-looking stone structure that fronted the river and invited lumbermen to re-lax along its veranda. The Bancroft House, the Fraser House, and the Occidental catered to the lumber dealers who were transient or semipermanent residents. At one time there were eighteen young, newly married wives of merchants and lumbermen living or taking their meals at the Occidental. These hotels maintained lumber price sheets in their lobbies and provided quiet "bachelor tables" or men's rooms for capturing the lumbermen's trade. Here lumbermen, com-mission agents, and buyers met to conduct business deals.[33]

As the lumbertowns grew, each community added more hotels that served the lumber and business clientele. There were also some second-rate establishments, along the Saginaw River and Muskegon Lake, that offered cheap accommodations to the transient woodsmen and workers. These were sometimes worse than boardinghouses and offered little but a shared room and a straw-filled mattress. Many, however, were reasonably comfortable and catered to businessmen and traveling salesmen who made their headquarters in the river towns while visiting settlements along the nearby tributaries. The Wolverton House, the Globe House, the Portland, and the Astor House in Bay City; the Everett House, Crowley House, and the Sherman Hotel in the Saginaws; and the National, Trowbridge's, and the Hofstra House in Muskegon were such establishments.

Company and privately owned boardinghouses supplemented the hotels and gave badly needed housing to unmarried sawmill workers as well as single women. As a matter of course, in the early lumber-ing era, many mill owners provided their workers with shelter and meals. Nearby the mill, a standard two- or three-story "railroad" boardinghouse, 30 x 80 feet, was quickly constructed. It usually cost $5 to $6 per week for room and board. In a relatively short time once the communities were established, most lumbermen sold or leased the company boardinghouses. Few saw them as profitable and they were at times unpleasant and unpopular residences. However, lumbermen or mill managers often directed workers from one board-inghouse to another for more expensive rentals ate up mill workers' wages and placed demands on the mill owners for higher pay.[34]

LUMBERTOWN "ENTERTAINMENTS"

One logging practice that supported several less reputable enterprises was the spring and fall bender that, according to folklore, rocked the foundations of the lumbertowns. Lumbertown "entertainments"—sa-loons, dance halls, and brothels—offered services to the shanty boys who headed to town each spring after six months in the woods. A whole literature has developed about the self-indulgence and de-bauchery of the loggers, and though much is probably true there is reason to suspect much of it is exaggeration.

When the logging camps closed down in the spring, the hands were paid off. Though there were exceptions, tradition testified that almost every shanty boy's stake "was usually spent in the river-towns in profligacy and intemperance."[35] John Fitzmaurice, logger, news-paper reporter, and temperance lecturer, wrote in 1889 that "if there is an honest dollar spent more foolishly than another, it is frequently the dollar of the shanty boy!" Fitzmaurice thought—perhaps accu-rately after having spent twenty-eight years as a logger—that the transient lumberjack was innately thriftless when it came to the an-nual spring orgy:

> I have seen men in camp so mean and penurious that they would pull threads out of an old coffee sack to mend their worn out socks. Half sole a sock with a mit, and mit with a sock. Go to their work poorly clad, and suffer the worst pains and penalties the woods could inflict. Borrow beg and steal tobacco to keep their "van" bill down, and all to have a big stake in the spring. And when camp breaks up, they go in to town. First the lad rigs himself out in a new suit of clothes and sports a cheap watch and a ring, and possibly a pair of patent leather shoes. He then meets a "chum," and together they make for the low boarding houses.

The hard earned dollars roll away, till in ten days or two weeks at the farthest, all the boy's money is gone. His watch and ring is gone. The side is out of his new shoe. His new coat is torn down the back, and sick in body and soul . . . watching for some acquaintance to pass, from whom he may borrow enough money to take him back to camp.[36]

The saloon was the foremost enterprise that catered to the visiting shanty boys. These establishments were extraordinarily commonplace in the lumbertowns. In 1878, with populations of 10,064 and 8,747, there were 138 saloons in East Saginaw and 66 in Saginaw City. In 1860 a clergyman counted 84 "grog shops" in Muskegon. Although by 1870 when the town numbered 6,001, the number of saloons had shrunk, perhaps more accurately to 62. The *Muskegon Chronicle* recorded that "there were generally 60 to 85 saloons in the city during the lumbering days."[37] In 1880 when Bay City had nearly 27,000 residents, there were 162 saloons. Most of these were in Bay City proper where, as Fitzmaurice recalled, in 1875 within a 300-foot radius of the notorious Catacombs 40 saloons could be counted. "Any one cognizant about facts," Fitzmaurice implored, "will bear me out when I say that I have not exaggerated in the least. In Bay City and East Saginaw, saloons and 'cribs' stood for blocks, side by side."[38]

As soon as a trainload of shanty boys pulled into the station, "runners," hired by individual saloons, met each man and offered wooden nickles or other inducements. The taverns to which the men trekked off varied considerably in respectability. They ranged from the usual dark and dank, sawdust-strewn, narrow brick buildings to the more elegantly decorated establishments serving businessmen. Most of the more disreputable grog shops were in zones of vice "far from the respectable portions of town." These saloons were usually along the waterways and offered more amusements than mere drinking. In Muskegon, the bars on Ottawa Street catered to the loggers and river men and were considered rougher than those along Western Avenue. East Saginaw's loggers frequented the establishments along Potter Street and nearby Water Street, although reportedly "houses of intemperance or licentiousness" were located throughout that city.[39] In Bay City, the Catacombs, a confusing series of interconnecting basements and exterior wooden walkways along the river at Third Street, has been immortalized in lumbering lore for its violent and debauched clientele.

The Catacombs and Muskegon's Canterbury House epitomized the extremes of saloons, resorts, and gambling dens. The Bridge

Block was perhaps the most infamous of the structures in Bay City's Catacombs. It is described in vivid detail by Fitzmaurice in 1889:

> Here were found every facility for drunkenness, debauchery and gambling, all or singly, associated with deeds of robbery and even murder. Here, in the darkness made visible by the flare and glare of dirty lamps, day and night alike, were found congregated the lowest and most degraded of both sexes. Here, the most horrible and obscene orgies were carried on with perfect impunity—for woe to the officer who alone would attempt a "raid" upon the "Catacombs," it was virtually as much as his life was worth. The second story of the building was occupied by saloons, a trifle more respectable than that in the pit beneath. It fronted upon Water Street, and carried an air of outside decency. But within the vileness was simply unspeakable! Here every convenience was afforded for fleecing the shanty boy, with liquors of every description, from the best Hennessey brandy to the fatal black bottle, drugged for the final drink, to be given the poor fool who would then be thrown upon the street penniless. "Pretty waiter girls" were in attendance, every one of whom was a prostitute of the most depraved and unscrupulous class, with her apartments in the same building, where her fascinated dupe would soon unload his winter's "stake." In the third story was a variety theater, where the plays presented were of the character suited to the vilest and most depraved taste, and the "wine room" attached to it was the receptacle of rotten moral corruption, impossible to even here hint at.[40]

The Canterbury House, outside Muskegon proper, contained many gambling tables, a large hall with stage and orchestra pit, a barroom, and about thirty-six rooms on the second floor. Rousing dances, boxing matches, cockfights, and other sporting events were held at the Canterbury.[41] Because of its distance from town it not only escaped police raids but also catered to some of Muskegon's prominent citizens.

Establishments favored by persons other than the shanty boys included Herman Vos's saloon and George Schubert's establishment on Western Avenue in Muskegon. These places were "larger, orderly and well conducted. Little hard liquor was sold here; the free lunch was good and one could always join a game of cards or billiards."[42] Other saloons were known by their clientele. The Dynamite saloon on Ottawa Street was the rendezvous for booming company employees in Muskegon. Fishermen, railroad workers, and dockwollopers in Bay City and Saginaw had their favorite haunts. Billy Taylor's saloon in Muskegon was the gathering place for politicians.

Prostitution was a second lumbertown enterprise closely associated with the tavern business. Despite the seasonal nature of the loggers' entertainment sprees, prostitution was a year-round operation. Arrest records for Bay City indicated that May was the most active month followed by June, October, September, and December. The Christmas season was surprisingly busy as some shanty boys returned to the city for the holidays, sailors and fishermen remained in port during the winter months, and others in festive spirits celebrated extravagantly. The year-round prospect of securing a livelihood, plus the twenty or so years of the lumber era's existence, created a permanent, hard-core legion of prostitutes in the lumbertowns.[43]

Women most often plied their trade from one of the hundreds of saloons in the Sawdust Flats, White Row, or Catacombs. Many of these drinking spots employed two or three "pretty waiter girls." The girls usually entertained their customers in sectioned dark apartments in the basements. The price was sometimes as little as fifty cents but more commonly ranged between two and five dollars.

As in so many frontier settlements, there are only estimates in the newspapers, pulp magazines, and personal reminiscences as to the number of prostitutes in the lumbertowns. Fitzmaurice stated that in the late seventies "Bay City and East Saginaw had between them 1,400 prostitutes."[44] Fitzmaurice's figures are probably high, but conservative estimates can place the number of prostitutes in the lumbertowns in the hundreds. The many saloons, dance halls, variety theaters, and resorts support the conclusion that prostitution was much more pervasive in the lumbertowns than in most western frontier settlements.[45] If, of the 162 saloons in Bay City, only half employed the minimum of two or three waiter girls, the number of prostitutes would rest in the hundreds. Similar numbers can be attributed to Muskegon where twenty one houses of ill repute conducted business, dance halls dotted the lake, and the general atmosphere was as tolerant as Bay City. East Saginaw approached the problem more openly, and in the 1880 census inquiry city officials admitted having thirty two houses of ill repute in the city. Bay City reported three and Muskegon acknowledged only four houses. East Saginaw, which experienced recurrent reform waves, was much more dedicated to investigating and reporting illicit activities.[46]

The lumbertown dance house was another entertainment emporium. These large wooden buildings primarily provided female companionship. Dance halls were more acceptable places for men of varied social backgrounds to mingle with ladies of easy virtue. Prominent lumbermen were known to partake in some expensive "entertainments." The third floor of Bay City's Catacombs served as a dance emporium and theater. Admission was five dollars, more costly than the common dives along nearby Water Street. The Canterbury House in Muskegon contained a large dance hall with stage and orchestra pit. Mollie Garde and Jennie Morgan, colorful ladies of the evening, ran the establishment. As entrepreneurs they devised more ways than one to tap the shanty boy and mill worker for his hard-earned wages.[47]

Although the businessman's ethic brought many diverse elements of lumbertown enterprise together, and entrepreneurship often determined the vitality of the settlements, the nineteenth-century system of free enterprise bred predatory capitalism on many levels. Working with a limited natural resource, logging and lumbering encouraged aggressiveness, ruthlessness, social turmoil, and individual disasters. The manufacturing of lumber, booming, and salt manufacturing, because the entrance requirements were higher in investment, talent, and technology, brought out the strengths and weaknesses of those involved. On all levels, though, entrepreneurs were in agreement on the twin goals of rapid community growth and the accumulation of wealth. They shared a view of society that stressed individualism and competition. But much of this individualistic success was achieved by the exploitation of a sizeable force of laborers in the lumbertowns. Unskilled workers on the lower end of the occupational ladder would soon realize that the entrepreneurs and enterprising businessmen were the only ones who experienced success.

A Ferry crossing the Tittabawassee River in the village of Freeland, near Saginaw City, in the 1870s. The Tittabawassee was the most important waterway for moving logs from Michigan's interior woods to Saginaw's sawmills. (Courtesy of the Historical Society of Saginaw County.)

The Tittabawassee booming grounds. Twelve miles of "pens" near Saginaw were used to store logs floated down the Tittabawassee and its tributaries. The Booming Company employed over five hundred men in peak years. (Courtesy of the Historical Society of Saginaw County.)

Gardner Williams & Brothers Mill, Saginaw City. In 1835 the Williams brothers built the first sawmill on the Saginaw River. They also were the first to use steam driven machinery in their mill. This is the fourth Williams sawmill, c. 1885. (Courtesy of the Historical Society of Saginaw County.)

The Michigan Lumber Company was directly across the Saginaw River from the Williams mill. Log rafts from the booming pens were stored in the mill pond prior to being cut into lumber. Drying lumber can be seen stacked on the right. (Courtesy of the Historical Society of Saginaw County.)

The Bliss & Van Auken Sawmill, Saginaw City. Owned by A. P. Bliss and Wills Van Auken, this was the last sawmill in Saginaw and was in operation until the 1950s. The eighty foot high refuse burners burned scrap lumber, and the derrick structures housed brine wells used in manufacturing salt. (Courtesy of the Historical Society of Saginaw County.)

The George Rust & Company sawmill, East Saginaw. Wooden water barrels were often kept on the roofs of the sawmills to offer some protection from frequent fires. Firms also hired fire boats that fought fires from the river side of sawmills. (Courtesy of the Historical Society of Saginaw County.)

Strable Manufacturing Company, Saginaw, 1900. At the end of the white pine era the lumbertowns temporarily manufactured hardwood products. This was a carry-over industry until automobile related manufacturing was introduced. (Courtesy of the Historical Society of Saginaw County.)

Strable's lumberyard, Saginaw, c. 1910. Strable's yard employed a number of recent Polish and German immigrants. Black workers in the nineteenth century usually worked in sawmills as "firemen" tending the coal boiler fires.

Matilda and Julius Schubert, pioneer German settlers in East Saginaw's Germania. This photo was taken around the turn of the century. (Courtesy of Connie Hartley.)

The First Bismarck, in East Saginaw's Germania. This was a more respectable drinking establishment catering to German merchants and workers. (Courtesy of the Historical Society of Saginaw County.)

Interior of The Jefferson saloon with lunch counter, East Saginaw. (Courtesy of the Historical Society of Saginaw County.)

CHAPTER THREE

Sawdust Cities

In a few years these impenetrable forests will have fallen;
the sons of civilization and industry will break the silence
of the Saginaw; its echoes will cease; the banks will be
imprisoned by Quays; its current which now flows on
unnoticed and tranquil through a nameless waste, will be
stemmed by the prows of vessels. More than a hundred
miles sever the solitudes from the great European settle-
ments, and we are perhaps the last travelers allowed to
see its primitive grandeur.

—ALEXIS DE TOCQUEVILLE

Between 1870 and 1890 the lumbertowns suggest in many ways the economic and physical landscape that Alexis de Tocqueville had envisioned fifty years earlier. One change associated with the lumber era was population growth. The Saginaws by 1880 numbered 29,541 residents; the Bay Citys, 27,040; and the Muskegon area, 11,262. Men and women had come to the lumbertowns searching for what was supposed to work in life: family, friendship, commerce, and industry. Many found what they were looking for. Workers, entrepreneurs, and lumbermen vigorously engaged in creating a townscape that offered new opportunities and perhaps, eventually, a new sense of community.

Throughout this time developers talked endlessly of individualism. It was the intense individualism that Tocqueville witnessed: "They own nothing to any man, they expect nothing from any man; they acquire the habit of always considering themselves as standing alone, and they are apt to imagine that their whole destiny is in their own hands."[1] The lumbertowns developed a milieu of contradictory extremes. Entrepreneurs who had unlimited desires depended on a unity with other men for their success. Some men were examples of complete individualism, but far more, while brazenly defending individuality, joined hands to build lumbertown communities.

For a while at least, especially during the halcyon days of rapid growth and prosperity, a sense of community developed—a willingness to set aside diversity and work together to affect common circumstances positively.

The three major lumbertowns thus did not simply just grow. The town promoters who settled the area were only the first in a long line of newspapermen, merchants, lumbermen, and citizens who combined their efforts to attract residents and businesses. Although strategically located and assured by nature of prosperity, locational advantages did not always guarantee urban dominance. Special efforts were constantly needed to ensure that settlers and businesses did not locate at a rival locale. For every Saginaw, Bay City, or Muskegon, there were scores of competing settlements striving for economic dominance. Controlling the hinterland commercially, and later industrially, became the key to continued expansion. Having once gained the proper integration of river, sawmill, and entrepreneurial interest, the townsfolk discovered that the struggle to persevere was an on-going effort requiring energetic leadership, ambition, influence, and money.

As in other Midwestern cities, town promotion in the lumbertowns followed a pattern.[2] However, there were exceptions to this pattern in towns engaged in extractive industries. Commerce, because of the need to ship lumber east and west, was easily established. It grew rapidly, moreover, as outside markets expanded. Eastern lumbermen who moved into the Saginaw Valley brought with them established lumber markets and well-traveled pathways of commerce. Further, industry did not supplant trade as these cities grew but developed concomitantly. Still, many other lumbertowns shared these advantageous patterns of growth. The leading lumber settlements, though, succeeded and grew more rapidly because promoters and lumbermen-entrepreneurs demonstrated leadership that coupled foresight with aggressiveness in their quest for economic advantage.

Town Growth and Transportation

Once commerce and industry were established and the lumbertowns grew slowly but steadily before the lumber era, the physical shape of the townscape became an important entrepreneurial consideration.

Along the Saginaw River, East Saginaw continued to prosper, and as
populations grew, the city expanded in 1865 by adding two 640-acre
sections, one to the north and another southward. In 1873 the village of Salina with three thousand residents was annexed to East
Saginaw.

On the other side of the river a new plat was adopted for Saginaw
City in 1857, and in 1865 several sections were integrated with this
plan. Thus, though in size the two Saginaws were comparable, the
more aggressive boosterism of east-side residents attracted more people to the newer city. By 1880 East Saginaw recorded 19,016 residents and Saginaw City, 10,444. Throughout the lumber era, an
intense and sometimes bitter rivalry developed between the two cities. East Saginaw because of its topography—swamps, mosquitoes,
and periodic floods—battled vigorously to build public improvements and provide more attractive urban amenities than its cross-
river rival. The "older residents" of Saginaw City, according to one
observer, developed "a keen hatred of all persons in any way identified with the remarkable progress of East Saginaw."[3]

Bay City was engaged in competition for settlers not only with its
downriver neighbor but also with Henry Sage's settlement directly
across the river. After Lower Saginaw changed its name to Bay City
in 1857, efforts were made to incorporate the village of Portsmouth
into Bay City in 1859. Water Street was connected with its counter-
part in Portsmouth, and streets were planned to integrate the two
communities. However, when Bay City was chartered as a city in
1865, Portsmouth was not included. It was reunited with Bay City in
1873. In the meantime, Bay City expanded its grid pattern eastward
at right angles from the river in contrast to the settlement of Portsmouth, which followed a traditional north-south grid arrangement.
In between these conflicting street patterns a narrow strip of land
was settled haphazardly.

Across the river, Wenona grew steadily after incorporating as a
village in 1867. Sage's company town expanded by integrating plats
of various speculators who built residential subdivisions adjacent to
the company's original 116 acres. From 1871 to 1875, especially after
Bay City annexed Portsmouth in 1873, efforts were made by the
larger town to convince Banks, Wenona, and Salzburg to join Bay
City. However, Sage and many residents on the west side resisted,
fearing higher taxes because of the need for inevitable west-side improvements. In 1877 the state legislature approved a plan to consolidate Wenona, Banks and Salzburg as West Bay City. Though a

rivalry emerged between the two Bay Citys, it apparently never reached the intensity that characterized the competition downriver at the Saginaws. West Bay City remained a smaller, less well-developed settlement, never competing vigorously with its larger, cross-river neighbor.[4]

In Muskegon the original four small settlements scattered around Muskegon Lake developed into nine separate urban districts, although nine-tenths of the population lived in Muskegon proper.[5] Little effort was made in the Muskegon area until toward the end of the lumber era to consolidate the settlements. As the lakeside community grew—it added about 26,000 people during the lumber period—most of the residents continued to locate near the lake. Muskegon proper spread out in a linear grid pattern along the southern shore of Muskegon Lake.

All three lumbertowns grew by annexing linear patterns of streets that appeared adjacent to the Saginaw River or Muskegon Lake. The attempts at integrating several waffle-iron, rectilinear patterns often led to townscapes that were not conveniently laid out for crosstown commerce. However, because water was for so long the primary means of travel and transport, little foresight was put into logical town planning. Natural, geographic contours—swamps, hills, and streams—were largely ignored, and towns were built simply to prepare land for sale amid the lumber boom. Thus, geographic obstacles often separated areas in a lumbertown and prevented the social and economic cohesiveness on which cooperative communities were based. The problems of social and, to some extent, economic separation that were present at first along the Saginaw because of cross-river rivalries were exacerbated by unplanned growth.

Though some town expansion into the hinterlands may have been unplanned, promoters of the lumbering towns were anxious to guarantee avenues of settlement and commerce by improving transportation. As noted above, Norman Little in East Saginaw and Martin Ryerson in Muskegon chartered plank road companies in mid-century. Bay City, surrounded by swamps and poorly drained soil, was not connected by road to Saginaw until 1861. Pioneer town-builder James Fraser and lumberman William McEwan financed Bay City's first road, the Tuscola Plank Road. West Bay City built a road westward into the hinterland to connect with Midland in 1866.

Plank roads were cheap to construct in the lumber manufacturing centers and the ideal material to cross the many swamps in the Saginaw Valley. Despite gravel roads supplanting plank roads in other parts of the state, wood turnpikes were maintained in the central state area until late in the nineteenth century. Lumbertown road networks, though, were never a primary avenue of travel. Because long wet seasons made many of the roads impassable, the settlers more often used the waterways for travel. Logging and lumbering were water dependent, and most of those associated with this enterprise quickly adapted to water travel in summer as well a winter.[6]

As the lumber industry grew, efforts were constantly made to improve the Saginaw and Muskegon rivers and Muskegon Lake for water transportation. Lumbermen financed much of the clearing that took place along the Saginaw and Muskegon rivers. Snags and obstructions that interfered with the movement of logs were removed, the waterways deepened, and wharves and docks constructed. The channel entrance on Muskegon Lake to Lake Michigan was shallow and occasionally silted. In 1863 contributions raised $40,000 to build wharves along the channel and construct protecting piers fifteen hundred feet long into Lake Michigan. Most subscribers were familiar lumbermen including Ryerson, Charles Hackley, T. Newall, and several others. The channel was dredged and widened to accommodate large, heavily loaded lumber schooners and passenger ships.

It is difficult to underemphasize the vast amount of freight—lumber, salt, and wood products—shipped from the lumbertowns throughout the era. By the 1880s Muskegon became the second largest port on Lake Michigan rivaled only by Chicago; the Saginaw River was easily the most active port on Lake Huron. Between 1879 and 1889 an average of three thousand vessels cleared Muskegon annually; and in Bay City, during the peak six months shipping season in 1883, an average twelve large transport vessels cleared port daily. Passenger transport records indicate that for five dollars, a person could depart the Saginaw River by one of four steamers leaving for Cleveland weekly. Regular lines served Tawas, Au Sable, Au Gres, and Port Austin; a boat left Bay City for Saginaw every two hours. Excursion ships and lumber boats also carried thousands of passengers between Muskegon and Chicago. Martin Ryerson discovered that by adding traveling quarters in his lumber steamers, passengers could be booked on return trips from Chicago to Muskegon at bargain rates. Waterways became the main arteries of an integrated transport system in the lumbertowns.[7]

In contrast to its importance in most Midwestern settlements, railroad building was met with some disinterest and apprehension by lumbertown residents and lumbermen. Despite considerable building activity in the southeastern part of the state, railroads had not even entered the lumber settlements until the end of the Civil War. Railroad building did not at first attract the interest of lumbertown promoters for three reasons. Foremost were the entrenched patterns or habits that favored water transport. The lakeside location of the sawmills and an established system of commerce that shipped goods to markets by water dissuaded many from eagerly supporting railroad construction. Moreover, a few mill owners who also became tug and steamship operators were unwilling to invite competition by subsidizing railroads. Lastly, "some lumbermen were antagonistic toward the railroads in part because of a feeling that the roads were discriminatory in their rates, in part because of a fear that the roads, if allowed to expand, might frequently cause fires in stands of timber."[8]

Regardless of their early reservations, many lumbermen by the Civil War heralded the railroads as a means of tapping new markets in an ever expanding hinterland. Still, it was not until the years after the war that railroads began to connect towns in the state's lumbering heartland. One exception was East Saginaw. Continuing the aggressive promotional policies of Norman Little and Jesse Hoyt, several promoters began to clamor for a railroad before the war started. After the land grants appropriated to the states in 1857–58, a company was formed in East Saginaw in 1857 intending to build a road from Saginaw to Flint and across the state to Ludington. This was an ambitious plan. No road yet connected to Detroit and the undertaking would be an effort to build out from an embryonic sawmill town into the western hinterland as well as to southern population centers.

An investment of $10,000 was spent on grading and laying rails between Saginaw and Mount Morris. Construction and financing moved slowly, but in January 1862 the first train ran from East Saginaw to Mount Morris and Flint. Until 1864, however, the line remained a spur going nowhere. From Flint passengers had to take a stagecoach to Holly where rail connections were made to Detroit. It took another ten years to run the Flint and Pere Marquette railroad across to Ludington.

Yet town promoters in East Saginaw had achieved their goal. East Saginaw became the terminus for rail passengers arriving from all southeastern Michigan. A large, handsome, brick railroad station was built near downtown East Saginaw on Potter Street. Businesses and saloons soon spread down Potter Street and along Water Street. More important, when the Pere Marquette was extended across the river into Saginaw City in 1867, bridge locations were far to the north of that city and avoided its population center. Terminal connections also were largely determined by east siders. As the line extended westward it passed through the heart of the pine forest and eventually had more than a hundred miles of spurs running into the woods. Although these feeder lines did not bring in much raw timber until later in the lumber period, they served as crucial supply lines to the lumber camps and small clusters of houses, saloons, and general stores that cropped up in the interior. Scores of businessmen and lumbermen in East Saginaw profited by extending their trade into the railroad's hinterland, and, as one early Saginaw observer noted, the Flint and Pere Marquette "served as an invaluable asset and contributed vastly to the growth and settlement of East Saginaw."[9]

Saginaw City was effectively cut off from this first railroad venture. Although asked to participate in early planning and promoters had planned a railroad bridge to connect East Saginaw with Saginaw City, the older community resisted because it was the second city on the line coming from Detroit. Several intransigent Saginaw residents, including real estate promoters Peter C. Andre and George W. Bullock, insisted that the bridge cross the river well south of East Saginaw and come into south Saginaw City first. Promoters in East Saginaw, antagonized by an arrogant rebuff, replanned the line and located the main terminal to the far north on Potter Street, the farthest possible point from Saginaw City. Saginaw City remained without a railroad connection until 1867, when the Jackson, Lansing and Saginaw Railroad Company completed a spur northward from Owosso. This eventually gave Saginaw City connections to Chicago.[10]

Bay City businessmen and some lumbermen began to plan for a railroad as soon as the connections from East Saginaw were completed in 1862. Yet any entrepreneurial enthusiasm was tempered by those who stated it was virtually impossible to build a roadbed through the swamps between Bay City and East Saginaw. After three years of planning and temporizing, the editor of the Bay City Journal expressed his frustration with the lack of progress:

> Do the people of this city think that business prospects of a road to this point are sufficient to induce some company to build it without any effort being made here? If so, we opine, that we shall continue to travel through mud and mire to reach the outer world. . . . Let them [the business leaders organizing the road] call a meeting to stir up the

people, something, anything, everything, rather than sit down in the mud as we have been doing for years past.[11]

The county board of supervisors soon appropriated $75,000 to aid those who had privately financed the East Saginaw and Bay City Railroad. In early 1866 the board expressed its dissatisfaction to president James Birney, Jr., that little was being done and threatened to withdraw its appropriation unless the line was graded by the end of the year. Apparently their threat had an effect, for in January 1866 Birney advertised for railroad ties and hired A. S. Munger to supervise construction. The railroad bed was built on dredgings from the swamps and completed to East Saginaw in November 1867. The twelve-mile spur was financed completely by private contributions and Bay County.

Movement in Bay City prompted Wenona to develop, as the Bay City Journal reported, a case of "railroad on the brain." Henry Sage, his partner John McGraw, and Salzburg investor Daniel Fitzhugh contracted with the Jackson, Lansing and Saginaw road at Saginaw City to build an extension along the west side of the river to Wenona. The lumbermen agreed to build the line in exchange for $80,000 in railroad stock.[12] More support came from a village bond to finance railroad improvements in the town. Sage foresaw, much like the promoters in East Saginaw, the importance of running a line to the west side. He pressured town officials to extend and improve the construction of new slips and docks along the river as an integral part of the railroad network. He also encouraged the railroad company to run spurs north and west and hinted that he would help finance these extensions. Sage saw the importance of a west-side connection into the interior. These westward lines would not only aid his lumber business but also stimulate trade for his company stores and in the long run boost property values in the interior where Sage owned valuable timberlands.[13] By the 1880s West Bay City and Bay City had important railroad connections running along Lake Huron northward, northwest toward Grayling, and westward to Midland.

Railroad fever developed slowly in Muskegon. The distance to the major population center (Chicago), the lack of a nearby connecting line, and the swampy terrain—much like Bay City—over which a road would have to be built slowed early interest. However, as lumbertown rivals across the state completed rail lines, some Muskegon residents began to clamor for a railroad. In January 1869 an association was incorporated to build a link between Muskegon and Ferrysburg, twelve miles to the south. Lumberman Lyman G. Mason was president. Other directors included Hackley and Chauncey Davis, both lumbermen; a lawyer, Frederick Nims; and Alex Rodgers, a foundry owner. They invested $80,000 to construct a roadbed and connect to the line at Ferrysburg. Although there were some intermittent arguments over location of a depot and more financing, the road was completed in January 1870, and Hackley's business office on Eighth Street became a temporary depot. The Muskegon and Ferrysburg Railroad merged with the Michigan Lake Shore Railroad that connected to Grand Haven, Holland, and Allegan. In 1871 connections were finally made to Chicago. Although Muskegon and nearby hamlets extended the railroad northward for some miles, the Lake Michigan port city did not undertake extensive railroad building into the interior until the 1880s. [14]

Lumbermen and businessmen in all three communities were instrumental in financing and constructing early railroads. They undertook railroad construction primarily to ensure community growth but also to acquire access to new timberlands as well as pathways to old markets. Once rail connections were complete, most lumbermen were content to quickly sell their railroad interest. Despite economic acquiescence, lumbermen maintained considerable control of local railroad interests. In the lumbertowns the railroads never had the economic or political power to drastically manipulate freight rates, determine settlement patterns, or promote rival town sites to sell railroad lands. Unlike towns developing in the plains states, railroad management could be counted on to be relatively supportive of lumbertown growth and promotion.

City Services, Culture, and Leisure

Although prominent city dwellers invested their savings in railroads and factories, almost all lumbertown citizens were willing to subscribe their time and money to improve municipal services. The most pressing services throughout the lumber era were fire protection and law enforcement. All three lumbertowns organized into legal municipalities primarily to enact laws and hold special elections to safeguard the settlements from the costly threat of fire. Sawmills and stacks of drying wood along the waterfronts were under constant threat of fire. Cheap timber also dictated that early buildings were constructed of wood. A single spark could easily kindle a whole town. Each lumbertown suffered several disastrous fires, and as a result, the authorities enacted stringent fire codes and constantly sought new equipment. Most of the lumbertowns' budgets went to pay fire wardens and to purchase fire-fighting facilities.[15]

Although Bay City had taken early steps to buy hand-drawn steam pumpers and make regulations against future wooden business buildings, an entire business block burned in 1865. Two years later a large sawmill and several downtown businesses were destroyed in separate conflagrations, and shortly thereafter a downtown business block was saved from another disastrous fire only by dynamiting several buildings to isolate the inferno. To combat these and other fires, lumbermen in Bay City took progressively more involved and expensive steps to provide fire protection. Mill owners, who had perhaps the most to lose, encouraged legislation and donations to purchase fire-fighting equipment. In Bay City H. M. Bradley, owner of one of the city's larger sawmills, was appointed the first fire chief. Likewise, after several fires in 1865, the citizens voted a bond issue of $6,000 to purchase a steam fire engine.

Similar developments took place in Muskegon. In the early sixties several prominent lumbermen met and submitted an ordinance to the village council to safeguard the city against fire. The city marshal was to supervise fire-fighting activity, and $100 was appropriated for equipment. When a fire broke out in Muskegon, all sawmills were required to give twelve short blasts on their whistles. At this signal every laborer was expected to drop his work and run to the fire. In these early years, "fire-fighting was a community affair. This interdependence bred friendliness hard to find in the more organized society of today."[16]

Volunteer, and soon professional, fire departments were established in all three lumbertowns. By the early seventies East Saginaw and Bay City had built waterworks primarily to supply enough water pressure in case of fire. Muskegon debated the need in 1871 but took action only after a major fire devastated a quarter of the town's business section and two hundred homes in 1874.

Besides the fear of fire, lumbertown residents were at times apprehensive about one another as well as transient visitors. Despite the earlier "rioting and carousing" of Indians, traders, and trappers, not until the rowdyism of the lumberjacks became widespread did the lumbertowns create police forces. Like so many frontier towns where law enforcement was lax, the fighting and vandalism of the shanty boys at first prompted vigilante action. East Saginaw, before the lumber boom, had experienced the shooting and death of a deputy marshal in 1864 as well as a series of fires that led to the formation of a "Vigilance Committee." Committee members were later appointed as "Special Police" by the town council and given the authority to arrest suspicious "incendiaries." Apparently the legitimization of vigilante action lasted more than a year in East Saginaw. In 1865, in the village of Portsmouth, a group of citizens met at the local school and formed a "Committee of Safety" to "protect the citizens of this place from acts of violence." Violence and rowdyism had become a fact of life in Bay City and was frequently mentioned and deplored in town newspapers. Likewise, near Muskegon, the village of Casnovia organized a "Vigilance Committee" in 1870 "for the purpose of ferreting out perpetrators [sic] of law and order." Yet despite these early incidents, local authorities in the lumbertowns held the vigilante alternative in check and rarely experienced protracted vigilante action. Nowhere in the lumber settlements does it appear that vigilantes usurped local police functions and exerted complete or prolonged control as law enforcement agents.[17]

Laws passed to regulate disorder and morality differed only in minor details from one lumbertown to another. The enforcement of selected statutes was directed primarily at fire code enforcement, drunk and disorderly conduct, and excessive fighting. Judging by arrest records, real efforts were also made to prevent rowdy and drunken lumberjacks from engaging in raucous activities after hours, on Sundays, and especially in the more respectable areas of the cities. These enforcement efforts kept the small police forces busy, especially during the spring, summer, and early fall months. In the winter, the lumber municipalities would frequently lay off policemen and direct the marshal or chief to fulfill his other responsibilities: fixing wooden sidewalks, cleaning alleys, filling potholes with sawdust, inspecting chimneys and flues, and collecting various vice-related fees.[18]

Municipal contributions to support policemen usually constituted the second largest lumbertown expenditure, though local marshals and their staffs collected less than ten percent of the city expenditures. In specific salaries, East Saginaw was probably typical. In the early 1860s salaries for the marshal varied from $150 to $500 per year without fees. The marshal augmented his salary by acting as tax collector and fire warden. By 1868 East Saginaw had appointed a marshall who was paid $1,500 per year; a chief of police, $1,000; and a force of seven men, paid $2 per day. In 1873 a revised city charter established a metropolitan police system and a Board of Police Commissioners. There were seventeen men in the department and salaries were: marshal, $1,200; captain, $1,100; and patrolmen, $825 per year. However, the marshal and his men were frequently paid in money orders rather than cash, and the money orders were often reduced ten or twenty percent by local merchants.[19]

Aside from fire and police, the lumbertowns also provided a meager and inadequate tax base to support pest houses, county poor farms, and local relief. The care of the sick and injured was usually provided by donations or private enterprise. Lumbering and logging were dangerous occupations and even a casual reading of lumbertown newspapers will confirm that many laborers were injured each year. The *Northwestern Lumberman* published a weekly column that detailed personal injury accidents and deaths in the camps and sawmills. A Muskegon paper reported that in the spring of 1882, forty five men had been killed and perhaps two or three times as many injured in the Muskegon area alone.[20]

Despite this apparent need for medical care, the lumbertowns were slow to develop hospitals. Medical care was usually provided in private homes or doctors' offices. People infected with contagious illnesses or incapable of taking care of themselves were moved to county poor farms or "pest" houses.

John Fitzmaurice and East Saginaw generally take credit for establishing the first lumberman's hospital. Fitzmaurice, with characteristic immodesty, wrote:

> The writer can take credit of being among the first to inaugurate the establishing of a woodsman's hospital. In 1872 he was associate editor of the East Saginaw Courier. The picture of destitution presented by the sick and wounded shanty boys, when brought in from the woods, was simply distressing in the extreme. There was no place for them to go, save the rough boarding house, where—if they had money— they were taken some kind of care of, but when their means were gone, they were "toted" off to the county house. With this picture of distress for a subject, he began to write and agitate in this interest, and after the publication of articles, showing the necessity for an hospital, the business men of East Saginaw took the matter up, and the result was establishment of what is known as St. Mary's hospital, in that city, under the care of the Sisters of Charity, and where hundreds of "shanty boys" have since found a good home and kindly care from these charitable women.

St. Mary's and the subsequent hospitals that replicated its beginnings operated on insurance plans that sold for four or five dollars
per year certificates that guaranteed the holder "care, board, lodging, and medical treatment, for one year . . . whenever sick or
hurt."[21] Bay City Hospital opened above a store in 1878. However,
Muskegon did not begin its first subscription hospital until the City
Missionary Society organized a facility in the declining, postlumber
year of 1889.

The quality of the early subscription hospitals varied from town
to town. St. Mary's in East Saginaw was reputedly a dependable
institution. Moreover, Fitzmaurice "retired" as associate editor of
the *Courier* and became the hospital insurance ticket salesman.
His popularity with loggers and determination to trek throughout
the woods in winter selling policies or hospital tickets brought
St. Mary's an enviable reputation and a profitable existence. Compared with other lumbertown's inadequate medical facilities, a
case can be made that Fitzmaurice's boosting and selling of St.
Mary's encouraged shanty boys who sought summer jobs in the
sawmills to trek to East Saginaw. Saginaw City did not have a facility until 1889. Bay City's subscription hospital appeared to be
more interested in selling tickets and franchises for other lumbertown hospitals than in providing sound medical care. The Bay
City hospital soon had branches in Cheboygan, Marquette, and
several Wisconsin cities. The original facility in Bay City moved frequently from one rented building to another, changed management
several times, and disappeared from the city directories in the mid-
eighties. Lumbermen and businessmen in the community at first
took some interest in starting subscription hospitals; however, not
until the postlumber era did individual lumbermen donate land
and money to construct substantial, public facilities in the declining
mill towns.[22]

To a large extent the cultural activities of the lumbertowns, beyond that associated with public schools, were also a result of private
support and subscription. Lumbertown residents were torn between
the practicality of providing the bare essentials of survival, the all-
consuming drive to excel financially, and the need to reflect characteristics of civility. The arts and literature required an amount of
leisure and monetary or public support to prosper. Such provisions
were scarce in the lumbertowns, and cultural pursuits witnessed
many vicissitudes. Many of the early cultural undertakings were performed, as the *Saginaw Enterprise* noted, by "itinerant monstrosi-

ties," touring groups that catered to the loggers and laborers. Yet, in the halcyon years, the accumulation of wealth and more leisure time did encourage some cultural endeavors. However, the efforts of lumbertown "connoisseurs" to bring culture to the community were often of dubious worth, and were vigorously pursued only late in the era when declining mill towns saw cultural amenities as necessary to attract new people and new industry.[23]

Forerunners to the prominent public libraries that lumbermen built in all three cities in the eighties were membership libraries associated with organizations or public libraries housed in local schools. Norman Little had started a public library in 1837 in Saginaw City when that community was little more than a paper city. East Saginaw's original public library was a part of the Central High School until Jesse Hoyt left $100,000 for the grand library edifice opened there in 1890.

In Bay City, which James Birney described to Harriet Beecher Stowe in 1853 as an "area that was not distinguished as a reading one—rather the contrary I think," the first library was owned by W. H. DeLisle. In the 1868 City Directory, DeLisle advertised a "Circulating Library" that loaned books for ten cents a week. A "Library Association" was founded in the seventies, and in 1874 $2,899 from penal fines was used to purchase from the association all its books. Not until 1922, however, did a grant from the Carnegie Foundation provide Bay City with its first permanent and separate library building. In contrast to the parsimony of Bay City's lumbermen, Henry Sage culminated his career in West Bay City with a gift of $60,000 to pay for the site, buildings, and books for the Sage Library. The library opened in 1884 and later provided branch libraries throughout the West Bay City area.[24]

Muskegon's library system developed much like those across the state. During the early years a public system was organized by Muskegon Township where books were circulated free of charge. By 1869 a private subscription library known as the Muskegon Library Association had been established in the offices of a local attorney. In 1876 this library became part of the city public school system and later became the nucleus of the collection of the Hackley Library. Charles H. Hackley contributed $100,000, plus $25,000 for the purchase of books, for the construction of the grand Hackley Library, which was dedicated in 1890.

Besides literature, lumbertown citizens also sought more participatory forms of culture and entertainment. Many of the saloons offered nightly entertainment, usually music and dancing. There were higher orders of diversion at variety theaters where patrons could drink while enjoying an amateurish stage play. But for the lumbermen and the so-called better classes, several opera halls provided legitimate theatrical entertainment and music.

In the early years concerts, plays, musical shows, and lectures were presented by local groups; occasionally a touring professional company would perform. In time, however, music academies and elaborate opera houses were built through subscription and donation. The Woods Opera House opened in Bay City in 1886. This magnificent three-story building that held fifteen hundred people was built from a fund of nearly $60,000 raised through subscription and contributions. Likewise in Muskegon, the Temperance Reform Opera House, constructed in 1878 as an alternative to Muskegon's bawdy entertainments, was purchased by a consortium of lumbermen a few years later and became the Grand Opera Theatre. In East Saginaw cultural activities took place at the Academy of Music. Bordwell's Opera House was a fancy honky-tonk where some legitimate shows were staged; however, more often than not "naked women danced on the tables and the upper crust didn't attend."[25]

Culturally, a pattern of localism emerged. Each lumbertown tried to establish and support a full range of cultural institutions: newspapers, lecture societies, fine hotels, libraries, and opera houses. Although these institutions had wide community participation, they certainly did not maintain a uniform or communitywide set of cultural standards. Culture and entertainment more often followed social and ethnic status rather than highbrow standards set by the town elite.

After a generation of prosperity, of phenomenal city growth, the lumbertowns were certainly conscious that they were "municipal entities" rather than mere transient natural-resource towns. Yet as Bayrd Still noted of other Midwestern towns, their ability to function as urban communities was more in response to the problems of size "than a changed philosophy" of the role of the individual in the community. However, the pursuit of cultural amenities, cooperation through taxes, and subscriptions for the promotion and improvement of the cities indicated that some social responsibility was in evidence. The "interdependence of city life certainly had fostered a group consciousness. . . ." Nevertheless, "municipal consciousness" would not develop fully until populations began to stabilize and new economic needs pressured some of the lumbertowns to adopt more aggressive means to persevere.[26]

LUMBERTOWN BOOSTERISM

"Town boosterism" was often the most visible and aggressive activity that involved many—although primarily newspapers—who tried to make the most of their community's prospects. Boosters tried to link the climate of individual opportunity to the collective destiny of each lumbertown. Despite the clamor for individualistic responsibility by lumbermen, entrepreneurs, and residents and the popularity of laissez-faire capitalism, many were also supremely capable of generating community spirit.

In the lumbertowns boosterism was usually identified with the competition that ensued between cross-river rivals or other nearby lumbertowns. However, because urban prominence was in part decided by geographic location and an abundant natural resource, town boosterism was not necessasry to guarantee continued existence. Boosterism was not part of the life-and-death struggle for survival that characterized many of the agriculture or cross-roads settlements in the Midwest. Competition for railroads and for public and state facilities such as colleges, asylums, and prisons was unnecessary. More commonly lumbertown boosterism came naturally from nineteenth-century beliefs in progress and individual social mobility. The lumbertown would flourish as it provided unlimited opportunity for individualistic achievement. Not until the timber was gone and sawmills were closing did the booster ethos become imminently tied to the much more substantial and pragmatic efforts focusing on survival and reindustrialization.

Despite their apparent economic security, lumbertown boosters were nevertheless eager to proclaim the need for a public spirit or a unity and progress necessary to provide future prosperity. The *Saginaw Enterprise* as early a 1872 inspirited "the interest of the Valley to encourage manufacturers. We have every facility. Our railroads and river navigation afford abundant facilities for transport. The forest[s] that lie contiguous can easily be made to contribute to the success of such an undertaking." An important corollary to the public spirit argument, especially in the lumbertowns, was the growing awareness that industrial boosterism was necessary and that any factionalism or economic jealousy would only lead to failure and disintegration. The editor of the *Muskegon Chronicle* in 1875 in a column headed "Why Not Pull Together" admonished his readers that

> if all of the business men and property owners in Muskegon had worked together in the past as they should, Muskegon might just as well be a city of 20,000 inhabitants today as to have only 10,000 people. There is no good reason why Muskegon should not grow rapidly and increase in wealth and prosperity, but in order that it may grow our citizens will have to learn the lesson that what is good for any part of the city is good for all parts.

He concluded by urging businessmen in the community to combine and "form an organization if necessary, for the promotion of the public interest. Let our citizens pull together."[27]

Local boosters also devoted much attention to deliberately discrediting rival towns. Muskegon, which had no nearby urban rival, apparently never engaged in the heated newspaper antagonisms that characterized other lumbertowns. However, editors in Muskegon, as in other towns, constantly kept the public informed of rival lumbertowns' river conditions during the spring drives, cutting totals, wood stockpiled and lumber shipped. Any misfortune in another lumbertown—low water, fires, strikes—might often lead to increased profits in the home port.[28] One town's success often took place at the expense of its rivals.

East Saginaw and Bay City, though, carried competition further, and the local press often engaged in bitter attacks on its nearby rival. East Saginaw newspapers relished publishing reports about Bay City crime and its toleration of prostitution and vice. The *Saginaw Courier* devoted several columns describing in detail the trial of Bay City's town marshal, who was up on charges of owning a resort and unofficially "taxing" other prostitutes. At other times the editor of the *Courier* noted that little was accomplished in Bay City because the community spent too much time on "police matters." Or again, all vagrants picked up along East Saginaw's railroads were not doubt on their way to "Tramp Heaven—Bay City." Bay City newspapers, on the other hand, were prone to remind their readers that East Saginaw was built on a swamp and subject to periodic flooding, mosquitos, and mud.[29]

More pragmatic efforts at boosterism were seen in the efforts made to induce immigration into the towns and nearby hinterlands surrounding the lumbertowns. Several agencies besides the newspapers became involved in fairly highly organized campaigns to speed up settlement. Lumbermen who had stump-strewn lands for sale were eager to attract immigrant settlers. They also periodically recruited immigrant sawmill workers. Railroad companies that retained government land grants sought prospective farmers, and a diversity of local interest including real estate operators, the press, and the local merchants, advertised and encouraged immigrant settlers. Finally, the state in the 1870s and early 1880s hoped to fill its territory with settlers to simply advance statewide prosperity.[30]

The Saginaw region especially benefited from the state's efforts to recruit German immigrants. The first and only commissioner of emigration for the state of Michigan sent to Germany was Max H. Allardt of East Saginaw. Allardt set up an office in Hamburg where, among other activities, he published an eight-page guide to Michigan. Between 1869 and 1874 when Allardt was recalled, he was successful in attracting several thousand immigrants, many of those to the Saginaw area where he was familiar with the land and the city. German immigrants who had little money were encouraged, as a state emigration officer wrote, "to give up such preposterous ideas as farming," and "look out for work in the cities or villages . . . among the lumbermen."[31]

Boosterism, though, throughout the boom years of lumbering remained sporadic and contradictory effort. Newspapermen were torn between their desire to criticize internal divisiveness and laxitude—town failure to compete with rival settlements—and their duty to relegate town shortcomings and project a common, enterprising public spirit. Lumbertown boosters never tackled town promotion in a well-planned, collective effort. Boosterism was more often done privately to serve the special needs of economic interests. Sporadic dabbling with the booster ethos ended, however, when the lumbertowns began to lose their grip on the sole source of their economic livelihood. External circumstances changed boosterism from a causal, individualistic practice to a conscious, aggressive, and collective strategy of town promotion. In the postlumber era the rhetoric of growth and progress became consciously and determinedly involved with the quest for economic survival.

For many town boosters the most urgent civil goal was to create a climate that invited prosperity. The sense of belonging to a local community, though, varied from town to town during the early years of growth and prosperity. Socially, the drive to succeed, in an open economic environment that benefited a good many entrepreneurs,

caused the successful to typically identify with the town that gave
them success and status. In the Saginaws and Muskegon people
could fairly comfortably believe that the important decisions for
these lumbertowns were being made by men who had built their
lives in and of those cities. In Bay City and West Bay City, individual ownership occurred often enough to balance some of the dangers
of absentee ownership. Yet crucial decisions were often influenced by
Sage, McGraw, Fitzhugh, and E. C. Litchfield, resident New Yorkers
whose own self-interests were, in their minds, the key to community
welfare. To those promoters the health of the community was measured almost solely by property values and real estate improvements.
Sage admitted as much when, on the occasion of the dedication of
the Sage Library in West Bay City, he remarked, "I have helped to
build your churches, your schools, your railroad, and in all ways, so
far as in me lay, to promote your interest, while promoting my own."
Often the absentee promoters of Bay City had to command the community support necessary to protect their own self-interest. Economic coercion and dominance of absentee owners hindered
boosterism and discouraged the development of a sense of community in Bay City.[32]

Physical Growth and Residential Patterns

The most obvious of the changes associated with the phenomenal
growth of the lumbertowns was the altered physical appearance
brought on by industrialization. Surely the townscapes changed considerably between 1870 and 1890, but what effect, if any, did the
new town environments have on the way of life in each settlement?
What did the distribution of homes, stores, and sawmills reveal
about the community? How did the spatial structure of the towns,
which now came to reflect contemporary industrial cities, influence
peoples' perception of their community?

Although the several separate cities that made up Saginaw, Bay
City, and Muskegon were not consolidated until the declining years
of lumbering, it would be a mistake to regard each individual lumbering settlement along the Saginaw or on Muskegon Lake as a separate locality. Their common geographical location and economic
base created a remarkable degree of interdependence and much similarity in their physical appearance. Despite the efforts of town

boosters to paint an attractive town landscape, and drawings depicting idyllic bird's-eye views of thriving industrial and commercial
centers, the lumbertowns were not universally attractive urban settlements. From the railroad station, a newcomer could look over
industrial waterfronts of sawmills, warehouses, salt blocks, railroad
sidings, and stacks upon stacks of drying lumber. By 1875 there were
at least 120 mills—sawmills, shingle mills, iron factories, several
makers of logging equipment, shipyards, breweries, tanneries, and
dozens of other industries subordinate to the lumber business along
the twenty five miles of the Saginaw. A similar, if not so numerous,
industrial scene characterized Muskegon's lakefront. The rivers had
lost their pristine clarity. Log rafts, bark, sawdust, sedimentation
from years of upstream alteration by loggers, and brine run-off had
created polluted waterways. Brownish water flowed into Saginaw Bay
and discolored Muskegon Lake. The sounds of whirling saws and the
odor of burning wood confronted the senses day and night.

Despite industrialization, the frontier was still evident. An immigrant to Muskegon in the mid-seventies was struck by the "blackened stumps of the recent wilderness that still stand in her principal
streets."[33] Across Muskegon Lake or on the Saginaw's Ojibway Island
Indians still gathered, smoked fish, and traded as they had for centuries. Hunting and fishing parties departed daily for the nearby forest interior. Along the industrialized waterfront, children still swam
in the rivers on hot summer days, trapped beaver in the fall, and
speared sturgeon and walleye pike in the spring. There were now two
worlds—the new industrial and the old frontier—in which the settler could find individuals searching for stability and prosperity.

The patterns of town development during the lumbering era suggest spatial structures that resembled larger, distinctively urban
places. As in most industrialized cities specialization had developed
and whole sections of the town were associated with industry, trade,
or business. Because lumbering was entirely dependent on water
transportation, the sawmills and woodworking industries were located along the waterways. Mile upon mile of waterfront consisted of
man-made docks and wharves paralleling and projecting into the
waterways piled high with drying boards.[34] Periodically log-holding
ponds broke the monotony of seeing wall upon wall of stacked
boards. Except for a few scattered industries located away from the
water's edge (for example, cigar manufacturers and breweries), almost all subsidiary lumbertown industries were located within a few
blocks of the Saginaw River or Muskegon Lake. Unfortunately, in-

dustrial locations along the waterfronts destroyed the one outstand-
ing natural geographic attraction the lumbertowns possessed. An
aesthetic riverine environment was subverted early because of economic need.

Stores, saloons, and restaurants were the principal types of establishments in the commercial districts. Most of the general merchants, clothiers, jewelers, and dry goods stores in East Saginaw
were along Washington and Genesee streets near the downtown area
(see map 5). Across from the Pere Marquette station on Potter
Street, several fashionable clothing stores were opened in the 1880s.
On the other side of the river in Saginaw City, the commercial center began along Hamilton and Mackinaw streets and ran north to
Court and west to Michigan Avenue. A smaller commercial center
was located several blocks west of the downtown along Court Street.

A similar pattern of commercial development characterized Bay
City and West Bay City (see map 6). The commercial center in Bay
City extended along Water, Saginaw, and Washington streets between Third Street to the north and Sixth Street to the south. City
offices were in the downtown commercial blocks as were several hotels. Because the river formed a bend around downtown Bay City,
the commercial center was hemmed in on two sides by sawmills,
flour mills, and other woodworking industries. At the old Portsmouth settlement, a few commercial establishments were located
along Water Street. In West Bay City, a small commercial center
was built along Midland and Linn streets. Sage sold lots in his original plat and financed several businessmen in building commercial
blocks. Choice locations along main streets sold within a few years
for more than $1,000.[35]

In Muskegon proper, the commercial district ran along Western
Avenue and Ottawa Street (see map 7). Yet unlike Saginaw or Bay
City, several small businesses were scattered throughout the community. The downtown was destroyed by a fire in 1874 that swept
through twelve city blocks and destroyed seventy businesses. A new,
much more substantial downtown commercial center was subsequently constructed. In the eighties Muskegon also built a smaller
industrial center, occupied by furniture manufacturers southwest of
the original city and about one and a half miles from the waterfront.

Characteristic of many nineteenth-century cities, areas of vice or
zones of hard drinking, gambling, and prostitution were also allowed
to develop in the lumbertowns. East Saginaw, Muskegon, and espe-

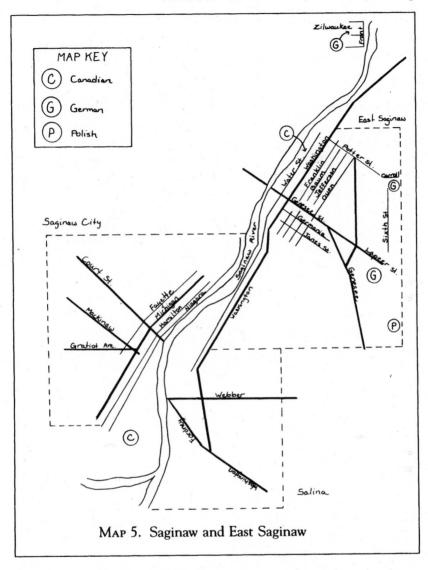

MAP 5. Saginaw and East Saginaw

cially Bay City developed reputations for having the three toughest vice zones on the Great Lakes. Muskegon had its infamous Sawdust Flats, an area of "unspeakable whoredom and violence," built on sawdust fill and running six solid blocks along the lake near Western and Ottawa streets. In East Saginaw, White Row was the "roughest, toughest, fightingest spot in the Saginaws." Beginning along the junction of Genesee and Water streets, saloons and bawdy houses

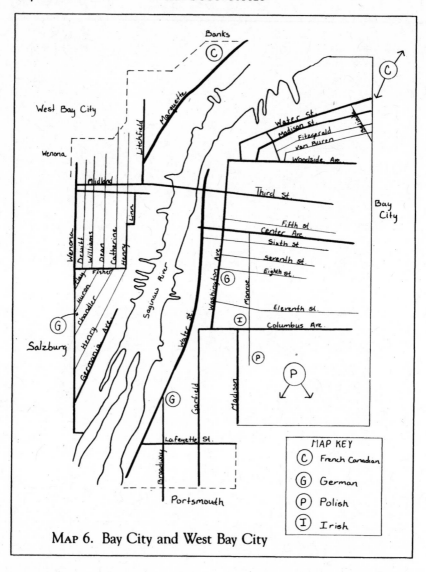

MAP 6. Bay City and West Bay City

ran for blocks south about a block from the river and across from the sawmills. Downriver in Bay City the aforementioned Catacombs "undoubtedly was the toughest place anywhere along the Saginaw River." It developed such a reputation for whoring, murder, and robbery that even today it is difficult to separate fact from fiction. There were about twenty six hotels, thirty seven saloons, and two liquor stores located in this four-block area.[36]

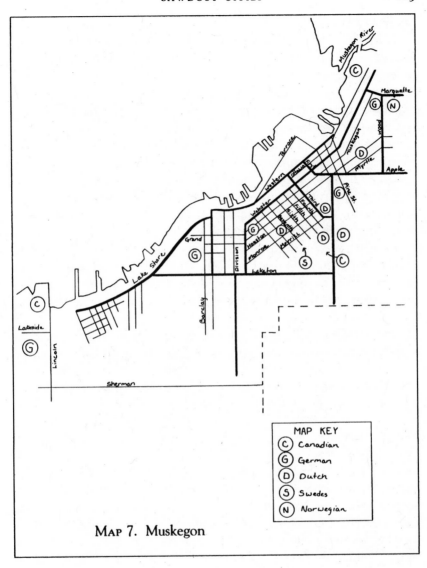

Map 7. Muskegon

The areas of vice were tolerated because the lumberjack and the sawmill worker spent much money in town. During the spring townspeople seldom ventured into the Flats, the Row, or Catacombs; certainly "proper" women remained well outside the boundaries. Yet, because they were actually mixed areas of hotels, boarding-houses, restaurants, and barbershops, as well as saloons and brothels, it would be a mistake to conceptualize these zones as isolated and rigidly enforced areas of vice. Except for the spring migration of lumberjacks who crowded into the vice zones and kept the saloons going all day, seven days a week, during the rest of the year a relative calm prevailed in these notorious areas.

As with most industrial cities, the lumbertowns developed the broader patterns of specialization in which commercial and industrial sections were separate from residential areas, and in which residential sections were differentiated from one another in desirability. By the early eighties patterns of residential segregation had developed in all three towns. Outside the saloons, restaurants, and resorts, the most prominant feature that a visitor to the lumbertowns would notice were the mansions built by resident lumbermen. As in most nineteenth-century industrial centers, families of greater means lived near the center of town. In East Saginaw there were many fine homes on Jefferson, Owen, and Washington streets, all within a few blocks of the commercial center. Likewise, in Saginaw City the main street, Michigan Avenue, had several mansions. In Bay City, Center Avenue remains to this day a promenade characterized by elegant residences. The lumbermen of Muskegon built many fine homes in the southwestern part of the city along Webster Avenue. Large oaks and a slight elevation separated them from the industrial and commercial waterfront areas of the city. In all three cities, the lumbermen remained within walking distance of their river mills.

Directly behind the lumbermen the merchants and professionals built their homes. Although several of the greater merchants built ostentatious homes along the main roadways next to the lumbermen, a distinct decline in decoration and size is evident in the nearby homes most merchants built on the first blocks off "Main Street." Thus, in Bay City, Fifth and Sixth streets, which ran on each side of Center Avenue, contained many large houses owned by merchants and professionals. Likewise in Saginaw City, Fayette Street, behind Michigan Avenue, and Franklin and Baum streets near downtown East Saginaw had many businessmen's residences. In Muskegon some merchants remained near their businesses in the downtown area and built homes along Muskegon Avenue, Houston Street, and Monroe Street within walking distance of their places of work. Nearby these neighborhoods the sizeable middle class that emerged in the lumbertowns (sawmill managers, foremen, engineers, insurance agents, lawyers, and doctors) built their homes.

Skilled workers sometimes lived in their place of business or next to it, and their residences were scattered throughout the lumbertowns. However, by the peak lumber years few of the skilled and semiskilled workers worked at home. Most left their residences each morning and walked to nearby sawmills, woodworking shops, and machine shops. As one drew further away from the lumbermen and merchant classes, these workers owned homes six or seven blocks away from the main thoroughfares. Still, almost all residential areas were close to the river sawmills and when the men left their homes in the morning they did not go very far. In many ways life did not become dramatically separated into workday and home life. Children would come down to the sawmill during the summer sawing season or perhaps even work alongside their fathers. Many workmen often came home for a midday meal. The segmentation of the domestic from the workaday, economic life had not enveloped the industrial lumbertown.

Thus, the residential patterns of the greater and middling classes in the lumbertowns resembled the concentric zone theory of urban settlement laid out in a linear pattern along the waterways. The wealthy resided close to the center of the town integrated and surrounded by entrepreneurs. Nearby, in a larger circle, were the professionals, skilled, and semiskilled residents.

Working-class residential patterns, however, destroyed the symmetry of the concentric zone. The influx of immigrant laborers in the early seventies created areas of concentrated immigrant populations as most newcomers sought low-cost housing close to their places of employment. Sawmills often hired individuals from nearby ethnic enclaves thereby encouraging the development of ghetto residential quarters. No other lumbertown had ethnic residential boundaries as well defined as Bay City.

The original French populations in Bay City engaged in fishing and continued to live near the mouth of the Saginaw River. The Banks area on the west side and Dolsonville (Frenchtown) directly across the river and to the north of downtown Bay City remained predominantly French. Frenchmen continued to fish and others worked at the nearby Dolson, Chapin and Company sawmill. German workers concentrated along Eighth Street in Bay City and in Salzburg on the west side of the river and worked in the salt blocks and mills of Sage, the Cincinnati mill, and Laderack and Bros. mill. Irish settlers lived just beyond the Germans in Bay City along Monroe and Twelfth streets. They trekked five or six blocks to work alongside the Germans at several mills and industrial works in the southern end of Bay City. In the early seventies Polish settlers arrived in Bay City and settled in the extreme south end (Ports-mouth); many were hired at John McGraw's sawmill. Precise geographical boundaries, churches, schools, and nearby employment reinforced ethnic residential cleavages in Bay City well beyond the lumber era.

Although certainly not as pronounced as Bay City, Muskegon also experienced narrow lines of residential ethnic segregation that per-sisted throughout the lumber years. Muskegon's largest ethnic minor-ity, the Dutch, settled in Muskegon proper; Rotterdam was located around Third and Merrill avenues and Dutch Town between Myrtle and Spring streets. Swedish and Norwegian newcomers who decided to stay in Muskegon built residences near Killgrubbin or Norwegian Hill located up Ottawa Street and along the lakefront. Lakeside was also an area of Swedish settlement. Although Germans immigrated to Muskegon and many settled near the Lakeside area, they more often scattered throughout the city. The French settled with the few Indians near Pickettown at the mouth of the Muskegon River. Most Frenchmen were river men who in the summer months worked for the booming company.

In East Saginaw and Saginaw City residential concentration was least pronounced. There were also fewer immigrant groups living in Saginaw. The Germans turned much of East Saginaw to the south and east of downtown into a new Germania, and many French set-tled on the east side along the river. Later in the lumber era a few Polish settlers located on the southern edge of East Saginaw. How-ever, despite immigrant churches and settlers, residential patterns were considerably more mixed in the Saginaws than in Bay City or Muskegon.

Because industry in the lumbertowns was not confined to a cen-tral core, workers did not have to concentrate in high density ghet-tos near their places of work. Moreover, building materials in the lumbertowns were relatively inexpensive; lumbertown workers could buy or build single-family residences not far from their places of em-ployment along the waterways. Home ownership and neighborhood living provided a respectable way of life for many newcomers. These factors also explain why the lumbertown's immigrant neighborhoods persisted well into the twentieth century.

New residential patterns and commercial expansion changed the character and appearance of the streets and buildings in the lumber-towns. The early village lumber settlements, where scattered sawmills stood amid stump-strewn streets and yards, virtually disappeared by the late seventies. Dirt and sawdust roadways gave way to plank and wooden block pavements. The commercial streets now became lined with unbroken rows of two- and three-story commercial buildings. Whole business blocks, sometimes ostentatiously decorated with arches, sculptured friezes, and contrasting stonework replaced many log and wooden buildings. Although public architecture was not monumental, architectural firms opened offices in both East Saginaw and Bay City and designed public and private buildings that celebrated and advanced the prosperity of the lumbermen-entrepreneurs.

Still, new residential and commercial patterns of growth in the three lumbertowns did not markedly affect the geographic spread of the towns' populations. Suburbanization, for example, was not important in the changing spatial structure of the towns. Each lumbertown continued to display a spatial separateness and incorporated new people easily by annexing contiguous land developments. Transport remained limited or water oriented, and throughout the lumber era the towns remained pretty much pedestrian cities. Horse-drawn streetcars were in use along the Saginaw River by the late sixties; however, Muskegon did not lay tracks for a street railway until 1882. Nevertheless, these early lines ran parallel to the river, served the businesses and sawmills, and did little to spread settlement into outlying developments. When electric streetcar service was introduced during the late 1880s, the lumber era was almost over and, though these newer, faster conveyances served a few new industrial areas, they at first ran to recreational centers along the Great Lakes beaches.[37]

The need to build lakefront recreational facilities resulted from a dramatic change in the quality of the waterways next to the lumbertowns. The sounds and smells rising from round-the-clock logging reflected the change in the public's relationship with the river or lake environment. Access to the waterways became restricted by sawmills, millponds, and drying docks. As early as 1865 a group of citizens petitioned the Bay City Common Council to reopen an access on the river at Eighteenth Street. A lumber millpond built there prevented cattle from being watered, boats from being launched, and driving teams from getting onto the ice in winter. The petitioners demanded that "free access to the channel of the Saginaw River be given as was intended when the place was first platted."[38] One of the basic reasons people settled in Bay City was because of its river access, and now so successful were the economics associated with the river that freedom of access was being restricted by flourishing enterprise.

The complicated machinery of sawmilling, which consisted of steam boilers, burning refuse, oil slicks, salt spills, drifting logs, and plant wastes being dumped into the waterways, affected the quality of the Saginaw River or Muskegon Lake. Saw ash settled on the river, and sawdust fills in low marsh areas at the water's edge were common. Fills were built to create space along the water to stack drying wood. The river and lake received the sewage and drainage from several population centers. Residue left from salt production often found its way into the Saginaw River. The lumbertown waterways took on a different complexion because of industrialization. The Saginaw River came to resemble a sluggish, "center of town river." Muskegon Lake lost its clarity. Fish life changed dramatically from what had been present not long ago. Spawning grounds were altered through drainage, forest clearance, siltation, and the resultant warming of the waters eliminated several species. Trout and whitefish disappeared. Lower species, adaptable to poorer gradients of water, proliferated. Sucker, pike, and perch persisted, and as one resident near Saginaw recalls, "the carp held sway over all kinds of fish on the river."[39]

The appearance of the waterways also underwent noticeable deterioration. No longer attractive to the hunter or fisherman, they became clogged with logs, strewn with acidic bark, churned by tugs, steamships, and ferry boats. The waterways became polluted highways of commerce. A sanitary survey report in Saginaw in the postlumber era described the river as "muddy, slimy and generally repulsive in appearance."[40] Although much of the damage done by the lumbermen to the waterways was impermanent, later industrialization prevented the aquatic environment from ever recovering. The lumbermen had left a legacy of exploitation; however, theirs was a transient greed. If only time had intervened, the trees and the waterways could have recovered. But the lumbering era left a legacy of brine wells, more people, and industries.

Yet, the men and women who came and settled along the waterways seeking economic opportunity had, to an encouraging degree found it. They built mill towns and machines that fed on the wilderness and transformed the frontier into a flourishing community of smokestacks, brine wells, and the hard steel of rails and saws. These cities and machines were built on the values of free enterprise in a highly individualistic and competitive society. And though these values brought prosperity, they also led to a long history of collective anxiety for many others in the lumbertowns.

CHAPTER FOUR

Adjusting to Violence

Within a radius of 300 feet from the "Catacombs"
could be counted forty saloons of the lowest character,
with from three to ten "pretty waiter girls" in each. . . .
The horrors and atrocities nightly chronicled . . . were
of such an astounding nature that the good men and
women of Bay City were simply paralyzed, and rendered
perfectly helpless to stem the torrent of wickedness. Busi-
ness men looked on and laughed, where they did not take
part in the "saturnalia" nightly enacted.

—JOHN W. FITZMAURICE, The Shanty Boy

Regardless of Fitzmaurice's observation, the "good men and women" of the lumbertowns were obviously not "paralyzed" into inactivity by the torrent of town wickedness. As Fitzmaurice implies, lumbertown business and professional men accepted interpersonal violence as a societal norm—not unlike entrepreneurial capitalism—that became part of their daily lives. The entrepreneurial ethic may have clashed with the violence that became a part of lumbertown society; periodic efforts to rid to the towns of vice were often made by citizens from various socioeconomic strata. However, in reality the presence of raucous shanty boys was good for many businesses. Businessmen and town authorities did not want to create an "unfriendly" environment that might drive the logger—the consumer—to another lumbertown. The challenge, as seen by many businessmen, was not to rid the settlements of "visitors prone to violence, but to suppress the violence while retaining the visitors."[1] Thus, local authorities took reasonable action and made efforts to control, if not suppress, violence by transient shanty boys. The official outlook remained simple: keep enforcement compatible with public welfare. Much would be tolerated so long as it did not interfere too much with business. Considering their reputations and the length of time they flourished as raucous sawmill towns, the lumbering settlements' town authorities and businessmen performed the task of preserving the shanty boys' trade exceptionally well.

Although the lumbertowns did not become armed communities like some Western settlements, physical violence—brawling, fighting, and an occasional homicide—were part of the cult of masculinity identified with logging. Gentlemen and loggers alike held that there were times when an individual had no recourse but to resort to physical violence to redress a wrong. Moreover, gang brawling during the annual spring and fall benders put on by the shanty boys became an endemic pastime in the lumbertowns. In popular literature unwary visitors to the lumbertowns often found themselves at the mercy of violent shanty boys, rowdy and drunken transient loggers, or mill workers. Early twentieth-century authors literarily enlarged the areas of vice in each lumbertown and painted urban landscapes that resembled nineteenth-century "gin rows."[2] Throughout the era, all three major lumbertowns suffered from violent reputations that became part of their cultural mystique long before their careers as lumber centers came to an end.

Observations about lumbertown violence, however, remain incomplete to the student of nineteenth-century logging and lumbering lore. Although historians can easily agree that the lumbertowns were violent places and can match the Western cow towns and mining settlements blow for blow with action, mayhem, violence, and tragedy, they are troubled by the fact that lumberjacks and lumbermen have been largely ignored as part of the American frontier saga. Few authorities have critically examined the most notorious features of lumbertown society. How violent really were the lumbertowns? Do the Michigan logging centers truthfully belong in the genre of frontier violence popularly associated with Western cattle towns and mining camps?[3]

Law Enforcement

Embryonic cities such as these Michigan settlements took time to develop orderly government, a police system, and a tradition of habitual consent to authority. The lumbertowns' first efforts to make the adjustments to the violence associated with the shanty boys were fairly conventional. By the time the lumber boom began in the late sixties, all three towns had been incorporated as cities. The immediate impetus for legal organization in East Saginaw was partly its rivalry with Saginaw City, a compelling necessity to institute fire regulations, and a desire to control the many Indians, trappers, and traders who populated the city.[4]

Fire seems to have been the most imminent threat requiring legal structure in Bay City. However, city ordinances against "gaming and other lewd curiosities" and the formation of a vigilance committee in 1865 to protect against "acts of violence" indicated that the disruptive activities of the itinerant shanty boys were also common concerns in Bay City.[5]

Muskegon, incorporated in 1869 just as the lumber era began, likewise began legal organization out of fear of fire and concern for transient violence by the lumberjacks. The city was at first organized in an attempt to absorb the neighboring village of Pinchtown, a narrow strip of land between Muskegon and Lakeside that housed Jim Robinson's Lakeview House. Never closing, the Lakeview house carried on boxing matches, cockfights, and prostitution. It attracted all sorts of unsavory characters as well as the shanty boys, who spilled over in their drunken revelry throughout Muskegon. Authorities could never close Robinson's saloon. Robinson was elected township clerk and his political power, coupled with the growing desire for places of entertainment, enabled him to forestall action against his "sporting house."[6] Men like Robinson demonstrated early in logging town existence that the businessman-entrepreneur was not only willing to tolerate violence but also apparently experienced community political support notwithstanding his unsavory entrepreneurial practices.

Thus, in the lumbertowns, rudimentary municipal governments may have indirectly encouraged violence by not punishing it consistently, whether consciously or out of weakness. Municipal statutes passed in the early years of incorporation in the lumbertowns did not vary greatly from those in other parts of the country including the Western cow towns and mining settlements. Towns throughout the country enacted laws that forbade vagrancy, disorderly conduct, intoxication, fighting, discharging a gun, and public indecency. The state of Michigan prohibited the sale of liquor, gambling, and houses of ill repute. So much for the statutory limits on order and morality. Routinely, lumbertown policemen were given instructions to "enforce this or that law" and act "as if the violation of others might be winked at."[7]

The establishment of police machinery was an important if not a haphazard function of early lumbertown municipalities. In the early years, law enforcement was provided by the county sheriff and village marshal. Before the lumber era all three settlements appointed city marshals upon incorporation. East Saginaw hired a marshal in 1855, Bay City in 1859, and Muskegon in 1861. They were given specific law enforcement functions, but only in Muskegon was the first marshal directed to keep order when the loggers and river men arrived in town. Besides fire code enforcement, the marshals in each city were charged with street repair and construction and tax collection.[8]

Most of the towns' budgets went to pay fire wardens and to purchase fire-fighting equipment. The local marshal and his staff collected less than ten percent of the city expenditures. Unlike the cattle towns, which spent nearly forty percent of the town's total budget on policemen's salaries, the lumbertowns subordinated law enforcement and considered fire a more imminent threat to survival.[9]

City councils in both the cattle towns and lumbertowns manipulated expenses by reducing the police force in the winter months and adding policemen each summer. The cattle towns, however, not only appropriated greater portions of their budgets to law enforcement and provided larger salary incentives but also hired more law enforcement personnel on a per capita basis. In several Kansas cow towns a ratio of about one law officer to every 200 to 400 citizens was maintained. The Colorado mining settlement of Leadville employed one officer per 344 residents. In Michigan, Muskegon's ratio was one to 2,200; East Saginaw's, one to 1,189; and Bay City had one officer per 2,222 inhabitants.[10]

Budget priorities, larger populations, and "zones of crime" explain the lumbertowns' willingness to spend less on law enforcement. Fire prevention was the first priority, and the lumbertowns expended much money on fire personnel, facilities, and public waterworks. Second, average populations by the mid-1870s ranged between six thousand and ten thousand people, much larger than the cow towns. Unlike the cattle towns, a feeling of permanence had developed. Most lumbertown citizens were no longer mere transients hoping to make a few dollars or find a little excitement. Many had an investment in the community and an interest in preserving law and order. For most residents a large, watchful police force was unnecessary. Third, when violence and criminal activity did take place, it was often confined to the Sawdust Flats, White Row, or Catacombs— zones in which the police acted with some leniency. Lumbertown businessmen and authorities did not discourage the shanty boys from celebrating and willingly took their money, but, in doing so, enclosed the lumberjacks in a defined section of the city. In the West, the cattle towns depended on the cowboy as a source of income; the lumbertowns, much like the industrialized Western mining settlements, tolerated their transient laborers but did not see these visitors as the primary source of revenue. Thus law enforcement was both selective and geographically limited. City officials in the lumbertowns did not need to hire as many policemen per capita nor watch as closely as did the cattle towns the costs or quality of law enforcement personnel.

Policemen in the lumbertowns, as in the West, often were transients and men of questionable character; more solid citizens were deterred by the low pay and by the physical and political harassment. Men were often dropped from the police force through the influence of a politician or councilman, and appointments were similarly obtained. A change in municipal leadership or political party could cause a complete change in the police force. Drunken policemen were common, and lumbertown newspapers frequently deplored their presence on duty. In Muskegon a few negligent officers were replaced.

Yet it was difficult for the authorities to chastise law officers for faults also common among their superiors. In 1876, for example, Judge A. H. Giddings, the popular circuit rider, frequently missed sessions of court because of "sudden illnesses" or "having gotten lost on the train to Muskegon." In 1877 the Muskegon marshal was caught visiting a saloon after hours and reprimanded by the city council. The editor of the *Muskegon Chronicle* deplored the city council's refusal to fire the marshal and described him as "useless, inefficient, and bullheaded." A few years later, a new marshal was admonished by council for "visiting and drinking after hours in a house of ill repute."[11]

East Saginaw's chief of police, Truman B. Fox, resigned his post in 1867 when the town council refused his request to dismiss two drunken officers. Several years later chief of police and East Saginaw marshal, T. Daily Mower, was "bounced" as chief for failing to file an annual report, lax enforcement of the gambling laws, and taking junkets at city expense while escorting prisoners to other towns. Two years later Mower was back at his post as chief and marshal. In 1875 the marshal of Bay City, D. H. McCraney, was accused of blackmail and drunkenness by members of the common council. McCraney had been charging Bay City prostitutes and their proprietors fees to operate. If either failed to pay, a raid would be ordered. During the inquiry it came to light that McCraney himself owned a brothel and frequently spent his off-hours there. Despite the evidence, a tie vote of the council failed to remove the chief from office. Trouble plagued Bay City's police force. In 1877 four policemen were tried before the local circuit court on charges ranging from "failure to pay over fines" to "resisting and obstructing arrest." A year later five more policemen were tried on similar accounts. Two officers were sentenced to serve eight months and another one year in the state prison at Jackson.[12]

The unreliability of the lumbertowns' police forces arose, in part, from the city councils' reluctance to insist on rigid enforcement of the law. City officials were often downtown businessmen, men like Jim Robinson, who were cautious when it came to overzealous law enforcement. In 1876 the Muskegon common council was criticized for dismissing policemen although "thieves were running rampant" in the city. The Muskegon Chronicle also accused the marshal and town officials of instructing policemen not to enforce Sunday closing laws. The men were told "just see that front doors were closed—not back." In Bay City, Fitzmaurice recalled that the city "was largely governed by the 'Catacombs' influence, and the tools of vileness and unblushing crime were in positions of power and trust in city and county. The chief of police was hand and glove with the miscreants." Police activity thus was mitigated by the economic necessity of maintaining the lumberjacks' trade; the businessman-entrepreneur often exerted influence to curb legitimate police activity.[13]

Not all lumbertown policemen acted with such scant respect for the law. The lumber centers employed a few officers who were dedicated, reasonably honest, and enforced the law with an efficiency and style like that of the romanticized Western lawmen. Remembered in East Saginaw was Marshal Charles Meyer, a Civil War veteran hired in 1871 to bring some order to the burgeoning lumber settlement. Meyer, an ex-cavalryman, devised a highly successful method to quell "free fights." When fifty or more lumberjacks began to slug it out in a saloon, Meyer would arrive astride his horse, ride inside the saloon, and "like a Cavalryman uses a saber," flail away with his nightstick while his horse pranced about among the brawlers.[14]

Patrick Kain was another East Saginaw officer who developed a reputation among lumberjacks as one of the toughest law officers in the sawmill towns. Kain, a blacksmith from Flint, was treated early in his career "to the favorite outdoor sport of the lumberjacks": testing the mettle of any new policeman. Confronted by a half-dozen near-drunken woodsmen, Kain, employing his nightstick, viciously subdued the mob. Repeated displays of Kain's prowess convinced the shanty boys of the new man's ability. His beat, along the infamous Potter Street, soon became "as orderly as any business street." Kain served twenty years as a policeman and later became a much respected chief of police.[15]

Muskegon's Patrick Ryan, a veteran officer of several years, developed an extraordinary sense of reasoned judgment. Newspaper accounts mention his careful investigations and cautious apprehension of criminals. In one episode Ryan permitted a drunken lumberjack to fire at him six times without returning a shot. When the assailant's gun was empty, Ryan calmly approached, clubbed the man, and hauled him off to jail. Questioned by a reporter, the officer matter-of-factly replied that he did not return fire "because the man was drunk." Yet, despite these individual exceptions, the police forces throughout the lumbering period generally remained suspect. Some order and stability resulted when the cities organized boards of police commissioners in the late 1870s and early 1880s. The boards mitigated political manipulation and the capricious dismissal of officers was made more difficult. However, except perhaps in Bay City, political reorganization did little to improve the quality or integrity of individual recruits.[16]

If the police were suspect and seldom made serious efforts to eliminate vice, drunkenness, and rowdyism, the courts were equally indulgent. As in the cattle towns, judicial authorities in the lumbertowns realized that discretionary penalties were best for business. "Soft-eyed" judges pragmatically moderated prescribed punishments and adopted a live-and-let-live disposition.[17]

Furthermore, enforcement of statutes by local police courts, rather than the district court, would result in fines being extracted that accrued to the city treasury and not to the county or state. Small fines regulated, not prohibited, and the perpetrator came back again to add to the city coffers. In Muskegon, for example, of the 195 cases brought before the police court in 1878 only 9 were sent to district court. If these misdemeanors were especially offensive or the transgressor perpetually indigent, he or she would be housed in the local jail for several days and then placed on a boat for nearby port cities along Lakes Michigan or Huron.[18]

The same leniency was also given those who engaged in fatal and near fatal encounters. As in the cow towns and mining settlements, few individuals guilty of homicide or severe assaults were sentenced to the maximum penalty. Michigan had outlawed capital punishment when it became a state and, unlike the Western towns, those committing a violent death were spared a violent retribution. The courts accepted a wide range of extenuating circumstances. Youth, intoxication, being a foreigner, ignorance of the law, and self-defense would often bring exoneration or moderate sentences from the courts. Intoxication appeared to be an appeal that mitigated severe sentencing especially if both the victim and offender were residents or habitual visitors to the Row, Sawdust, or Catacombs areas. James Gordon of Muskegon was let off on a charge of shooting and nearly beating a peddler to death. "If Mr. Gordon had been sober," mused the editor of the *Muskegon Journal*, there would have been no question in the case for the court to try." Townsfolk were also inclined to be forgiving if the perpetrator was from a good family and committed a crime against a transient lumberjack or foreign mill worker. Leniency also often resulted from the lack of witnesses and trials that often ended in acquittal by hung juries. Because of the costs involved, few prosecutors were willing to pursue new trials.[19]

Throughout the twenty years of the lumber era in the three lumber counties of Bay, Saginaw, and Muskegon, 112 murders were reported by the Michigan attorneys general. Only six individuals were sentenced to imprisonment for life, and one, a Muskegon woman, was pardoned within two years by the governor. Sixty-three of the homicides are known to have ended in acquittal, discharge, hung juries, fines, or discontinuance. Thus, fifty-six percent of the capital offenses ended with no punishment being imposed.[20]

The leniency of the lumbertowns' courts and society compares favorably with the circumstances in the Kansas cow towns and several Western mining settlements. In five representative Kansas cattle towns between 1870 and 1885, forty-five homicides were committed. Only three persons received the death sentence and none of these, despite capital punishment in the state, was executed.[21] Tolerance, as well as legal circumstances, contributed to create a fairly permissive nineteenth-century society. Permissiveness was encouraged by economics. The businessman, the entrepreneur, the lumberman, and town authorities may not have liked the shanty boy's antics, but they realized that their profits necessitated acceptance and toleration to ensure the shanty boy's continued presence in the lumbertowns.

PROSTITUTION

Experience indicated that prostitution, gambling, and intoxication were the three main causes for much of the violence in frontier communities. Acting under such an assumption, it would seem only natural that efforts be made to curtail, if not stamp out, prostitution and gambling. There were extensive efforts to regulate these vices through taxation in the Western cattle towns and mining settlements.[22] However, in the Michigan lumbertowns taxation of prostitution was virtually nonexistent. Statutes effectively placed taxes on saloons, liquor sales, and gambling devices, but the lumbertowns never grasped the opportunity to add to the city treasuries by taxing illicit sex.

Failure to tax, in fact, may have encouraged prostitution to flourish in the logging centers beyond the regulated trade in the Wild West settlements. The lumbertowns did not tax prostitutes because it was not an economic necessity. In the West, taxation was imposed on prostitutes not only to regulate but also to dilute some of the tax burden placed on the saloons. In the logging centers, however, there were so many saloons and prostitution was such an integral part of their existence that to tax both would have been excessive and cumbersome. Taxes on saloons ranged from $20 to $25 per month; however, as the towns grew and saloons and attendant vice flourished, the taxes reached $100 by the mid-eighties. Fees levied on saloons brought in enough money (Muskegon collected $7,923 in 1878) that more taxes were unnecessary. Considering that in 1880 total police expenditure in Muskegon was $3,036.86, the tavern license fees more than carried the cost of law enforcement.[23] The fee system also ensured a semblance of control by providing a convenient pretext for investigations and official inquiries, but the regulation of prostitution was sporadic. Like many large cities, the lumbertowns succumbed and accepted prostitution as a necessary evil.

The number of saloons, dance halls, variety theaters, and resorts supports the conclusion that prostitution was more pervasive in the lumbertowns than many Western cities. In the Western mining settlements during the sixties and seventies, forceful steps were taken to rid many of the smaller communities of prostitution.[24] Later, however, as toleration and acceptance became the norm, some Western mining towns became less hostile to cribs, dance halls, and parlor houses. The cattle towns, however, never matched either the industrailized mining and lumber settlements in sheer numbers of prostitutes.

There are only estimates as to the numbers of prostitutes in all kinds of frontier communities.[25] Carefully interpreted census data can help put these numbers into perspective, however. In the 1880 census enumeration for Bay City, occupations characteristic of prostitutes appear frequently within certain geographical areas. "Laundress," "waitress," "dance-hall girl," "domestic," and "servant" appear on the census list and have often been linked to the occupation of prostitution. In Bay City eight boardinghouses along Water and Third streets each housed from six to fifteen girls claiming such occupations. If only half of these women were prostitutes, the Catacombs area housed at least forty women of pleasure. The census records also indicate another half score of boardinghouses along nearby Adams, Woodside, and Jefferson avenues where prostitution also flourished. To calculate it another way, if half of the 162 saloons that existed in 1886 employed a minimum of two or three girls, the number of prostitutes would be in the hundreds. Similar numbers are evident in Muskegon and East Saginaw where twenty-one and thirty-two houses of ill repute were in operation in 1880.[26]

Though there was apparently less transience among the lumber bawds, migration nevertheless did take place. Surprisingly, as the cow towns played out, pioneer women trekked eastward to the pineries in Michigan and Wisconsin. Easterly migration is evident in lumbertown census data, although the birthplaces of those women residing in notorious boardinghouses were mostly Canada, the New England states, and other parts of Michigan. Muskegon, because of its proximity to Chicago and Milwaukee, had more women from the West. Ethnic origins are those of the more established stock in the country: English, Irish, French-Canadian, and German. Except in Muskegon, where some Hollanders practiced the trade, recent female immigrants to the lumbertowns apparently did not become wanton. Black prostitutes, who invariably settled in every Western town, were practically unknown in the lumbertowns.[27]

Records of arrest and newspaper accounts affirm that prostitutes were an integral part of the lumbertowns' crime statistics. After common laborers and sailors, prostitutes represented the third most frequently arrested occupational category in the lumber settlements. A careful reading of Muskegon's newspapers between 1869 and 1889 reveals that there were about twenty-one murders committed. Of these, three, and perhaps four, directly involved prostitutes: two in

which the girls died after abortions; one violent, though unexplained, prostitute's death in a Muskegon "hell-hole of shame"; and
another in which a suspected prostitute was shot by a woman she
had accused of living in adultery. A dance hall was the scene of at
least one murder. About one-quarter of Muskegon's violent deaths
were related in varying degrees to prostitution.[28]

Several suicides were also associated with prostitution. Again
looking at Muskegon, the early years of settlement were nearly void
of violent, self-inflicted deaths. Yet between 1875 and 1887 there
were about twenty-seven suicides in the Muskegon area. Three were
known prostitutes who poisoned themselves with either laudanum or
morphine. Another waitress committed suicide by poisoning, and a
fifth killed herself because apparently false rumors had associated her
with a house of ill repute. A sixth drowned herself in Muskegon
Lake because her daughter lived in a city brothel. One-quarter of all
recorded suicides directly or indirectly involved prostitution.[29]

All authorities agree that whoring and violence also mixed freely
in the Western cattle and mining towns. In the Kansas cow towns
studied by Robert R. Dykstra, three of forty-five homicides may have
been linked to prostitutes or dance halls. A study of violence among
prostitutes in the mining towns of Aurora and Bodie reveals that
although much mayhem took place, few whores participated in
deadly encounters. However, a recent examination of Virginia City
indicates that at least six prostitutes were homicide victims and
many more constantly involved in police matters. Evidence indicates
that prostitutes in the lumbertowns were as violent and perhaps involved in more violent deaths than the women in the West.[30]

Despite the association of prostitution with violence, the lumbertowns and their Western counterparts made scant efforts to eradicate
prostitution. When the red ribbon temperance crusade swept
through the logging centers in the late 1870s, a short-lived, partly
successful campaign closed some saloons and brothels. Despite the
inordinate claim of sometime temperance lecturer Fitzmaurice that
"all the low 'dives' had been forced to shut," few disappeared. By
1880, after the "rapid declension and final demise of the red ribbon
movement," most houses of ill repute were back in business.[31]

Journalists periodically clamored for moral reform, but most agitation was selective and sporadic. Newspapers sometimes urged removal of houses that were too close to schools or churches or that
were the scenes of excessive rowdyism. The *Muskegon Chronicle* rec-
ommended ridding the city of the houses of ill repute by having the

police release the names of the men found in such places as well as
the women. Yet when such information was available, the paper remained discreet in the male names it published. During the height
of that city's pine era, the police commission reported to the common council that "it is impossible to rid the city of houses of ill
repute." The commission's only recommendation was to make an effort to eliminate those that are "abiding places of disease."[32]

Organized commercial sex was too profitable and too necessary to
the lumbertowns' social and economic fabric to provoke vigorous
regulation. Saloon keepers, some businessmen, and even community
leaders often fought to maintain prostitution because it was good for
business. Besides that, why would anyone interfere with consensual
sex when people were dying in sawmill accidents, beating one another up in the streets, and generally misbehaving on a daily basis?
As in so many nineteenth-century urban areas, prostitution in the
lumbertowns became a standardized product. It was no better, and
perhaps not much worse, in the lumbertowns than in other burgeoning industrial, frontier towns east and west. Local authorities in the
logging centers failed to enforce statutes not only because the Sawdust, Catacombs, and Row districts brought revenue into the towns
and segregated vice but also because many people believed prostitution to be a trifling impropriety that did not require abolition.

GAMBLING

The professional gambler was a legendary fixture in frontier towns,
but gambling apparently never assumed significant dimensions in the
lumbertowns. The state and the logging municipalities had drawn up
codes forbidding gaming houses as they had outlawed houses of ill
repute, but legislation was of little avail if enforcement was lax. Authorities in the lumbertowns enforced antigambling laws selectively
and usually permitted games of chance.[33] Yet despite legal tolerance,
the logging towns only infrequently attracted the card sharks or engaged in gambling practices that encouraged mayhem and violence.
If the shanty boy was on his way to hell, he apparently was content
to drink and whore his way there. Gambling was an afterthought;
though he might participate, the woodsman never tarried too long
at the green table.

The lumbertowns taxed games of chance, not to raise revenue but
simply to provide some control and supervision over saloons and

their gaming tables. As in the West, municipal ordinances and police practices were designed to protect the backwoodsmen from being fleeced by professionals or crooked tables. The lumbertowns generally permitted card tables, bagatelle, and billiard tables in the saloons, resorts, and barrooms. Each table was taxed between $15 and $25 per year, but some municipalities later lowered even these minimal fees $10 per annum. In contrast, the Kansas cow towns charged similar amounts but collected them monthly. Again, gaming taxes in the cattle towns were used to raise revenue. In the lumber settlements saloon taxes provided enough income to meet municipal law enforcement costs.[34]

The professional gambler did, at times set up shop in one lumbertown or another. However, local authorities, perhaps to protect the neophyte woodsmen, usually acted quickly to urge these "knights of the green" on their way. Muskegon attracted a number of professionals in 1872, and the local newspaper alerted the town officers that these men had become "bold and brazen" and had gone "unwhipped of justice too long." Shortly thereafter the county prosecutor issued several arrest warrants in an attempt to put a stop to the "nefarious practices" of the gamblers.[35]

Throughout the entire twenty years of the white pine era, very few arrests were made for gambling or illegal gaming. In eighteen of the years for which arrests were reported to the attorneys general by the three Michigan counties, only 3.8 arrests were made each year for gambling and fewer than one per year for keeping gaming houses. Penalties usually were moderate. Seldom were jail terms meted out. Fines of $100 were common for gambling—probably intended to discourage the professional—but fines for local operations using illegal devices were considerably less.[36]

Violence was seldom associated, at least publicly in newspaper accounts, with lumbertown gaming. If it did occur, it was often inflicted on the itinerant gamblers who won too much money or used unscrupulous practices to fleece unsuspecting lumberjacks. There were reports of gamblers being beaten by gangs of unknown toughs.[37] Perhaps the lawlessness that prevailed within the Row, Sawdust, or Catacombs was enough to keep the trained professionals away from the lumber burgs. Illegal gaming generally meant that shady saloon keepers drugged or clubbed a green shanty boy engaged in a game of chance. Authorities investigated such establishments but apparently not often enough to completely eliminate violent practices associated with gambling.

Lumbertown arrest records, newspaper accounts, and police reports give evidence that gambling never became the public nuisance or provoked the violence that came to be associated with the "sport" out West. Perhaps a larger immigrant labor force, the frugality of some shanty boys with families, or a willingness to waste their wages on more mundane sports led the lumberjacks away from gambling. The lawlessness within the zones of vice and the hostility that the shanty boys displayed toward itinerant gamblers may have discouraged the professional from settling into the lumber settlements. The woodsmen's lack of interest in gambling, though, should not convey an image of righteousness; they participated in many less sophisticated but violent sports.

ROWDYISM, BRAWLING, AND FIGHTING

The one form of violence that separated the lumbertowns from their Western counterparts was brawling. The "national pastime" for the shanty boy was fisticuffs, and though he may not have raised his sport to an art, he engaged in it often enough to establish a ritualistic pattern.

Rowdyism began on the spring journey from the interior logging camps. Not all the jacks became river hogs and worked the spring drive. Many purchased an infamous "ticket to hell" and boarded a train to Muskegon or the Saginaw Valley. Pushing, cursing men, carrying their "stake" and worldly possessions in a "turkey" (a sack or bound-up kerchief), packed into the train's passenger cars like cattle off to market. By the time the train reached Bay City, Muskegon, or Saginaw most of the day coaches' windows were shattered, and the loggers were drunk, blackened, beaten and torn from the brawling during the journey.

Embarking from the train the "red sash brigade" headed for the nearest taverns and bawdy houses determined to catch up quickly on the winter's fun they had missed. Fortified with whiskey, the jacks swaggered along the wooden sidewalks marching, singing, and shouting from one saloon to the next. When one brigade confronted another, there was a moment's hesitation, after which there might be a joyous reunion or a pitched battle. Often even a joyous reunion quickly degenerated into the all-too-common "free fight," and twenty or more shanty boys would have at it in a so-called friendly battle. Legend had it "after the dust settled from the fight they all became buddies. Fighting was as much a part of the lumberjacks' lives as drinking, working, and wenching."[38] In the early years of the lumbertowns' existence there evolved a method of fighting and brawling that gave the logging cities much of their colorful notoriety.

Weekends, especially during the spring and fall, and even through much of the summer during the later years of the lumber era, were made for fighting. The *Bay City Tribune*'s Monday column, "The Weekend's Activities," detailed the fights and arrests of the three previous nights. Despite frequent arrests, as with so much violence that went on in the lumbertowns, there was much official tolerance. Parker Owen, a policeman who shared the notorious Potter Street beat with Patrick Kain, explained his responses to the rowdy lumberjacks and the Saturday night action:

> They weren't a bad lot, not at all, they were just a lot of big, strong boys, their pockets bulging with money and their thirsts made keen by long months in the woods, far from the sort of civilization offered by the cities.
>
> They were full of life, tired of their work in the woods, and intent on having one grand and glorious blowout before heading back for the pine forests and weeks on end more of the hard work of getting out the logs that fed Saginaw's roaring mills.
>
> There were many things they missed—liquor, the companionship of women and a fight or two or three—and most of all they loved a fight. They weren't especially nasty about it, but if there wasn't an invitation for a fight they'd issue the invitation themselves—always with plenty of takers.[39]

Besides the brigades, there was the free-lance combatant who roared into town and challenged one and all.[40] Newspaper accounts, as well as literature, affirm the existence of the rough and tumble fighter who came along and proclaimed he "could whip the best man in Muskegon," or wherever. The same accounts also confirm that many of these braggarts inevitably landed in the local jail.[41]

A few of these shanty boys became well known for their violent acts. Literature about the wicked lumbertowns tallied a familiar list of logging town bad men. The "fightingest of all lumberjacks" was "Silver Jack" Driscoll. He acquired an unenviable reputation for brawling in East Saginaw until robbery sent him off to the state prison for fifteen years. Silver Jack engaged in the lumbertown fight of the century in the early 1870s with Joe Fournier, another "noisy, quarrelsome, notorious tough." Fournier not only lost the fight but a few years later was reputedly pounded several inches into the ground by a wooden mallet after a fight in Bay City's Catacombs. The trial of Fournier's killer, in which the dead man's skull was used as "evidence," became the trial of the decade. Another bad man, T. C. Cunnion, the "man-eater" from Bay City, chewed bloody cow's liver to frighten opponents, but in later years was forced to fight bulldogs in sawdust pits. A well-known fighter who apparently lost more often than he won was "Brick" Thomas, who claimed to have been arrested 299 times in Bay City.[42]

Although there were several well-contrived methods of engaging in brawling, most frays were individual affairs resulting from too much cheap whiskey. In contrast to romanticized accounts of these friendly contests, many led to bloody and battered heads and stab wounds. Many intoxicated, overconfident, and angered lumberjacks engaged in grudge matches that ended tragically. Of the twenty-one murders committed in Muskegon during the lumber era, eight were directly related to arguments, drinking, and fighting. In East Saginaw fully one-third of the homicides resulted from similar confrontations. All too often the one common element that inflated the murder rate in the Michigan lumbertowns was "fighting merely for the hell of it."[43]

Local authorities, when they were aware of the event, generally permitted the combatants to have at each other until one or the other dropped of exhaustion. Parker Owen recalled that "unless someone other than the lumberjacks themselves seemed in danger, or unless the danger took on a murderous tinge, the police seldom interfered, except to make sure the fighters got fair play, and that their caulked boots didn't play too great a part in the fray." Policemen, who themselves often became the object of the shanty boys' hostility, were understandably reluctant to step hastily into an especially violent melee. "The favorite outdoor sport of the lumberjack was to test the mettle of any new police officer. If he lasted a couple of months he was pretty sure to stay on the job."[44]

Yet, despite the risks, lumbertown authorities did attempt to bring those guilty of violent assault to justice. East Saginaw, which made a more determined effort than Muskegon or Bay City to control crime and vice, placed Judge DeWitt C. Gage on the circuit bench. Gage developed a reputation as a "terror" for assigning stiff sentences with little or no mercy to those brawlers branded as "bad characters." Attempts by the local police to control rowdyism also appear in the reports of the attorneys general for the three counties. The crime most frequently precipitating arrest was "assault and battery." If charges of "simple assault," "assault with intent to kill," and "disorderly"—all crimes associated with fighting and brawling—were added, about one-half of lumbertown criminal activities involved rowdyism, fighting, and brawling.[45]

Western towns also experienced fighting and brawling, but it never became as pervasive or as interwoven in Western culture as it did in the lumbertowns. Where statistics are available, it appears that in the mining settlements during the sixties and seventies fewer personal assaults occurred than in the lumbertowns. However, later in the century, larger boom towns, such as Virginia City, Cripple Creek, and Leadville, experienced widespread rowdyism. In some of the cattle towns fighting took place, but arrests for assault and battery seldom matched those in the lumber settlements; such activities were commonly ignored by cow town officers. Sketchy comparative data on assault and battery make it difficult to compare accurately the extent of rowdyism, brawling, and fighting. Nevertheless, like gunplay and shootouts in the cattle towns, fighting and brawling vividly branded the lumbertowns as havens of endemic mayhem and violence.[46]

Violent Deaths

In a society where vicious physical confrontations were everyday events, violent deaths were certain to occur. Yet, as in the Wild West, homicides in the lumbertowns were not frequent. Recent studies of Western violence note that in most mining camps, cow towns, and boomtowns, "within a remarkably short time" violence diminished and frontier settlements were relatively free of serious crime.[47] There were not many killings in the lumbertowns either; however, rather than decreasing, homicides occurred more frequently as the logging centers became larger and more settled. In the early years, when law enforcement was supposedly ineffectual, there were fewer violent deaths in the frontier lumber ports than in later years. The patterns of logging-town homicides resembled those in Eastern municipalities and turbulent Midwestern port and river settlements rather than Western frontier towns.

In the twenty years of the lumber era about 112 murders took place in Bay, Saginaw, and Muskegon counties. The murders were reported by county prosecutors to the state attorneys general and reflect countywide statistics, but many of these homicides did occur in the counties' three principal cities where most of the population resided. See table 4, in which figures begin with 1868, a year which lumber productivity accelerated, and end with 1888, about four years into the decline of the timber business.[48]

Newspaper accounts confirm many, but not all, of the reported homicides. Violent deaths occurred infrequently enough that they were prominent, newsworthy items. Yet some remain merely statistical deaths and explanatory details are unavailable, such as the so-called unknown floaters pulled from the Saginaw River and Muskegon Lake. Although some of these died violently, details were seldom known. Accounts of these findings sometimes went unreported in the local press. Nevertheless, the frequency of such discoveries in the waterways and evidence available as to the cause of death indicate that homicide figures in the logging towns should be higher.[49]

The number of lumbertown homicides manifested "wave" dimensions, mirroring an image of sporadic but violent internal conflict that characterized Western cattle towns. However, the violence in the lumbertowns was completely unrelated to internecine community conflict, and, furthermore, no homicide was committed as part of a multiple murder episode. All deaths occurred as individual affairs, and, while this makes it difficult to determine causation, it demonstrates that murder was somewhat more pervasive and affected many social groups. More than half of the homicides were recorded in the years 1881–86, turbulent years marked by a decline in lumber productivity and labor turmoil. Although no deaths were directly or indirectly associated with labor unrest, there was considerable violence, and economic insecurity obviously affected social and personal interactions. Economic uncertainty in part explains the trends toward violence in the lumbertowns' latter, declining years rather than in their formative, frontier periods.[50]

Saginaw County experienced twenty homicides—fifteen of which occurred in East Saginaw—in 1881, and Muskegon witnessed a homicidal rampage from 1884 to 1887. In 1884 the editor of the *Muskegon Chronicle* noted the "epidemic of crime" and that the list of persons charged with murder "has become frightfully large." However, although he commented on the "horror which the long list of deeds inspires," the editor was more concerned with the "enormous expense which will occasion the county." Thus despite the plague of murders, he deplored human suffering but simultaneously bemoaned financial loss.[51]

TABLE 4.
Lumbertown and Cattle Town Homicides

Place	1868	1869	1870	1871	1872	1873	1874	1875	1876	1877	1878	1879	1880	1881	1882	1883	1884	1885	1886	1887	1888	Total
Bay County	nr	1	3	3	0	1	0	1	3	0	0	0	0	0	4	1	3	0	0	0	4	24
Muskegon County[a]	1	1	0	2	0	1	0	0	0	1	1	0	0	2	0	2	6	2	7	5	0	31
Saginaw County	0	nr	0	0	1	2	0	4	5	1	0	2	1	20	0	1	6	5	8	1	0	57 / 112
Abilene, Kansas[b]	2	3	2																			7
Ellsworth, Kansas[b]				1	5	0	0															6
Wichita, Kansas[b]				1	1	1	0	0														4
Dodge City, Kansas[b]								0	5	2	1	1	0	3	2	1						15
Caldwell, Kansas[b]									2	2	3	1	2	2	1							13 / 45

nr: No report turned into the attorney general.

[a] In Muskegon, 1881–84, no reports were filed. Numbers are from newspaper accounts of homicides.

[b] Dykstra, *The Cattle Towns*, p. 144.

It is hard to identify any connection between the homicides and the lumber business. The clubbing of Joe Fournier and the ax murder of one lumberjack near Muskegon are the only two recorded cases directly involving lumberjacks. However, when their occupations were listed, most assailants were described as "laborers," a significant portion of whom were in one way or another involved with logging and lumbering. By far the one common element associated with many lumbertown deaths was drinking. About one-quarter of all violent deaths involved persons who were either drinking or in saloons or dance halls. Interestingly, only six homicides took place in the three cities during the four years of the red ribbon temperance crusade, 1877–80.[52]

Although drinking was associated with the murders committed in the Western towns, the traditional participants in Western violence—law officers, gamblers, and "bad men"—played only minor roles in lumbertown homicides. Gamblers were periodically abused, but evidently none was murdered or committed murder in the lumber cities. Joe Fournier was the only well-known bad man to suffer a violent death, and despite their reputation for brawling, no bad men apparently committed murder in the logging centers. One East Saginaw law officer was the victim of a fatal gunshot wound while apprehending a wanted criminal, and a private guard in Muskegon shot a suspected general store robber. The lumbertown police, however, used uncharacteristic discretion in the use of deadly force. They were more willing to resort to the baton than the pistol.[53]

Except for the common association with drinking, the circumstances surrounding homicides varied considerably in the logging towns. Most were private quarrels over wronged honor, unpaid debts, or careless insults. Unlike the cattle towns and mining settlements, it is impossible to group lumbertown homicides into a few common categories. The larger, more socially and economically complex logging towns had homicides more like those in settled, urban centers. Thus, while deaths evolved from private confrontations, robbery, and accidents, they also involved poisoning for profit, infanticide, patricide, jealousy, and many unknown causes. When family disputes that ended violently is added, the pattern is more like that of contemporary homicides rather than the bloody events characteristic of the nineteenth-century West.

In the choice of weapons, however, the lumbertown assailants emulated their Western contemporaries: guns were the principal medium of death. Where means of death are determinable, about one-half of all lumbertown murderers used guns. Surprisingly, unlike the Western settlements, which early on outlawed the carrying of arms in town, the lumbertowns in their heyday did not legislate against concealed weapons. The availability of guns was not only reflected in the homicide rate but also in the number of suicides, nonfatal shootings, and accidental deaths involving guns. In 1885, after four murderous years and the senseless killing of a fifteen-year-old boy, the *East Saginaw Courier* demanded a city code prohibiting the carrying of concealed weapons. However, the revised city charter for that year failed to provide any provisions outlawing firearms. Outside of gunplay, in towns where brawling and fighting were endemic, it is not surprising that stabbings and clubbings with various instruments would account for the second most common means of killing.[54]

The number of homicides in the lumbertown did not compare closely with the number of similarly violent deaths occurring in the Western cattle towns and mining settlements. Lumbertown deaths were not as dramatic, did not involve famed bad men, and generally reflect a bloody narrative more reminiscent of complex and larger urban settlements than of the Wild West. The crime rate for the frontier communities, which may rightly include the lumbertowns, "was lower than it was in regions which always have been considered as settled down, civilized, and law abiding."[55]

In general, the lumbertowns were not a great deal more or less violent than their Western counterparts. In prostitution, fighting, rowdyism, and homicide, the lumbertowns could boast of a heritage that placed them in the mainstream of America's violent frontier tradition. And like other frontier communities, the lumbertowns lent a respectability to their forms of violence. Fighting and brawling, which they practiced with a traditional style, gave the lumber settlements a certain notoriety. The legend of lumbertown violence, though, does the settlements some injustice. Popular histories negate and give short shrift to the less colorful and orderly side of life, transform violent characteristics into glorified virtues, and deny the complexities of nineteenth-century urban life.[56]

CONCLUSION

The acceptance of some strains of violence and tangential activities that encouraged various degrees of violence say much about economic values, class, and laboring conditions in the lumbertowns. Authorities and many members of society supported economic practices that tolerated vice districts where illegal and morally questionable actions flourished. In these zones, men and women provided one another with social, as well as economic, support for their marginal activities. In the Catacombs, White Row, or the Sawdust Flats a marketplace evolved in which illegitimate and legitimate activities were carried on as an integral part of the towns' entrepreneurial structure.

Violence and vice did not hinder lumbertown prosperity and growth. Their violent reputations notwithstanding, all three towns grew rapidly throughout the lumber era. Bay City's often unfit law enforcement personnel and its notorious Catacombs area may have encouraged a few respectable citizens from settling in that community. Saginaw citizens tried, although with little success, to be more visible in their efforts to repress violence. These efforts, coupled with incessant public references to its notorious downriver neighbor, may have attracted a few more settlers seeking security to East Saginaw rather than Bay City. Muskegon prospered despite being the roughest town on Lake Michigan. Citizens knew, though, that much of the money spent in the saloons remained in the community. Local barkeeps, saloon owners, restauranteurs, brewery workers, and "working girls," as well as the businessmen-entrepreneurs created an economic reciprocity in the lumbertowns. The quest for profits and prosperity encouraged a collective adjustment to the unsavory aspects of town life.

Regulation and law enforcement activities were closely tied into the towns' economics. Police forces were small and the policemen of questionable character because city officials were reluctant to spend money to provide for enough or qualified personnel. Local authorities never encouraged strict law enforcement because many saw the need to remain hospitable to the shanty boys. Consequently, punishments were light and taxation of crime-related vice activities was almost nonexistent. Violence and vice were tolerated and, like entrepreneurial capitalism, became accepted values in lumbertown society.

For the sawmill worker and the shanty boy the saloon in the Catacombs, White Row, or Sawdust often represented a rejection of some of the standards of the dominant classes. Here they could find mutuality, conviviality, and collectivity. There probably were few U.S. cities where violence and prostitution were related as closely to a respectable labor force as they were in the lumbertowns. In nineteenth-century sawmills and lumber camps men were often treated like interchangeable parts in the machines that ran the mills. Shanty boys and mill workers worked long hours under conditions that often led to fatal accidents. Dangers at work and boredom in cramped lodging houses and camps created tensions that were partly dissipated through brawling, carousing, drinking, and whoring. Public rowdiness may be interpreted as a rejection of, or a release from, the discipline and danger that lumbertown workers faced on the job. Celebration eased some of the pain of life under the exploitative economic system characteristic of nineteenth-century society. The distinctive patterns of lumbertown violence demonstrated a set of values accepted by the workingmen that in some ways challenged those of the economic hierarchy. Violent episodes and entertainments certainly revealed social tensions and a stratified society. A society that was divided was going to have trouble developing a community consensus about the goals of acquisitive individualism.

CHAPTER FIVE

Lumbertown Barons

The typical lumberman possessed a strong sense of personal integrity. He met financial obligations promptly and was imbued with an underlying optimism and tended to be kindly and generous. He took pride in his achievement, regarding himself as a good steward who was making a modest fortune and by his labor furthering the progress of the country.

—FREDERICK W. KOHLMEYER, "NORTHERN PINE LUMBERMEN: A STUDY IN ORIGINS AND MIGRATION"

They were a thieving crew addicted to muttonchop whiskers and piling up vast sums of money. Time, however, had given them the status of empire builders, and their larceny is remembered only by a few diligent historians, who do not count.

—LEWIS CHARLES REINMANN, *Incredible Seney*

Violence, brawling, and vice were activities that ostensibly contrasted keenly with those values associated with entrepreneurial capitalism. The contrast did make clear, though, that there were two distinct societies in the lumbertowns. Elite society was dominated by the lumber barons, and, like the rich everywhere, they have been the subject of frequent inquiry and evaluation. A few attempts have been made by historians to discern the real nature of the lumbermen; however, the debates have never satisfactorily resolved the query: "robber barons or industrial statesmen?" As recently as 1983 Charles Twining again raised the issue and concluded that "such a question is unanswerable."[1] It may be impossible to ever achieve a consensus about the values and methods of the nineteenth-century lumbermen, but it is possible to discover the role these operators played in the drama of lumbertown social, cultural, and economic development.

The historian in trying to discern the nature of the lumber barons is encumbered by a reluctance on the part of these men to make much of their contributions. Few American businessmen exemplified Tocqueville's definition of "ambitious men in democracies," who "care much more for success than for fame," better than the lumber barons. As early as 1898 George Hotchkiss, the self-proclaimed historian of Great Lakes lumbering, noted a hesitancy on the lumbermen's part to realize "the importance of their work." Certainly their wealth, and in some cases their gaudy excesses, made it unlikely that the lumbermen themselves were unaware of the importance of their contributions. Even with this apparent awareness, they remained extremely reticent to write about their experiences.[2]

As a result, the frontier lumbermen have received only scant attention from professional historians. Yet, despite historical oversight, lumber operators were important in the development of Michigan's lumber mill towns.[3] They formed powerful interest groups that greatly influenced the social, political, and economic evolution of the lumbertowns. To a remarkable degree, the men of Saginaw, Bay City, and Muskegon reflected the attitudes and values of the entire generation of lumbermen-entrepreneurs who came to power during the Gilded Age. In this critical period of cultural change, these entrepreneurs were among the ruling elite of the lumbertowns' social systems. Who then were the sawdust barons? Were they outsiders or natives? What were their social origins, and more important, what were their beliefs, values, and attitudes toward the workers and communities in which they earned their fortunes? Was it possible, paraphrasing E. Digby Baltzell, that the lumbertowns were largely shadows of these leading men? Did different values and entrepreneurial practices create different communities?[4]

Although no specific study has been done on lumbertown barons, regional studies offer some broad assumptions and a framework for a more detailed comparative analysis.[5] We know, for instance, that lumbermen were often imbued with certain assumptions about the nature of society. Underlying their public statements and operational behavior was a shared value system that provided a collective identity and defined their actions toward labor and their surrounding community. Yet individual manifestations of these beliefs varied, and in the twenty-five years of the lumber era enough time was allowed for change in common ideology. Although lumbermen seldom expressed their social beliefs openly, they inadvertently left records in private correspondence, newspaper accounts, and professional publications.

The Lumbermen

Concern about the cohesiveness and stability of urban leadership is an issue that has involved scholars in protracted debate and is a question crucial to understanding the economic development and leadership of the lumbertowns. This study of lumbertown elites suggests traditional explanations—that lumbermen stabilized society by operating in "island communities," or a fluid society existed that altered the industrial community's social class patterns—are inadequate.[6] More recent explanations, which assert that social and economic networks are largely dependent on regional ties, are more relevant to understanding the lumbertown elites.

Occupational mobility as a force for change is likewise challenged. Established leadership often can easily absorb new members who came from a regional network made up of cities and towns in surrounding areas. The extent to which these migrants or new leaders "share socioeconomic and ethnocultural characteristics with established leadership" is often the most important indicator of continuity or change in town leadership.[7] Recruitment, demanded by rapid growth, may have reinforced dominant leadership if the new investors reflected the same social background of the established elites.

For lumbertowns, economic and social exchange went well beyond the context of established trading networks in the lumbering communities themselves. Markets consisted of, and investors came from, towns and cities that encompassed a region extending throughout the Great Lakes states. Past studies of regional leadership networks, for example Stuart Blumin's study of Kingston, New York, or Edward Davies's examination of towns in the Pennsylvania anthracite region, rely primarily on the presence of resident elites. Some of the lumbertowns, in contrast, had economic leaders who were absentee owners or seasonal and part-time residents. To the extent the upper classes were necessary to commit resources to the continued economic growth of the lumbertowns, especially considering the limits of an exploited natural resource, nonresident investors often determined the economic futures of individual settlements. Thus, regional networks are important to understanding lumbertown society, but absentee ownership presents an overlay that complicates the picture.

The method of identifying the lumbertown's elite is occupational positional. Individuals with economic power are identified as those who served as a charter member of an incorporated lumber company or subsidiary lumber industry. This technique is used because it is best suited to discovering not only overlapping dimensions of power but also those who exercised economic and political influence but were nonresidents. An approach focusing on individual wealth and participation would fail to reveal many absentee owners.[8] Because lumbering represented nearly eighty percent of the industrial base of Saginaw, Bay City, and Muskegon, identifying leaders by position provides a list that is almost totally inclusive. The list of 223 lumbermen for whom some biographical data could be obtained is constructed from lumber firms operating during the mid-eighties near the peak years of lumbertown enterprises. Most of these men enjoyed the halcyon years of lumber production and were still operators as the lumber business entered its precipitous decline.

We already know some things about the men who pioneered in the development of the Great Lakes and Michigan lumber industry. Frederick W. Kohlmeyer surveyed the lives of 131 lumbermen, mostly from the western Great Lakes states, and Barbara Benson examined the careers of the 133 lumber manufacturers in Michigan who entered the business before 1856 and another 161 who entered before 1870. Despite Kohlmeyer's efforts to create a rags-to-riches characterization of his lumbermen, there is a remarkable similarity among the lumber entrepreneurs surveyed.

Great Lakes lumbermen were overwhelmingly native born. Nearly ninety percent of the samples taken represented individuals born in the United States. Less than three percent were natives of Michigan. Most of the manufacturers came from New York. In considering regional networks note that the New York-New England influence emphasizes a lateral migration to Michigan. This narrow geographic range, following Erie Canal-associated transport routes, eased the transference of technology and capital.[9]

Early studies also revealed similar family backgrounds of lumbermen. Few came from socially prominent or wealthy families. More than half, for example, in both studies were sons of farmers. A study of lumbermen's educational backgrounds reveals contrast of emphasis. Kohlmeyer stressed the limited educational achievements of his lumbermen; Benson revealed "a modest surprise in the number [of Michigan men] who received more than a rudimentary education.[10]

Benson does not address absentee ownership, but Kohlmeyer sees migration westward as a condition of success. He notes that nearly all leading lumbermen migrated a second and third time and shifted their center of operations elsewhere. Younger operators, Kohlmeyer says, might often change residences, but older operators only "gave direction to enterprises founded in new regions." Kohlmeyer agrees that after 1890 Michigan's market, Michigan's capital, and Michigan's lumbermen were "released" to move west. Ironically, Kohlmeyer concludes his study by insisting that lumbermen "grew deep roots in the locale in which they lived during their prime, and the community they helped to create. They gave their time to the solution of civic problems and their money for civic improvement."[11]

How do the lumbermen of Muskegon, Bay City, and Saginaw compare with these early pioneers? Were there any differences between the lumber elites of the three communities? (See table 5.)[12] Although New York still dominated, there were more foreign-born lumbermen in the lumbertowns, especially Bay City, in the latter period. There were also more lumbermen born in Michigan and the Midwest. Many of these inherited lumber operations started by pioneer settlers. Indiana-born Charles Hackley took over his father's business in Muskegon, and W. B. Mershon and Arthur Hill grew up in Saginaw about their fathers' lumberyards. One-fifth of the

TABLE 5.
Birthplace of Lumbermen, 1860–1895

Birthplace	Muskegon N	Muskegon %	Bay City N	Bay City %	Saginaw N	Saginaw %
New England		31		26.5		28
Maine	2		8		1	2
Vermont	6		3		6	10
Massachusetts	4		3		4	7
New Hampshire	—		—			2
Connecticut	1		3			2
Mid-Atlantic		29		25		30
New York	12		16		18	
Pennsylvania	1		4		—	—
New Jersey	2		1		—	—
Midwest	3	7	3	4.6	6	10
Michigan	7	17	5	7.8	12	20
Other countries		7		28		13
Canada	1		2		3	
Germany	—		1			
Great Britain	2		10		4	
Switzerland	—		2			
Other	—		3		1	
Total	41		64		59	

lumbermen-entrepreneurs of Muskegon and Saginaw were natives of Michigan. In contrast to Kohlmeyer's observation that the younger men changed residence and moved west, the lumbertowns demonstrate that native sons, though often expanding operations to other parts of the country, frequently remained loyal residents in declining mill towns.[13]

Not surprisingly, the latter generations also had advantages of birth that ensured economic success (table 6). More came from family backgrounds with lumbering experience. In contrast to Kohlmeyer's lumbermen, among whom less than 40 percent had prior lumber experience, the lumbertowns more accurately agree with Benson's latter group where 55.5 percent of the leaders had prior lumbering experience.[14] In Saginaw especially, 60 percent of the successful mill owners were schooled in the lumber business. Likewise, the lumbertown barons were better educated. In an era when common school education was the norm, more than half of the lumbermen exam-

TABLE 6.
Social Characteristics of Lumbermen, 1880–1890

	Muskegon	Bay City	Saginaw
Occupational Experience (%)			
Lumbering	48	56	60
Farming	25	8	9
Merchant	7	13	14
Bookkeeper	13	10	0
Other	7	13	17
Education (%)			
No education	4.5	25	3
Common School	23	20	35
High School	32	15	16
Academy	5	15	16
College	14	25	29
Ethnicity (%)			
English	42	31	25
Scot	10	17	—
Irish	5	6	10
German	22	25	15
Canadian	16	13	25
Other	5	6	25
Political Affiliation (%)			
Republican	70	85	88
Democrat	26	15	12
Other	4	—	—

ined in this study had high school educations. More than a third were fortunate enough to have had experienced private academy or college education. Saginaw had a solid core (45 percent) of lumbermen trained beyond high school.

Ethnically, there was more diversity in the lumbertowns' entrepreneurs. Although English and traditional European stock continued to dominate, there were Canadian-born lumbermen, a few Irishmen, and even a black, ex-slave William Q. Atwood of Saginaw, who achieved success. The early agriculture migration of Germans into the Bay City area is reflected by the numbers for that city. Nevertheless, despite a sizeable labor force in the sawmills consisting of southeastern Europeans and Scandinavians, no one from these nationalities achieved lumbermen status.

Regardless of the exceptional ethnic or racial anomaly, the members of the lumbertowns' leadership still demonstrated a remarkable similarity in social characteristics. The cities' leaders were overwhelmingly Protestant and especially Episcopalians, Presbyterians, Congregationalists, or Methodists. Religion reflected their British or New England descent. Only two Catholics were found and one avowed agnostic with "atheistic tendencies," D. A. Blodgett. Many, though, were apparently indifferent to organized religion. Politically, as Kohlmeyer noted, the lumbermen were Republicans, although Muskegon had fewer Republicans and fully one-quarter were Democrats. The lumbermen's diversified allegiance is reflected in Muskeon's local politics, which were early-on characterized by fusion and third party tickets.

Another trend (confirming Benson's study) was that the ownership of lumber firms changed from proprietorship to partnership and incorporation. Of 161 firms surveyed in the three lumbertowns between 1880–90, 118, or seventy-three percent, were formed in partnership or corporation. Increased capital requirements and an expanding scale of production made this trend inevitable.[15] Likewise, it was not uncommon for firms to have multipartners or for one individual to be invested in several different firms. Few capitalists had the entrepreneurial nerve to shoulder the full risk of such investments. Many of these multipartner firms were family affairs like the Hackleys, Rodgers, and Wilsons in Muskegon; the Rusts, Grants, Bliss, and Hills in Saginaw; and McEwans, Eddys, Averys, Watrous, and the five Laderach brothers in Bay City. Other firms numbered three or four unrelated partners. Multipartner firms evolved as companies added manufacturing or marketing, built new sawmills, or transferred operations to other cities. Frequent fires probably encouraged some lumbermen to protect their investments by starting separate firms within one city. John Torrent in Muskegon had partnerships in three separate firms that bore his name, and Aaron Bliss was a partner in at least four separate operations in Saginaw.

Partnerships and incorporation had the effect of opening the lumber business to many new investors. Some lumbermen simply trained specially selected, promising bookkeepers or tallymen to run their firms as invested partners when civic, personal, or community activities took them from their sawmill. Hackley trained Thomas Hume to run his operation as he became absorbed in personal legal matters and efforts to reindustrailize Muskegon.[16] Absentee ownership also affected the recruitment of new entrepreneurs as mill managers working for distant owners often became partners or established their own business. The Hoyt family and Henry Sage started the careers of lumbermen like Lewis C. Slade, W. B. Mershon, and William McClure, all of Saginaw.

Many of these new leaders, sixty percent, were recruited from New England and New York. Couple this with the number of Michigan-born lumbermen—who were mostly sons of those who migrated from the East—and fully eighty percent of the lumbermen had ties eastward. A regional network reached eastward tracing the lines of commerce established early in the lumber era. Capital and technology followed this narrow lateral migration route westward. The lumberyards at Detroit, Tonowanda, Buffalo, and Albany were supplied and sometimes owned by lumbermen who processed lumber along the Great Lakes. The transfer of labor and capital from the eastern lumber region ensured that those becoming leaders in the lumbertowns shared a common culture and background.

Family ties were probably the most obvious contacts facilitating the continuance of a common leadership. Of the lumbermen surveyed, twenty-five percent were brought into the lumber elite by fathers, brothers, or immediate relatives. Marriage ties were another avenue toward leadership that perpetuated economic control among members of a regional upper class. Among those lumber concerns that expanded through marital ties were Pitts and Cranage, Murphy and Door, Smally and Woodworth, and McEwan and Fraser in Bay City; Farr and Storr in Muskegon; and Briggs and Cooper, Ring and Merrill, and Merrill and Palmer in Saginaw. Local leading families and absentee lumbermen often maintained control of stock majorities through inheritance.[17]

Several of the well-known lumber barons whose charity is well remembered in their communities achieved success through deaths of relatives or partners. Charles Hackley became primary owner of C. H. Hackley & Company when his father and brother died leaving the operation to him. Likewise in Saginaw, Arthur Hill inherited his lumber business when his father and brother both died in 1887.

Although regional and family ties were important in recruiting members into the lumbertown leadership, there were individuals who achieved success through traditional drive, determination, and good fortune. Enterprising and promising young men were often selected by lumbermen for special training. Thus Hackley so impressed his original employer, Gideon Truesdall, that he sent the young man to a Chicago business school. When he returned to Muskegon, Hackley was put in charge of the company store. Several years later Hackley financed Thomas Hume's entry into the lumbering business.[18]

The lumber business was still expanding rapidly enough to permit the occasional truly self-made man to appear. Perhaps no career was more remarkable than that of William Q. Atwood. An escaped slave, Atwood fled to Ohio, attended Berea College, panned for gold in California, and then settled in East Saginaw. He found work as a timber cruiser, and in time, as he was compensated in land, his timber holdings grew to respectable proportions. In 1874 he opened a sawmill along the Saginaw River and was personally worth more than $100,000.[19] Other entrepreneurs shared Atwood's experience, but as the century came to an end and the lumber era peaked, the demand for capital and the start-up costs for sawmill investment made it difficult for the self-starter to achieve wealth in the lumbertowns.

Self-made men and an occasional rags-to-riches success story reaffirm that the lumber business was not a closed industrial society. Until late in the nineteenth century, the industry remained less centralized and more open to entry from below than most American enterprises of that period.[20] However, new partners, owners, and managers were seldom newcomers climbing the ladder of success. Despite Kohlmeyer's assertions, the experience of the lumbermen reaffirms the historians who have demonstrated that the saga of the self-made man was partly myth. Most lumbermen were cut from the same cloth. The members of Muskegon's, Saginaw's, and Bay City's leadership demonstrated a remarkable similarity in social characteristics despite the varied avenues they followed toward success. A

regional recruitment network and introductions into lumber-
entrepreneurships through kinship or apprenticeship preserved and
sustained an upper class that reflected a common social and cultural
background. Taking off from the starting gate and running the race
to success was fairly easy. The next-to-impossible task for many was
merely getting to the starting gate itself.

One observation that cannot escape serious examination is the
number of absentee lumbermen owning sawmills in the lumbertowns
(see table 7). Muskegon and Saginaw reflect a core of resident leaders; Bay City stands out in its number of absentee owners. More
than half of Bay City's lumbermen were nonresident owners. Although historical monographs sometimes comment on absentee ownership in natural resource towns, few authorities have quantified its
extent or carefully evaluated its effect on community. Only a limited
basis for historical comparison exists.[21]

The total effect of absentee ownership is seen more accurately
when the production capacity of sawmills is identified by residence of
owners. In Saginaw and Muskegon ownership according to production capacities and mill size closely reflects the percentage of resident and nonresident lumbermen in the towns. However, in Bay
City the largest sawmills with large work forces and sizeable production rates were controlled by absentee owners. Nearly sixty-one percent of Bay City's lumber was cut in sawmills owned by outsiders.
One-half of this lumber was cut in the mammoth mills owned by
Henry Sage, Thomas McGraw (Birdsall & Barker), the Rusts, and
the Keystone Lumber Company—all absentee-owned firms.[22]

The fact that many absentee owners invested in the lumbertowns
reaffirms the regional nature of the lumber business and reveals
clearly the interregional network that helped shape lumbertown
leadership. The comings and goings of these absentee owners helped
others to move into economic leadership. Business ties were often

TABLE 7.
Residence of Lumbermen, 1880–1894

Status	Muskegon		Bay City		Saginaw	
	N	%	N	%	N	%
Resident of lumbertown	28	53.8	31	37.8	56	62.8
Absentee owner	19	36.5	43	52.4	26	29.2
Left lumbertown in declining years	5	9.6	8	9.7	7	8
Total	52		82		89	

forged and new partners brought into local operations from regions beyond the lumbertowns. Moreover, as in Bay City, absentee owners were often the wealthier lumbermen with economic and cultural ties eastward. These regional relationships preserved a common leadership.

Although the data on the social origins of the lumber barons are indicative of several broad trends, and do not provide a complete picture of attitudes and behavior of the group, such information does cast light on the social, economic, and institutional context from which labor and community policies in the lumbertowns evolved. By and large, the men who ran the sawmills in the peak production years were independent, fairly well educated, and predominantly middle and upper middle class. The commonality of cultural background and social characteristics helped create and sustain upper-class institutions. Several of these institutions touched almost every aspect of life among the lumbertowns' upper classes.

UPPER CLASS INSTITUTIONS

The visibility of the upper classes was nowhere more apparent than in the lumbertowns' exclusive residential districts. Lumbermen usually lived in several bounded areas near the downtown sections of each city. The greatest concentration was in Bay City. Here the elite neighborhood was especially conspicuous; nearly eighty percent of the city's resident lumbermen lived in a six-block area along Center Street. Saginaw's and Muskegon's leaders were more dispersed. In Saginaw most lived along Washington, Jefferson, or Owen on the east side, and along several blocks of Michigan Avenue in Saginaw City. Likewise in Muskegon, leaders lived near downtown along Terrace and Market streets, but others lived in scattered tracts around Lake Muskegon.

Many wealthy lumbermen and other leaders built splendid mansions, several of which still stand as reminders of the Gilded Age. Because their social circles were large, but amusements limited, lumbermen often built houses with entertainment in mind. The mansions were big, tall, and elegant. The largest houses had ballrooms on the third floor and enough bedrooms to accommodate several overnight guests. They often tried to outdo one another by constructing larger and more ostentatious homes than their neighbors.

Often taking up whole square blocks—William B. Mershon's took up eight blocks in Saginaw—these elegant homes sat away from the street and were commonly fenced by uniquely designed picket or wrought-iron fences.

In these residential districts, the leaders participated in several activities. The leading Protestant churches were within a five-minute walking distance. Lumbermen, like Alex Folsom in Bay City and S. C. Hall in Muskegon, built churches for nearby congregations. Their children were married in these edifices, the lumbermen were buried from these same churches, and interred, like most members of the upper classes, in the same, nearby cemeteries. The presence of these institutions helped preserve the upper-class character of the neighborhoods and reinforce their attractiveness to newcomers recruited into the elite classes.

Within this milieu, lumbermen carried on social functions. The letter books of William B. Mershon, whose father, Augustus H., had been prominent in Saginaw since the early 1850s, describe a constant interaction among members of the upper classes. Mershon, an avid sportsman and conservationist, had a private railroad car that became headquarters for him and his lumbermen companions whether on business or hunting and fishing excursions. He not only traveled with the Morleys, Lintons, and Fordneys of Saginaw but also with early auto pioneers from Detroit. In his notes are comments about social calls, dinner invitations, and political gatherings.[23]

The diary of William C. McClure of East Saginaw is notable for its account of the cultural activities that the lumbermen attended. Whenever he was home in East Saginaw and not traveling about visiting his timberlands and sawmills or buying and selling lumber, McClure took his family and others to the Music Academy in Saginaw or to the Bay City Opera House. His tastes were not elegant. He "simply wanted to be amused not wrought up with excitement." McClure did not "like the highly emotional plays." The opening of *Faust* was "no doubt a good play" but one that he "did not enjoy." Yet, educated and well-traveled, he knew enough about theater to comment that performances were "amusing because they were full of ludicrous mistakes" or that another was "nothing, and the characters were miserable."[24] The lumbermen's patterns of association and entertainment not only indicated intimacy among the upper classes but also reflected their interest in simple entertainments that enabled them to escape the burdens of industrial management.

Even in their entertainments, though, the lumbermen could not escape individual rivalries. They liked good horseflesh and built a racing park in East Saginaw and another in Saginaw City. Rivalries between Saginaw City and East Saginaw were intense, and races between horses owned by men living in the separate cities were frequent. In the winter they cleared a race course on the Saginaw River and continued their sport. Horse racing was almost as exclusive as the lumber barons' other social activities.[25]

Rivalries were set aside in more serious times. Births reflected a time of close association between community leaders. Upper classes on occasion incorporated the names of a lumbertown leader who was a close friend or associate when they named their children. For example, Captain Seth Lee named his son Charles Henry Hackley Lee after his friend and business partner in Muskegon.[26] Marriages occurred among prominent lumbertown families and helped strengthen economic ties or create new ones. However, the next life cycle stage, which would have seen sons and daughters intermarry, did not reach the lumbertowns until the late eighties and nineties when the towns were experiencing economic decline. Prominent families moved on or, more frequently, offspring made contacts outside the declining lumbertowns that took them to greener economic pastures. In death also associations persisted. Funerals for lumbermen found other barons serving as pallbearers and reading eulogies for fellow lumbermen.

After the mid-eighties philanthropic acts were another visible activity that separated the lumber elite from the town and even from one another. Few people could give money away on the scale of the lumber barons. "Muskegon's Carnegie," Charles Hackley, perhaps gave away more than any other Michigan timber baron; more than six million dollars was donated to institutions in Muskegon, many of them named after their benefactor. Saginaw received the largesse of many benefactors. Most notable was the competition between East Saginaw's Wellington Burt and Saginaw City's Arthur Hill. Rivalries carried over into philanthropic competition. Manual training schools, high schools, hospitals, and auditoriums were built because of these two lumbermen's attempts to outspend each other.[27] Bay City, perhaps because of the number of absentee owners, never experienced the philanthropy of her sister lumbertowns.

Thus members of the upper classes engaged in familial and institutional practices with one another that preserved and separated the lumbertown elite from the community at large. Their conformity and exclusivity revealed a stiff class consciousness. Though they might have been competitors, and a few lumbermen did not hesitate to grab a quick dollar, the members of the lumbertown families never really confronted one another as economic enemies. Common leisure pursuits and philanthropy enabled them to develop and reinforce a community of interest that visibly strengthened class solidarity. In their common expression of cultural and social attitudes, the lumbermen were not unlike other industrial entrepreneurs at the turn of the century. They wielded power over all aspects of the local community that directly supported their business enterprise. Leisure, like so much that they did, coordinated and reinforced class awareness.

However, leisure and institutional activities were only two narrow dimensions of their involvement in lumbertown society. The lumbermen were businessmen first and their economic practices and ideas had an equally profound influence on the lumbertowns.

LUMBERMEN-ENTREPRENEURS

In his pioneer days in Muskegon, Charles Hackley was a hard drinker who mingled freely in the shanty boys saloons and river dives. He and other rugged individualists who became lumbermen acted brashly and brazenly. Curtis Emerson was not invited to a grand party at the Bancroft in Saginaw. As the legend goes, he appeared in the ballroom on the night of the party, jumped to the table top, and walked its length kicking dishes and crystal left and right. In the early years the relationships between economic interests—the social responsibilities and attitudes of the lumber operators—were not well cultivated.

Pioneer lumbermen seldom thought about the problems of labor management or societal obligations that they might have had to the community. As the industry matured, though, and the number of sawmills multiplied and the lumbertowns became urban centers, the lumber producers developed life-styles and policies that responded to the demands of a new industrial age. Old-time loggers became lumbermen and then lumber barons. Newcomers, recruited into the industry in its peak production years, came as educated offspring or investors with an established bourgeois tradition. The success of the lumber enterprises bred two distinct societies in the lumbertowns; as a result, certain values and underlying assumptions now dictated the daily actions and activities of the lumbertown elite.

Two mind-sets evolved in late-nineteenth-century industrial society that, although antithetical, molded the social and labor attitudes of the lumbermen. Many of the old-time loggers and resident lumber barons adopted an attitude of paternalism; many large operators—vertically integrated and often absentee owners—reflected the new tenets of social Darwinism. The paternalistic operator developed a sense of responsibility toward his workers and his community. His wealth was to be used in part to help benefit and protect the workers from the vicissitudes of life. Those who became social Darwinists emphasized the struggle for existence, laissez-faire, and competition in the developing social order. The relationship between the lumberman and the mill worker was reduced to purely economic levels. Wealth and poverty were only reflections of differences of ability and effort, and by hard work, frugality, and individual improvement, the poor could always improve their lot. These operators were principally interested in the business and technical aspects of lumbering. In labor or community involvement, they responded only to the needs of the moment.[28]

Because of their contributions, charitable activities, and community benefactions, most lumbermen adopted a paternalisitic attitude toward their community. Even preceding Andrew Carnegie's famous article on "Wealth" in 1889, these lumbermen evolved toward a theory of stewardship or trusteeship for the public. Their money should be used not only to correct hardship and misfortune but also to benefit the industrious who wished to improve themselves. No lumberman personified the belief better in life as well as in words than Charles Hackley. In an interview with the *American Lumberman* at the turn of the century, Hackley reflected on his role and the responsibilities of wealth:

> After making due allowance for talent, enterprise and the faculty for improving opportunities, I consider that a rich man to a great extent owes his fortune to the public. He makes his money largely through the labor of his employees, and keeps it only through the protecting laws of the state; consequently I think his obligation to devote at least part of it to the public is manifest. Moreover, I believe that it should be expended during the lifetime of the donor, so that he can see that his benefactions do not miscarry and are according to his intent, applied for the general good. . . . To a certain extent I agree with Mr. Carnegie in a remark he recently made to the effect that it is a crime to die rich.[29]

Hackley had his counterparts in Muskegon and several in Saginaw: Wellington Burt, Arthur Hill, Aaron T. Bliss, Arthur Eddy, and others. One is hard pressed to find similar largesse in Bay City.

Still, many lumbermen adopted a social Darwinist outlook of society. Clearly in each lumbertown there were several fortunes made by individuals who remained obscure, uninvolved, and apparently not very philanthropic. Because few of these men left written records, it is difficult to piece together their ideology. However, Henry Sage, the absentee owner in West Bay City left records that epitomize the social Darwinist faith. To Sage, economic hard times were not the fault of businessmen, who "are enterprising—industrious and accumulators—for these things are right—but because of the purely animal instincts of men—& not their higher moral natures, have been placed in command."[30] According to his biographer, Sage's sentiments were indeed "that of the social Darwinist." Strongly influenced by the teachings of Henry Ward Beecher, Sage accepted the belief that the rich could not aid the poor without decreasing the national wealth; therefore, they had no social responsibility to the less capable members of the community. He was able to dismiss the failure of his one-time partner—to whom he was unwilling to lend money—as evidence of his associate's incapacity. Sage thoroughly "absorbed the social application of Darwinism."[31]

Certainly it is simplistic to conclude that the social attitudes of all lumber operators could be dichotomized into two outlooks. Most wavered or made their own private compromises between the two philosophies. The very nature of the unregulated and competitive lumber business required common economic practices that tempered diverse individual attitudes. There were shared views, for example, that power and authority belonged to those who demonstrated ability through success; that business success required control over community life; and that all labor union activity should be resisted. Still, individual lumbermen maintained differing social attitudes and economic practices. Although it is difficult to know precisely these varied beliefs because of the dearth of personal writings, it is possible to discern by actions and results the varied social attitudes and economic activities of the lumbermen. How did these varied attitudes and activities affect individual lumbertown fortunes? If Muskegon and Saginaw were dominated by resident lumbermen who were paternalistic, did these practices markedly direct town development? In contrast, is it possible to conclude in Bay City that many absentee mill owners, some of whom may have been social Darwinists, adversely affected the community's fortunes?[32]

The varied practices and beliefs of the lumber barons were reflected in several ways. Perhaps the division among philosophies is least discernible in the attitudes toward labor. Most mill men saw labor as simply an item in the cost of production. Wages were set by market conditions, and costs and profits were largely dependent on wage rates. This impersonal formula permitted the lumbermen to disregard the question of their responsibility for the conditions of the workingmen. Many lumbermen agreed with Sage that their only obligation to the workers was to provide jobs.[33] Often they accepted a social Darwinist division of men into "fit" and "less fit" and assigned a subordinate position to the laboring man because he had demonstrated an inability to assume responsibility by the lack of his own achievements. Moreover, labor unions or conflict between labor and capital were unnatural conditions because the capital class was by evolution the best to judge the needs of the workers. As one Saginaw Valley lumberman put it: "I will never submit to have anybody dictate to me how long my mill shall run or what wages I shall pay."[34]

The lumberman's implicit contempt for the less meritorious worker undoubtedly grew in part from a learned ideology, but it also developed from the attitudes that prevailed in the interior logging camps. Irresponsible, transient, and troublesome shanty boys were treated to rigid rules of conduct. As Norman Clark noted of the lumber camps, "no liquor was allowed—for workers are irresponsible; no weapons—for wage earners cannot reason; no conversation at meal times—for common men have no discipline."[35] The impersonal association common in the woods was easily transferred to the sawmills where a seasonal and largely transient work force seldom could establish a relationship with the mill owner. The edge was maintained in the lumbertowns where, for example, rigid rules were maintained ensuring prompt payments on rents in company-owned housing and immediate dismissal was guaranteed for union activity. Absenteeism was often unforgiven and injury on the job was invariably viewed as the result of employee carelessness.[36] Wherever they worked the shanty boy or mill worker was often seen, as the *Saginaw Courier* reminded its readers, as having "embraced his calling not from choice, but to escape the penalties for the commission of various crimes and misdemeanors."[37]

Still, even the most ardent social Darwinist held out some hope that the laboring man could be advanced if he took advantage of his opportunities, disciplined himself, and practiced frugality. Especially after the temperance movement swept through the lumbertowns in 1877, the lumber operators came to support the virtues of hard work, frugality, and sobriety in their relations with employees. The temperance campaign is seen by one historian as a turning point in the community life of Muskegon.[38] Several lumbermen became active in the campaign and now related to their men on a more intimate but formal level to win them over to temperance. Hackley became an avid convert, largely because of the death of his brother to alcoholism, and held socials and free lunches in his mansion to upgrade the workers' quality of life. In Bay City, Sage also argued for the closing of "Sunday grog shops—and houses of ill fame."[39]

The involvement of Hackley and Sage in the temperance crusade was, in part, a reflection of the efforts of middle and upper classes throughout northern industrial cities to reform, reshape, and restrict working-class cultural practices. Sponsored by local Protestant churches, Dr. Henry A. Reynolds swept into all three lumbertowns in 1877 and launched a "Dare to do Right" temperance crusade. In Muskegon, Reynolds was financed by the local Baptist church and two prominent lumbermen, J. W. Moon and J. B. McCracken. Temperance and religious activity in the lumbertowns were intended to affect outward control as much as self-control. Lumbermen were sure that abstinence and the elimination of the saloon would ensure industrial discipline and maintain social order. The economic order would be strengthened and, in the long run, the city would benefit financially. John Fitzmaurice, newspaperman and temperance crusader, observed the results of the movement in Bay City: "Law and order again resumed legitimate rule. Business men had more time to give to trade, and as a consequence, made more money. Mechanics soon began to get themselves homes. The restoration of such a mass of labor to its legitimate belongings, cannot be over estimated, nor can the amount of money—diverted from its proper use of intemperance and again restored to its proper channel—be fully measured or calculated." The crusade "served not only to fire endeavor, but also to cement the masses of people firmly together." Thus, as Clark has observed, temperance was used by the lumbermen, both absentee and resident owners, to develop among the mill hands a sense of individualism rather than the communalism of the saloon, and an affirmation that the middle-class home was the highest fulfillment of American life. The saloon and its values had to be regulated because to the lumbermen it represented a blatant attack on the the bourgeois values of an entrepreneurial-industrial society.[40]

In all three towns thousands of workingmen took the pledge and became visible foot soldiers in the red-ribbon crusade. Fitzmaurice reported that not only had "hundreds of shanty boys donned the 'red-ribbon,' but lawyer, doctor, merchant, judge, clerk, mechanic, and laborer all joined hands together." The movement in the lumbertowns, though, was short-lived. The independent and seasonal work habits of a frontier and immigrant work force made it difficult for the workers to accept the new ethics of the lumbermen. The churches, as Fitzmaurice complained, turned the crusade into a religious revival. The working class resented the Protestant religious fervor of the movement and remained highly resistant to repression, reform, and regulation.[41]

Despite this collective disapproval of workers' values, there does appear to be a difference between absentee and resident lumbermen in their treatment of labor. An example may be made of company housing. Because he was an absentee owner, and perhaps because his investments were widespread—Ithaca, Toledo, Albany, Wisconsin, and Canada—Sage certainly did not take any special interest other than financial in West Bay City. Repeatedly, in his correspondence to his managers in West Bay City, Sage, when referring to the settlement, uses the phrase "your people," "your streets," or "your arsons." Company housing was merely one part of a large business investment in that city and as such, it was built to return a profit. Sage built several boardinghouses for his single men and a large, four hundred-by-twenty-foot, two-story tenement house, with twenty-five apartments for his married workers. Sage rented out the boardinghouse to independent managers but kept a careful eye on prices and profits. He gave orders to "eject tenants that don't pay—uniformly—relaxing only in cases where there is a moral purpose and disability through sickness."[42] The tenement block came to be notorious as "headquarters for rats, mice, cockroaches, bedbugs, and lice." To live in what was popularly called "the barracks" invited social ostracism by others in the community. Sage remained unwilling to spend money on improvements despite the reputation of the barracks. When the building was destroyed by arson in 1875, Sage was distressed by the village's complacency toward seeking out "the villains" who set the fire. Similar attitudes also characterized the practices of absentee owner John McGraw in his larger operation across the river in Bay City. [43]

In contrast to Sage's use of company housing, Hackley also built a tenement building and several cabins to house married workers; however, Hackley's journals and ledgers indicate that he did not see these buildings as sources of profit. They were built and maintained as a service to his employees because of the housing shortage in the community. Like Sage, though, Hackley did not put much effort into keeping up the housing. He saw them as temporary structures until the men found alternative housing. [44]

In Melbourne, the company town built by Wellington Burt near Saginaw City, an even more paternalistic attitude was evident. Burt's town had the largest sawmill in the world for a while, rivaling that of Sage and McGraw in the early seventies. He built forty-five houses for married men and two boardinghouses. Yet, unlike Sage or McGraw, and perhaps because Burt lived nearby, he almost immediately built a library and public school in the town. Burt effected a policy of primarily hiring married men because they were a more stable work force. Melbourne's employees remained, as one source noted, "contented and well satisfied with conditions in the town." As an early chronicler of Saginaw history noted, that city's lumbermen "lived within a few minutes walk of their work, and these mill owners provided comfortable houses for their married men who too preferred to live close to their work."[45]

Absentee lumbermen also disrupted community life by importing and hiring immigrant laborers. Before the 1870s, mill hands in Bay City were largely native and Germans. Increasingly in the seventies "Polanders" and a substantial number of "Frenchmen . . . from Canada, and Irishmen . . . from everywhere" were hired in Bay City's sawmills. Foreign workers were employed because of a strike by mill hands in the summer of 1872. Although the strike lasted only a few days, Sage fired most of his workers including nonstrikers and hired a new crew that consisted largely of immigrant workers. [46] Sage was infuriated by the strike and was determined to let "the whole laboring community feel the burden of the strike till there grows up in their midst a sense of their folly."[47] He ordered his managers to collect rents promptly from strikers or remove them from company housing. The men who were fired had no choice but to relocate.

In Bay City, John McGraw's mammoth mill burned down in 1872 and was replaced by an even larger complex. When the mill was reopened, McGraw employed a recent Polish immigrant, Ludwik

Danielewski (Daniels), as an agent to recruit Poles to work in the mill.[48] During the depression years of 1873–74, other mill owners in Bay City hired foreign laborers at reduced wages. These practices alienated the community against not only the newcomers but also "the money grasping lumbermen." The Poles, especially, incurred the displeasure of the citizenry for "they did shove the average [wage] down to almost unlivable scale and boosted the fortunes of Bousefield [a mill owner] and his ilk."[49] Sage's and McGraw's entrepreneurial attitudes and practices were shared by both absentee and resident lumbermen in Bay City. Community antipathy toward the "money interest" in Bay City was developing by the mid-1870s.[50]

Downriver at Saginaw some immigrant labor was recruited during the 1870s; however, the percentage of foreign workers in that city's mills never matched the number in Bay City. There is no evidence that lumbermen in Muskegon deliberately recruited European workers. Whether or not resident lumbermen in these towns were more sensitive to their community and workers, neither Saginaw nor Muskegon lumbermen experienced the wrath of the citizenry for hiring immigrant employees.

Besides lumbermen's attitudes toward labor, the contrasts between paternalistic and social Darwinist beliefs and between resident and nonresident lumbermen can be seen in three more ways. First, resident lumbermen in Saginaw and Muskegon had city loyalty; they were more likely than outsiders to start new local businesses and services. The Mershon family, for example, not only built a sawmill but branched out into the manufacturing of sawmill machinery, helped build the city's waterworks, and founded the Saginaw Country Club and Canoe Club. William Mershon became an avid protector of the state's wildlife, and worked diligently to restock fish and game in streams and cutover lands damaged by lumbering practices. Likewise, Arthur Eddy and his brother Walter, sons of Saginaw lumberman C. K. Eddy, used their lumber money to fund the Consolidated Coal Company, Saginaw Milling Company, and the Saginaw Plate Glass Company. These same men and others also worked to beautify their adopted city. Parks—Rust Park, Hoyt Park, Bliss Park, Fordney Park—were built on land donated by resident lumber barons of Saginaw and East Saginaw.

In Muskegon the core of lumbermen who worked with Charles Hackley in the halcyon days of the lumber era saw rather early that urban revitalization was necessary. As early as 1879, Hackley and others began to support new, lumber-related businesses. The Temple

Manufacturing Company, which made curtain rollers, opened in that year. Lumbermen financed the Wood Package and Basket Company and a new furniture factory that opened in 1884. Moreover, these same men saw the importance of building a physically attractive city as well as one that could be proud of its public institutions to attract new businesses and settlers. Hackley and his friends built parks, beautified them with statues, opened a manual training school, and subsidized the hospital. These capitalists were committed to Muskegon and they helped the city grow.

Bay City was not without lumbermen who possessed city loyalty, but that city consistently lagged behind recruiting new business and providing public amenities. Absentee lumbermen closed their saw-mills, packed their machinery, and moved on to new pinelands. The largest mill in the valley, Thomas McGraw's (Birdsall and Barker) burned in 1884. McGraw ignored his contract with his partners and refused to rebuild. Other leading lumbermen like N. B. Bradley and Newell Eddy moved their operations northward. Sage closed his mill in 1892. Nonresident owners set a pattern in Bay City for all lumbermen. Unlike Saginaw and Muskegon where resident lumbermen reinvested in the community as well as in new pinelands, Bay City's resident lumbermen followed the pattern of the large, absentee investors and moved their plants and machinery to virgin forests. The loyalty of the absentee owner to the community was that of an investor. He participated in a cycle of investment and exploitation, and when the trees were gone he moved on. But in Bay City the economic success and example set by the absentee owner was emulated by those lesser men who wanted to achieve great things.

Second, paternalistic mill owners helped cities diversify. Entrepreneurship was needed because the lumber industry had only a small multiplier effect. Early loggers were often satisfied simply to cut rough-sawn lumber and ship it for finishing elsewhere. In time, to better control their own prices and eliminate middlemen, the mill owners built their own planing mills. Planing mills soon evolved into manufacturers of wooden building materials: doors, window blinds, moldings, sash, and flooring. Bay City led this early woodworking diversification. Located at the mouth of the Saginaw River, hardwood, used in manufacturing many finished wooden products, could be easily brought by ship into Bay City. Hardwood did not float well down the rivers; it was cut along the shores of the Great Lakes and shipped to Bay City. Saginaw and Muskegon continued to reply primarily on the abundant supply of pine floated from their network of interior tributary streams.

Bay City had thirteen planing mills in the late eighties, and the number increased to eighteen in the nineties while other towns were closing their mills. Several large flooring plants, woodenware, and shipbuilding concerns were also built in Bay City.[51] Muskegon had only four planing mills and a clothespin factory. Bay City's entrepreneurship, however, was fairly conservative. New industries were largely producers of wood products, and though they may have prolonged Bay City's lumber era, these industries did not prepare the town for the postlumber years. Local owners did not start new industries unless they were lumber related. As one city historian noted in 1905: "Bay City was too busy cutting timber and making salt to bother about permanent industries."[52]

In contrast to Bay City, lumbermen in Muskegon showed their interest in diversification in the early eighties when the Lumbermen's Exchange, a trade and pricing group, reorganized as the Muskegon Board of Trade. The board inaugurated a newspaper-advertising campaign to promote Muskegon as a place for industry. They brought two new railroads into the area and stressed the need to establish nonlumber-related industries. Several firms were started with capital from lumbermen or with support from the Board of Trade. These companies included Chemical Fire Company, Muskegon Cracker Company, Sargent Manufacturing Company, Chase Brothers Piano, and the Muskegon Rolling Mills. Lumbermen, principally Hackley, invested in all these concerns and served on the boards of directors. None of the new industries were based on lumbering, and though not all survived, their presence indicated that Muskegon's mill owners were risk-takers and farsighted enough to plan beyond wood-related reindustrialization.[53]

In Saginaw, local owners tied the city's diversification into machine shops and foundry works. By 1880 there were already seventeen foundry machine shops in the city and fifteen tin and copperware industries.[54] These firms, like Mitts and Merrill, W. B. Mershon, and Wickes Brothers, were started by lumbermen to make sawmill equipment, tin and sheet-metal products. There was also a large plant that made files for sharpening saws. Saginaw and Muskegon lumbermen were venturesome entrepreneurs who, as resident owners, wanted to build a city. They promoted diversified economies, created active boards of trade, and encouraged newcomers of talent to prosper in their towns. Bay City's absentee and conservative lumbermen simply wanted to preserve their economic positions. That city's leaders failed to pursue the ingredients necessary to perpetuate a thriving industrial economy.

Third, Muskegon and especially Saginaw possessed strong local elites who worked to bolster the political and civic life of the community. In politics the lumbermen tried to influence local, state, and sometimes even federal laws that would improve the economic environment in their towns. Muskegon's sawmill owners were active in local politics from the very beginning. When the first city charter was adopted in 1870 several young lumbermen tried to create a non-aligned, "Young Men's" ticket to eliminate partisan city politics. Although they lost the election and became part of the regular party structure, lumbermen exercised their influence and held public office throughout the lumber era. Chauncy Davis, a pioneer lumberman, was a state representative from the Muskegon district and later the city's first mayor. Hackley ran unsuccessfully for mayor in 1873 and again in 1877, but he served several terms as alderman, city treasurer, and school board member. Between 1870, when the first city mayor was elected, and 1889, nine of the twenty mayors in Muskegon were lumbermen or closely associated with the lumber business.

Mill owners in Saginaw seldom lost control of local politics and often went on to exert state and national influence as well. On the local level, lumbermen frequently held the mayoral seats in both Saginaw City and East Saginaw. Arthur Hill and Lyman Bliss served three terms each as mayor of Saginaw City. Other lumbermen politicians included Wellington Burt, William Webber, H. H. Hoyt, William Linton, and Mershon. Saginaw mill owners also became national political figures. Aaron T. Bliss, for example, was a member of the state senate in 1882 and 1883, a member of the U.S. Congress in 1889–90, and governor of the state from 1901 to 1904. David Jerome, another Saginaw lumberman, also served as governor from 1881 to 1883. Several national representatives served as effective lobbyists for the lumber interest. In the early seventies, Saginaw resident, Representative John F. Driggs, who was financed by Sage after suffering hard times financially, worked to secure choice and inexpensive pinelands for his mentor. Later "Sugar Beet" Joe Fordney, a wealthy lumberman from Saginaw, became chairman of the House Ways and Means Committee where he consistently supported high lumber and sugar tariffs to protect his and fellow lumber scions' interests in the Saginaw Valley.[55]

Political involvement of the lumbermen in Saginaw grew out of the rivalry between East Saginaw and Saginaw City. Norman Little and Jesse Hoyt had originally established East Saginaw with an aggressiveness to compete with its older neighbor. In the 1880s, during the boom years, East Saginaw lumbermen, such as Mayor John Estabrook, began another broad scheme of public improvements. Streets were paved and electric streetlights installed to make East Saginaw "the metropolis of the Valley." Lumbermen Arthur Hill and Lyman Bliss promoted similar improvements in Saginaw City.[56] Although this competition became expensive and eventually resulted in consolidating the two cities in 1889, the rivalry, especially the example set by the lumbermen in East Saginaw, created a recipe for urban growth, prosperity, and responsible leadership that prepared the towns for the postlumber era.

In the early years Bay City lumbermen were active in local politics. Nathan B. Bradley was the first mayor of Bay City in 1865 and later served as state senator and U.S. congressman. Other pioneers, such as W. C. Fay and J. J. McCormick, also held political office in the early seventies; however, after that no one from the lumbering elite held positions of prominence in Bay City. The lumbermen did not resign that modicum of power their economic positions enabled them to wield in the community. However, because they were often absentee owners with widely scattered investments, these lumbermen did not concentrate exclusively on Bay City politics as did those lumbermen who worked and resided in Saginaw or Muskegon.

When the absentee lumbermen showed interest in Bay City's political affairs, it was not all-pervasive power like the lumbermen in Saginaw or Muskegon. Sage's experience in West Bay City may be indicative of some of the political challenges that confronted absentee owners. His letters to the H. W. Sage Company in West Bay City and the comments of Sage's biographer give a vivid glimpse into absentee-community relations.

Conflict between owner and community arose primarily over the issue of taxation. In the early years when West Bay City [then Wenona] was gradually becoming less of a company town, Sage maintained a core of employees who served on the village council and generally supported his interests. As the community grew, however, politics became partisan, and the Republicans (allied to Sage) and the Democrats vied for power. When the Democrats were in control, Sage viewed these politicians as "Wenona's Tweeds" and saw taxes placed on his holdings based "on greed and for . . . enriching political cliques."[57]

Sage successfully defeated plans for new sewers that would have placed $7,000 of a total $9,723 tax on his holdings. He also fought against the removal of a platform sidewalk that was on his property and found to be a public nuisance by the village council. Although this matter was eventually adjusted with compromise, the conflict caused Sage to explain his role in the community:

> What seems strange to me is that any one can think it wise for the authorities to be in constant conflict with the largest taxpayers and property owners. . . . We ought to work together there—as a unit. . . . If we are to have improvements involving outlay of capital there *must be* a reasonable acceptance that there will be no unjust official action with reference to it. . . . Without a reasonable assurance on the point I would never invest another dollar there for Rail Road or improvements of any kind—Nor will McGraw or Litchfield. . . . How much of the prosperity of Wenona thus far has been dependent on what we have done?

Sage even threatened to withhold his benefactions to the community if the local politicians did not acknowledge their economic link with him:

> It has been my intention to build there a Public Library—and to so endow it that all the citizens of Wenona would have forever the means of education and culture—but I can have no thought to do even a good or necessary work when all my interest and purposes are met with hostility.[58]

Sage allied himself both politically and financially with Bay City Republicans. He became a supporter of Mayor Nathan Bradley and later loaned him $7,000 when he was a member of Congress. After 1873 the Democrats captured political control of Wenona and Sage found himself once more struggling with the taxation issue. A new effort to build sewers along the river and to tax him for about three-quarters of the costs enraged Sage in 1874. He called on McGraw and Litchfield to aid him in blocking the proposal. These three men represented the largest property interest in Wenona and they were all absentee owners. This time Sage was again able to put the project on hold for several years.[59]

By 1876, and especially after 1877 when West Bay City was created, Sage tried to reestablish his control over town politics. "Perhaps we had better take hold of politics a little and learn some of our present masters that they can't have all their own way," Sage wrote in 1875. The growth of the village, the advent of more complex political issues, the coming of the Greenback party, and the

defection to the local community of some of Sage's earlier lieuten-
ants prompted aggressive action. In the fall of 1876 he entrusted one
of his representatives in West Bay City with $100 to "keep the Dem-
ocrats from control." Although his effort to defeat the Democrats
failed, Sage managed to get his agent in West Bay City, W. I. Tozer,
elected to the town council every year until 1881.[60]

After 1877 Sage took a more conciliatory approach to local politics. He agreed to the paving of streets in 1881 and finally built the
long promised library in West Bay City in 1883. Eventually the relationship between absentee owner and the community became
complementary. To secure profits from his investments, though,
Sage and others had to struggle to command the support of vocal
and involved individuals in the community. In most cases of conflict
over taxation Sage obtained the relief he sought. As his biographer
points out, his holdings were consistently undervalued, and Sage
probably did not pay his fair share of taxes.[61]

What is clear from the experience of Sage and others in Bay City
is that absentee owners partly alienated themselves from the community. They were not benevolent nor paternalistic to the extent
that they worked for the constant betterment of their community.
Although he had built the community and the economy on which
the working and middle class was dependent, the goal of the community was profit. In many instances the community sacrificed internal improvements because the investment would not fulfill the
profit motives of the absentee owners. Unlike Saginaw or Muskegon,
there were few lumbermen in West Bay City or Bay City who were
involved in local politics with the intention of adjusting and prepar-
ing the city for the future. Moreover, resident lumbermen in Bay
City tended to emulate the conservative political and economic
practices of the largest sawmill operators—the absentee owners. Bay
City's elite simply wanted to preserve their economic power.

Although there are different types and degrees of absentee ownership, its effect on the lumbertowns was to resist change and limit
diversified reindustrialization. Municipal improvements were often
opposed and when absentee owners did upgrade socioeconomic conditions in their settlements, they were done primarily to improve
personal property or profits. Incomes from lumbering were seldom
used for local internal improvements. They were invested in distant
timberlands and often in the hometowns of the absentee owner.
Lumbering was a speculative investment rather than a way of life.

There was no economic incentive for the distant owner to alter the traditional economy of the sawmill town. As long as adequate, if not substantial, financial returns from the sawmill were sustained, there was little reason to tamper with the economic structure. When returns declined as the trees disappeared, it was part of the process to simply move the entire operation to a new frontier.

Nonresident owners like Henry Sage journeyed to their holdings three or four times a year. Yet, their indirect association with the lumbertown demonstrated a disinterest in local community. Their principal economic pursuits and social and political milieu lay elsewhere. As a result, lumbertown operations, especially in Bay City, became a tangential economic pursuit; the episodic visit to the sawmill was an obligatory function, not an affectionate or nostalgic trip.

Absentee ownership, to use Veblen's characterization, gave the owner the power to "sabotage at a distance."[62] Large lumber operators had no incentive to improve operations or raise mill workers' wages. That their interest did not lie in maximizing community is explicit in the practice of exhausting the forest and subsequently abandoning their sawmills at the expense of workers and community. Throughout all of this the worker and community suffered. In the competitive environment of the Saginaw Valley lumber business, the lumbermen sought to continually lower production costs, and this was largely done at the expense of the sawmill worker. All employees suffered, but those operators not tied to community could more easily "sabotage" the lumbertown that was merely a resource for making money, not goods, lives, or community.

Absentee ownership, as J. Rogers and Ellen Jane Hollingsworth have pointed out in their study of medium-size towns, permitted business and labor leaders to fill positions in local government as nonresident lumbermen abdicated political responsibility. Although this tended to create a less autocratic and more fluid political process, it did not necessarily prepare Bay City well for the future. Bay City lumbermen, unlike those in Saginaw and Muskegon, did not view their enterprise as immobile. They moved once, and they could always move again into the West. When they moved on, they took with them the money and skills necessary to rebuild the declining mill town. In contrast, the lumbermen who planned to remain, as in Saginaw and Muskegon, took a more active interest in local politics as a means of protecting their vested interests. These elites witnessed citizen participation in the political process evolve gradually as populations increased and economic growth and social diversity created a more heterogeneous society. In the long run, these paternalistic lumbermen made decisions *with* the community that prepared Saginaw and Muskegon to become integrated into the larger economic society of the twentieth century.[63]

James Fraser, a Scotch immigrant, was an early land speculator and founded the Sagina Bay Company, or Lower Saginaw, the original paper town of Bay City. He also owned a sawmill and fishing vessels in and around Bay City. (Courtesy of the Bay County Historical Society.)

James G. Birney, Liberty Party candidate for the presidency in 1844, was a speculator and developer in Lower Saginaw in 1842. Birney was instrumental in establishing government and attempting to bring law and morality to Bay City.
(Courtesy of the Bay County Historical Society.)

Hitchcock & Bailey's sawmill at Cass Avenue in Bay City, 1882. Many of the sawmills were near workers' residences and children often brought their father's lunches to the mills at noontime. (Courtesy of the Bay County Historical Society.)

Franklin House Hotel on Sixth Street in Bay City. A number of hotels along Sixth Street catered to the large transient population of loggers, mill workers, sailors, fishermen, and salesman that made Bay City their temporary residence. (Courtesy of the Bay County Historical Society.)

Bay City police force, 1888. This photo was taken soon after the creation of the Metropolitan Police Force, an effort at reorganization to eliminate corruption and politics in the department. Saloons, transients, and gambling and fighting made the understaffed police force hard pressed to maintain order and respectability in the lumber era. Policemen were required to "lick the tar" out of any ruffian. (Courtesy of the Bay County Historical Society.)

Bay City's notorious Water Street, looking north from Center Avenue. The Fraser Hotel is on the right. Along the west side of the street were the saloons, hotels, and stores that collectively made up the "Catacombs." In 1884 there were sixty-five saloons or hotels selling liquor in this four block area. (Courtesy of the Bay County Historical Society.)

West Bay City fire station at Linn Street. Despite the ever-present threat of fire, early departments were loosely organized groups of volunteers. They took great pride in their horse teams and the skill and training of the department's driver. (Courtesy of the Bay County Historical Society.)

Kolb Brothers Brewery, in the Salzburg area of West Bay City. The number of Germans living in Bay City prompted the establishment of several breweries. (Courtesy of the Bay County Historical Society.)

Bay City as viewed from West Bay City, 1909. Twenty years after the lumber era log pilings and abandoned drying docks still marked the waterfront. The shorelines of the lumbertowns remained unattractive and depressed as industries moved away or closer to interior rail lines in the twentieth century. (Courtesy of the Bay County Historical Society.)

Bousfield & Company, the world's largest woodenware factory in the 1880s. Located in Bay City's south end, it produced wash tubs, wooden churns, and butter, lard, water, and tobacco pails. At its peak Bousfield produced 20,000 pails every day. By the early twentieth century woodenware gave way to metal and cardboard containers and most wood related industries closed in Bay City. (Courtesy of the Bay County Historical Society.)

William McEwan's house, 702 Center Avenue, Bay City. McEwan and his brother had extensive logging interests and camps in Clare County. Lumbermen often purchased entire blocks along Center Avenue in Bay City and built homes that rivaled each other in ornate style and elegance. (Courtesy of the Bay County Historical Society.)

Four prostitutes who worked the interior forest just north of Bay City, c. 1880s. (Photo taken from *Michigan's Timber Battleground* with the permission of the author, Forrest B. Meek.)

Advertisements for Polish businesses in Bay City's south end, 1901. After a generation in Bay City, the Poles developed their own business community and neighborhood identity. (Courtesy of the Bay County Historical Society.)

Workers in the Mill Towns

*We had only one class—all were equal—the rich and
the poor. They shared together. You saw the mill owner
and his wife eating at the same table with the mill hands.
There were no classes as now.*

—FERDINAND DIETRICK, *Muskegon Daily Chronicle,*
27 May 1899

Ferdinand Dietrick's observation of the changing social conditions
was a candid acknowledgment of the new industrial order that transformed the lumbertowns during the halcyon days of the 1870s and
1880s. Twenty years earlier the forests had stood in solitude. The
lumbertowns were small settlements with only a few sawmills scattered along the rivers. Life on the whole was simple, relatively quiet,
and devoted to a slow, laborious turning of logs into boards.

By the 1880s, however, the ascendancy of lumber had brought
sudden and dramatic changes to the towns and people. A panoramic
view of the lumbertowns picturized the transformation to the new
order. Unpainted boardinghouses, sawmills, brine wells, and drying
wood piles lined the riverbanks. Teepee burners belched smoke, and
mounds of sawdust and piles of discarded sawmill waste lay about.
The once majestic rivers were brown and ugly, clogged with runoff
from brine wells, bark, splintered logs, and boards. Sawdust covered
everything during the summer months. Railroads now sent tracks in
all directions, and long lines of timber cars came from the North;
long lines of passenger cars arrived from the South. The quiet
sounds of village life had been replaced by a cacophony of industrial
sounds and foreign languages. Industrialization had created the lumbertowns and had caught up the populations in the rush to progress.

Even more so for the mill workers than the lumbermen, the town
had become the dominant institution of community life. Nourished
by the profits of industrial expansion, the lumbertowns experienced

phenomenal growth in the 1880s. Saginaw, 29,541 people in 1880, burgeoned to 42,845 by 1884 and 46,322 in 1890. Bay City numbered 27,040 people in 1880, 38,902 in 1884, and 40,730 by the end of the decade. In Muskegon the populations increased from 11,262 in 1880 to 17,835 in 1884 and 22,702 in 1890.[1]

The lumbertown was not only the site of one's summer employment; it became a vital social center around which the mill worker's life evolved. The town now became the location of many permanent, working-class residences, introduced many newcomers to organized community life, and also became the milieu in which attitudes, values, and social institutions developed, changed, and conflicted with one another. The mill hands and shanty boys had participated in this "progress," but for the most part profits had failed to accrue to them. When it became clear to many that the halcyon days of lumbering were going to end, and end precipitously, the winds of optimism dissipated and antagonisms and social turmoil propelled events toward the ten-hour strikes of the mid-eighties.

Who were the workers who came to share the profits but, in the short run, found only general anxiety over the exhaustion of the timber supply? Where did they come from? What cultural traits did they bring with them into the towns that now often determined their fate? What was life like in the sawmills, and how did work habits and cultural attitudes affect the economic futures of the lumbertowns? Did the nature of the exploitative society make economic conflict inevitable, and, in the end, how did this conflict affect entrepreneurial efforts to reindustrialize at the close of the pine era? An understanding of lumbertown workers, coupled with our knowledge of the lumbermen, may go a long way in explaining the economic conflict and industrial turmoil that plagued the lumbertowns for several decades.

THE LUMBERTOWN LABOR FORCE

After opening a sawmill and beginning the cutting of the trees in the interior, the lumbermen turned to the problem of recruiting a labor force.[2] Most of the shanty boys, who were also summer mill hands, belonged to one of three distinct groups: (1) local, primarily native, agricultural workers and sons of farmers drawn from nearby settlement, (2) native New Englanders, Canadians, and French Canadians who migrated in the 1860s after the depletion of the Eastern forest, and (3), after 1870 emigrants from Scandinavia and southern Europe.

Native-born workers dominated Michigan's early lumber industry. This is borne out in several studies. George Engberg noted that more than fifty-one percent of the workers came from the New England states, New York, nearby Great Lakes states, and Michigan.[3] Still, a considerable number of immigrants migrated to the industry in the 1860s, particularly from Canada, the British Isles, and Germany. In Muskegon, in 1870, only thirty-eight percent of the male adult work force was native born. In Saginaw, about forty percent of the work force was native born, and in Bay City native-born represented thirty-five percent of that town's workers.[4] There were more foreign-born in the three lumbertowns in 1870 than would have been true of the state as a whole.

Local farmers, native and immigrant, often provided the most convenient source of labor for many early sawmills. Sons of farmers drawn from a relatively close radius also provided sawmill employees. The seasonal nature of lumbering made it especially easy to hire farm laborers for the winter logging season; however, as the demand for mill hands grew, local rural sources could not supply all the workers needed. Lumbermen then began to recruit laborers from other parts of the state and the Great Lakes region. As technology in the sawmill became more developed, skilled hands from Eastern sawmills were sought.

Like many other preindustrial hands, the local settler and migrant farmer found it difficult to adjust to the routines of industrial production.[5] Despite the chronic shortage of labor, wages in the mills remained low, and many of the mill hands were casual, unskilled, and unmarried. Lumbering has always been a mobile and unstable occupation. Nearby agricultural laborers would sometimes work in the sawmills during the summer to supplement farm income. However, work was often undertaken for only a brief period to replenish family finances, and once this was accomplished the farmer would return to the land. It was also common for local workers to take off for family functions, hunting, and fishing trips. Yet, although these practices may have clashed with the work ethic of the lumbermen, early operators did little to stabilize the work force. Henry H. Crapo, a lumberman from Flint in the Lower Saginaw Valley, wrote to his son recruiting laborers in the East that, as far as permanence and reliability, it was "of little consequence. . . . I merely want their bone and muscle and when they do not earn their wages I discharge them."[6]

Crapo, though, was more concerned that skilled hands remain and show willingness to become permanent workers. As sawmilling grew, machinery improved and the milling season became longer, a more reliable work force was needed. The owners' attitudes toward all labor gradually changed. Wellington Burt in Saginaw hired predominantly married workers; Sage and Hackley built tenements to house families. Canadians were recruited to work in the forest, and many, in turn, came into the towns for summer employment in the sawmills. They made up about twenty-four percent of the lumbertown work force in the 1860s. During the same period skilled New England and a few English settlers entered the lumber industry. Germans, especially in the Saginaw Valley, and Scandinavians, around Muskegon, also hired on at the sawmills. Many of these people were capable supplements to native labor. They were typically hardworking, industrious, and sometimes skilled people easily employable in the jobs associated with lumbering. The Scandinavians and Canadians often had experience in lumbering, for it was an important industry in their homelands. The cyclical nature of the industry also suited many of these newcomers because it was a continuation of the natural rhythms common to farming.

Nevertheless before the boom years of the seventies and eighties, the efforts at stabilizing the work force were sporadic and largely unsuccessful. The three lumbertowns' populations continued to reflect transience characteristic of frontier settlements. The persistence rate for adult laborers in the three towns from 1860 to 1870 remained between fifteen and twenty percent. Not surprisingly, the most persistent settlers were native-born Americans, followed by the Germans in the Saginaw Valley, and the Irish and the Scots. The most transient workers were the Scandinavians and especially the Canadians.[7]

High transience made for a relatively poor population, especially the foreign-born populations. The census listings of personal wealth in 1870 make it possible to ascertain average or mean wealth by major ethnic groups in the lumbertowns. There are few surprises in these statistics. Two groups, native-born Americans and the few Scots, are clearly above the community mean. Both contained the wealthy lumbermen and owners of considerable real estate. The Germans of the Saginaw Valley and a few in Muskegon, though below the mean, achieved some economic success over their long period of persistence. Englishmen likewise did well. Almost all foreigners, though, were poor. The newly arrived French Canadians and Scandinavians claimed little property or personal wealth. The Dutch in Muskegon began to accumulate a little, but still remained well below the community standard. As Blackburn and Ricards noted of nearby Manistee, property and wealth distribution in the lumbertowns "scarcely supports the typical American image of the frontier as the land of promise for the poor, ambitious young man."[8]

Although most of these natives and newcomers eventually conformed to the new industrial system, the lumbermen could not wait for the labor force to adjust to the highly competitive and rapid growth of the 1870s and 1880s. Operators began to search for more workers. Between 1872 and 1884 lumbermen hired agents or worked with state immigration authorities to lure potential mill workers to the northern Michigan mill towns. Attracted by glowing descriptions of the possibility of farm ownership after a few years work in the woods and sawmills, thousands of European immigrants were brought into the towns. Germans, Poles, and French Canadians flooded the Saginaw Valley; Dutch, Swedes, more Canadians and Scandinavians arrived daily in Muskegon. In this way the population grew rapidly and the ethnic composition of the lumbertowns changed further as the peak years of lumbering approached.

IMMIGRANT WORKERS

Though the population makeup of the communities changed, traditional attitudes toward the workers remained. Many of the lumbermen, especially in the Saginaw Valley, continued to view the mill workers as "thickheaded" and "ignorant rabble".[9] Despite these condescending attitudes, lumbermen continued to recruit foreign help in the sawmills. The question remains, though, did the ethnic makeup of the lumbertowns' work force influence the decisions made by the lumbermen that determined future economic development? Did their social Darwinist viewpoints toward the laboring classes, reinforced by the violence associated with the ten-hour strikes, convince many lumbermen to avoid reinvesting in declining sawmill towns? More important, if ethnicity did sway entrepreneurial beliefs and hence investments, were these attitudes based on valid assumptions about the efficiency, reliability, and quality of each town's ethnic labor force? Or were the lumber barons' predispositions merely conclusions drawn from assumed "inferiority" of European immigrants? A cultural-historical analysis of the immigrant labor force in the three lumbertowns may offer a clearer insight into the dynamics of community economic development.

The proportion of immigrants in the lumbertown populations grew significantly by the decade of economic turmoil, 1880–90. Bay City's foreign-born represented 44% of its population, and the foreign-born were about 40% of Saginaw's and Muskegon's populations. In comparison with other well-known immigrant cities (Milwaukee, 39%; Detroit, 39%; Poughkeepsie, 40%; and Troy, 40% foreign-born), the lumbertowns' percentages were slightly higher. Between 1884 and 1894, there was a decline in the foreign-born residents (about 4% in each town). This may be explained in part by the reluctance of the lumbermen to hire immigrant workers after the ten-hour strikes of 1882–85, and the general lumbering decline of the late eighties. Economic instability affected recently hired immigrants more than native-born settlers.[10]

In examining individual ethnic groups (table 8), Bay City clearly represents a community that contained a polyglot population, although three nativity groups, French Canadians, Germans, and Poles, made up about 71% of the foreign-born population in 1890. In Saginaw, French Canadians and Germans dominated, making up 81% of the foreign born. Muskegon, statistically as ethnically diverse as Bay City, was dominated by northwestern European stock.

TABLE 8.
Source of Immigrant Population in the Lumbertowns in 1890

Country	Bay City (%)	Saginaw (%)	Muskegon (%)
Norway	—	—	8.5
Sweden	2	—	17
Poland	12	2	—
France	7.8	—	—
Canada	41	42	22
Ireland	5	5	4.7
England	8.2	5.2	5
Germany	21	39	16
Holland	—	—	22
Russia	1	—	—
Scotland	2	2	—
Denmark	—	—	3.8
Other	1	4.8	1

Source: Eleventh Census of U.S., 1890, 6: Populations, 464–80.

The Swedes, Norwegians, Dutch, and Germans made up 65% of the immigrants. In all three communities the Irish, many of whom emigrated from Canada, made up a larger percentage than is represented in the table. Correspondingly, the Canadian representation is inflated.

For developing an understanding of entrepreneurial investment based on assumptions of community ethnicity, generalizations about each lumbertown can be made. Observations of historical and contemporary sources reveal curious contrasts in the images ascribed to Bay City and Muskegon. Bay City was described as a city with several diverse ethnic groups including a percentage of southeastern Europeans who did much of the heavy labor in the lumber mills.[11] The Poles bore the brunt of ethnic discrimination. They were resented by other laborers because they were originally imported as scab and cheap laborers during a minor strike in 1872.[12] They later were important in the 1885 strike only to experience, as a result, threats and blacklisting by lumbermen. As late as 1932 the Poles continued to be described by one local chronicler as a "distinct type," and "backwoodsy." John O'Neill, writing on Bay City lumbering and labor, regretted that "there had been no attempt made to keep them [the Poles] in bounds," and "even though the younger generations are prone to intermarry, the impression of their race, however, will not be lost."[13] Germans, too, were active in the 1885 strike. Couple the Polish and the German strikers to the large and transient Canadian work force (that preferred work in the woods rather than the sawmill) and it is not surprising that the lumbermen in Bay City threatened to blacklist immigrant workers after 1885.

Muskegon, in contrast, had few southeastern European workers. The dominant northern Europeans were seen as industrious, efficient, and trouble free. A belief that one historian noted as late as 1935 permitted local employers to view "the Scandinavian and Dutch laborers as superior to Slavs, Hungarians, Poles, and Italians. Fortunately, perhaps, the latter groups always have been small in Muskegon." Low turnover of laborers and home ownership among the Dutch and Scandinavians are also mentioned as factors that encouraged economic stability in Muskegon.[14]

Saginaw was less ethnically diverse than either Bay City or Muskegon. The Germans—who were perceived as thrifty and industrious—dominated the work force. Although there were some French Canadians, they apparently are never characterized in historical records as difficult laborers.

To validate these assumptions about the ethnic work force, it is necessary to examine the antecedent cultural roots, the realization of occupational mobility, and commitment to community—permanence, education, and home ownership—of several dominant immigrant groups in each lumbertown. All three towns attracted some ethnic workers in common. The French Canadian element was important, and there were similar as well as distinct traits displayed by these settlers. Likewise, each lumber settlement had a number of Germans, especially Saginaw. Yet, what clearly stands out and requires analysis is the situation of the Poles in Bay City and the Dutch and Swedes in Muskegon. An examination of the livelihood, goals, and aspirations of the lumbertowns' ethnic groups will provide a more precise and accurate understanding of subsequent socioeconomic development.

Settlement patterns for all ethnic groups emerged quickly in the three towns. Local historians have frequently defined the boundaries of ethnic residential neighborhoods for the lumbertowns; and any resident could easily direct a visitor to Rotterdam in Muskegon, Germania in Saginaw, Frenchtown or the Polish Southside in Bay City. Historians generally agree that by the late nineteenth century, rapid industrialization, the demise of the walking city, and the increased immigration of unskilled labor (especially from eastern Europe) contributed to the formation of these ethnic ghettos.[15] Although some authorities have argued that the so-called Old Immigrants were less likely to form ghettos, historians have shown that of these immigrants, the Germans of Milwaukee and the Dutch of Grand Rapids settled in and identified with strictly defined neighborhoods. The newcomers not only wanted to live together, but migration chains from the old country and common occupations and incomes dictated similar residential locations.[16]

The lumbertowns reflected a similar pattern. Ghettoization was encouraged by employers who hired workers into the mills from nationalities that lived nearby. Thus, McGraw and Bousfield brought predominantly Polish laborers into their factories in south Bay City; Dolson and Chapin, and Pitts and Cranage hired primarily French workers from nearby "Frenchtown"; and the five or so firms in Salzburg hired German workers. Likewise in Muskegon the mills in Pickettown hired Frenchmen, and the Lakeside yards employed Swedish and nearby Germans. Workers were also brought directly from Europe to the lumbertowns. Max Allardt recruited Germans to the Saginaw Valley, Poles were imported as strikebreakers to Bay

City, and whole colonies of provincial Dutch settlers moved into western Michigan. The migration chain was uninterrupted; cultural assimilation did not begin until settlers arrived in the lumbertowns. Here they were able to build cheap housing because of the ready supply of milled and scrap lumber. Thus, all the elements—job location, homogeneity, and cheap housing—were present and influenced residential concentration in the three lumbertowns.

Although an index of dissimilarity could be used to examine residential segregation, outside of Saginaw such an analysis would be untenable. In Bay City and Muskegon, several ethnic groups, along with native-born settlers, concentrated in working-class wards. The area of a ward usually included several ethnic neighborhoods, and thus segregation indexes by ward would be misleading. In Saginaw, however, where most of the east side was German, an index would undoubtedly indicate many German residents. Bay City and Muskegon likewise evidenced residential ethnic segregation, but it usually was limited to specific geographical areas. Instead of trying to discover extreme ghettolike concentration, one can look for subtle forms of ethnic dominance in which a group of immigrants exerted influence in this defined area.[17] Simple percentages of immigrants living in clusters in the heart of the immigrant areas will show the degree to which a single nationality occupied well-known ethnic areas in the lumbertowns. Most important, a comparison can be made from these percentages to determine the degree of homogeneity that existed in each community.

French-speaking *Canadiens* were the earliest settlers in all three lumbertowns. Engaged originally in the fur trade they later became fishermen. However, with the advent of lumbering they were eagerly sought as experienced woodsmen. Experience in Ontario, Maine, and New York enabled *Canadien* lumberjacks to become foremen and river drivers in the lumber camps. In time many moved into the lumbertowns and became mill men in the summer and fall and returned to the woods as lumberjacks in the winter months.

Although the few English-speaking Canadians in the lumbertowns assimilated more quickly, the French *Canadiens* remained socially and geographically isolated through much of the lumber era. In Bay City, two distinct settlements developed. In Banks, on the west side of the Saginaw River, the *Canadiens* fished and labored in three nearby sawmills. Here in 1880 about ninety percent of the residents in the cluster sampled were *Canadiens*.[18] Directly across the river was Dolsonville, or Frenchtown, where the large Dolson and

Chapin sawmill was located. Along Campbell Street in a cluster between Dolson and Belinda, *Canadiens* represented eighty-eight
percent of the residents. In Muskegon, Bluffton, a French settlement
"dependent principally upon the mills," and Lakeside evidenced
concentration percentages of seventy percent *Canadien*. Pickettown,
on the mouth of the Muskegon River, was occupied by trappers, Indians, and *Canadien* employees of the Muskegon Booming
Company.[19] Saginaw had the most *Canadiens*. The original *Canadien*
settlers located along the river, especially on the east side south of
the town center. Here along Water Street in the First Ward, sixty-
five percent of the residents in the cluster were *Canadien*.

Lutheran missionaries were the vanguard of German settlement in
the Saginaw Valley. The successful and prosperous agriculture settlement at Frankenmuth, established in 1845 in southern Saginaw
County, was a lightning rod to attract other Germans to the valley.
Saginaw came to have the most Germans outside Detroit. Although
many of the original German settlers were engaged in agriculture,
after the Civil War more started in industrial work to secure money
for an eventual farm. The state of Michigan recruited German immigrants who were seen as ideal settlers. They were described as
"industrious, religious, often educated, and if not, interested in establishing educational institutions, and fairly easily assimilated."[20]

Although many Germans viewed their employment in the mills as
a temporary necessity to save for a farm, thousands adjusted and
found their livelihood in the sawmills. East Saginaw became the new
Germania. Clusters along Seventh, Eighth, and Ninth streets between Carroll and Janes had ninety percent German concentration.
Other Germans were attracted to nearby Zilwaukee north of Saginaw
City's limits. Near Bay City, the residents from the agricultural area
of Frankenlust gradually spread into the city and created the
German neighborhood of Salzburg, which was sixty-six percent German. Across the river from Salzburg, Portsmouth attracted other
German settlers. On the west side of the state, although the German population was not as large as in the Saginaw Valley, Muskegon
had a sizeable German settlement near Brewery Hill. Several sawmills were here and most of the residents, about sixty percent in one
cluster, were German.

Muskegon also had northeastern European immigrants that were
not present in large numbers in Saginaw or Bay City. The Dutch,
much like the Germans in Saginaw, were the first settlers who immigrated in numbers to Muskegon. In 1847 the first Dutch colony

was established near Holland and from this embryonic beginning other Dutch settlements sprang up along Lake Michigan. Most of the Dutch settlers in Muskegon, though, arrived in the decade after the Civil War and came from the province of Groningen. Sources of Dutch history repeatedly emphasize that most came as poor laboring men who had few skills outside those gained on the farm.[21]

In Muskegon, the Dutch settled in the city proper. Rotterdam, around Third and Merrill avenues, had a Dutch concentration of eighty-five percent, and Dutch Town between Myrtle and Spring streets had a concentration of ninety-six percent. One local historian noted: "The residents were rather slow to mix outside of their own neighborhoods and the absorption of these districts was gradual over the years."[22] By 1888 there were about five thousand Hollanders living in Muskegon, nearly one-third of the town's population.

Muskegon also attracted Swedish and Norwegian immigrants. Grand Rapids was frequently a point of embarkation for many Swedes who were recruited by the Continental Improvement Company to work in the furniture industry. Others were contract laborers emigrating to work in the Upper Peninsula copper mines. However, using the "Cousin Jack" principle, the Swedes and Norwegians used informal channels of communication to the old country to alert friends and relatives to the opportunities in west Michigan.[23] Eventually many found work on the logging crews where they were reportedly "unexcelled" as lumberjacks. After the long drive, invariably the loggers drifted to the mill towns and found seasonal employment in the sawmills. Apparently many decided to stay in Muskegon. Killgrubbin, or Norwegian Hill, up Ottawa Street in Muskegon proper attracted the Norwegians, and Lowertown west of Sixth Street was an area of Swedish settlement.

There was one other large ethnic group in the Saginaw Valley sawmills: the Poles. The last of the immigrant groups to arrive, by 1910 they came to represent the largest non-English-speaking ethnic group in Bay City. In the early seventies, about two hundred Polish families located south of Bay City to work in the sugar beet fields; however, as lumbering expanded and the fields were absorbed by urban growth, many Poles became lumbermill workers. Polish farm laborers and immigrants were also encouraged to serve as strikebreakers during the 1872, short-lived, ten-hour strike in Bay City. The Polish took up vacant land in the southeastern part of Bay City along Seventeenth and Eighteenth streets between Fitzhugh and VanBuren. They embraced the geographical area as evidenced by clusters that registered eighty-four percent Polish concentration.

Ethnic concentration was highest in Bay City. All three major immigrant groups dominated by more than sixty-six percent. The Polish and *Canadien* neighborhoods were nearly solid and isolated ethnic enclaves. Saginaw's Germans, largely because they were so many, lived in several intensely concentrated ethnic clusters. The *Canadiens* in Saginaw were likewise concentrated, but much of this concentration was because so many boardinghouses served primarily single, male *Canadien* mill workers. Muskegon's ethnic areas never reached the intensity of the ethnic concentration evidenced in the cross-state lumbertowns. The inhabitants were distributed according to an irregular system of dominance, with only a few traces of intense ghetto formation. Except for the Dutch, Muskegon's ethnic relationships were not as necessarily individualistic. It was a multi-ethnic city with strong ethnic ties, but the lines of division were often more subtle than, say, in Bay City, and the transition from one neighborhood to another gave evidence of a more complex interaction among different groups.

The force that contributed the most to persistent isolation of ethnics in Bay City was urban geography. The Polish Southside was once the original settlement of Portsmouth. It was separated by the river on the west, swamps to the south, and a pattern of irregular streets to the north that divided it from Bay City proper. Frenchtown, along both sides of the Saginaw River at the north end of town, was made up of the old settlements of the Banks and Dolsonville. Both areas had nonintegrated street patterns that demarcated Frenchtown from the rest of Bay City. The Germans at Salzburg on the west side were likewise isolated in a triangular village that stood apart because of the river and street arrangements. The number of distinctly separate concentrations reinforced by geography encouraged lumbermen to hire nearby ethnics. The journey to work had few constraints. The Polish, French, or German workers in Bay City developed a powerful sense of group identity and created institutional ghettos that maintained cultural continuity and later fostered political and economic interest-group identity.

In contrast to Bay City, the geography of Muskegon or Saginaw never was used to create complex ethnic isolation. Ethnic neighborhoods in Muskegon were often in the city proper and only a short walking distance from the business district or sawmills along the lake. Any group in the region, regardless of how concentrated, could not have avoided contacts, residential or otherwise, with other groups. Thus, although ethnic identity remained strong in Muskegon, considerable structural assimilation took place in the workplace and marketplace. Saginaw was even more homogeneous than Muskegon. The east-side Germans were not separated by precise geographic boundaries. Sheer numbers, relative prosperity, and rapid settlement all encouraged concentrated neighborhoods. However, numbers and imprecise geographical boundaries also encouraged the Germans to move out and assimilate sooner than similar groups in Muskegon and especially in Bay City.

Each ethnic group brought to the lumber settlements cultural characteristics that affected assimilation.[24] It would appear on the surface that the French *Canadiens* had the experience and background to succeed in the burgeoning sawmill towns. During the post-Civil War period, the rapidly developing economy in Michigan lured many *Canadiens*. Spurred by falling agricultural prices and the reluctance of the Canadian government to open undeveloped timberland for settlement and exploitation, thousands of French *Canadiens* in Quebec and Ontario came to believe that a job in a lumber camp or sawmill was far better than an uncertain future in Canada.

Aggressively recruited by lumbermen to work in the woods, *Canadiens* brought to Michigan much of the lore and legend associated with the white pine era. Lumbermen respected the French woodsmen and advertised in Canadian newspapers for experienced river hogs, wood choppers, and teamsters. A French *Canadien* "riverhog" was in a class by himself. Few could challenge the French at riding logs during the wild spring drives to the sawmills. In the sawmill towns, however, the French laborer apparently took on a different disposition. Long viewed even in the Eastern textile mills as "industrious" and "docile" laborers, the French were recruited for the sawmills. The French were used as scab laborers in the early lumber strikes, and French boom company workers helped break the 1885 strike along the Saginaw River. Although familiar with primitive lumbering machinery from the Northeast and Canada, Frenchmen viewed lumbering and logging as an out-of-doors occupation. They did not adjust comfortably to life in the sawmills. French *Canadiens* preferred outdoor work, such as riding the logs downriver, and were the most transient of the lumbertowns' ethnic groups. When fall approached, the French *Canadien* quickly packed his bags and headed into the woods to resume the life of a shanty boy.

The German settlers who came to the Saginaw Valley had an "eye for the soil." They had an "uncanny" ability to select good farmland, and many intended to remain in the valley just long enough to earn money to buy land outside the city.[25] However, after the Civil War, few came with money, and much of the land in the valley was already bought up. Subsequently, the Germans who continued to come settled in the city and readily found jobs in the sawmills.

Many of the Saginaw Valley Germans were Lutherans from Franconia; however, by the late nineteenth century almost all areas of southern Germany were represented in the valley. These settlers were primarily farmers and outside their skill with some primitive agricultural machinery, they carried over little experience adaptable to the sawmills. However, once settled in the city of Saginaw, they developed the reputation of eagerly supporting education. The ability to read and write encouraged many German laborers to strive for something more permanent than seasonal sawmill work. Saginaw also was home for a few thousand Volga Germans. Skilled craftsmen from Hesse expatriated to Russia, they could not practice their trades in Russia. In the 1870s Russian hostility forced the Volga Germans to emigrate. Although many of these emigrants became farmers and settled on farms around Sebewaing, Michigan, others found work in the wooden industries of Saginaw. In Muskegon the first German settlers came from Prussia, but by the mid-eighties southern and Catholic Germans were dominant.[26]

The Dutch, who comprised most of Muskegon's foreign-born were, like the Germans, farmers who came to Michigan after the Civil War with no particular skills. However, many Dutch immigrants also brought with them woodworking experience. "One of the furniture factory officials in Holland (Michigan) insisted that the Dutch were the best furniture craftsmen in the world." Most of the skilled Dutch immigrants settled in Holland and Grand Rapids; however, some drifted northward and found jobs in the woodworking industries of Muskegon.[27]

Though many of Muskegon's Dutch were not skilled woodworkers, they were thought to possess the Dutch *werkkracht*, "the ability to work." The Dutch were viewed as careful, painstaking workmen who could easily adapt to woodworking manufacturing. By the early twentieth century, 25.7% of the nation's furniture labor force was represented by Dutch workers.[28] Dutch workers may also have been sought out because of their thrift and frugality. Because they led simple lives, their wage demands were not excessive. Being highly individualistic, Dutch settlers were generally opposed to unionism. The Dutch Christian Reform Church throughout its history opposed union membership. In more ways than one, antecedent cultural roots made the Dutch attractive workers in the lumbertowns as they converted from sawmill to woodworking manufacturing industries.

The Polish who settled in the lumbertowns came from a divided homeland where few peasants could acquire property rights. Primarily rural laborers in the old country, Polish peasants were often seen by their German landlords as indolent and cunning in their efforts to escape work. Many Poles had been shifted around by political change and remained landless migrants before departing for America. Although some Poles had been skilled in the potash industry of northern Poland, this experience benefited only a few Poles in the nineteenth-century lumber mills. By and large, their immigration experience was difficult. An accumulation of political, economic, and social deprivations uprooted a village folk by the thousands forcing them to emigrate to a country fully embarked on industrial expansion.[29]

The Poles who settled in Bay City were the first to arrive in the lumbertowns. Most emigrated from Prussian Poland, or Poznania, and they came as agricultural workers to "top" sugar beets on the farms owned by Volga Germans and other Germans. Men, women, and children, unlike the German and Dutch immigrant families, worked together as laborers in the fields. Yet, like the Germans, many hoped to save to buy a farm. When they were recruited as scab laborers for the lumber mills, however, the Poles left the farms to locate in the city and take advantage of better wages. In time, remembering their peasant backgrounds, the Poles found life in the mills acceptable. Their lack of practical experience and education made mobility harder to achieve. The seasonal nature of sawmill work coupled with the difficult low-paying jobs assigned to the Poles also delayed future prospects for many.

As sawmill workers and early scab laborers, the Poles were often given the "lowest grade of work."[30] Subjected to low pay and, as newly hired workers, frequent dismissal, layoffs, and wage cuts during slack timber seasons, the Poles organized and joined labor movements. These activities were aided by the strength of ethnic bonds developed in the lumbertown churches. Brotherhoods and fraternal organizations, centered in the Catholic churches, coordinated activ-

ities to raise money, financed school buildings, and provided sickness and death benefits for many Polish laborers who were without
other protection.[31]

The Poles "occupied the out-lying districts of both Bay City and
Saginaw and were content to leave the rest of the citizenry alone."
Most Poles "did not consider emigration an opportunity for 'upward
mobility' but a sacrifice necessary to preserve their culture and elements of life they held dear—family, farm household, village, and
community."[32] The clannishness and their first occupations as scab
laborers reaffirmed a less than positive image associated with the
Poles in the Saginaw Valley. However, their efforts to build a community and develop social meaning in their neighborhoods
confirmed their long-term commitment to their new country. Antecedent culture and racial prejudice encouraged the Poles to find a
space where they could be autonomous and isolated citizens in an
environment of their own.

DEMOGRAPHICS AND PERSISTENCE

Can the observations about the lumbertowns' ethnic populations be
supported quantitatively? In pursuing a quantified comparison between immigrant groups, it is crucial to determine if existence for
one ethnic group in a lumbertown was markedly different from the
existence of other immigrants in other towns. Because Muskegon's
Dutch were seen as ideal, docile, and committed workers, did that
city reindustrialize as lumbermen willingly exerted economic leadership predicated in part on their beliefs in the reliability of the Dutch
work force? In contrast, were Bay City's Poles and other immigrants
troublesome and unreliable workers? Was there anything unique
about Saginaw's immigrant labor force that aided assimilation and
subsequent successful reindustrialization?

Before examining the immigrant work force, further demographic
characteristics of the lumbertowns may be drawn. The decade 1880–
90 witnessed the peak years of lumber production, the tumultuous
ten-hour strikes, and the beginnings of the precipitous decline of the
lumber industry. Populations grew rapidly in the first half of the decade, stabilized, and then began to fall off in the 1890s. Muskegon
suffered a rapid decline after 1888; Bay City and Saginaw lost population in the 1890s. Likewise, the number of wage earners decreased

rapidly in Muskegon as the lumber business experienced a rapid demise. The towns' economic and demographic changes wrought social uncertainties.

Throughout this tumultuous decade changing demographic characteristics can also give a clue about the stability of the lumbertowns' work force and an overview, perhaps like that developed by the lumbermen, of labor's reliability, permanence, and tractability. During the peak lumber years, males represented a preponderance of the populations in the mill towns. In 1880 Bay City and Muskegon, and to a lesser extent Saginaw, were represented by a majority male population reflective of the lumbering economy (Bay City 55.4% male, Saginaw 54%, and Muskegon 55.6%). By 1894 all three communities experienced a movement to the state norm (51.77%) indicating a "settling-in" of the populations. Muskegon's progression during these years was more normal than the fluctuations of Saginaw and a little less precipitous than Bay City's. If anything can be concluded from these slight variations, Muskegon may have experienced a more consistent and stable evolution toward traditional male-female distribution.

Likewise, an examination of the average age of the male population in the lumbertowns reveals that all three communities had a younger working population than the state median (table 9). Bay City, even as late as 1894, when lumbering was well into its decline, maintained a relatively young, male work force. Those under twenty-five are frequently alone, unattached, and isolated. Persons with few ties are not likely to persist in the community. They do not supply a dependable work force, especially a skilled group needed to aid the transition from lumbering to diversified industry. Moreover, young, unmarried workmen spent much of their spare time amid the crowds of idle men frequenting the saloons, billiard halls, and brothels that marked Bay City's famous Catacombs. In contrast to Bay

TABLE 9.
Average Age of Male Population in Lumbertowns, 1870–1894

Location	1870	1884	1894
Muskegon	24.09	25.19	26.54
Saginaw	23.81	25.74	26.76
Bay City	23.24	24.58	25.06
Michigan	24.91	26.47	27.54

Source: *Census of Michigan, 1894.*

City's younger population, Muskegon and Saginaw were represented by populations that reflected some stability. An older, less transient work force provided Muskegon and Saginaw entrepreneurs with more experienced laborers.

The preceding observations are reinforced on viewing the married populations in the lumbertowns (table 10). Saginaw and Bay City had married populations that fluctuated as lumbering prospered and grew to large-scale industry. There was a decrease in married persons as lumbering burgeoned and many transient workers, male and female, sought opportunities in the lumber settlements. During the declining years, as the transients moved on, those who had married likely persisted and found jobs in new industries or managed to subsist off their wives' wages during the lean years. Again, in contrast to the fluctuations of Bay City and Saginaw, Muskegon's residents were marrying at a consistent rate that contradicts the traditional demographic image of a frontier, industrial boomtown. During the peak year of economic activity, 1884, when the migratory ebb and flow should have been greatest, Muskegon mirrored a steady maturation of population. No apparent invasion of unmarrieds occurred, and a consistent percent of the population sought the stability of married life. Bay City in 1884 represented the historical ideal. As the economy stretched beyond bounds, many single persons flooded Bay City seeking opportunities. Even as late as 1894 Bay City was marked by a large number of young, single males and females.

General demographic characteristics have revealed tentative conclusions about the three lumbertowns' labor forces. Muskegon's appears consistent, advancing in a stable and regular patterns toward social maturity. An older work force, tied by kinship lines of marriage and family, offered the Muskegon mill owners permanence and

TABLE 10.
Percent of Married Persons to Total Population in Lumbertowns,
1864–1894

Location	1864	1874	1884	1894
Muskegon	37.26	38.80	39.68	39.28
Saginaw	37.14	36.35	36.06	38.91
Bay City	37.82	36.95	35.92	37.63
Michigan	36.24	38.86	40.37	40.25

Source: *Census of Michigan, 1894.*

dependability. Moreover, because kinship and marriage ties were frequently more binding than occupation and property holdings, a part of Muskegon's labor force developed community attachments. Permanence and commitment to community also created in Muskegon's workers a reticence to engage in labor activity that would jeopardize employment. The Lake Michigan lumbertown could be viewed as having a docile and compliant work force. These observations are verified in part by the low average daily wage paid to Muskegon workers. Muskegon's daily wages were the lowest in the state, even below those of Grand Rapids, a city commonly known for "low pay and scab labor."[33]

Bay City, however, was a community in which a young, less frequently married work force gathered. Probably transient and with fewer kinship ties than Muskegon's employees, the sawmill workers in Bay City could afford to be militant in their demands for higher wages and shorter hours. But these demographics and higher wages did not encourage entrepreneurial investments in Bay City. Saginaw existed between the extremes of Muskegon and Bay City. Its population was comparable in the number of males to Bay City's, although Saginaw's people were older and correspondingly more settled than its downriver neighbor. Still, while Saginaw did not represent the conservative social milieu that characterized Muskegon, in the long run it pursued industrial revitalization as successfully as its cross-state rival. Other demographic factors involving the lumbertowns' ethnic populations may offer further clues to explicate Saginaw's comparable success.

With the aid of "population pyramids" constructed for Muskegon, Saginaw, and Bay City, the lumbertowns' immigrant populations may be visualized. Using a representative number of foreign-born residents from ethnic wards in the 1880 United States and 1884 Michigan census, a portrait emerges that challenges some nineteenth-century assumptions about the nature of the immigrant populations (see graphs 2, 3, and 4). Muskegon's Dutch, as contemporary accounts had indicated, do represent a stable force in the community. Although there were only slightly fewer women than men, the pyramid, especially if native-born children of Dutch parents are added at the bottom, begins to take on the classic triangular configuration representative of family groupings (graph 2). The French Canadians and Swedish, however, are represented by the peculiar deck-gun profile indicative of frontier settlements with populations heavily dominated by males in their twenties and thirties.

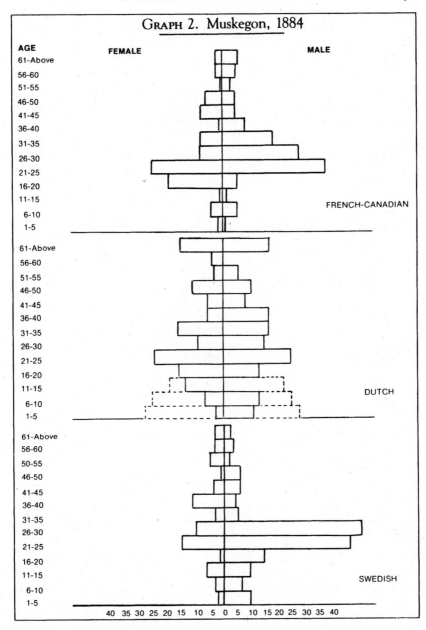

GRAPH 2. Muskegon, 1884

On the basis of these configurations, Muskegon's transient laborers were the French and Swedish immigrants. The Dutch represented an important part of the foundation on which the community built its stability. It is not surprising that Muskegon's lumbermen singled out

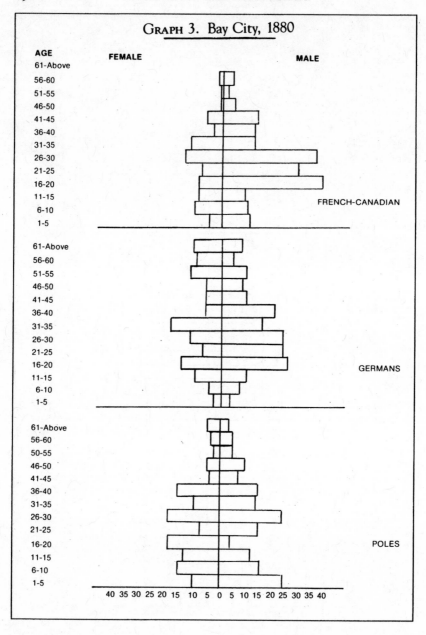

GRAPH 3. Bay City, 1880

the Dutch for their dependability and efficiency as persistent and desirable sawmill workers.

Bay City's immigrant work force likewise had a core of stable, family-oriented workers (graph 3). The Germans and the Polish

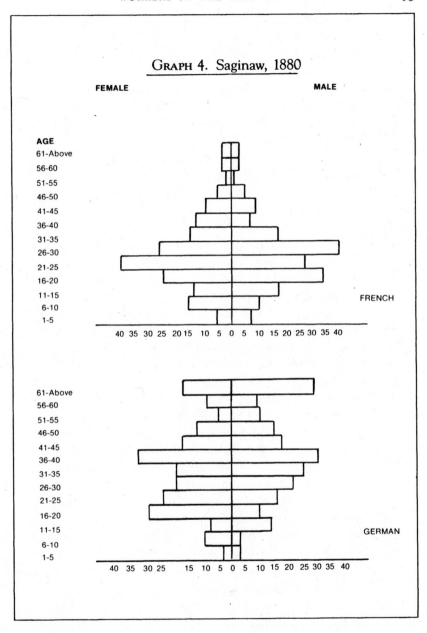

GRAPH 4. Saginaw, 1880

populations are represented in the pyramids as substantially settled immigrant groups. The German pyramid, representing an older and slightly male-oriented population, is probably misleading because many German families moved to rural farm areas in Bay County.

Nevertheless, there were some single, male German immigrants working in the sawmills. The Poles, like the Dutch, arrived in Bay City in family units. The many foreign-born children and adults in the thirty to forty age-grouping affirms the observation. Again, as in Muskegon, the French Canadians were dominantly male and young, and thus most likely to be transient. In reality, because the French represented forty-one percent of Bay City's immigrants and twenty-five percent of the city's lumbering work force, in all probability these workers contributed to the transient, less dependable generalization descriptive of Bay City's sawmill workers.

The French Canadians in Saginaw projected a configuration unlike Muskegon or Bay City (graph 4). Both sources of immigrant workers in Saginaw show a substantial balance between male and female. Germans and French, who made up eighty-one percent of the immigrants in Saginaw, cast a configuration indicative of a settled and fairly dependable labor force, and the French, especially, closely emulated the triangular pattern of a settled community. These two immigrant groups alone present a picture that confirms Saginaw's sawmill workers antipathy toward the 1885 ten-hour strike and the willingness of the city's lumbermen to reinvest in a community void of troublesome and transient workmen.

The conclusions drawn from configurations presented in the population pyramids are reaffirmed on examination of persistent rates for the varied immigrant groups in the three lumbering communities. Transience was common in lumbertown society in the nineteenth century. In an industrial environment that was by nature seasonal and geographically mobile—from winter logging to summer milling—it is not surprising that the lumbertowns' populations were far from stable. Yet between 1870 and 1890 the burgeoning logging communities offered opportunities that ensured permanence for many. Throughout this period, as the cities nearly tripled their populations, opportunities for work expanded rapidly. In short, there remained a contradictory work environment: many job opportunities available in purely seasonal occupations.

The rate of immigrant persistence over a decade (1875–85) is significant in that in all three communities it falls below the norm for other nineteenth-century cities (see table 11). In cities, towns, and rural counties of all sizes in the United States, the rate of persistence over a decade normally hovered between forty and sixty percent.[34] However, if the persistence rate of Muskegon's (40.5%) and Saginaw's (40%) immigrant populations were figured alongside the more

TABLE 11.
Persistence of Immigrants in Michigan Lumbertowns, 1875–1895

City and Ethnic Group	Number Persisting						% Total Persistence
	1874–76	to 1880	to 1885	% after 10 years	to 1890	to 1895	
Muskegon							
Germans	200	92	84	42	70	50	25
French Canadians	100	53	36	36	33	20	20
Dutch	200	102	92	46	80	66	33
Swedish	200	82	76	38	58	38	19
				40.5 avg.			24 avg.
Saginaw							
Germans	200	98	82	41	58	51	25
French Canadians	200	86	66	33	52	40	20
							22.5 avg.
Poles	50	20	14	40	8	5	10
				38 avg.			18 avg.
Bay City							
Germans	200	82	64	32	56	42	21
French Canadians	200	38	20	10	16	14	7
Poles	200	82	76	38	58	38	19
				26 avg.			15 avg.

stable native-born population, persistence in these towns would likely fall within the norm. In Bay City, which had more foreign-born, the persistence rate would remain below the norm despite adding native-born persons to the low persistence scores of that town's immigrants (26%). These observations about the percentages of "persisters" help explain Muskegon's and Saginaw's success at reindustrialization. These communities offered a stable core of laborers, who more than likely had some skill to offer diversified manufacturing. In contrast to Stephan Thernstrom's observation that a "rooted" work force unwilling to migrate to seize new employment opportunities can retard local economic growth, comparisons of Muskegon and Saginaw with Bay City indicate just the opposite.[35] Bay City, having a more mobile work force, apparently failed to attract new resources or skilled persons to promote economic redevelopment. In lumbertown industry, where reindustrialization moved from lumber to woodenware and wooden products to machined goods, a stable, skilled work force was conducive to industrial diversification.

Equally important, persistence study allays the belief that Bay City's Polish workers were unreliable and impermanent. Outside Muskegon's Dutch and German immigrants—claimed to be the most reliable workers—no other ethnic group persisted over the first decade to the degree that the Poles did in Bay City. Coupling this persistence rate with the profile projected in the population pyramid, an image emerges that depicts the Poles as stable, family and community-oriented workers. Statistical revelation makes it difficult to accept the popular nineteenth-century generalization that Poles were responsible in part for lumbermen's unwillingness to reinvest in Bay City's economy at the end of the white pine era. Of the three major immigrant groups in Bay City, more Poles persisted in the first decade than Germans or French.

It may well have been the French Canadians in Bay City who contributed significantly to that city's transient work force. Ninety percent of the French left within a decade. In contrast, the French in Saginaw and Muskegon remained consistent in their rates of persistence. The high rate of attrition among the French creates the low persistence rate in Bay City, and, because the French Canadians accounted for about a quarter of the workers, it is not surprising that the entire labor force in Bay City was seen as unstable and unreliable.

Persistence in Muskegon easily reaffirms a more stable immigrant work force. Even after twenty years, a third of the Dutch remained and a quarter of the Germans. This long-term commitment to one community entails all the trappings of permanence, family, and housing. Considering their determination to remain in Muskegon, it is evident that the Dutch, especially if reasonable opportunities for advancement were available, would remain dependable, docile, and enterprising workmen. The Dutch, and Muskegon's immigrants in general, remained an attractive work force to that city's lumbermen.

Saginaw, like Muskegon, offered an economic climate that kept many of that community's immigrants in the city. The French Canadians, for unexplained reasons, evidenced a higher and more consistent persistence rate in Saginaw than Bay City. Couple their reliability with that of the only other major immigrant group, the Germans, and Saginaw offered a work force comparable in permanence to Muskegon's. Even by 1895, after two decades, about a quarter of Saginaw's immigrants remained. If the twenty-year persistence figures in Saginaw and Muskegon are compared with Bay City's, where only a quarter of the population remained after ten years, it is not difficult to envision a local economy in Bay City besought by turmoil and instability.

IMMIGRANT OCCUPATIONAL STRUCTURE

An examination of occupational mobility from 1875 to 1895 more clearly reveals the labor situation during the peak, transition, and declining years of the lumbertowns' economies. The survey (table 12) traces individuals of known occupations in 1875 by observing their occupational changes in a twenty-year period. Tracing is a straightforward approach to occupational mobility. It involves a simple methodology of tracing a representative sample of ethnic names in city directories over a selected period. Beginning in 1875, individuals were traced at five-year intervals, their names, residences, and job status recorded.[36] A hierarchical scale of occupations based on Alba M. Edwards and improved on by Stephen Thernstrom provides a tool for analysis (see chart 1).[37] The highest classification, "high white collar" (HWC), includes most of those used in the Edwards/Thernstrom classification. However, "lumberman," classi-

TABLE 12.
Occupation Mobility (Percent) for Foreign-Born
in Michigan Lumbertowns, 1875–1895

Community and Nativity	Occupational Level					
	HWC	LWC	Skilled	Semiskilled	Labor	N
Muskegon						
Dutch, 1875	2.5	16	15.3	6.4	59.6	200
to 1880	8.5	15.8	15.8	4.8	54.8	102
to 1885	5.4	18.9	17.5	5.4	51.3	92
to 1890	11.1	23.8	9.5	11.1	44.4	80
to 1895	9.0	29	16.3	5.4	40.0	66
Germans, 1875	3.5	14.2	17.8	16	48.2	200
to 1880	3.4	20.6	17.2	10.3	48.2	92
to 1885	5.4	14.8	16.8	18.5	40.7	84
to 1890	9.5	14.2	12.2	11.5	50.3	70
to 1895	6.2	18.7	25	12.5	37.5	50
French, 1875	0	13.3	23.3	10	53.0	100
to 1880	0	18	19.5	11.6	50.9	53
to 1885	0	25.4	20.7	4.8	50.1	36
to 1890	0	24.7	15.8	4.6	54.9	33
to 1895						
Swedish, 1875	2.4	7.3	17.0	14.6	58.5	200
to 1880	8.5	9.4	13.2	15.1	54.2	82
to 1885	9.3	14.7	9.3	18.75	47.7	76
to 1890	8.3	19.7	7.7	12.3	52	58
to 1895	13.3	20.0	6.6	11.3	48.6	38
Saginaw						
Germans, 1875	1.9	12.4	35.2	8.5	41.8	200
to 1880	4	20	49.3	9.3	17.3	98
to 1885	4.4	20.5	47	10.2	16.1	82
to 1890	5.1	20.6	46.5	12	15.5	58
to 1895	5.8	21.5	47	7.8	17.6	51
French, 1875	3.3	6.6	18.3	15.3	56.6	200
to 1880	3.5	3.5	25	10.7	53.5	86
to 1885	4.5	9	31.8	13.6	35.9	66
to 1890	0	6.6	33.3	20	40	52
to 1895	0	16.6	33.3	15.3	38	40
Bay City						
Germans, 1875	6.8	19	20.4	13.6	40.2	200
to 1880	8.1	34.4	32.7	4.9	19.6	82
to 1885	6.2	30.5	33.3	8.4	24.6	64
to 1890	4	35.7	33	5.7	21.6	56
to 1895	4	38.6	30.2	7.2	20.0	42
Poles, 1875	0.6	8	3.2	22	67.2	200
to 1880	0	13.1	3.9	20	63	82
to 1885	0	12.3	6.2	19.4	62.1	76
to 1890	0	14.5	6	21.5	58	58
to 1895	0	18.3	5.2	17.1	59.4	38

TABLE 12. (Cont')

Community and Nativity	Occupational Level					
	HWC	LWC	Skilled	Semiskilled	Labor	N
Bay City Cont'						
French, 1975	3	7	24	16	50	200
to 1880	10.5	10.5	26	10.5	42	38
to 1885	20	10	20	20	30	20
to 1890	12.5	12.5	12.5	25	37.5	16
to 1895	14	14	14	28	30	14

fied in Thernstrom as "unskilled laborer," is actually "HWC" and represents the epitome of social-economic success in the lumber-towns. The lumberman-entrepreneur was the owner of the sawmills and forestlands that provided the livelihood for so many laborers. To "low white collar" (LWC) was added such sawmill jobs as "ink-slinger" (record keeper), engineer, and tallyman (tallied board feet). Also in the three succeeding classifications, "skilled," "semiskilled," and "laborer," several other occupations peculiar to lumbering operations were added. The placement of some of these occupations was determined by the average daily wages paid. A survey of wages was given in the 1886 Third Annual Report (Michigan Bureau of Labor and Industrial Statistics), which surveyed the 1885 strike in the Saginaw Valley.[38]

Before examining similarities and contrasts by nativity, some broad observations can be made of the towns' economic opportunities. The survey of Muskegon shows a remarkable similarity of opportunity. There are no pronounced success stories or evidence of drastic deprivation or economic limitation. Saginaw's more diversified economy apparently provided opportunities for movement into the middle classifications, especially the skilled trades. In Bay City, the transient nature of the work force is evident, and the limited economic opportunities affected most nativity groups. In all three towns, the closing of the sawmills is reflected in some downward mobility in the later 1880s and 1890s.

Examining individual communities and nativity groups, it is not difficult to ascertain why the Dutch were considered ideal employees in Muskegon. Not only did they persist in significant numbers, but they also evidenced slow but steady occupational mobility. Escaping the lumber mills, the Dutch bounded beyond semiskilled or skilled

Chart 1. Rankings of Lumbertown Occupations

High White Collar

Lumberman	Manufacturer
Clergyman	Attorney
Teacher	Editor
Doctor	Banker, Executive
Builder	Lumber Dealer
Contractor	Architect

Low White Collar

Accountant	Grocer
Teller	Agent
Bookkeeper	Conductor
Canvasser	Tug owner
Clerk	Engineer (in sawmill)
Saloon keeper	Superintendent (in sawmill)
Self-employed	Capitalist
Stove dealer	Peddler
Foreman	Minor government official
Musician	Surveyor
Salesman	Printer (newspaper)
Lumber inspector	Ink-Slingers (in sawmill)
Tallyman (in lumber yard)	Land dealer

Skilled

Baker	Boilermaker
Blacksmith	Bookbinder
Mason	Cabinetmaker
Carpenter	Jeweler
Watchmaker	Machinist (in sawmill)
Mechanic	Millwright (in sawmill)
Pattern maker (in sawmill)	Painter
Shoemaker	Cooper (in sawmill)
Tailor	Upholsterer
Plasterer	Tinsmith
Harness maker	Boot maker
Bricklayer	Butcher
Brewer	Cigar maker

Semiskilled

Barber	Teamster
Bartender	Sash maker (in sawmill)
Janitor	Sawyer (in sawmill)
Driver-drayman	Joiner (in sawmill)
Sailor	Planer (in sawmill)
Fisherman	Pumper (in sawmill)
Watchman	Fireman (in sawmill)
Edger (in sawmill)	Scaler (in sawmill)
Potash maker (in sawmill)	Setter (in sawmill)

CHART 1. (Cont')

Laborers

Workman	Boom man
Laborer	Ditchdigger
Salt worker (in sawmill)	Helper
Sorter (in sawmill)	Street cleaner
Dryer (in sawmill)	Chimney cleaner
Miner (in sawmill)	

occupations and settled into the low white collar classifications. Most who rose became owners of small businesses, and a few small businesses became large concerns over the years. Surprisingly, in the sample survey only one Dutchman took advantage of assumed antecedent skills acquired in Holland and became a furniture manufacturer. The limited numbers of Dutch workers who moved into skilled occupations challenges the assumption that the Hollanders relied on prior skills as carpenters and cabinetmakers to become occupationally mobile. The individuals who moved into the white-collar occupations relied more on business acumen or education to achieve success. The upper classification—represented by teachers, a minister, a student who became a physician, several clerks, two bookkeepers, a salesman, an architect, the county treasurer, and county surveyor—reflect mobility through practical or formal education. The entrepreneurs who gained success usually started businesses: several meat stores, two boiler works, several groceries, a jeweler, a dairy, a bookbindery, two hardware stores, one lumber inspector, a lumber dealer, and one furniture manufacturer. Antecedent skills apparently were not significant in Dutch upward mobility. Instead they valued business skill and persistence. Doubtless, because a few Dutch settlers did well in Muskegon, others witnessed success stories and remained in the community hoping to emulate their fellow countrymen. Permanence and reliability made the Dutch attractive laborers for diversified industry.

Other immigrant groups in Muskegon reflected occupational mobility. The Germans, who persisted almost as consistently as the Dutch, settled into unskilled and skilled occupations. The German workers' forte was machinery, and occupations such as engineer, blacksmith, saw maker, millwright, boilermaker, and sawyer represented avenues to success. The French sample, where attrition was at first larger than the others, is sketchy at best in its representation. Nevertheless, the French Canadian found it more difficult to escape the laboring class and impossible to move into the HWC category. The antecedent skills that the French brought from the logging camps and mills of Canada did enable several French settlers to become foremen, lumber inspectors, and engineers in the Muskegon sawmills. The relatively high number of French in the LWC classification is reflective of these individuals. In reality, though, their skills as woodsmen probably retarded French mobility and kept them working as experienced laborers rather than businessmen or educated professionals. The Swedish immigrants' mobility patterns were like those of the Dutch, although more Swedes settled in the semiskilled classifications and fewer escaped the status of laborers. In the declining years of lumbering, 1888–95, the Germans, Swedish, and French skilled hands experienced some downward mobility into the laboring classes. The Dutch escaped this decline, perhaps indicative of their reliability and permanence as employees and businessmen. If the highly mobile French were statistically set aside, persistence and gradual but steady mobility by the Dutch, Germans, and Swedes supports the conception that Muskegon as a declining sawmill town continued to maintain an efficient and dependable work force.

Examining the Saginaw Valley immigrants in table 12, the similarities and contrasts are apparent. Saginaw had a persistent core of German settlers who gravitated into skilled trades and LWC occupations. Coming into the community frequently with some savings, many of the Germans avoided labor occupations and steadily moved into skilled categories. In no other lumbertown did the Germans so dominate skilled trades. The French Canadians also managed to acquire semiskilled jobs and apparently one-quarter to one-third became skilled hands. However, more remained laborers and unlike Muskegon, few moved into LWC classifications. Also unlike Muskegon, few Frenchmen became foremen or engineers in the mills. Instead, the skilled occupations they engaged in, represented in the survey, were those of carpenter, cabinetmaker, cooper, and drayman—designations not usually associated with French lumberjacks. Still, traditional avenues of mobility existed; three Frenchmen in the sample became lumbermen. Thus, the two largest immigrant sources of labor in Saginaw persisted long enough and evidenced enough occupational mobility to compare Saginaw's labor force favorably with that in Muskegon.

Bay City represented different mobility patterns. As has been demonstrated, the workers in Bay City were the most geographically mobile. Moreover, the Polish and French immigrants stand out quantitatively. Attrition among the French was so great that statistical generalizations about occupational mobility are almost meaningless. The survey here ends up tracing primarily skilled and upper-class French workers. The Poles, however, were indeed workers who did the "lowest grade of work for the lowest pay." They had the most persons in the laborer classification and in semiskilled. As semiskilled workers in the sawmills, the Poles were still assigned difficult and dangerous tasks: firemen (tend salt boiler fires), boilermakers, sawyers, and setters. A few Poles were potash makers in the mills, evidence perhaps that some antecedent skills from northern Poland did find applicability in the Saginaw Valley. Very few Poles became skilled workmen, although a few managed to become proprietors of small businesses. Not one Pole managed to ascend into the HWC rankings.[39] The Germans, however, represented the most established stock in Bay City and evidenced mobility comparable to that of their countrymen in Saginaw and Muskegon. As in Saginaw, many Germans in Bay City became skilled hands and self-employed proprietors. Germans also were often seen as engineers and inspectors in the sawmills. The rapid mobility of the Germans in Bay City, however, may have been aided by the considerable attrition in the laboring classes.

Statistical representation of mobility in Bay City may help explain the Poles' proclivities toward labor protest. Like the Dutch in Muskegon, the Poles persisted in Bay City, and by 1885 they had planted their feet firmly on the lower rungs of the occupational ladder. The Polish culture was slow to change, but it was not static. The expected rewards for persistence and hard work were either unavailable or more difficult to come by, and condescending racial hostility made the Poles objects of job discrimination. Coming from peasant backgrounds, the Poles were slow to realize and develop entrepreneurial skills. Trapped in semiskilled and menial tasks, perhaps even experiencing rising expectations, the Poles, nevertheless reflected little upward mobility. It is not surprising, then, that Polish workers led organizational drives in 1885 for shorter hours, bimonthly pay, and higher wages. They sought to improve their status through militancy if necessary.[40] With some accuracy, therefore, the activism of the Bay City work force can be ascribed to the Poles. Couple this with the high transience of the large French Canadian work force and it is possible that Bay City lumbermen, imbued with social Darwinistic racism, viewed the local work force as troublesome and unreliable.

JOBS, EDUCATION, AND HOUSING

Despite apparent transience and infrequent occupational mobility, working-class immigrants engaged in other activities that when examined provide a clearer picture of the economic structures in the lumbertowns and differing ethnic reactions to urbanization. Polish militancy, for example, was brought on by job discrimination and an ethnocultural reluctance to strive for immediate upward mobility. Even though the Poles may have been the latest immigrant group to arrive in the lumbertowns, they had been present since the early 1870s and increased their numbers significantly in the 1880s. The Poles' upward mobility throughout this period into the skilled, LWC, and HWC classifications was severely limited. Part of the explanation for this limited mobility would have to rest on job discrimination. Isolated on the south side of Bay City and slow to assimilate, the Poles were seen as outside the community. Representing only twelve percent of the labor force, they did not have the numbers—as they did after 1900—to achieve demands or representation in the sawmills. The Poles seldom rose to assume leadership roles in the sawmills (see table 13). The lack of internal occupational mobility may well explain Polish job frustration and willingness to join labor

TABLE 13.

Random Sample of Lumbertown Persons in Positions of Authority by Nativity, 1885–1890

Occupation[a]	German			French Canadian			Dutch	Poles		Swedes
	M	S	BC	M	S	BC	M	S	BC	M
Lumbermen	2	3	1	0	3	1	0	0	0	1
Lumber Inspector	0	4	1	3	2	1	2	0	0	2
Engineer	4	7	4	0	1	2	2	0	1	1
Foreman	2	7	6	4	3	1	1	0	1	1

[a]N equals 100 in every instance.
M is an abbreviation for Muskegon, S for Saginaw, and BC for Bay City.
Source: City directories, 1885–1890.

movements. In Bay City, the Germans who had skills and long-term commitment made incursions into leadership positions. Native-born residents, though, continued to dominate positions of authority in the sawmills. Saginaw offered considerable opportunity for Germans and French to assume leadership in the mills.

The inability of the Polish and French-Canadian immigrants in Bay City to achieve mobility into the LWC and HWC classifications may also reflect their economic inability to keep their children in school. The Canadians were generally too transient, and in Polish families frequently all the members were wage earners (see table 14). Children of French Canadian and Polish families in Bay City went to school proportionately less often than those of native-born American families.[41] The same comparison between immigrants and natives is true in Saginaw and Muskegon. Workers in the lumbertowns often relied on children's wages to supplement the father's income. However, in Muskegon the percentage of Dutch sons and daughters going to school was even lower than comparable immigrant groups in Bay City or Saginaw. The Dutch families apparently valued education less and often kept their children out of school and in the work force. The Dutch moved into HWC and LWC classifications by filling jobs that required some business acumen but apparently

TABLE 14.
Children's Status in Selected Ethnic Group in Lumbertowns, 1900

City & Ethnicity*	Sons 12–20			Daughters 12–20		
	School	Work	Home	School	Work	Home
Saginaw						
American-born	37	60	3	54.6	26.6	18.6
French Canadian	26.6	62	11.2	29.1	43	27.7
Germans	31.4	61.7	6.7	37.5	34.7	27.7
Bay City						
American-born	40.2	56.5	3.3	57.5	18.1	24.2
French Canadian	20.2	75.6	4	34.5	38.3	27.2
Germans	34.5	47.2	18	46.1	34.6	19.2
Polish	26.3	53.3	20.3	24.1	37.9	37.9
Muskegon						
American-born	46.6	43.3	10	66.1	7.4	26.4
French Canadian	17.8	76.7	5.3	48.8	26.6	24.4
German	30.1	68.8	1.1	52.9	20.5	26.4
Dutch	19.7	70.4	9.8	11.7	43.5	44.7

*Having two foreign-born parents. N equals 200 in every sample.
Source: U.S. Manuscript Census, 1900.

little education beyond the basics. Native-born children, although employed in the lumbertowns almost as frequently as some immigrant children, found employment as bookkeepers, clerks, bankers, and engineers, occupations that reflected earlier training or education.[42]

Home ownership may be another criterion that determined the nature of the immigrant work force. Although home ownership is commonly considered a sign of entrance into the middle class, Olivier Zunz concluded that owning one's home was more an ethnocultural phenomenon than one of class.[43] As has been suggested, some immigrant groups acquired homes by having the entire family, except for young children, employed.[44] Zunz's findings for Detroit are largely replicated in the study of lumbertown home ownership (table 15). Immigrant families owned their own homes more often than native-American workers. Moreover, a comparison of German and Polish in Bay City with Dutch and Scandinavian wards in Muskegon indicates that the Bay City workers owned their homes almost as frequently as the Dutch and Scandinavians. The Dutch even more so than the Poles and Germans encouraged their children to seek gainful employment at an early age. Despite the question of home ownership as representative of upward mobility, owning one's home,

TABLE 15.
Home Ownership for Selected Ethnic Groups in the Lumbertowns, 1900

City & Ethnic group	Owned	Mortgaged	Rented	N
	%	%	%	
Saginaw				
American-born*	41	5.8	53.1	239
French Canadian	40.8	13.2	45.9	196
German	50	31.5	18.4	190
Bay City				
American-born	31.6	13.4	54.8	587
French Canadian	19.2	14.2	66.6	530
German	42.8	14.6	42.5	369
Polish	39.5	16	44.4	256
Muskegon				
American-born	22.5	4.8	72.5	224
French Canadian	33.3	13.8	52.7	266
Dutch	34.1	37.1	28.6	264
German	43.5	15.2	41.1	185
Swedish	42.1	10.5	47.3	238

*Head of household born in U.S. of two or more U.S.-born parents.
Source: U.S. Manuscript Census, 1900.

nevertheless, represented permanence and stability. Thus, where the Dutch were seen in Muskegon as an attractive labor force because of home ownership, the Poles had the same commitment in Bay City. However, Bay City's natives and immigrants were less permanent than either Muskegon's or Saginaw's. Saginaw had nearly sixty percent of the sample registered as homeowners. Thus, Saginaw and to a lesser extent Muskegon in 1900 evidenced a stable population that may have been a result of lumbermen's early efforts to diversify industrially.

A second factor was the many immigrants who held their homes mortgage-free. Many Germans, Polish, and Swedish settlers, especially, built their own homes. Following a pattern characteristic of sawmill settlements, cheap scrap lumber provided the material to build a home that was solid but inexpensive. Most important, when he was eventually done, the homeowner was free from rent and debt. Owning property was the easiest way to accomplish a semblance of social mobility.

Most of these houses, which still can be seen today, were designed by the carpenter-resident and imitated unimaginative, Midwestern, one-and-a-half story, two-bedroom styles. Crowded together, they were oriented toward the sidewalks and streets. The houses invariably had front porches, and the living rooms also faced the street. Immigrant residents wanted to belong to the neighborhood. They did not erect barriers to neighborliness and ethnic identity. Though the houses were made of cull lumber and often painted in garish colors, they nevertheless remained neat and clean. The Polish, German, and Dutch neighborhoods stood out as places where the homeowner could pass his life in work, comfort, and relative contentment.

Although mortgage-free homes were common to all three lumbertowns, Saginaw had the highest average (44%). Muskegon followed closely (41.1%), and Bay City was a distant third (33.2%). For immigrants in Saginaw and Muskegon, and for the Poles and Germans in Bay City, owning a home was perhaps the only way to gain security and build stability. A home, often built by himself or his fellow countrymen, was how the immigrant could contribute to city-building. City-building, if one can judge by the extent of mortgage-free homes, was most successfully carried on in Saginaw and Muskegon. In Bay City, this stability could perhaps be gained only in the framework of one's ethnic group—in the Polish or German neighborhoods. Home ownership, though, enabled the immigrants to build neighborhoods in Bay City that provided a basis for their form of community organization.

Immigrant occupational mobility, jobs, education, and housing all affected the economic directions the three lumbertowns would take. In Muskegon where there was responsible, resident ownership of the sawmills, limited occupational mobility, permanent residents, and entrepreneurial growth, an economic environment evolved that encouraged an eventual reconciliation between the demands of labor and those of rapid industrialization. Saginaw had a homogeneous labor force and a core of resident lumbermen who had early on undertaken some industrial diversification. When the inevitable conflict materialized between labor and capital in 1885, many skilled workers, both inside and outside of lumbering, refused to participate, and the lumber oligarchy never lost control of the reins of community control. Authority and community successfully stifled any incipient, large-scale labor unrest. In contrast, at Bay City, a community of absentee owners, where there were fewer opportunities for mobility, a labor force that was statistically more transient, with fewer home owners, a climate conductive to labor unrest and worker dissatisfaction evolved. The 1885 ten-hour strike began in Bay City among the Polish and German workers and spread to Saginaw. It represented in many ways the frustrations evident in a community where there was little leadership and no community building. The strike began a period of labor-capital conflict in Bay City that was to persist for more than a decade.

CONCLUSION

Did ethnicity affect lumbertown industrial policy during and after the white pine era? Ethnicity effected positive results in Muskegon. Dutch and Scandinavian workers, having some few antecedent woodworking skills and the *werkkracht*, "will to work," were viewed by entrepreneurs and local historians as ideal laborers on which to risk capital investments. Moreover, using the Dutch as an example, community stability and reasonable occupational mobility was achieved by immigrant workers in Muskegon. Continuity and religious conservatism discouraged labor organization. Family men and home owners, Dutch workmen, who were unhappy in the sawmills, could strike out on their own and often achieve mobility and independence as proprietors of small businesses. Furthermore, practical and sometimes formal education became a resource to open other avenues toward upward mobility. It is not surprising, therefore, that Muskegon lumbermen, several of whom were also more visionary than their contemporaries, would be willing to spend capital to bring industries into the declining sawmill town.

Saginaw, like Muskegon, was marked by a fairly reliable work force dominated by Germans and French Canadians. These workers were reasonably stable and occupationally mobile. Many became skilled hands with homes and families in Saginaw. However, Saginaw's workers were not docile and they affiliated with labor organizations. Yet that city's economy was more mature and industrially diversified than either Muskegon's or Bay City's. Although lumbering remained the main industry, in the declining years lumbermen diversified into metal and woodworking plants and created other forms of employment. Saginaw lumbermen, like Muskegon's who largely lived in the community, had already undertaken industrial diversification before the end of the white pine era. Despite some later labor agitation, the town's diversified economy and entrepreneurial foresight, coupled with a fairly reliable and skilled work force, created an economic climate that continued to attract local investment.

The responsibility for Bay City's protracted and meager efforts to reindustrialize cannot be placed on the backs of immigrant workers. Polish and Germans in Bay City persisted and settled in Bay City at a rate comparable to the much admired Dutch workers in Muskegon. These groups actively participated in the 1885 strike, and French workers protested working conditions by simply migrating in and quickly out of Bay City. If a comparative analysis of Bay City's work force reveals anything, it should indicate that the town's economic problems were not the fault of its laborers. Social Darwinistic and largely absentee lumbermen—Bay City's financial elite—did not develop at any stage a commitment to continued lumbertown prosperity. Absentee ownership, conservative economics, and racism toward workers, not an uncooperative and militant work force, prevented Bay City from achieving industrial revitalization comparable to its sister lumbering communities.

The study of immigrant workers in the lumbertowns reaffirms that antecedent cultural traits were important in determining life-styles for newcomers to industrial communities in America. Although prior skills and cultural dispositions toward education, family, affiliations, and mobility were important, attitudinal predispositions toward immigrant cultures also determined New World life-styles. Not only did some Dutch and Scandinavian immigrants have woodworking skills, but they were viewed as hard workers and dependable employees. In Muskegon quantified analysis questioned whether the practical skills associated with the Dutch were significant in their occupational mobility. More important was the image they had as hard workers that led to Muskegon's later prosperity. At the same time, Bay City's Poles, also hard and committed workers, carried over a cultural baggage that depicted them as unreliable peasant laborers. Entire Polish families worked, while sacrificing education, to build home and neighborhood.[45] These predispositions and practices made it more difficult for the Poles to achieve occupational mobility. The Poles' involvement in the 1885 ten-hour strike confirmed racial views toward the Poles and permitted them to be used as scapegoats by lumbermen unwilling to reinvest profits in Bay City. The seeds of distrust and discrimination sown in the boom years helped prevent Bay City from ever extending economic prosperity beyond the lumber era.

The immigrants in the lumbertowns failed to develop a real class consciousness. What should be clear is that economic dislocation was often mitigated by cultural and newly emergent institutions of each immigrant group. Most of the immigrants in the lumbertowns clustered in homogeneous enclaves, which comprised segregated areas. The decision to associate together was voluntarily brought on by common culture and religious and historical experiences. As important, external forces—discrimination, labor exploitation, and poverty—also produced residential ghettos. Homogeneous residential settlements reinforced a sense of ethnic identification. Victimization produced an ethnic consciousness rather than a class awareness.

Ethnic consciousness, nevertheless, enabled immigrant groups, depending on the degree of minority victimization and exploitation, to adopt several different political and economic responses to oppression. Where oppression was intense and included ethnic and economic exploitation, labor market disadvantage, and even anti-Catholic discrimination, an ethnic group, like the Poles in Bay City, responded by insulation or withdrawal. Because of economic and minority disadvantages, such an immigrant group could develop elements of class awareness and organize into movements that rely on ethnic as well as class consciousness. But where abuse was less intense—like the Dutch, or Saginaw's large French and German populations—accommodation and integration, orthodox political action, and assimilation strategies often developed. Immigrant response, though, regardless of the extent of victimization, usually followed two steps: (1) the attempt to improve material conditions by directly confronting the entrepreneurial classes, and (2) the attempt to use the political process as a mechanism to accomplish economic equality. The Muskegon and Saginaw Valley ten-hour strikes trace the evolution of the confrontation between labor and capital in the lumbertowns.

"Ten Hours or No Sawdust"

---

*The crowd, now increased to probably 800 . . . all had
clubs and were shouting; men went into the mill; they
were ordered out, and went. Loaded carts attempted to
come out, and the crowd commenced throwing clubs at
the . . . drivers. . . . Both myself and my officers were
hit. . . .*
*The crowd were all sober. The leaders were generally
Polanders, who were shoved to the front by their more
cunning backers.*

—STATEMENT OF MARTIN BRENNAN,
SHERIFF OF BAY COUNTY, 1885

*My dock and salt sheds are full, and I don't care to
run. It would be a benefit to me if the strike did not end
for a month.*

—STATEMENT OF W. B. ROUSE,
MILL OWNER, BAY CITY, 1885

In the spring of 1882 Saginaw lumbermen who gathered around the
tables in the card room of the Bancroft Hotel should have been con-
gratulating themselves and looking forward to another profitable
season. They were beginning their fourth year of prosperity after
weathering the 1873–78 nationwide panic. In the four years since,
they had revolutionized the lumber business. The logging railroads,
brought to Michigan in 1876, reached the woodlands and brought
trainload after trainload of heretofore inaccessible timber to the
riverbanks. Sawmill towns had become mechanized contrivances in
the wilderness. Sophisticated steam engines powered new and speed-
ier crosscut, band, and gang saws. Small, inefficient mills closed and
large modern sawmills cut nearly one-half of Michigan's pine. Still,
the lumbermen who met at the Bancroft that spring could not hide
their apprehensions; the new year began inauspiciously with strikes,
lower profits, and a foreboding that the nation was about to slip

again into a period of labor unrest and depression. The lumbermen had heard of the strike threats made by "radical workingmen" in Muskegon the previous fall. Those that returned from Detroit recalled the angry voices of the Knights of Labor demanding ten-hour workdays. In West Bay City the salt block workers at H. W. Sage & Co. struck for five cents more per day. A few weeks later, despite Sage's dismissal of the salt workers, the coopers at his mill started yet another strike. Most alarming were the rumors in the newspapers that the men were forming unions.[1] Whenever they discussed business in the sawing season of 1882, the lumbermen found that they often nervously considered the prospects of social upheaval.

Adversarial relations between labor and capital in Muskegon, Bay City, and the Saginaws were largely a reflection of changing economic conditions that affected the industrial society in the era. Events in the lumbertowns were part of the national experience evident in the late nineteenth century that witnessed repeated attempts by capital to bring order and stability to the work force. A slight rise in real wages and the emergence of the industrial logging towns as places of permanence encouraged workers to assert demands for shorter hours and better working conditions. Although these were the halcyon years for lumber production, by the early eighties it was clear that the locus of lumber production would once again shift westward. When a decline in demand in the mid-eighties forced a cut in wages, workers feared the future and resisted a return to old standards. In Bay City especially, absentee and resident lumbermen were determined to maintain traditional work patterns and relationships. Likewise in Muskegon and Saginaw, paternalistic lumbermen inhibited organized, working-class activities and worked with public officials to maintain order. When strike action developed, the lumbermen transformed potentially dangerous labor conflict into more traditional local political activity.[2]

To a significant degree a similarity in causation, strike patterns, and results can be ascribed to the ten-hour movements that plunged Muskegon in 1881–82 and the Saginaw Valley in 1885 into strike activity. However, despite apparent commonality—identical economic foundations, similar size, and comparable population structures—each lumbertown responded very differently to labor unrest. While Bay City, and to a lesser extent Muskegon, offered firm support for the strikers, the Saginaws acquiesced quickly to employer pressure and demands. State and local authorities also differed in their responses to strike action. Moreover, community and authority response to the strikes further reveals the social and economic machinations in each lumbertown that permitted Saginaw and Muskegon, and not Bay City, to reindustrialize successfully at the end of the lumber era.[3]

SAWMILL LABOR

Despite the economic promise of 1882, the period of vigorous, undisciplined expansion in the Michigan lumbertowns was about to end. Though lumber output increased tremendously during the eighties, the profit margin declined significantly. Lumbermen's costs were rising dramatically. Cutting, logging, booming, driving, sawing, and taxes all increased in the early eighties. Between 1877 and 1882 the total cost of production per thousand board feet rose from $8.02 to $13.50.[4] Increased costs were simply a result of a dwindling supply of quality pine trees. Prime timber in the Lower Peninsula had disappeared and what remained was often of poorer quality and on land that was swampy, hilly, or at a distance from railways or river transport.[5]

Faced with a diminishing supply of good lumber, increased transport costs, competition, and an unstable economy, lumbermen turned to reducing costs of production. Although many costs were fixed, the one unit that was flexible and easily adjusted was labor. The mill owners held fast to the old maxim that, as Sage said, "a reduction in the costs of making lumber . . . must come through cheaper and more efficient labor."[6] As lumber became more expensive, rising wages after 1878 first leveled off and then began to drop, especially when depression hit the industry in 1884 (see table 16). The wage level was responsive to the increased costs of lumber production and declining prices.

Average wages for sawmill workers in the Saginaw Valley and Muskegon compared favorably with wages in other industries and states. Though the pay may have been less than several industries in Detroit, it was comparable to other sawmill towns, and as the *Lumberman's Gazette* demonstrated in 1877, they matched wages earned by the iron workers in Troy, the New England woolen industries, and Erie Railroad employees.[7] Nevertheless, most of the sawmill workers were not employed throughout the year and even more were unskilled laborers who earned less than average wages. When they received their pay, some sawmill men were not paid entirely in cash, but received scrip or credit at company-owned stores.

TABLE 16.

Average Daily Wages of Common Sawmill Labor

Year	Amount
1876	$1.31–$1.46
1877	$1.21–$1.38
1878	$1.23–$1.46
1879	$1.27–$1.38
1880	$1.27–$1.46
1881	$1.31–$1.55
1882	$1.38–$1.74
1883	$1.38–$1.75
1884	$1.31–$1.62

Source: *Bay City Tribune*, July 8, 1885.

A declining and undependable wage scale was not the only concern of the common laborer. The mill worker in Saginaw, Bay City, and Muskegon worked about occupations structured with a high degree of insecurity. The seasonal supply of logs meant that he was employed only six or seven months in the late spring, summer, and fall. Even after logging railroads were brought into Michigan, they never drastically altered the seasonal work patterns. Winter employment in the woods for mill workers was often difficult to secure, for their competitors—farmers, miners, and boom men—often got a head start in the fall. The sawing season was usually not completed until late October or early November, and lumbermen often paid workers the final month's wages only after the logs were all cut. A mill worker who left for the woods early could not reclaim his old job next season. As a result, sawmill employees often went the winter without work.

During the sawing season the men worked six days a week, eleven or twelve hours per day. At Hackley's mills in Muskegon the workday usually began at 5:45 A.M. and ran until 8:45 in the morning when the workers received a fifteen-minute break. The breaks were brought on more by the necessity to replace dull saw blades than to rest the men. From 9:00 A.M. until noon the mill workers resumed work. During the half-hour lunch break, saw blades were again replaced. There was a third change of blades and a fifteen-minute break at 3:30 P.M. The mill shut down at 6:15 P.M. The workers were paid for the time spent working: 11.5 hours per day.[8]

Unlike Gutman's accounts of a leisurely twelve-hour day for some workers in Eastern industries, the sawmill workers in the lumbertowns were driven to put in a good day's work. New, highly efficient, and complicated machinery thundered in the sawmill. "The men are part of these machines," noted a Bay County attorney in 1885. "They could not even stop for a drink of water but must keep up the labor just as fast as the inanimate machinery. The men are a cog in a vast machine." Most mills were small enough that supervision could be constant. The short sawing season and the need to saw all the logs before winter encouraged the lumbermen to push the workers. Drinking on the job and shirking work would bring immediate dismissal. However, hangovers and alcoholic consumption, despite the dangers of the work, were common.[9] The long hours, dangerous saws, drive belts, and machinery often made mill work a bloody occupation.

The casual reader of any lumbertown newspaper during the summer sawing might find several men per week who fell into the equipment, perished in the salt boiler fires, or were maimed amid the whirling saws. Driven by lumbermen who often boasted of cutting thousands of feet per day, it was inevitable that eventually many mill men would feed blood and bone to the lumbermen's quest for efficiency.[10] Sawmill workers about the lumbertowns were known by missing and misshapen fingers and hands. Chemical vapors from the brine water caused further afflictions. Asthma, breathing problems, and stomach disorders were endemic in the saw towns. Outside the hospital policies started in the early seventies in East Saginaw, there was seldom any accident insurance to provide for the injured or their families. Only a few employers made gifts of money or provisions to the injured; the mill worker was usually considered responsible for causing his injury through carelessness.

The laborers in the lumbertowns were at the mercy of their employers. Low wages and unsafe conditions could be maintained because the sawmills employed unskilled men, boys and young men, drifters, and a disproportionate share of foreign immigrants. Many of the foreigners were usually poor, unskilled, and ignorant of the American way of life. They were willing to accept jobs for lower wages and longer hours. The lumbermen knew this and promised jobs to Polish and French Canadian immigrants. In 1885 sixty percent of the work force in the state's lumber industry consisted of foreign-born.[11] All this had the effect of creating a constantly changing work force. Immigrants brought into the sawmill work habits and values that were not acclimated to the industrial work ethic. They became victims of the system. Some, like the French Canadians, moved from place to place; some, like the Poles, adapted older patterns of work and life to the new society; others, like the

Dutch and German, shed some of their ways and adjusted to the entrepreneurial scheme of things. All though, chafed at the restructuring of old habits and beliefs; and, as a result, they sometimes collectively challenged the emerging socioeconomic system.[12]

The sawmill workers only rarely protested in a collective way. Most did not at first plan to stay in the lumber mills long. Regardless of ethnicity, these men had come to the lumbertowns and joined a seasonal work force with the intention of saving enough money to buy a farm, start a small business, or return to their homeland.[13] Some Dutch, German and Polish workers saved small amounts of money and quit the sawmill for small businesses or skilled occupations. The general passivity of the unskilled worker, though, was reinforced by the practices of the lumber barons. The frequent turnover of the labor force, the wholesale firing of disruptive workers, language problems, fines and penalties, and the opportunity to eventually escape the sawmill kept the work force submissive.

However, when recessions, recurrent unemployment, fluctuating wages, and a declining log supply caused expectations to wither, a worker consciousness and status group camaraderie developed. The sawmill workers sustained wildcat strikes and protested low wages and long hours to the lumbermen. Strikes in the lumbertowns, especially in the Saginaw Valley, took place with some regularity in the 1870s and early 1880s. Mostly, though, they were limited in scope and involved only a few skilled hands.

The lumber workers in Bay City struck unsuccessfully in 1872 demanding a ten-hour day and higher wages. The mill operators immediately fired their workers and tried to run the mills by finding workingmen willing to meet their conditions. The mill owners tried, as Sage forcefully stated, "to let the whole laboring community feel the burden of the strike." Angered and exasperated, Sage next ordered that his supervisory staff members be fired because they probably secretly sympathized with the strikers. In ten days imported skilled hands and Polish immigrant laborers had many of the mills back in operation. The twelve-hour day remained and the "discontented demagogues," "the sinister and selfish" workers who created the strike were "debarred from work." In 1873 employees at the Tittabawassee Boom Company struck because of 12½ percent wage cut. The strike was dealt with by simply replacing all the men. There were sporadic labor strikes in 1876, a salt block workers strike in 1882 in Bay City, and a coopers strike in the Saginaw Valley in 1882. Most of these protests were ineffective; mill owners could usu-

ally find a gang of idlers, drifters, or immigrants to replace the striking workers.[14]

Little organized union activity took place until the Knights of Labor moved into Michigan in 1879. Joseph Labadie organized Detroit
shoemakers in that year, and from there the order grew rapidly
throughout the state. By 1882 there were several "Local Assemblies"
(LAs) in the state. Saginaw was "the home of many assemblies,"
Port Huron had "a flourishing branch," "while Bay City had four
locals" in 1883. Outside these cities, Manistee and Menominee had
small, local chapters. The Bay City District Assembly was the second largest after Detroit in the state, and Saginaw trailed Bay City
and Grand Rapids. Muskegon's sawmill workers had a couple of local
assemblies before the 1881 strike.[15]

The Knights also had important converts in Muskegon and Saginaw. A young Muskegon attorney, Francis W. Cook, with Thomas
Barry, a member of the National Executive Board of the Knights
from Saginaw, became influential spokesmen for the mill workers.
They became members of the state legislature and were instrumental
in getting legislation approved in 1884 that legalized labor unions,
and, later in the same session, they also authored the state's first
ten-hour law. The Knights and representatives like Cook and Barry
breathed life into the sawmill labor movement. Their concern with
the social and economic questions of the day provided the planning and leadership that sustained the lumbertowns' (and the state's)
first large-scale organized attempt by workingmen to direct their
own lives.

"Ten Hours or No Saw Logs": Muskegon, 1881–82

Francis W. Cook's involvement with the labor movement began
when he took advantage of spontaneous strike action precipitated by
the boom and pen men along Muskegon Lake in 1881.[16] Employees
of the Muskegon booming company were responsible for sorting and
penning logs on the lake boom and then rafting them to sawmill
ponds. The 1881 season had been prosperous for the lumbermen,
and late in the season a large supply of logs remained in the river.
The boom men desired a share of this prosperity and began to com-
plain about wages, working conditions, and monthly pay schedules.
They had strength in numbers, about three hundred, and they con-

trolled the flow of logs to the sawmills. The boom employees petitioned the mill owners for a wage increase from $1.75 to $2.00 per day and full pay for the days they could not work because of poor weather.[17]

Mill owners capitulated readily to the workers' demands for increased wages; however, they refused to comply with the request for wages on foul-weather days. On September 17 the boom men refused to work and lumber production quickly halted. Surprisingly, though, only three days into the strike, the lumbermen relented. The company hired back all the strikers, agreed to pay them for lost days, and even compensated the boom men for the days they were on strike. The lumbermen acted not out of benevolence but out of the pressing, though short-term, need to get the remainder of the logs to the mills before the end of the sawing season. They merely passed the increased costs on to the mill owners. On the afternoon of October 1, the boom and pen men went back to work. Strike activity, though, was far from over.

The next day attorney Francis Cook and his law partner, Nelson DeLong, spoke to a crowd of three thousand sawmill workers gathered at First Street and Western Avenue. DeLong, who was county prosecutor, ran the meeting.[18] The success evidenced by the boom men clearly influenced Cook, DeLong, and the mill workers. The attorneys proposed that a petition, already prepared, be adopted and presented to the lumbermen. The circular requested that "the mill owners . . . reduce the number of hours of labor so that the employees will not be compelled to labor more than ten hours each day." DeLong and Cook were well inculcated with the values and goals of Terence Powderly, Grand Master Workman of the Knights of Labor. As young lawyers, the men had moved to Muskegon in the early 1870s. They developed reputations as well-spoken trial attorneys and politicians who allied themselves early on with the causes of the workingmen. Throughout these early rallies DeLong insisted that he and Cook opposed strikes and that his primary goal was to implement ten-hour workdays so that the mill workers "exempted from toil" would have more time for "recreation and mental improvement." Like Powderly, DeLong and Cook took a gradualist, conservative view, holding out for evolutionary social-welfare unionism and worker improvement.[19]

However, Muskegon represented merely one front in the battle for union representation. In 1881 the Knights of Labor, partly in response to the charismatic leadership of Powderly, gained nearly twenty thousand members, and local assemblies were exercising their newfound power throughout the industrial states. The *Chicago Tribune* reported as much on October 6, 1881, when they noted "the Lumbermen of that city [Muskegon] are now affected with the series of labor troubles which are growing in magnitude every day." Like labor leaders everywhere, DeLong and Cook also experienced the hostility of the local conservative press and outspoken lumbermen. They were accused of being "demagogues, political opportunists, and of misleading the workers."[20] Although they apparently had little to do with the strike at the boom company, Cook and DeLong had prepared for and called the first meeting on October 2 that precipitated the second phase of the 1881 ten-hour strike. They largely directed labor activities for the next eight months and became the recognized spokesmen for the laboring men in Muskegon. Indeed, they were political opportunists.

Political opportunism, though, did not preclude dedication to the workers' cause. Although these leaders may have been making "tools of the workingmen" to further their careers, the mill hands were willing to be led. There were no efforts made to repudiate their leadership, and they consistently spoke to large, sympathetic crowds of workingmen throughout the months of labor agitation. After the strike(s) Cook and DeLong remained popular public figures (both would soon serve terms as mayor) and continued to represent the workingmen. Years later a local newspaperman wrote in retrospect:

> While the DeLong and Cook administrations were criticized severely and good folks of the conforming mentality readily accepted the theory that they were dangerous demagogues, as a fact viewed as a whole and measuring their achievements, Muskegon has reason to be grateful to them for their sincerity in supporting the workingmen's movement at that time cannot be disputed. There was no big reward in sight for them. The fact that in the polls, notwithstanding heroic efforts on the part of the conservatives, their platform was so overwhelmingly endorsed, even after it was known that the opposition candidate was sympathetic toward the ten-hour movement shows that they expressed public opinion in their campaign utterances. . . . Cook and DeLong were not demagogic radicals. They never preached anarchy or even socialism in any phase. In fact they were moderate men politically.[21]

The influence of Cook and DeLong represented the significant cross-class undercurrents in the Knights of Labor throughout the country. These middle-class spokesmen for labor, like so many in the order, saw an opportunity to advance themselves and others on the fringes of American economic and political life. These men were "neither physically or experientially far removed from the working poor." As such they were "educated and sympathic mediaries between working-class neighbors and the larger community." The presence of the middle class in the Knights gave the movement in Muskegon articulate and influential support and reflected the workers' drive toward political power.[22]

DeLong and Cook accepted Powderly's goals of reduced hours and made it the focal point of the Muskegon strike for several reasons. Working conditions were not good. The recent addition of the gang saw and newer, faster, and more efficient, but extremely dangerous circular saws increased the likelihood of on-the-job injuries. Most injuries occurred late in the eleven- or twelve-hour working day. Shorter hours also were supported by many businessmen, especially saloon keepers, because the men would have more time to spend wages. The Knights of Labor desired fewer hours to enable more unskilled laborers to find work.[23]

Though the mill men went back to work on Monday, October 3, after Cook's and DeLong's Sunday mass meeting, strike fever was spreading rapidly. During the week the lumbermen of Muskegon rejected the petition for shorter hours.

The following Sunday, October 9, Cook and DeLong organized another rally at First and Western. So many mill hands turned out, nearly four thousand, that the crowd had to reorganize at nearby Mason's Park. The sawmill workers were ready for a fight. They had received their monthly pay the day before and many had time to visit the saloons Saturday night and fortify their discontent.[24] Worker agitation was quickly transferred to the speakers. Cook and DeLong and Levi Beardsley, another local attorney, spoke to the crowd. The immigrant work force was well represented and some speeches were made in French. Leaders ignored the moderation of a week earlier. Beardsley now called the lumbermen "Shylocks, who oppressed labor"; Cook said that the lumbermen would work their men "12 or 13 hours if they thought your muscle and bones could stand it"; and DeLong singled out Charles Hackley as one lumberman who still worked his men twelve hours. DeLong ended his impassioned speech by declaring, "I did say I would not be among you if this was a strike—but I don't care now whether it is a strike or not."[25]

The speakers exhorted a strike and encouraged the men to form a union. Shortly thereafter a vote for a strike was overwhelmingly approved by the assembly, and two separate—a skilled and nonskilled—unions organized. Two days later more than twelve hundred members had paid their dues. The *Muskegon Daily Chronicle* estimated that the strike put six thousand employees out of work. Planing mills, the boom men, sash and door factories, and other industries shut down. The link of skilled and unskilled labor was crucial to the development of political events in Muskegon. Wherever the Knights achieved political success, as they would in Muskegon, an alliance of new and old workers, skilled and unskilled, immigrants and women was inevitably necessary. The mixture provided for an accumulation and transfer of wisdom from older to younger workers.[26]

During the week, DeLong and Cook led delegations of men around the lake to close sawmills still operating. On Wednesday, October 12, after another mass meeting at Mason's Park, a delegation of six hundred men, led by a band, crossed the bridge into North Muskegon to close down the last working sawmill. Barricades were put up around the mill entrance, but DeLong and several men were permitted to go inside to talk to the men still working. The crowd outside grew restless; they stormed the sawmill. Sheriff Waters and his deputies were overrun by the strikers; the sheriff was beaten and robbed of $105. Strikers sacked part of the sawmill and succeeded quickly in shutting off the machinery. Although they closed the sawmill, violent activities turned the law and some public sympathy against the strikers.[27]

The next day the sheriff arrested several strikers and called on the governor to send two companies of state militia to Muskegon. The *Chronicle,* which to this point had supported the strike, now deplored the violence. DeLong and Cook also cautioned the men against using force to prevent others from working. The strikers then went out and serenaded the militia on its arrival. However, the presence of the militia permitted some mills to reopen.[28]

Although a delegation of workers met with the lumbermen again, neither side modified its position. Gradually, though, as early as October 15, some lumbermen began to open at ten hours. A few mill owners conceded to the demands because they had contracts to fill. Others, principally the larger operations, remained closed.

By the following week, workers were beginning to run low on money. Families had few provisions and some mill hands began to return to work regardless of hours worked. Others simply left Muskegon and headed into the woods to secure winter employment. On October 17 owners from thirty-eight mills held a meeting at the boom company and reaffirmed their intentions of running eleven-hour workdays. They created an organization of lumbermen and united in their determined opposition to resist further labor activity.[29]

Almost as quickly as it began, the strike subsided. Despite the inflammatory rhetoric, both lumbermen and sawmill workers were forced by economic necessity to compromise. DeLong's and Cook's union movement waned, and men began to go back to work. Some lumbermen ignored their pledge to abide by eleven hours, and with labor in short supply, they agreed to finish the season working ten hours. The sawing season was nearing an end and those mills with logs in their millponds had to get it cut before winter set in. Sawmill laborers wanted one more paycheck before the end of the season and they returned to work regardless of hours. The end of the 1881 season brought no victory to either side.[30]

Throughout the winter months, the frustrations over hours and working conditions in Muskegon's sawmills led the working class to pursue fairly classical evolutionary patterns in the development of class awareness. Exploitative working conditions led to anger and frustration. From this resentment evolved rallies, strikes, collective confrontations with mill owners, and trade union activity. Ultimately the worker, in the ideal pattern, developed a group consciousness that was channeled toward the political arena. Despite this apparent fit in Muskegon between the classical Marxist paradigm and the political behavior of the sawmill immigrant groups, there remained important inconsistencies.

For one, most of the sawmill workers had departed the town for winter logging work. It was difficult for the group to develop a consciousness when they were scattered throughout the north country. Political activity instead became the goal of the ten-hour movement's resident leaders. Shortly after the end of the fall strike, De-Long vacationed in the Dakotas. When he returned he began to plot his campaign for mayor. By early March, when the workers were trickling into Muskegon from the woods, DeLong announced his candidacy on the "Workingman's Ticket." He and Cook invited from Detroit the outspoken labor organizer Richard Travellick. In mid-March, Travellick, DeLong, and Cook began the campaign for the ticket and its principal platform goal, the ten-hour day.[31]

Traditional political elements in Muskegon became alarmed by the third-party movement. The Democrat and Republican organizations fused and organized a "Citizen's Ticket," represented by several

leading lumbermen and businessmen. Although it would appear that
the traditional parties had the strength, resources, and community
support to win the election, DeLong, and Cook, and Travellick
worked enthusiastically for the Workingman's party. All three were
extremely capable speakers, and they persuaded almost every returning mill worker that the ten-hour cause required political
involvement.[32]

In the April election, the Workingman's Ticket carried all four
wards in the city. DeLong defeated Loftus King for mayor by a three-
to-one majority, and the workingmen carried almost all minor offices. "Never in the history of the city," reported the *Muskegon
Chronicle*, "was there an election in which a ticket was carried by
such majorities."[33]

At a large election eve rally, DeLong, Cook, and Travellick spoke
urging the mill men to hold out in the spring for ten hours. Two
days after the victory, April 6, the ten-hour strike was rekindled.
Although the river was still clogged with ice and only a few mills
had started up production, the boom men precipitated the strike by
refusing to begin working unless ten hours were agreed on. Other
sawmill workers, likewise, quickly joined the boom men. Most of the
men were returning from the woods with their winter's pay. They
came to participate in the annual spring orgy of drunkenness and
revelry along the Sawdust Flats. Few were in the frame of mind to
submit to the lumbermen. Thus, not all the shanty boys who voted
in the spring elections evidenced a class consciousness brought on by
alienation, frustration, or anger over economic exploitation. The
movement not only had capable leadership but it began when social
and economic circumstance permitted many workers to disregard
nominal economic consequences.[34]

The lumbermen were also in a strong position. They had some
lumber left from the previous fall and could continue to fill contracts. Unwilling to concede the costs involved in implementing a
ten-hour day, the mill owners remained content to wait out the
strike. Hackley, in fact, early on envisioned a long strike.[35] To many
lumbermen the seasonal nature of cutting simply made it illogical to
concede a ten-hour day.

Negotiations began ten days after first strike action. The boom
company offered the men an eleven-hour day with a twenty-cent pay
hike. The boom men responded insisting on the ten-hour provision.
The company made no counteroffer and ignored the Workingman's
petition to continue negotiations. A few days later they rescinded all
previous offers and decided to wait things out.[36]

Out of desperation and anger the Workingman's Union now tried to close the remaining sawmills still running around the lake. The *Muskegon Chronicle* later recalled the April 24 episode:

About 250 men marched in a body from Rifenburg Hall at Terrace Street and Western Avenue to the McCracken, Hovey, and Company mill, where there was a full crew working 11 hours. Word of their coming had preceded them, so the mill owners were prepared. They had taken up about 10 feet of a bridge near the mill, piling the planks as sort of a barricade. Behind this barricade were J. B. McCracken, H. N. Hovey, A. F. Temple and others. Finally, after some parley between the two factions, a committee of five was let into the mill to talk to the workers. While their representatives were gone, the men outside grew restless, removed the barricade, and then some of them surrounded the mill while others went inside. Considerable damage was done, and the workers who could not be intimidated into striking were kicked out or knocked out. Later the Workingman's Union sent an apology for the damage done, reasserting its intention to abide by the law and respect private property. [37]

Besides the apology of the Workingman's Union, Mayor DeLong sent an official letter reminding the men that forcefully closing sawmills was unlawful, and that if they persisted, he would have to offer protection to the lumbermen. [38]

Ironically, DeLong as mayor was placed in a position of defending and protecting those whom he had been fighting against for eight months. DeLong was no radical of the new order; he represented the laboring classes but was not willing to put one class against another. Frustrated by the intransigence of the lumbermen and his own inability to effect a favorable outcome, DeLong's reform movement in Muskegon was faltering. He not only met the opposition of the lumbermen but also found members of city government against him. In early May he suspended City Attorney Andrew B. Allen, an old political opponent, and tried to unseat Alderman A. Doran who had consistently voted against DeLong and his allies on the city council. Both Allen and Doren, in retaliation, brought charges against DeLong for continuing to act as prosecuting attorney besides mayor.

DeLong resigned his seat as prosecuting attorney but was soon confronted with other charges that he solicited bribes from petty criminals in exchange for pardons. Subsequently, the governor ordered an investigation into these and other allegations. [39] Cook became the nominal leader of the strike once DeLong was preoccupied with city politics. As the strike dragged on, though, Cook was hard pressed at times to maintain order among the more militant hands.

DeLong's troubles and the violence associated with the strike caused some to turn against the strikers. The *Muskegon Chronicle*, all the time lukewarm in its support of the ten-hour movement, began to paint a negative picture of the strike's effect on the community. They warned that "capitalists were going elsewhere" and that the laboring men should get rid of DeLong and Cook. In contrast the *Muskegon Mail*, a labor journal started by Cook, said businesses that opposed the strikers should be "busted and smashed." Violent words worked against the Workingman's Union.[40]

The booming company, likewise with an insensitivity to the community, brought strikebreakers into the city and began to build "soup shanties" along the booming grounds to house them. When the crowds of strikers welcomed the first trainload of eighty workers from Toronto, the "scabs," claiming ignorance of their terms of employment, returned home. Later, though, more Canadians were imported and housed at the booming grounds without interference. By late May, 232 new workers were running the booms eleven hours a day. When crowds of workers threatened to close those few sawmills working, a platoon of well-armed Pinkertons was brought in to protect the mills. The same day that scabs arrived, Governor David Jerome visited the city to survey the situation. Sporadic incidents of violence, though, were not serious enough to warrant state troops.

On May 25 many boom men met and agreed to accept the booming company's terms. Those that could be employed were hired back on the 26th. The next day, recognizing dissolution of the strike was near, the mill owners issued a pledge that they would concede one-half hour and universally work 11-hour days instead of 11½ or 12. All men, regardless of their involvement in the strike, were promised work if they signed on by June 1. Wages would be paid semi-monthly or weekly and old hands would have priority being rehired. The lumbermen, though not fully acquiescing to the workingmen's demands, offered an attractive proposal. With the boom running full time, logs were being delivered to the millponds. The mill owners were willing to make concessions to begin processing logs.

On May 25, eight weeks after it began, the strike was over. Even when they were well organized and directed by effective leadership, the strikers could not overcome the Muskegon sawmill owners. A really effective, long-term strike in Muskegon, rather than softening the mill owners with fear for their profits and concerns for their security, would probably have resulted in many mills being closed for good. Most lumbermen would not produce in an environment where their gains were limited. They could simply pack their machinery and ship it westward. The lumber business, in the 1880s, was a competitive industry that could not become a humane system. There were too many logs, too many mills, too many machines, and too many workers.

The ten-hour strike in Muskegon never became a class struggle. Although the rhetoric and actions of the workers make it evident that there was a class awareness, the transience, divisions between boom men and laborers, and the importation of foreign laborers worked against protracted class conflict. The leadership of DeLong and Cook remained conservative. Secure in the their middle-class occupations, they sought to gradually open new avenues of class mobility. There was an easier way toward middle-class security than union militancy or class warfare.

The political, avenue was the most obvious. Cook and DeLong fortiified their base of political support through the summer of 1882. In November they allied with the Democrats to form the Democrat-Workingman's party. Cook ran for the state legislature and became the first state official ever elected in Michigan on a Workingman's ticket. In the legislature, Cook, with Thomas Barry from Saginaw, introduced the Michigan Ten-Hour Bill. Cook also was responsible for the creation of the Michigan Bureau of Labor, and introduced several other bills supportive of the laborers' cause.

DeLong was reelected mayor in 1883, and Cook became mayor in 1884.[41] The Democrat-Workingman's party effected peaceful change that charted an easier route toward social amelioration. DeLong built a new city hall and guided the construction of the city's first horse-drawn streetcars. During his term, electric street lighting was installed in Muskegon, streets were graded and paved for the first time, a new water main and lines were added to protect sawmills, and a city sewage plan inaugurated. DeLong worked hard to upgrade the city police and fire departments. When he left office in 1884, Cook as the new mayor continued the civic improvements begun by DeLong. Although taxes went up during the Workingman's years, population growth of nearly five thousand people required new expenditures. DeLong and Cook still left a surplus in the city treasury upon retirement.[42]

Years later the *Muskegon Chronicle*, having forgotten that it had once called DeLong and Cook "two shyster lawyers," acknowledged that the Workingman's officials had inaugurated the city's extensive program of civic improvements.[43] The workers' revolt in Muskegon was no social upheaval; it was a response to economic exploitation that sought redress and reform through accommodation, integration, assimilation, and orthodox party politics. It was a forerunner to that urban liberalism that used the power of government to stabilize economic life and fulfill social welfare demands.

From the strike there also emerged a new sense of community by the lumbermen. The Lumberman's Exchange, which evolved out of strike activities in early 1882, became an effective force for joint action not only to combat the strike but also to plan effectively for the city's and its primary industry's future. After successfully weathering the strike and making some concessions, the mill owners signed the agreement not to seek retribution. The following year, before Cook's ten-hour law was introduced, the lumbermen of Muskegon voluntarily went to a ten-hour day.[44] In 1883–84 the Lumberman's Exchange was reorganized as the Board of Trade. The board included not only lumbermen, but businessmen and Republican and Democratic party officials. The board began an advertising campaign to promote Muskegon as suitable for new industry. Education for the workers in the form of a manual training school and the Hackley Library became part of the program to reindustrialize Muskegon.

Evidence confirms that, despite the workers in Muskegon continuously articulating political issues, mobilizing for elections, and occupying public office, the lumbermen continued to exert a paternalistic influence throughout the community. An entrepreneurial democracy evolved in which business, industrial, and civic activity became coterminous. Many resident lumbermen remained paternalistically committed to the lumbertown. These economically dominant persons needed to be involved in local politics to protect their well-established investments. The creation of the Board of Trade, voluntary industrial associations, and evolving civic responsibility are signs of a paternalistic elite maintaining entrepreneurial democracy.[45] At the same time workers subordinated class interest to job interest and remained willing to settle strike activity democratically. Interclass relationships of varying degrees of deference were maintained in Muskegon after the strike and into the postlumber era. A cross-class community evolved that was rooted in paternalism, a large degree of resident ownership, ethnic homogeneity, and middle-class leadership in the labor movement.[46]

The strike, rather than hardening lines of class conflict in Muskegon, expanded opportunity. By 1887 subtle traces of a sense of community began to crystallize. New buildings, parks, and several new rail lines betrayed no scars of the industrial strife or primitive, transient industrial life of frontier logging days. Ethnic differences blended into a predominantly northern European complexion. Permanence, new industry, and new buildings indicated a new social-economic life-style and an energy that would soon meet new and more pressing economic issues.

"TEN HOURS OR NO SAWDUST": THE SAGINAW VALLEY, 1885

"The Great Strike in the Saginaw Valley" originated when many of the seven thousand mill hands in the valley demanded a reduction in working hours from eleven to ten per day.[47] In the spring of 1885, when the mills opened for the season, owners notified workers that wages would be twelve to twenty-five percent lower than in 1884. Wages ranged from $1.00 per day for slab pilers, lumber pilers, and other unskilled laborers to between $5.00 and $6.00 for a few foremen, sawers, or filers. All workers had averaged $1.98 per day in 1884 but were now cut to an average of $1.77 in 1885.[48] A moderate drop in the price of lumber was advanced by the mill men as justification for the wage cut.[49] When the mills opened at lower wages, all hands accepted the new scale. While accepting the new pay rate, however, workers made an effort to compensate for the wage loss by demanding a one-hour reduction in the dangerous working day. In May a "Workingman's Committee" of the Knights of Labor passed a circular among mill owners indicating that they desired a meeting with them to discuss a possible ten-hour day. Nothing resulted from the petition.[50]

In the meantime, between the spring opening of the mills and the outbreak of the strike in July, more complaints arose. About one-half of the mill hands were paid monthly. This taxed the worker's ability to budget and frequently forced him to request credit from the company store. A demand for pay twice a month encouraged other workers to join the strike. Payments of wages in store orders, though affecting only about one-fifth of the valley's mill hands, also encouraged participation. The worker's primary goal, though, was to recoup some lost wages by shortening the working day. The refusal of mill owners to discuss this goal solidified the workers and prompted strike action.

Historical opinion implies that the strike was prompted because Saginaw Valley workers misunderstood the implementation date of a new, statewide, ten-hour law.[51] In June the Michigan legislature passed a ten-hour law, which would become effective on September 15. A few valley newspapers failed to mention the implementation date. Consequently, some men assumed that it became law on July 1. This misunderstanding is perhaps overemphasized as a cause of the strike. Local labor leaders, like Thomas Barry who had co-authored the law, definitely knew of the effective date.[52] More important, they were also aware that ten-hour workdays in September, when mills would soon be closing, would provide little comfort to workers employed a full season at reduced wages. Lastly, characteristic of most nineteenth-century hour laws, the Michigan statute contained an escape clause. A contract for longer hours between employer and employee would void the ten-hour provision. Effective hour regulation, therefore, was not legislated. The worker still had to bargain individually with his employer over hours. Despite the law's shortcomings, sentiment for shorter hours had been fermenting since spring, and the owners' refusal to bargain with the workers was the key in precipitating the strike.

Strike action began in Bay City on July 6. W. B. Rouse, a mill owner, described the incident:

> My mill was closed on Monday, July 6, for the purpose of cleaning out the boilers. Some six or seven of the men who were about the mill took their dinner pails and started for home. One man took a bandana handerchief [sic] from another man's pocket, fastened it to a stick, and as they were near McEwan's mill, waived [sic] it in the air and shouted "Hurrah for ten hours." McEwan's mill was not running, some of the men not having got over the "fourth," and the others were around the mill. The shouting of the men started them going and the strike began.[53]

Throughout that day and the next, workers roamed the city closing mills. Violence erupted on July 8 when five hundred men tried to close the Rust Brothers mill and were met by the sheriff and twelve deputies. The law officers suffered cuts and bruises in their failure to halt the closure, but they managed to arrest three of the ringleaders.[54] Officers delivered the men to the city jail, whereupon the chief of police clubbed one of the prisoners. Word of this action spread through the crowd gathering outside the police station. Threats were exchanged, but peace was restored when Bay City

Mayor George H. Shearer, a sawmill owner, ordered the men released. The vengeful response of the police chief, coupled with the apparent capitulation to the strikers' demands to free the prisoners, was a turning point in the strike. Public interest and involvement rapidly increased, and the strike soon spread beyond Bay City.

Flushed with their success of the previous day, striking mill hands succeeded in closing all Bay City's mills on July 9. Upriver around the two Saginaws there was no strike action and, except for a minor "dockwollopers," or longshoremen's, strike going into its third day, all was relatively quiet. The *Saginaw Courier* reported that the Bay City strike had "no organization, no leaders. It would not spread to this city."[55]

The *Courier's* surmise that the Bay City strike lacked leadership was hasty. On the evening of July 9, the day after the jail house violence, a mass meeting was held in Bay City's Madison Park. The main speaker was D. C. Blinn, outspoken editor of Bay City's *Labor Vindicator*. From the earliest stages of the strike, Blinn was the central figure of the agitation and the driving force behind events in Bay City. A member of the Knights of Labor, Blinn was constantly in contact with workers through his paper and was seen frequently in the vanguard of crowds closing mills. He urged workers to maintain their vigilance, yet to avoid violence.

Among leading spokesmen for the workers, Blinn came closest to depicting the strike as a class struggle, a conflict that pitted the entire laboring community against the mill owners. He rejected the owners' demand that mill workers deal individually with their employers. Angered by the apparent arrogance and unwillingness of the owners to negotiate with "outsiders," Blinn called for a general strike. He urged workers "to let the millmen feed their own horses; let their wives cook their own meals. . . . Let all persons who labor quit, and see how they can get along without labor."[56]

Whether Blinn displayed a militant class consciousness or desired drastic reform of the economic system is impossible to determine from quotations in the *Labor Vindicator*.[57] Nevertheless, he remained the most outspoken agitator in Bay City, and judging by the opposition he engendered he was a leader who could upset the tranquil status quo. The Knights of Labor, who had not been officially involved in the first efforts to close the mills, rose against the editor after one of his volatile speeches and, as the Bay City sheriff later put it, "shut down on Blinn." Once repudiated by the Knights, his position as self-appointed leader diminished only slightly. His

frequent arrests and virulent attacks against this "ranting political parasite" by the conservative press attest to Blinn's persistent involvement. His popularity with laboring men remained firm
throughout the strike.[58]

Also speaking to the crowd at Madison Park was State Representative Thomas Barry of Saginaw. Barry, who had previously confined his efforts to the Saginaw "dockwollopers'" strike, now
became the recognized leader of the lumber strike in the Saginaws.
A member of the Knights of Labor and a Democratic-Greenback leg-
islator, Barry had promoted passage of the ten-hour law in June. He
was an ardent supporter of workingmen and had proposed along
with Cook and DeLong other pro-labor bills in previous legislative
sessions. Less outspoken but more widely recognized than Blinn,
Barry had come to Bay City that evening with fifty or so dockwollopers to encourage and join with striking mill hands.

The ethnic makeup of the Saginaw Valley work force was diverse
enough to make beginning collaboration difficult. The Poles, for example, were never completely welcomed in the laboring community.
Many were still remembered as strikebreakers who were imported in
1872, and in 1882 several hundred more Poles had been brought
into Bay City by McGraw as cheap labor. Nevertheless, labor exploitation appeared to have at least temporarily supplanted ethnic group
loyalties, and a form of developing class consciousness emerged, especially in Bay City. In the early stages of the strike, Polish Catholics and German Lutherans were its backbone. Blinn's appeals for
concerted action particularly attracted the Poles. They did the "lowest grade of work . . . [and] received the lowest pay." Large families,
low pay, and long hours made the Poles eager to strike back at un-
sympathetic mill owners. During the first instance of violence and
mob action, the Bay City sheriff reported, "The leaders were mostly
Polanders, who were shoved to the front by their more cunning
backers. Most of the 2,000 men meeting at Madison Park were Polanders." A Mr. Buchkowski spoke to the crowd in Polish and reminded them that most Polish laborers got only $1.00 to $1.25 per
day and worked 11-½-hour days.[59]

Arrest records bear out that Germans were likewise conspicuous
participants in the strike. German names were scattered among
committees of workers sent to negotiate with owners. Speeches
given in Polish and German at public rallies support the view that
both ethnic groups dominated the strike's earlier phases. When the

strike later spread to the Saginaws, some French Canadians also participated.[60]

These strikers were joined by another minority. Unemployed mill hands, often called "loafers and idlers", may have started the original march to close the mills on July 6. As one businessman recalled, "The first day I recognized every 'bum' and every 'drunk' that I have seen around Bay City for years." This may have been a questionable characterization, but there is little doubt there were many unemployed workers in the valley in 1885. Early in the spring, labor journals had warned that Saginaw Valley was "a good place to stay away from." But the unemployed had an interest in the strike's success. The Knights of Labor, and probably Blinn in his journal, saw the advent of the ten-hour day as providing more work for more people. The *Detroit Labor Leaf*, official state organ of the Knights, noted: "Fewer hours would relieve the pressure of the unemployed which is what keeps wages low. . . . Increased pay cannot come as long as there is a large percentage of idle men in any calling."[61]

Unemployed mill hands, however, were not "transient unemployed." Because it was seasonal, lumbering in the valley made sporadic unemployment a chronic occupational hazard. During seasons of low employment, mill owners frequently extended credit at company stores and permitted rents to fall in arrears. In 1885, when employment even during the peak season was scarce, discontent grew. Many idle and indebted mill hands joined the ten-hour movement simply in hope of securing work. This might well explain why strikers demanded ten hours in July, rather than in September when layoffs would again take place. But to characterize unemployed during the strike as "loafers and idlers who didn't care whether the mills ever ran" was an extreme distortion. These men had a vested interest in the ten-hour day and were not "tramps" occupying idle time "doing mischief."[62] Many had stakes in the community and, perhaps prematurely encouraged by the ten-hour legislation and the implementation of ten hours in Muskegon, they were disappointed when enactment in local mills was not forthcoming.

The Knights of Labor also mustered in support of the strike. They had little to do with precipitating the strike, but once mills were closed in Bay City, the Knights influenced strikers' policies. Numerical and political strength made the Knights a force to be reckoned with. Of an estimated seven thousand mill hands in the valley, three thousand were said to be Knights. The many local assemblies were attached to either of two district assemblies in Bay City and the Saginaws or to the General Assembly. Typical of less industrialized areas, the composition of each assembly varied. Records reveal that Bay City had fifteen local assemblies, including an "Iron Workers" and a "Black" LA. The rest were labeled "Laborers" with a few "Mixed" LAs. Saginaw, in contrast, had twenty LAs including a "French," "Salt Workers," "Tailors," "Longshoremen," "Furniture," "Sewing Girls," and a "Telegraph" LA. Saginaw's more diversified industrial base was reflected in the Knights' makeup.[63]

Politically, the Knights had supported many elected city officials, although it does not appear that "nearly all of the city officials in Saginaw, East Saginaw, and Bay City were members of the order."[64] The Saginaw police chief and the county sheriff were members. Actions of other officials in Saginaw and East Saginaw, however, reflected little sympathy for either strikers or Knights. In Bay City, Mayor Shearer, a lumberman, supported the strikers' efforts; four city aldermen appeared often to speak at protest meetings; the ex-marshal, Ben Fox, was an active Knight; and the city treasurer posted bail bond for D. C. Blinn when he was later arrested for strike activity.[65] Thus, though the strike was neither officially organized nor led by local chapters, individual Knights, especially in Bay City, were influential.

In contrast to actions of individual Knights, local assemblies in their official proclamations reflected the conservative position of the national organization and urged strikers to accept ten hours and reduced wages. This sense of moderation plus the wide diversity of membership may have prompted the Knights to repudiate Blinn's unofficial leadership after one of his inflammatory speeches. Nevertheless, after the first week of the strike, Bay City Knights offered to mediate the dispute between mill owners and striking mill hands, but nothing came of this proposal. In the second week of the strike, the Knights organized relief committees and opened grocery stores. They passed out rent money to strikers and, in the end, enabled the men to hold out much longer than normally would have been possible.

Thus, the strike force gathered to listen to Blinn and Barry at Madison Park on July 9 represented an amalgamation of ethnic and occupational diversity. Barry and his fifty or so dockwollopers not only added support to the mill hands but, more important, urged them to come to the two Saginaws to spread the cause of ten hours. The next morning several barges carrying between twelve hundred and eighteen hundred men headed upriver from Bay City. Banners and slogans on hats proclaimed their cause: "Ten Hours or No Sawdust." Landing at East Saginaw, the crowd was met by Barry, the striking dockwollopers, and a band. Blinn and Barry both made speeches. After a dinner break the men began closing mills throughout the Saginaws. Most of this proceeded without violence, although in one instance some workers refused to leave a mill and were stoned and clubbed, and in another strikers set upon a mill foreman and severely beat him. All afternoon Barry was hard put to maintain order, and the police forces could not prevent the closing of mills. The crowd returned to Bay City by 10 P.M.

The next day, July 11, in Bay City, tired strikers met with a delegation of sawmill owners. D. C. Blinn, chairman of the committee of mill hands, presented the owners with a list demanding that ten hours constitute a day's work, wages be the same as an eleven-hour workday, workers be paid every two weeks, and all men be reinstated without discrimination. The owners retired to discuss the matter. Three hours later they returned and rejected the workers' demands. Representatives of the lumbermen stated they would "hire anyone back at old wages and comply with the 10 hour law in September."[66]

The attitude of the lumbermen was due to their belief that "mobs, or illegal combinations of men" were preventing many who were satisfied with present wages from working and also, more significantly, because their economic position was improved by the work stoppage. Lumber piled up on the docks during the depression of 1884–85, and attempts to limit production had been unsuccessful. Now this was being effected by strikers. Sage claimed that if all valley mills would close for sixty days, "that would do great good." As long as mills remained closed and lumber grew scarce throughout the Midwest, prices for good lumber would go higher. In fact, by the end of the strike some lumber sold for five dollars more per thousand feet. Thus, Sage was able to "welcome with joy an absolute shutdown of the mills for the whole of this season—it would enable consumption to overtake production and in that way restore values of property already produced."[67]

Despite this prevailing attitude, mill owners still feared destruction, and they did not remain complacent during the first week of the strike. Owners visited local authorities and petitioned for action. Some stated that they would hold local governments responsible for property damage. Their demands were met with indifference, especially in Bay City. At a special meeting on July 10, after the sometimes violent closing of some Bay City mills, several aldermen proposed to appoint fifty more policemen. The commission rejected the proposal by a vote of nine to three. Failing to obtain public support, several Bay City mill owners hired twenty Pinkerton detectives. They arrived by early train on Saturday, July 11, "each armed with Winchester rifles and two revolvers."[68]

Appearance of the Pinkertons brought an outcry of protest in the community. The *Bay City Evening Press* insisted the private guards "were not needed unless to increase strife and irritation and prolong the strike." Bay City aldermen viewed "with regret and indignation the introduction . . . of an armed force of alien mercenaries." They requested immediate removal of "this standing menace." Intense response to the Pinkertons, coupled with a vague promise from the Knights of Labor to guard the mills, resulted in dismissal of the private guards, who departed by train on July 12.[69]

Mill owners were angered by lack of cooperation from Bay City authorities. Sage was upset by this capitulation to "mob rule." "If the Bay City authorities had not been so weakkneed," Sage insisted, "the strike would never have assumed its present proportions."[70] Doubtless the reticence of authorities arose in part from their sympathy with the strikers and from possible affiliation of some officials with the Knights. But more realistically, and despite the owners' protest of mob rule, there was little evidence of extended violence requiring private police. The Bay City sheriff stated he had seen no violence since July 8. At this point in the strike, a remarkable unity of expression sympathetic to the ten-hour movement extended even into the ranks of authority in Bay City.

In the Saginaws mill owners faced fewer obstacles in securing enough force to protect their property. Although some authorities there exhibited allegiance to the Knights, the owners retained and exercised political influence to a much greater extent than their counterparts in Bay City. Mayor Charles Benjamin of Saginaw and Mayor John W. Estabrook of East Saginaw, owner of several mills, were allies of the lumbermen. Saginaw lumbermen, moreover, made a stronger case for protection by depicting their city as being besieged by an invading army of outside agitators. Saginaw responded more readily and forcefully than did Bay City to a situation less dangerous.

After the mills were closed by invading strikers from Bay City on July 10, the mayors of both Saginaws jointly requested one hundred Pinkertons. Although Mayor Benjamin admitted he telegraphed

Pinkerton on July 12 for fifty men, the first call must have gone out earlier. The *Bay City Evening Press* reported that eighty-three Pinkertons arrived in Saginaw from Chicago on the morning of July 12. In contrast to Bay City, officials in the Saginaws swore in Pinkertons as special police.[71]

On July 11, without consulting law enforcement authorities, Benjamin also "telegraphed the Governor that [the] situation was critical and asked for aid." Governor Russell Alger told him to call on state troops stationed locally. On the following day, Mayors Benjamin and Estabrook, police commissioners, and businessmen requested the Saginaw sheriff to call four more companies of troops. Sheriff McIntyre, a member of the Knights, reported his reaction:

> They requested me to make a requisition for four companies on the spot. Some thought they should bring in a Gatling gun and preferred the Lansing Company. I refused to do it, as I did not see any necessity for it. I told them I would order the East Saginaw company to be in readiness at their armory, and would ask the Governor to have two more companies in readiness.[72]

The sheriff's insistence on calling up the East Saginaw company was no doubt motivated by his knowledge that this company was headed by a fellow Knight. The Saginaws did not acquiesce totally to the demands of lumbermen.

In their quest for support, mill owners throughout the valley found a valuable ally in Governor Russell A. Alger. A wealthy lumberman with several mills in northern Michigan and part owner of a Saginaw mill, Alger acted steadfastly in favor of his colleagues. Alger, later secretary of war during the Spanish-American War, had served in the Civil War and risen to the rank of general. As governor he had strengthened the state militia, enlarging it by six companies and equipping it with Springfield rifles. Although not blatantly anti-labor (he refused to send militia a year later to arrest a railroad strike), Alger nevertheless appeared uncompromising and prejudicial when dealing with labor unrest in the lumber industry.[73]

Alger not only sent personal representatives to the Saginaw Valley when the strike started, but also on July 14 he arrived on the scene himself. His presence and direction helped Saginaw's lumbermen resist the strike and enabled them to overcome any remaining opposition from local police officials. In East Saginaw Alger issued a proclamation prohibiting all mass meetings or "unlawful assemblage." Authorities immediately sent deputized Pinkertons to the Pe-

noyer farm where they dispersed with threats and clubs a gathering
of strikers. Four more companies of troops were called from Flint,
Port Huron, Detroit, and Alpena. On the same day, Thomas Barry
was arrested and jailed for a few hours on orders from the governor.
Moving on to Bay City in the afternoon, Alger addressed a crowd of
strikers without incident. He reiterated his proclamation prohibiting
meetings and parades. After meeting with a committee of lumbermen and local businessmen at the Fraser Hotel, the committee
emerged to request that "the sheriff call upon the Governor for suf-
ficient aid to preserve peace." Five military companies arrived in
Bay City on the following day, and Blinn was arrested and jailed for
two days.[74]

Alger's actions provided an interesting story of management-
authority cooperation to diffuse and overawe strike action. His call
for state militia appears not to have been predicated on the principle
of preventing violence; instead, it was part of a determined effort to
reopen mills and intimidate strikers. The fear of widespread violence—as a rationale for armed intervention—hardly seemed justi-
fied in the Saginaw strike. There was little evidence of violence after
the July 10 invasion to close the Saginaw mills. Most state newspapers emphasized the absence of conflict. When the troops arrived
in Bay City, Colonel Robinson of the Detroit company "saw a quiet
town and was surprised at the call up." The *Alpena Labor Journal*
observed that the "mill-owning Governor regarded himself as the
servant of a few men" and had called out "the militia for no other
purpose than to intimidate the laborers in the interest of his brother
lumber barons."[75]

As an entrepreneur the governor reflected the widely held view
that the strike was merely a temporary rupture of relations between
the employer and his labor force brought on by a few "agitators" and
"political demagogues." In his speech to workers outside Bay City's
Fraser Hotel, Alger warned them against "listening to leaders who
are stirring up strife." Militia were necessary, Alger later asserted,
because "processions of men, headed by bands of music and bearing
banners and transparencies . . . paraded the streets and worked the
people up to a pitch of intense excitement." Some local authorities,
he added, "actually sympathized with the strikers." Alger predicted
that once disorder was quieted and Blinn and Barry were jailed, "the
workers who have been misled by their leaders will go back to work,
and the mills will start up in a few days."[76]

Michigan's Bureau of Labor and Industrial Statistics final report on the strike supported Alger's views that its origins were "attached directly to a few 'professional politicians.' " Doubtless, involvement of many foreigners in the strike reconfirmed Alger's strong nativist sentiments. Branded by one historian as a "native-bred flannel-mouth," Alger saw all immigrants as "bad people of all classes and conditions." Concurrent, sometimes violent strikes in the Cleveland Iron Works and Chicago Street Railway had large, especially Polish, ethnic elements. Alger knew of the involvement of Poles in the Bay City strike and responded vigorously to his own social Darwinistic beliefs that foreign elements were conspiring to disrupt labor relations. This was not the time to remain timid in the face of strike activity "by men from a foreign state who were invading Michigan." Alger believed that show of force would quiet protest in the valley and restrain immigrant labor unrest throughout the Michigan lumber industry.[77]

To what extent were Alger's actions predicated on the threat of personal financial loss? He admitted his opposition to the ten-hour law. In response to a Detroit newspaperman's question concerning a report that Alger's own lumber companies were requesting employees to sign contacts waiving the ten-hour law, he replied: "I presume it is [a valid report]. I gave orders to have such contracts sent to our camps . . . to have them signed."[78] Thus, there was legitimate concern that the ten-hour movement, if successful in the Saginaw Valley, would spread throughout the state. The Bay City Evening Press reported on July 14: "Men in Oscoda [location of one of Alger's mills] were awaiting results in the Bay City strike prior to trying a ten-hour movement there." Aware of this possibility, lumberman Alger reminded the crowd gathered outside the Fraser Hotel that he had not made any profit the previous year. He encouraged strikers to deal individually with their employers and return to work.

Alger's statements and actions are an incisive portrayal of management response to workers' protest movements. He perceived nothing inappropriate in his use of militia to prevent success of a labor uprising that might have jeopardized his own personal holdings. When local authority failed to maintain operation of the mills, the governor determined that decisive, immediate action had to be taken. He imported troops, jailed the strike leaders, and outlawed demonstrations. Such action would force mill hands to deal individually with the lumbermen and stifle further collective efforts. Labor organization would be avoided, and as Alger observed, the strike would come to its logical conclusion: "Gradually by two's and three's the striking men will become satisfied that the laws are going to be enforced and in a few days . . . they will go back to work."[79] Thus, at public expense the governor helped repress a potentially popular labor cause. These efforts succeeded in weakening the strike effort in the Saginaws; however, Alger failed to discern the strength of community support for strikers at the other end of the river.

Alger's actions—appearing on the scene himself, calling up more troops, prohibiting mass meetings, and having strike leaders arrested—may have encouraged militancy in Bay City. His words and actions were directed more at Bay City (than Saginaw) where the governor viewed local officials as well as the strike leaders as especially troublesome.[80] As a result, after the governor's visit immigrant workers, labor, and a few radicals intensified strike action. In the long run, Alger's actions may even have prompted labor to involve itself more in Bay City politics and resist the lumbermen with greater determination.

After Alger's importation of troops, events in the valley settled into relative calm. Public support for the strikers remained strong. Attempts to open various mills failed because not enough workers appeared. Skilled sawmill workers, especially in Bay City, maintained strong allegiance to the strike. As time passed and no violence erupted, public organs and residents questioned the need for troops. By July 21, seven days after his visit, Alger withdrew the militia. Troops departed a somber Saginaw Valley "after having a good time."

As the strike dragged on, mill owners hardened in their unwillingness to negotiate a settlement. On July 23 the employers in the Saginaws met and resolved "not to open their mills until employees reject demands of labor agitators and come back at hours and wages of pre-strike days."[81] The uncompromising attitude of Saginaw lumbermen was due to the understanding that some skilled hands in the area were willing to work. These men, many of whom were forced off the job, never participated in the strike. Soon after the ultimatum of the mill owners, skilled hands met and proposed to return to work at ten hours and reduced wages. Some owners relented and several mills opened under these terms.

Saginaw lumbermen also benefited from a ready supply of five hundred unskilled laborers who had been employed by the nearby Tittabawassee Boom Company. When the strike erupted, most of the company's men did not participate. However, the boom company was forced to shut down as the mills downriver closed. Many of these men became a willing reservoir of unskilled labor once the skilled hands returned to work in the Saginaws. Near the end of July mills began to find workers willing to sign on at old hours and wages. Resolve in the Saginaws weakened and the strike effort gradually diminished.[82]

Further defections among strikers resulted from the visit of Grand Master Workman Terence Powderly. On July 29 Powderly came to Saginaw and privately urged mill hands to return to work at ten hours and old wages. The Knights believed that hour reduction was the key to increased employment and higher wages. Powderly encouraged acceptance of half a loaf. His advice apparently impressed several local assemblies, and in Saginaw, at least, more men returned to work.[83]

In Bay City, however, strikers maintained a firm posture. Skilled hands remained off the job. One effort to start up a mill with inexperienced labor ended when unskilled hands cracked a circular saw. Authorities in Bay City, moreover, remained disinclined to interfere with the strike. Consequently, more mills were kept closed through intimidation. The business community also aided the strikers. The Knights reported that "enough support had been guaranteed to provide for the poor families for 30 days at least." In late July a Polish Catholic priest and a local mill owner spoke to eight hundred workers at the Catholic church and urged the men to go back to work at eleven hours. "Only three said they would." For a while it seemed that the strike might actually succeed in Bay City. As the mills reopened in Saginaw, however, Bay City owners began to ship their logs upriver for processing. Acquiescence in the Saginaws portended failure for Bay City mill hands.[84]

In early August, as more and more mills reopened, exasperated strikers once again resorted to violence. Aside from minor acts against individuals trying to return to work, major violence had been avoided since the first week of the strike. On August 6, however, as more mills reopened in East Saginaw at eleven hours, two hundred strikers tried to shut down a newly started mill. East Saginaw police, reinforced with deputies, waded into the crowd with swinging clubs. Several mill hands were injured and five were arrested. At Bay City a smaller crowd was dispersed the next day while trying to close a mill. The most violent confrontation of the strike took place a week later when a crowd of about two hundred tried to close the Eddy Brothers mill outside Bay City. When strikers refused the sheriff's orders to disperse, the police charged. A bullet creased the sheriff's forehead, and police responded in kind, wounding three strikers. The crowd scattered. Nine men, mostly Poles, were arrested. With tension high, Bay City authorities called out the local militia, the Essexville Peninsulars, to maintain order.[85]

The affair at the Eddy Brothers mill was the last effort of a dying cause. Although some strikers held out until September, more mills reopened during August. With the strike practically defeated in the Saginaws, and Bay City operators shipping their logs to the Saginaws for processing, more Bay City mill hands, fearful of not working at all before the winter season, began to accept the lumbermen's terms. By the end of August the strike was broken. In general the mills reopened at either the old eleven-hour day or at ten hours with a corresponding pay reduction. Some mills that had reopened early at ten hours and no pay reduction now reduced wages. When the September 15 deadline for enactment of the ten-hour law arrived, more firms complied but reduced wages by one-eleventh. Sporadic strikes took place as some mill owners ignored the law or tried to force contracts circumventing the ten-hour provision. Most of these were settled quickly, and by late September the valley returned to normal. Yet, the milling season was coming to an end, and a grim winter lay ahead for many workers.

Mill hands gained little from their summer's effort. Although the ten-hour day was widespread, reduced wages undercut the original goal of recovering the spring pay reduction through fewer working hours. Ethnic cohesion in the valley remained firm, and at no time during the strike did ethnic rivalry weaken the workers' resolve. At the end, as in the beginning, "Polanders" were the backbone of the strike. Ethnic solidarity, however, failed to weaken the lumbermen. In October several owners let it be known that they would not hire immigrant labor for the coming spring.[86]

Mill owners gained most from the strike. Wages were reduced, and more important, limited output through the summer months significantly increased lumber prices. Militant labor protest was silenced, and the few remaining years of lumber production in the Saginaw Valley were relatively peaceful.

That Bay City and Saginaw had taken separate pathways in their socioeconomic development was nowhere more evident than in community response to the Great Strike in the valley. That adjacent, nearly identical communities responded so differently to the strike further defines the two different economic worlds in which Bay City and Saginaw evolved. Bay City clearly provided active, communitywide support for the strikers and was a town in which laboring classes wielded some political power. Saginaw, however, displayed attitudes less hospitable to labor and more typical of the period.

Like many dominant businessmen in small industrial towns in the Gilded Age confronted by labor conflict, Saginaw Valley lumbermen reached outside their local environments and brought in state and private militia to restore order. Individual community response to armed intervention, however, was very different. Saginaw deputized and forcefully used the Pinkertons and also requested more aid from state troops. Bay City's aldermen, in contrast, voted to remove Pinkertons and did not request state aid until Governor Alger arrived in that community more than a week after the strike began. Without the governor's firm action it is unlikely that Bay City lumbermen would have found much local political support for efforts to overcome strikers. Thus, the way the two communities responded to limit the lumbermen's freedom of action says much about the political power that workers had achieved in these mill towns.

There is little doubt that mill hands participated successfully in the local politics of the Saginaw Valley. Workers in all towns elected their representatives to office, yet they were more successful in Bay City than in the Saginaws. The political influences of the workers and the contrasting community responses to the strike can be explained by dissimilarities in the social and economic structure of the communities. Saginaw and East Saginaw had a more diversified industrial structure than Bay City. The chief industry was lumber, but other enterprises such as coal mining, railroads, machine shops, breweries, and farming employed skilled and unskilled laborers. Occupational diversification moderated community support for strikers and prevented development of communitywide antipathy toward mill owners. There was less absentee ownership of sawmills than in Bay City. Sixty-five percent of the mill owners lived in Saginaw and many were active in local affairs. Such involvement enabled mill owners to maintain economic and political support from small businessmen, shopkeepers, and professionals of the community.

In Bay City absentee owners—about sixty percent of the lumbermen—caused shopkeepers, who were heavily dependent on mill hands for business, considerable distress by their willingness to keep mills idle for sixty days. They saw little sense of community responsibility being exercised by the lumber barons. Consequently, throughout the strike they supported the workers by donating provisions and offering to arbitrate settlements favorable to labor.

Local newspapers in these communities followed a similar pattern. Several of Bay City's journals, the *Evening Press*, the *Bay City Tribune*, and the *Courier*, reflected communitywide sympathy for strikers and frequently castigated mill owners for their arrogance and tactics. Bay City also supported Blinn's outspoken, pro-labor sheet, the *Labor Vindicator*. In the Saginaws the press was much less sympathetic toward the strikers' cause. The *Saginaw Courier* consistently emphasized the violence surrounding the strike and approved of the owners' request for state militia. Barry was so dissatisfied with the *Courier's* "misrepresentation" of the facts that he urged mill hands to boycott the paper. Likewise, the *Saginaw Evening News* drew labor's wrath for "coloring matters to the disadvantage of the strikers."[87] In a large way, the economic structure and the ideology of many residents, neither workers nor lumbermen, shaped the behavior of those citizens confronted by industrial conflict.

There may have been yet another reason, especially in Bay City, for widespread support of the workers. By 1885 the Saginaw Valley and its hinterland had been largely depleted of its timber supply. Mills in the valley continued to operate by shipping in logs from northern Michigan and Canada. As costs for shipping continued to rise and as mills nearer the timber supply competed for logs, it was obvious that the valley's mills could not remain open for many more years. Closure of the mills would devastate the area's economy. This possibility influenced community antipathy toward the mill owners, especially toward those who did not live in the locality. The high rate of absentee ownership in Bay City, coupled with its lack of industrial diversification, intensified workers' feelings of hostility and insecurity. At the height of the strike, absentee owner Sage threatened to close his "mill and all business there and not resume it" unless something was done to control the "rule of mobs."[88] Such intimidation could do little but influence community attitudes against the lumbermen.

The Saginaws, although also facing an inevitable decline of lumbering, demonstrated less support for strikers because of their industrial diversification and the more extensive community involvement of lumbermen. Fewer absentee owners and because several lumbermen diversified reaffirmed the belief that some Saginaw mill owners were aware that successful economic endeavors must be coupled with community stability. This sense of community responsibility might explain in part why Saginaw lumbermen and newspapers took exception to the closing of their mills by an army of invading mill hands. It also suggests why laborers could not claim as much political power in the Saginaws as they had in Bay City.

CONCLUSION

On the surface, the ten-hour strikes may be seen as comparable— taking place in communities sharing similar economic relationships; however, the social, ideological, and to a lesser extent, industrial structures of the three lumbertowns were profoundly different. Bay City maintained community support for the workers' cause because many elements of society, relying on definite lines of economic and social relations rejected the exploitative values of the mill owners. Bay City mill hands influenced local politics and garnered public, entrepreneurial, and journalistic support in their struggle against the owners. Here the lumbermen's power was not absolute. They could not overwhelm politically or legally the power of local government nor could they manipulate public opinion to their advantage. A declining mill town saw little reward in supporting absentee lumbermen already investing in distant timber frontiers. Yet, by the time the community expressed its sympathy for the workers, it was too late to affect the established patterns of industrial capitalism.

Economic exploitation had not only produced a high degree of class awareness but also a degree of ethnic consciousness in Bay City. When the strike was over, the approaching end of the logging era forced the workers into submission. If they persisted in their demands, as Sage threatened, absentee lumbermen would simply move on. As a result, in the few remaining years of prosperity, sawmill workers withdrew and insulated themselves from further contact with the dominant group of lumbermen. Ethnic group loyalties remained strong, brought on by social Darwinistic prejudice and discrimination. The Poles and French, and to a lesser extent, the Germans remained isolated ethnically and withdrew into enclaves that were geographically separate. Class loyalties were relegated to a sense of ethnic consciousness. Ethnic group loyalties and rivalries prevented the emergence of political beliefs based solely on class allegiances.

Still, ethnicity and class were often asserted simultaneously into political life.[89] Even when, as perhaps with Bay City, aspects of ethnic identity were politically dominant, socioeconomic influences could also be important in local politics. After the demise of the Knights of Labor following the Haymarket bombing in 1886, the politics of the workingmen in Bay City blended back into the regular parties of tradition. Ethnicity and class, though, continued to shape the lives of Bay City workers, often in contradictory ways. Immigrant wards and social differences militated against class mobilization in trade unions or radical political parties. Ethnic divisions coupled with the struggling economy in the postlumber era intensified rivalries between people who shared many of the same problems. Subsequently, insularity and separation of the three immigrant communities in Bay City limited immigrant working-class influence over local political and economic issues.

Likewise, the middle-class labor leadership in Bay City did not persist beyond the strike stage as it did in Muskegon. Thomas Barry remained an active Knight and became a member of the General Executive Board in Philadelphia. Though he remained a resident of East Saginaw, his immediate interest was national, and his energies were soon to be caught up in his struggle with Powderly. D. C. Blinn's socialist newspaper soon disappeared from Bay City as it failed to articulate the views of a declining, disappointed, and largely foreign labor movement. Without leadership, the short-lived labor movement in Bay City never regained the drive and cohesion brought on by the strike, and it could not transfer its organization successfully into political activity.

The lack of leadership and ethnic rivalries prevented the creation of unified approaches to community improvements. Bay City became bogged down in ward politics where individual ethnic groups were more concerned with the politics of status. They came to represent a public difficult to mobilize for the "greater" community aims found in policies directed toward community growth and expanded urban amenities. The economic elites offered no leadership either; they remained only as memories enshrined in street names and a few monuments. Bay City faced a bleak future.

The Saginaws were beyond staging legitimate community protest against lumbermen. Imaginative lumbermen-entrepreneurs had acted early to diversify their economic interests in the community before the timber supplies gave out. Thus industrial diversification largely prevented wide-scale community participation in the lumber strike.

Mill owners had not relinquished their ability to influence public opinion, and there was only passive sympathy for the strikers' cause. Although workers did exercise some political power, they could not modify the owners' efforts to restrain the strike.

Saginaw, because of an ambitious employer class and some industrial and agricultural diversification, had reached the "take-off" point toward becoming an urban center. By 1885 Saginaw City and East Saginaw, which were soon to be incorporated into one community, reflected the social environment of larger American cities. Citizens of the Saginaws displayed a characteristically impersonal disconcern for strikers and evidenced a more complicated existence. Thus, lumbermen in the Saginaws enjoyed greater freedom of action and more community support in their efforts to resist demands of mill hands.

Saginaw's ethnic consciousness never matched Bay City's, a city of fewer immigrants but with a large German population. Ethnics in Saginaw never experienced the discrimination nor isolation evident in its downriver neighbor. The Germans worked to secure political representation, and participated with the lumbermen in directing Saginaw into the postlumber era. Class or ethnic awareness never dominated local politics. But, most important, Saginaw's founding families remained prominent in the management of the town and its industries. Their desire to control their environment kept talent involved in local politics and urban improvements.

Ethnic consciousness never characterized economic strife in Muskegon. The city offered a homogeneous ethnic construct of Germans, Dutch, and Scandinavians. The French, who came as strikebreakers, remained isolated and largely transient. Many never considered Muskegon a permanent residence. In contrast to foreignborn in Bay City, the Dutch in Muskegon entered into civic life more as individuals than as ethnic spokesmen. Many gradually became prominent among the business elites. The Dutch and Scandinavians developed civic pride and a concern for the amenities of urban life. More important, during the ten-hour movement, the working class enjoyed intelligent and trained leadership. DeLong and Cook were elected officials who, despite their early rhetoric, eschewed radical, class-conscious solutions to economic exploitation. They participated in the traditional political structure and left a legacy that prepared Muskegon for the postlumber era.

The leadership of DeLong and Cook interacted well with the economic leadership of Muskegon's lumbermen. Although they were at odds politically, both factions cooperated often enough that Muskegon's path toward postlumber era readjustment was not obstructed by ward politics, ethnic rivalries, or intense class antagonisms. This amalgamation of class and leadership created a pattern of stability that prepared Muskegon to weather the storms of the postlumber era.

The experiences of Saginaw and Muskegon are like generalizations made about the labor situation in several other nineteenth-century industrial settlements. Throughout the strike, the press, much of the business community, and city government (even in Muskegon where DeLong and Cook ruled) maintained a deference to the lumbermen and their sawmills. Concessions by the lumbermen were important meliorative acts that restored relative calm but never permitted the laborers to break the shackles of social control that directed their lives. The most important factor, especially in Muskegon, that transformed a conflict potentially dangerous to the lumbermen was electoral politics. Local politics came to be coequal with the formation of unions as a method to redress worker grievances. Nowhere, perhaps, was this more true than in Muskegon. The rise into city officialdom of individuals like DeLong and Cook convinced wage earners that working-class representatives could gain power and respect. This legitimized the existing political system and enabled the working class to improve conditions without militant unionization.[90]

In Saginaw the ruling oligarchy was not static. The economic and social structure generally permitted the many resident lumbermen to have contact and communication with the local citizenry through churches, voluntary organizations, and unions of skilled workers. Moreover, a homogeneous population does not encourage a high level of political participation. The eruption brought on by the strike was only temporary and only slightly dented local oligarchic structures. The Saginaw lumbermen remained responsive to community demands, though they were not necessarily pressed, despite the strike, by ethnic or social classes to implement drastic change.[91]

The many foreign-born workers in Bay City created a heterogeneous population that was less likely to acclimate itself to the established political culture of the city. The militancy of the strike activity in Bay City might well have materialized because socialization in support of the political system was weakest. As a result, the sharper the ethnic cleavage, the more competitive the local party structure and higher the level of political participation in splinter, fusion, or (as in Bay City) geographical isolated groups. Thus, ethnic political enclaves developed in Bay City where immigrant workers shared experiences and found refuge from unemployment, poverty, and the pitfalls of industrialized life in America. "Community" came as territorial concentration. Progress was reflected in localized social and political organizations and not in citywide promotion, or social or economic integration. Politics in Bay City became the politics of redistribution of municipal resources; and ethnic cultural activities became the focus of community in contrast to the past when labor and class activities once had been, though briefly, the center point.

Lumbering camp of Hackley and Hume near Harrison, Michigan. Hackley and Hume employed over three hundred loggers by the mid-1880s. The mess barrels supplied pork, flour, dried beef, and lard for the cook. (Courtesy of the Muskegon County Museum.)

Shanty boys on the Muskegon River in the 1880s. Rafts, or wanigans, were the living quarters for men on spring log drives. Various firms were responsible for keeping the logs flowing freely over a designated stretch of the river. (Courtesy of the Muskegon County Museum.)

At the cataract, three miles above Big Rapids, during the last big log drive on the Muskegon River in 1887. Scenes like this were common along the Muskegon and Tittabawassee rivers every spring between 1865 and 1890. (Courtesy of the Muskegon County Museum.)

The Muskegon Booming Company's sorting grounds south of the causeway. Men using pike poles sorted logs according to their individual end log marks into booming enclosures. From the boom logs were later rafted to the sawmills. (Courtesy of the Muskegon County Museum.)

George J. Tillotson's sawmill and crew, 1888. Tillotson's mill was medium sized and cut about seventeen million board feet annually. (Courtesy of the Muskegon County Museum.)

The Beidler Manufacturing Company. Jacob and Henry Beidler built this mill in 1871. It shut down in 1886. (Courtesy of the Muskegon County Museum.)

Inspectors, or tallymen, who checked and measured all the lumber loaded or unloaded on sawmill docks in Muskegon. (Courtesy of the Muskegon Count Museum.)

Western Avenue, looking east from First Street. Town boosterism became a conscious, aggressive, and collective town strategy in the post–white pine era. (Courtesy of the Muskegon County Museum.)

The Muskegon Opera House, at Western Avenue and Second Street, in 1897. Originally the Temperance Reform Opera House, it was built by Muskegon lumbermen as a direct result of the red ribbon temperance crusade in 1877. The Opera House late became the Grand Theater, then the Elks Temple. (Courtesy of the Muskegon County Museum.)

Muskegon's first fire department, in front of the railroad depot on Ottawa Street in 1874. The most important city service in the lumbertowns' early years was fire protection. Because of wooden buildings and huge piles of pine lumber and sawdust, fires occurred frequently and spread rapidly. (Courtesy of the Muskegon County Museum.)

The burned district along Pine Street at Webster following the fire of March, 1887. A second fire in 1891 swept up Pine Street and destroyed seventeen city blocks and 250 buildings. (Courtesy of the Muskegon County Museum.)

Charles Hackley's house. The house was built for $50,000 and shared a large corner lot and carriage house with Thomas Hume's residence next door. (Courtesy of the Muskegon County Museum.)

Sawmill workers in Muskegon in front of a boardinghouse or bunk house. Workers' wives are in the second story windows. Boardinghouses were dirty and poorly maintained, making them unpopular places to live. Only the most transient workers resided in these quarters. (Courtesy of the Muskegon County Museum.)

Bridge Street boardinghouse where the town water pump was once located. This boardinghouse was also a saloon where mill men drank. The establishment was operated by Mrs. Peter Grossman (*in upstairs window*). (Courtesy of the Muskegon County Museum.)

Members of Carpenters and Joiners Union Local No. 100, Labor Day, (September 4, 1899) on the steps of the Courthouse, Terrace Street. (Courtesy of the Muskegon County Museum.)

Charles Hackley. This portrait hangs in the Hackley Library in Muskegon. (Courtesy of the Muskegon County Museum.)

Thomas Hume, December 26, 1917. He emigrated from Ireland in 1870 and in 1872 was hired as Hackley's bookkeeper. In 1881 he joined Hackley as a partner. (Courtesy of the Muskegon County Museum.)

CHAPTER EIGHT

End of the White Pine Era

One can ride through the heart of the pine country from Manistee on the west to Saginaw on the east, and see . . . miles upon miles of stumps. . . . The large operators have gone out of business or have shifted the scene of their operations to the forest of the Southern states or the Pacific Northwest.

— ARBOR DAY ADDRESS BY PROFESSOR A. A. CROZIER,
1896

The evolution of mankind has proved that human settlements . . . can have a better future if there are leaders who believe in the possibility of creating a future and convince others to follow them.

— CONSTANTINOS A. DOXIADIS, *Emergence and Growth of an Urban Region*

After the turmoil of the strikes had passed, it seemed that industrial conflict lost its sense of urgency and momentum in the lumbertowns. The class struggle itself never materialized. It failed not because industrialists acquired virtue or because significant social changes took place; instead, it diminished when the labor movement in Saginaw and Muskegon moderated and workers in Bay City lapsed into residential enclaves and ethnic consciousness. More important, industrial conflict dissipated when there was nothing left to cut. Exhausted timber supplies portended economic calamity for the lumbertowns. In this regard the ten-hour strikes represented more than ephemeral crises; they were an end and also a beginning.

The deluge began in the late 1880s. To the amazement of many the pine had suddenly vanished. Once again, as they had years earlier, the logging towns were faced with making a determined effort at the end of the white pine era to sustain "community progress." As viewed by economic historians, community progress is simply the ability of a town to effect population growth and continuous business and economic expansion. The lumber settlements had grown from small towns to industrial cities. The struggle, according to definition, should continue: most cities would be urban and metropolitan trading centers if they could. By the end of the nineteenth century these three lumbertowns, which had been shaped by the lumber era, were suddenly compelled to redirect themselves. The future was uncharted, yet courage, wisdom, fortitude, and good fortune enabled discouraged and nearly devastated communities to plot differing courses of economic recovery. What actions were undertaken by individual lumbermen, community, and government to sustain and stimulate local economies? Did lumbermen-entrepreneurs pursue an "adaptive response" or a "creative response" to profound changes in economic conditions.[1] The answer to these questions makes it clear why Muskegon and Saginaw could initiate rates of economic recovery that propelled them to heights unknown even during the halcyon lumber era, and why Bay City procrastinated and languished in the economic doldrums.

At the end of the white pine era it should be remembered that the lumbertowns' consciousness was not as responsive as it might be to similar, modern-day economic contractions. In all communities except Muskegon, the downturn was gradual and the subsequent occupational and entrepreneurial dislocation largely unnoticed. Lumbermen, even during the boom years, suffered bankruptcy and were forever opening and closing mills in the logging centers. The philosophy of "cutting all you can, cutting it as fast as you can, and moving on" was an accepted economic practice born in the woodlands of the Eastern seaboard.[2] Absentee ownership was not intrinsically irresponsible; it was simply an unfortunate aspect of nineteenth-century exploitative economic notions. Workers, too, did not expect much of the boomtowns. Sporadic and frequent unemployment was inherent in the lumber business. Transience did not encourage workers to establish roots in the lumbertowns. As the mills closed, many mill hands expected to move on to Western or Southern timberlands. The transient and exploitative nature of the business made it difficult to realize, let alone assert a willingness to counteract, economic decline. In the light of prevalent nineteenth-century attitudes, it is even more remarkable that Saginaw, Muskegon, and Bay City endured.

The Decline of Lumbering, 1888–1895

With the closing of the sawmills, Saginaw, Muskegon, and Bay City were threatened with the fate that had already overtaken many smaller lumbering towns: a nearly complete collapse of industry and commerce. Sawmills began to close in all the communities in the late eighties. By 1896 Muskegon had only three mills remaining. Saginaw and Bay City lost nearly one-half of their mills in the 1890s, though the attrition rate was not as precipitous as Muskegon's because of imported Canadian logs and the switch of some plants to hardwood manufacturing. By 1900 Saginaw had about eighteen mills remaining and Bay City twenty.

Each logging community evidenced demographic changes that varied in time from place to place, but by the early twentieth century all three towns experienced significant population decreases. Saginaw lost about four thousand people in the 1890s, or ten percent of its population. Bay City, near the mouth of the Saginaw Bay, subsisted on Canadian logs and fishing. It experienced only one-half of the population loss of its rival city up the Saginaw River, or roughly five percent. Muskegon's population fell from twenty-four thousand to eighteen thousand between 1888 and 1896, or a phenomenal twenty-five percent.

The first to leave were the lumber barons. Loggers, mill managers, and sawmill workers followed; they left the communities for other timber areas. Muskegon was the most seriously crippled of the lumbertowns. Once the timber was cut along the Muskegon River and its tributaries, there was no other source for logs. Production peaked in 1887, but already several sawmills were, according to contemporary speculation, "sold to the insurance companies." These sawmills were consumed by fires that appeared to be of "incendiary origin." The first to burn was the Eldred mill in 1885. Eighty men were thrown out of work and $40,000 lost; $30,000 was covered by insurance. In 1886, the old Farr mill, the East Shore Lumber Company, and the Beaudry mill were destroyed. In the next three years several more sawmills were consumed: the old Thayer mill, the Shippy shingle mill, and Dayton Manufacturing. A total of 13 sawmills burned in these years. The earliest mills that were closed due to fire—the Eldred mill, the Farr mill, the Beaudry mill, and the Thayer mill—were all owned by absentee lumbermen. While no one has ever proven arson by sawmill owners, it was a commonly accepted belief that many lumbermen facilitated removal and record keeping by burning their sawmills. Insurance companies began to contest payments in Muskegon by 1888 and afterwards fewer fires occurred, but the closings nonetheless continued.[3] Though resident lumbermen in Muskegon were often the last to close their mills, the death knell of the lumber era arrived in 1894 when the Hackley and Hume and the McGraft mills closed.

When the forests were cleared of pine along the Lake Huron shore, the big operators in Saginaw and Bay City also began to abandon the settlements in the late eighties and early nineties. An attempt to keep going was made by several mill owners who rafted logs across Lake Huron from Canada. The Canadian government, though, stopped this practice in 1894 by declaring that logs cut in Canada must be processed there.[4] Several remaining Saginaw firms now moved to Canada. The C. K. Eddy Company went to Blind River, Ontario, in 1893, as did Ralph Loveland, Benjamin Webster, and Wells and Stone in the early nineties. Mershon, Burt, and W. S. Grant all moved their operations west and expanded into copper and iron mining. However, many of these lumbermen and others who invested in timberlands in the South and West remained Saginaw residents. Arthur Eddy, Webster, Stone, Mershon, Burt, and others continued to direct their new operations from their hometown.

In Bay City, the out-migration began early; between 1884 and 1890 the population decreased by fifteen hundred people. Although its population loss began earlier, Bay City's demise was not as precipitous as Saginaw's or Muskegon's. The importation of Canadian logs, the hardwood industry, and fishing enabled Bay City to experience a less traumatic response to the closing of the mills. But large-scale, absentee owners never participated in the diversification to hardwood or wood specialization. The S. J. Murphy mill burned in 1884 and then shifted operations to Green Bay. McGraw's mill (Birdsall and Barker), the largest Bay City firm, was destroyed by fire in 1884 and moved its business to Wausau, Wisconsin. The McCormick brothers moved to Duluth; A. Chesbrough shifted operations to the Upper Peninsula. Sage closed his operations in West Bay City in 1892 and invested in southern pinelands. Resident owners, the Eddys, Moulthrop, and Jackson shifted operations to the Georgian Bay region of Canada.

When the lumbermen moved on, others soon followed the trek westward. Much of the migration involved young, single men, always a transient element in the lumbertowns. The movement of some ethnic groups likewise affected the demographic composition of the cities. The French Canadians were the first to leave and follow the logs. In Bay City the Canadian population shrank to twenty-five percent of the total. In Saginaw, where the French Canadians experienced more stability, the percentage changed little (twenty-two percent in 1900).[5] The Poles in Bay City, some of whom had been ostracized by mill owners after the ten-hour strike, moved into woodworking industries, and sugar beet work; some left for farms in the northern cutover. The Bousfield Woodenware Company in south Bay City employed many Polish workers who had formerly worked for McGraw's nearby sawmill. The Polish population, because of home ownership, remained fairly stable through the 1890s and resumed growth by the turn of the century (seventeen percent of the city's population in 1900). The German populations persisted, although a study of residences in Bay City and Saginaw indicates that the Germans began to spread throughout the city and into new, outlying districts.[6] In Muskegon many Dutch and Scandinavians who had become homeowners like the Poles in Bay City chose to remain and seek other careers as businessmen, woodworkers, and furniture factory employees. However, the French in Pickettown and Bluffton moved out. By the turn of the century, foreign-born and those of French parentage represented less than seventeen percent of Muskegon's population. Blacks in all three towns, who had secured steady employment during the lumber era as barbers, waiters, and laborers in the sawmills, were forced from these positions by competing white workers.[7]

The closing of the lumber mills also changed the appearance of the communities. Shipping facilities along the waterways fell into disuse. Abandoned sawmills and burned-out ruins gradually deteriorated. Lumber docks began to decay and soon much of the shoreline along Muskegon Lake and the Saginaw River presented a desolate scene of abandonment and ruin. Squatters moved into river or lake shanty towns. New industries often located away from the waterways and closer to the rail lines running into the cities.

Homes and boardinghouses near the closed sawmills became vacant as mill workers moved and company housing closed down. Little or no effort was made to keep property in repair, and a good deal reverted to the county for nonpayment of taxes. Some stranded homeowners remained along with a few renters of little means in the blighted areas. Property values declined and people could not sell their homes near the sawmills.[8]

The physical appearance of the commercial districts likewise became blighted. Public improvements were neglected; old wooden sidewalks decayed and little effort was made to pave sawdust or wooden streets. In Bay City, the citizens voted down a bond issue in 1888 to buy a commercial street-lighting plant. Once the decline set in, commercial functions and their locations likewise changed. Company-owned stores near the sawmills closed and no longer dominated the commercial field. Chain stores, catering to a population of more limited means, moved in. The infamous hellholes in the sawdust districts, drinking establishments, and restaurants became vacant. In time the buildings were replaced or remodeled to serve new retail establishments. The lumber business could not even find local markets as home construction and repair nearly ceased in the former boomtowns.[9]

To add to the physical malaise, all three communities suffered devastating fires in the 1890s. In May 1891 a fire swept along Pine Street in downtown Muskegon reducing seventeen city blocks and 150 buildings. Hundreds were left homeless and businesses destroyed. A year later, in June, Bay City's south-end residential area was consumed by a fire that left thirteen hundred persons homeless and about forty blocks burned. One year later, in May 1893, Saginaw's east side was engulfed in a conflagration that destroyed a thirty-block area, consumed 239 homes, and left eight-hundred persons homeless. The fires destroyed businesses and sawmills. Many made no effort to rebuild. Instead, they joined the exodus determined to seek employment in more prosperous cities.[10]

POLITICAL READJUSTMENTS

By the summer of the depression year 1894 the lumbertowns were no longer the burgeoning industrial settlements that they had been five years earlier. In that year the remaining factories were smokeless. There were no longer throngs of immigrants crowding the streets or milling about outside the sawmills seeking employment. There were fewer skilled carpenters in the woodworking plants. Many of the brine wells had shut down and Saginaw had to import salt. There were no clusters of men and women talking eagerly, excitedly about the future.

Yet economic gloom was not all pervasive. There were men of vision, especially in Muskegon and Saginaw, who had already begun to fan the coals of optimism. Economic and political leaders in these towns proved equal to the need to reorient themselves; by 1900 a relatively diversified commercial and industrial economic base had emerged in Saginaw and Muskegon. There were several reason for the success these communities experienced in the transition period: rail and water connections; the availability of prime manufacturing sites as centrally located sawmills closed; expanding agriculture in the area; the presence of skilled laborers; and, most important, considerable local capital for investment and the political will to develop public policy to effect economic revitalization.

All three lumbertowns' social and economic institutions were relatively well developed before the lumber era had ended. Each lumbertown also had enough capital to survive. However, the difference between successful reindustrialization and stagnation—between Saginaw-Muskegon and Bay City—rested with the dedicated citizens and economic elites who became concerned with how they might contribute to the well-being of their community's future.

These economic decisions were not made in a vacuum. Political structures had to respond to the lumbertowns' needs to develop a more complex, diversified economy. The lumber elites, to redirect their city's economy, sought municipal fiscal policy that facilitated and abated industrial redevelopment. To rebuild the lumbertowns, public financing as well as personal investments were necessary, and local government had to be willing to support a variety of policies regarding economic development. The city council and mayor could not merely confine themselves exclusively to caretaker policies.

Political changes that took place after the ten-hour strikes—the restoration of serenity and balance in politics—often aided reindustrialization. Where turmoil and turnover persisted, political heat obstructed economic development. In Muskegon and Saginaw the lumber oligarchy continued to dominate politics to protect their investments and guide reconstruction. As long as their investments were fixed, resident lumbermen in these towns were determined that local policies be directed by individuals who remained sympathetic to a lumber products–based economy. Though their commitment to community remained, they also became anxious to broaden Muskegon's and Saginaw's economic base as lumbering eventually declined. Among these leaders, it mattered little if elected officials were lumbermen, industrialists, or businessmen, for in a city where lumbering was paramount, everyone generally acted to protect the lumberman's interest.

In Bay City, the mobility of the lumberman and his capital discouraged widely diversified feeder industries. When diversification did take place, it was ordinarily narrowly within a lumber products–based economy. Primary investment capital went elsewhere. Both resident and absentee mill owners were aloof to city needs and took little interest in political events. Instead, in a city with such a large, concentrated immigrant population, there was considerable turmoil and turnover in the city political arena. Neither economic elites nor political factions envisioned city-building policies for Bay City.

In the postlumber era, all three lumbertowns maintained a relatively simple political structure. They had mayor-council forms of government with the mayor elected at large and having modest powers aside from the authority to make appointments. Aldermen were elected from wards, usually two per ward, for two-year terms. The mayor in Bay City was elected for a two-year term. In the Saginaws and Muskegon the mayor served only a year. The Saginaws continued this practice until they were united in 1889; Muskegon did not change to a two-year term until a new charter went into effect after World War I. In all three lumbertowns, as in most Midwestern cities, city governments did not practice effective long-range planning or rationalize municipal procedures. Not until the early twentieth century, with the shift to a more diversified economy and population stability, did the cities recognize the need for fiscal responsibility and professional management.

In Muskegon the progressive leadership of DeLong and Cook initiated municipal reform. Following the challenge of the Workingman's party, 1882–84, the lumbermen accepted political responsibility and reemerged to dominate city politics. After Cook's term of office, Republican businessman S. H. Stevens regained the mayor's office in 1885. Although an alliance ticket, the Workingman-Democrat, took city hall in 1886, for the next ten years lumbermen often held the top city office. Lumberman John Torrent served three terms (1887, 1888, 1892). James Gow (1893), Newcomb McGraft (1894) and A. F. Temple (1897), all prominent lumbermen, were also elected mayor. Even in their few losing efforts, the Republicans consistently nominated lumbermen like Torrent and Thomas Hume. The only Democrat who could crack the lumbermen's political oligarchy was the popular Dutch businessman Martin Waalkes (1889 and 1890). A relatively small cast of people were overtly concerned with being, or wanting to be, mayor in Muskegon.

Throughout the last decade and a half of the nineteenth century, the Republican or Democratic parties won every major election; after the Workingman's party's effort of 1886, there were never any serious third-party movements in Muskegon. The Workingman periodically fused with the Democrats in the late 1880s, or at other times ran separate tickets for minor offices. A People's party appeared as a minor third party in 1892 and tried with little success to mount a challenge to the lumber oligarchy. Reform waves also periodically appeared. A vocal Temperance Ticket ran in 1884, and although it failed to capture any political offices, the Republicans maintained that it divided their votes and cost them the election that year. Nevertheless, fusion or mass third party movements never seriously disrupted Muskegon politics during the postlumber era. The two major parties firmly controlled city politics, and as permanent structures they inevitably developed a sense of responsibility in city affairs.[11]

Lumbermen were spurred toward political involvement as soon as they began to make serious efforts—in 1883 with the formation of the Board of Trade—to diversify the city's economy. Though the lumber industry in Muskegon was not immobile and several lumbermen left to move to the South and western Great Lakes, many lumbermen-entrepreneurs viewed Muskegon as their hometown. Even if individuals like Hackley, Hume, Torrent, and McGraft chose to make investments elsewhere, they also continued to make local investments; and, as long as some of their investments remained in the community, they were unwilling for local policies to be determined by other people with less stake in the development of the community. Unlike other lumbertowns where the oligarchy may have persisted because of limited reinvestment options, Muskegon's barons had a sentimental attachment to hometown.[12] Their efforts to revitalize the community—their philanthropic and industrial contributions—were recognized by the town's citizens who often supported the lumbermen and their endeavors in popular referenda. Thus Muskegon's politics were relatively free of rancor and rowdiness. Mayors were often reelected and politics, despite ongoing economic readjustments, often remained docile enough that the Muskegon newspapers noted light voter turnouts.[13]

It is not surprising then that the most striking characteristic of Muskegon's municipal politics was the mayors' and city councils' willingness to employ a variety of policies regarding economic development and not confine themselves exclusively to caretaker policies.

One of the first significant economic development policies was the McGraft Park Fund, a city project in 1893 to raise $200,000 to finance new industrial development along the lakefront. In a sense the bonding issues, approved by the voters 2,093 to 367, set a precedent: though private groups—in this case the Chamber of Commerce—might initiate, own, or manage improvements, city government was expected to cooperate by providing money and moral support.[14] Since there was such overlap in personnel among lumbermen and commercial, industrial, and political leaders, this kind of cooperation was rarely challenged. The city council and voters were, for the most part, eager to provide business leaders with the financial support needed to upgrade public facilities to attract new industries. In 1890, 1892, and 1893 the voters overwhelmingly approved bonding issues for a new water supply, new roads, and new industries. Throughout the era, lumbermen-entrepreneurs boosted the city by vigorously attracting new businesses and manufacturers, and they inevitably did so with considerable public and governmental support.[15]

Public policy, though, of this sort was not without its critics. Mayor Waalkes ignored for two years lumbermen McGraft's efforts to involve the city in a bonding issue for new industries. Waalkes argued that low taxes were what attracted industry and that a city would never have low taxes with bonus payments. Others argued that money spent on schools, libraries, parks, and hospitals would make Muskegon a desirable city, and that manufacturers would come without special incentives. And because expenditures were offered at the time that the lumber industry was collapsing, there was even less money for caretaker policies in the late 1880s.[16]

To avoid neglecting the city, the lumbermen of Muskegon took much of the financial burden for reindustrialization and building city amenities upon themselves. They subsidized one-half of the first bonus fund, and Hume, McGraft, and Hackley built Muskegon's hospital, library, parks, and schools. Thus Muskegon avoided becoming over-bonded, and the city could fulfill caretaker responsibilities above minimal levels.

Participatory municipal government in Muskegon also created opportunities for labor and immigrants to be elected to public office. The ward system especially permitted the dominant class or status interest of each area to elect aldermen to the city council, and here they had a definite presence and even, at times—like the election of Mayor Waalkes—some political power. Yet, during the collapsing years of the lumber business, labor never mobilized itself or its allies to effect its political-economic goals. The best the workingmen could do after 1885 was to nominate a few fusion candidates and put pressure on the major parties to support the laboring man. Likewise ethnic blocs apparently were never harnessed by one party or politician. An analysis of voting patterns by wards reveals that on only one issue—the 1890 new water supply station bond issue—did workers in the First Ward reject a city expenditure and vote against an improvement measure. More often, workers and immigrants joined businessmen in pursuing issues that encouraged city-building in Muskegon.

In many ways, Muskegon's politics reflect Alan Dawley's description of how local electoral politics often transformed potential class or ethnic conflicts into less harmful, often cooperative endeavors. Dawley argues that in Lynn, Massachusetts, local capitalists never lost control of city government but permitted workers to participate in electoral politics. In doing so, political involvement often served as a safety valve to larger working-class discontent. The lumbermen in Muskegon maintained control of that city's physical form and exerted significant social control. Nevertheless, many workers became aldermen and demonstrated that wage earners could rise to positions of respect in the community. The successful electoral experience earlier of DeLong and Cook, and later of Waalkes, convinced many workers that the political system could be a means to alleviate discontent. Couple this election success with the economic readjustments taking place during the lumbering collapse, as well as the lumber baron's industrial reinvestments, and a reliable buffer developed that moderated working-class discontent in Muskegon. In a short time the labor movement, never ideologically strong in the first place, was completely absorbed in the efforts to rebuild Muskegon's industrial base.[17]

Muskegon, which eventually developed a reputation as an "open shop" town, never experienced a strong labor movement after 1885. In 1895 there were only two unions active in the city: five assemblies of the Knights of Labor and the Lumber Union. The union movement never took hold in Muskegon in part because Dutch and Scandinavian workmen were generally reluctant to affiliate with binding associations. The presence of many similar yet separate Dutch Reformed, Christian Reformed, and Lutheran churches offers support that these immigrants were reluctant to affiliate into large, monolithic congregations. Further, the Christian Reformed church opposed all forms of labor organization. Likewise, the French Canadians were an individualistic breed. Their culture did not encourage industrial protest. The hostile attitude toward organized labor in Muskegon was also evidenced in the employers associations that developed during the readjustment years. Because of the varying though substantial anti-union forces, Muskegon had few strikes after 1882 and none of significance until the 1930s. As one observer noted: "As long as such a [open shop] situation was maintained the community possessed a special advantage."[18]

The Scandinavian and German elements in Muskegon generally gave support to a political culture that expressed itself in the values placed on duty and commitment by the lumber oligarchy. The homogeneous ethnic structure was more inclined to accept than to manipulate authority; citizen political mobilization was uncommon. Moreover, religious beliefs common among the Dutch Christians and Reformed, as well as German Lutherans, stressed pietism. The orientation toward conversion, and personal piety—the emphasis on proper behavior for self and others—did not encourage large-scale political involvement. Likewise several church-related organizations and societies in Muskegon that served as stabilizing and assimilative institutions made it easier for the newcomers to be gradually absorbed into society despite trying economic times. The only issue that exacerbated community cleavages was prohibition. German wards and the village of Lakeside in 1884 (and on the statewide prohibition referendum in 1887) broke with other immigrants and the town's elite and supported local prohibition.[19]

Religious and cultural influences generally made the immigrant voter willing to acquiesce in the paternalistic practices of the lumbermen. Muskegon's political culture and policy reflects a blend of traditional personalism, paternalism, and practiced economic planning. This unique blend owed much to the town's socioeconomic structures and the lumber oligarchy. People expected little of government, more of their economic leaders, but brought few pressures on a sociopolitical system that evidenced little conflict in its efforts to reindustrialize and move into the twentieth century.

Political patterns in Saginaw changed modestly—not unlike those in Muskegon—as the economic and social structure became slightly more complex. Saginaw's dependence on wood products was never as extensive as either Muskegon's or Bay City's; nevertheless, local businessmen, politicians, and lumbermen left few stones unturned in their efforts to further diversify the economic base in the late nineteenth century. Reasonably well-favored by railroads and water links, Saginaw flirted with a host of schemes for enhancing its economic prospects: sugar beet growing and processing, coal mining, supplying products to the Michigan north country (which never developed as anticipated), and, most important, the manufacture of machines and foundry products. Although only some of these endeavors brought success, some kinds of economic activity were brisk enough to get Saginaw growing again and move steadily away from dependence on lumber products.

In trying to lure manufacturers and industries, businessmen and lumbermen in both Saginaw City and East Saginaw maintained the necessary interest in local politics. After the 1885 ten-hour strike, labor's support was sought by both major parties. In 1886 a Democrat-Labor fusion ticket successfully ran Henry Youmans for mayor in East Saginaw, and in Saginaw City a United Labor ticket fused with the regular Democrats. In 1889, though, when East Saginaw and Saginaw City united, fusion and third-party politics all but disappeared and the two major parties nominated candidates without forming alliances. Much like the creation of the Board of Trade spurred Muskegon lumbermen into concerted action in that city, the struggle for unification of the Saginaws brought lumbermen and businessmen into city politics. In 1890 a prominent Republican lawyer with lumber connections, George W. Weadock, became the first mayor of the united city.[20] At the next election, 1892, William S. Linton, son of a prominent lumber manufacturer and professional politician, became mayor. Linton had been in the state legislature in 1889 and authored the bill that led to consolidation of the two Saginaws. In 1894 another lumber baron, William B. Mershon, was elected mayor. Between 1896 and 1902 the Democrats held office electing real estate and insurance man William B. Baum mayor for three terms.

In many ways Saginaw politics were not especially partisan but much more personalized than the other lumbertowns. A consequence of the "nonpartisan" nature of politics was that "better people" from diverse leadership backgrounds were encouraged to seek political office. Although lumbermen were at first on the political playing field, they were willing to share power with other businessmen or lawyer-politicians who subscribed to their goals of reindustrialization and diversification. Most Saginaw citizens, like those in many middle-size American cities in the late nineteenth century, reasoned that businessmen were ideal to govern the city and lead its economic revitalization.[21] In political leadership, Saginaw evolved within a decade from a simple to a multiple-element oligarchy.

A further reason that Saginaw politics were rarely acrimonious was the virtual total overlap between business and political elites. Although Saginaw's political-economic leaders were less paternalistic than Muskegon's they nevertheless took some pains to remain in touch with other citizens. They spoke at public meetings for bond issues, and generally succeeded in their aim of keeping a broad political base. In 1894 the *Saginaw Evening News*, a Democratic newspaper, reporting on the election of lumberman Mershon as the new Democratic mayor, noted that he had "received hundreds of Republican votes. He was elected because business interests had confidence in him and voted for him irrespective of party." The *News* affirmed that Mershon's victory "was not a party victory. It was largely a personal victory."[22] Thus Saginaw citizens accepted very personalized politics. Political issues, though not absent in Saginaw, were seldom causes for much ire.

There was no strong organized labor movement in Saginaw politics. True, there were more unions in Saginaw than any other lumbertown—a glance at the City Directory in 1892 reveals twenty-seven different labor affiliations—but most of these represented skilled workers. Other townspeople considered skilled craftsmen respectable, middle-class citizens and did not view them as threats to the economic establishment. Because Saginaw's economy was more diversified, its workers more skilled, and they were not employed in a few large factories or sawmills (as in Bay City's sawmills, shipyards, or woodenware plants), there were no common conditions supportive of union activism. During the last five years of the 1890s, with the advent of coal mining, several new workers' unions were organized. In 1902 labor's presence became more visible when a Socialist Ticket ran candidates for all major offices in Saginaw. The ticket finished a poor third, and despite campaign rhetoric, the reform movement failed to mobilize any more voters than the normal turnout. During the crucial years of industrial redevelopment, organized labor activity did not discourage the town's efforts to reindustrialize. Labor, like most of the lumbertown's citizens, engaged primarily in politics of personality, not issues.[23]

Ethnicity was not important in Saginaw politics. Although Saginaw had many foreign-born, the Germans, who dominated, folded easily into the political system. The Germans had been migrating into the Saginaws since the late 1840s, and they arrived in several medium-to-small waves, rather than in a large mass (like Bay City's Poles). Gradualism and length of residence made it easier for local institutions to absorb newcomers. By the late nineteenth century the Germans were represented among the economic and political elites. There were German mayors, German lumbermen-industrialists, and German professionals. Because the French Canadians lost population in the postlumber era and remained transient, they never became a factor in local politics. Their less skilled occupations were rapidly being filled, after the turn of the century, by newly arriving eastern European immigrants.

Immigrant voters, because they were often property owners, became concerned with local public policy, particularly policies regarding taxes for bonus funds, sewers, and waterworks. The immigrants of Saginaw had become regular citizens unlike the transient woodsmen voters in Bay City or the clannish Dutch families in Muskegon. Apparently understanding the need to add jobs and city amenities, immigrant wards in Saginaw supported bond issues for sewers, a county poorhouse, waterworks, and a farmer's market.[24]

The public policies implemented by Saginaw were not extremely ambitious and usually were not much beyond minimal caretaker activities. Though the voters generally approved small bonding issues, expenditures for city improvements were often minimal, and problems with sewers and water supplies plagued the community well into the twentieth century. Conservative fiscal policy was the order of the day after consolidation in 1889. City business leaders had been the main force behind consolidation primarily because cross-river rivalries had become too costly. Consolidation, though, also brought with it unexpected expenditures for a new, centrally located city hall and three new bridges connecting the town. Saddled with bonded debt and a declining tax base as sawmills closed, Saginaw officials practiced "economy, retrenchment, and reform."[25] For the rest of the century, city government was prudent in bonding programs and frugal in ongoing expenditures. As long as the town's economy industrially advanced and public consensus about the general goals of caretaker government could be maintained, no one in Saginaw objected very vigorously.

Like Muskegon, hovering in the background was the willingness of several well-to-do lumbermen to aid Saginaw. The Saginaw Board of Trade—founded in 1863—sought to lure industry to Saginaw. Industry provided work for the idle, increased opportunities for skilled and unskilled hands, and gradually broadened the city's tax base. Lumbermen contributed land for several parks to beautify the city, raised contributions for bonus funds, and provided libraries, a hospital, swimming pools, and two manual training schools. Saginaw also benefited from the political clout that several of its public and private officials acquired. Lumberman Aaron T. Bliss, elected in 1888 to represent the Eighth Congressional District, herded along a bill that appropriated $100,000 for a federal building in Saginaw. William S. Linton, who succeeded Bliss, worked with postal authorities to secure an appropriation for a magnificent downtown post office and the dredging of the Saginaw River by the Army Engineers. Joe Fordney, who followed Linton to Congress, consistently engineered protective tariff measures for the lumbermen and sugar beet growers. With private and federal help and business organizations doing so much, city government did not have to allow for such items in annual budgets. Saginaw in the late nineteenth century is a good example of conservative urban municipal government of the time, and how private, not public, systems bore most of the responsibility to rebuild depression-era cities.

The interplay of labor organization and electoral politics after the 1885 ten-hour strike was more evident in Bay City. Though the lumbermen were beginning to depart the city, workers failed to take over city government; however, they continued to establish unions and supported splinter or fusion candidates. In 1887 labor successfully supported Republican-Greenback candidates for aldermen and a Democratic lawyer for mayor.[26] Two years later, the Democrat-Labor candidates split evenly with the Republicans for control of the common council. In 1891 three Labor Party aldermen were elected along with eleven Democrats and eight Republicans. After that election the laboring men in Bay City pursued either major party, supporting the Democrats or Republicans. Throughout the poststrike era, candidates from a fusion or labor ticket in one election might very well run on a regular party ticket the next year as fusion politics did not endure from one election to the next. However, fusion or third-party movements created an instability in Bay City politics. Though they may have encouraged political expression, the transient nature of fusion politics made it difficult to create strong political coalitions that over the long term could affect economic directions in the community.

Bay City experienced several unsettling strikes in its shipyards in the 1890s and early twentieth century; however, labor apparently could never transfer its economic interest to the political playing field and never became a force in redirecting Bay City. Even though party activity was intense and third-party movements surfaced, political parties in Bay City were never highly institutionalized or differentiated. Laboring wards would support the Democrats or Labor party for aldermen, but often voted for a Republican mayor. For example, in 1895 the Polish Eighth Ward, "heretofore almost phenomenal in its adherence to the Democratic party," elected two Republican aldermen.[27] Thus labor could never represent a separate political force in Bay City and redirect politics or policies toward its goal. The workers, nevertheless, introduced confrontation; however, unlike Muskegon or Saginaw, the economic elites in Bay City ignored the challenge. With labor unable to form a working alternative, and the lumbermen concentrating on pinelands elsewhere, Bay City's political leadership was represented by small businessmen, lawyers, doctors, and a few industrialists who often came up through the aldermanic ranks. They were often long-time politicians running on personality and persistence rather than progress and promises. Bay City's citizens consequently developed low expectations of municipal government and came to tolerate political mediocrity.

Lumbermen in Bay City, in contrast to Saginaw or Muskegon, did not create a political oligarchy that dominated municipal politics. Because their investments were often elsewhere, they were willing to acquiesce in political factions and abdicate personal involvement as long as the city fulfilled a primary caretaker function. Between 1885 and 1910 of the ten mayors in Bay City, only two were lumbermen. One of these was the Democrat, George H. Shearer, the owner of a small mill, who had sympathized with the strikers in 1885 and subsequently drew the wrath of fellow lumbermen Sage and Alger. More typically, Bay City was governed by persons like Dr. Hamilton Wright, who served three two-year terms. Wright, also a lawyer, was foremost a politician. During these years he served two terms in the state legislature and while mayor (1895–97) served concurrently as judge of probate (1892–1901). Besides Dr. Wright, William Cunningham, another M.D., served one term; a meat market owner, a coal yard owner, and a shingle mill operator also served as mayor.[28] Outside O. A. Watrous, who owned the shingle mill, there were few mayors who directly or even indirectly were motivated by the need to protect Bay City's lumber interests. As professional or small businessmen, most mayors did not have the vision or commitment to mobilize Bay City's postlumber era economy. Caretaker activities tended to dominate their concerns.

Bay City's lumber elite not only abdicated responsibility when it came to the city's economic and political future but they also resisted public efforts that were made, though infrequently, to modernize city and governmental services. An analysis of voting patterns at the ward level suggests that the elite consistently voted against proposed bond issues for urban improvements. Between 1888 and 1903 there were several citywide referenda on public improvements: in 1888, citywide public electric lighting; 1889, a city hall building; 1897, an effort to unite Bay City and West Bay City, and a proposal to build a farmers' market; and in 1903, a second greater Bay City unification proposal. In all three bonding issues (lighting, city hall, and the farmers' market) voters in the Third Ward, the "blue stocking" district as the editor of the *Tribune* referred to the residents along Center Avenue, cast ballots against the public improvements.[29] Only in 1905, on the third attempt to ratify unification of the two cross-river cities, did the elite support a modernizing proposal.

In contrast to the opposition of the "blue stocking" districts, Bay City's working-class wards almost always supported public financing referenda. The working-class wards along the river and the Polish Eighth Ward supported by large margins the city hall project, the farmers' market, and unification of the two cities. In 1889 workers supported the city hall project with such a majority (the Second Ward voted 172–18; the Fifth Ward, 81–7; and the Eighth Ward, 110–6 for the new building) that the Republican *Bay City Tribune* accused several transient boarders of illegally voting. Evidently, some citizens were concerned that loggers returning from the woods early were tilting politics against the economic interests of the community.[30] Nevertheless, the evidence suggests that the economic elites of Bay City not only were reluctant to reinvest in declining mill town industries but they also remained unwilling to be taxed to pay for public improvements. The elite of Bay City, not immigrant workers, were largely responsible for that community's failure to confront its changed economic environment.

Bay City Poles represent an ethnic community that gradually found a place in the political structure of the city. Although they remained geographically, socially, and religiously isolated, the Poles eventually used municipal politics to attain representation and deference. After 1889 they consistently elected two aldermen to the twenty-two-man city council, and by 1895 Ludwik Daniels was beginning his first of several terms as city treasurer. The Poles, like others in Bay City, deemphasized the importance of party affiliation and made politicians personally accountable. Though they certainly were cognizant of status group and local economic issues, voting patterns indicate that the Poles did not establish a narrow parochialism that neglected city-building schemes. The Polish worker used the ballot to gain a presence, if not real power. The record also indicates that their presence was progressive enough that immigrant workers cannot shoulder the responsibility for Bay City's inability to move with economic or political vision into the twentieth century.[31]

The interaction of politics and business was also evident in the struggles that surrounded efforts to consolidate the lumbertowns with their cross-river rivals or nearby environs. The late 1880s saw several twin cities across the nation, physically divided by waterways but joined by bridges, move toward consolidation that had the municipal advantage of administrative cost-cutting as well as the prestige of a larger community. More significantly, though, the changes in political and community boundaries in the lumbertowns were brought on by the contraction of the economy. Rivalries between communities for sawmills, businesses, railroads, public buildings and people during the halcyon lumbering period were too expansive to continue into the period of decline. Taxes for schools, sidewalks, sewers, and duplicate facilities were becoming burdensome. No longer were the once burgeoning lumber settlements engaged in competitive boosterism to attract new settlers. Instead, the decline required concerted action, and the first to realize the need for cooperation were the lumbertown businessmen who, especially, felt the excessive tax burden. Yet, petty politicians and local interests, despite the economic wisdom of consolidation, often resisted political union.

Muskegon was the first logging center to accomplish political consolidation. Muskegon proper, where about eighty percent of the area's population lived, annexed the tiny, nearby villages of Port Sherman, Bluffton, and Lakeside in 1889. These villages, which were largely lumber mill residential areas and resort homes along the lake, were hit hard by the lumber decline. They joined the city of Muskegon without much opposition to take advantage of the electric railway being extended along the south side of Muskegon Lake. Consolidation for a while made Muskegon the state's fifth largest city and was accomplished with far less conflict than in those communities along the Saginaw River. Business interest was not major in effecting consolidation, for Muskegon never felt keen competition from its village rivals. The only opposition to annexation was in Lakeside, a "dry" town, where local Swedish and German temperance agitators feared absorption by Muskegon would eliminate Lakeside's prohibition.

Saginaw City and East Saginaw began serious discussions toward consolidation in 1887, a few years after the lumbering boom peaked. Earlier efforts had been made but were voted down by residents of Saginaw City who feared the loss of their post office and separate identity and higher taxes. However, by the late 1880s businessmen in both cities were pressuring local political leaders to undertake consolidation. Again, politicians resisted and, especially Saginaw City's elected officials fearing the loss of political power, opposed the union. Finally, several prominent businessmen secured consolidation through an act of the state legislature, and in 1889 the two communities became the city of Saginaw. If local businessmen in the Saginaws sought consolidation to avoid expensive and duplicate facilities, however, unification was at first a failure. The legislature stipulated that a new city hall would have to be built between the two cities and three bridges connecting the communities at designated spots would also have to be constructed. East Saginaw residents carried their objections to the bridges all the way to the state Supreme Court, which in 1894, ruled in favor of a bond issue for construction of the bridges. Yet, despite the initial cost, in the long run consolidation enabled Saginaw to launch a more effective united effort to attract new industries.

Efforts were made between 1889 and 1890 to unite West Bay City and its cross-river neighbor Bay City but were defeated by strong opposition in West Bay City. West Bay City was very much a company town still largely controlled by Henry W. Sage. Further, the large Wheeler and Davidson shipyards there continued to prosper into the 1890s. Economics did not necessitate consolidation. Local leaders, those few who had remained in West Bay City, successfully convinced many resident workers that annexation would lead to higher taxes as civic improvements were legislated.[32] There were no further efforts at consolidation until Sage closed his mill and West Bay City began to experience the pangs of economic readjustment. In 1897 a second effort at consolidation was again defeated on both sides of the river. Not until 1903 did the two towns vote to unite, and even then opponents to consolidation introduced a "repeal" bill in the state legislature. The bill passed both houses; however, a committee of businessmen from both Bay City and West Bay City persuaded the governor to veto the repeal bill. Finally, in 1905 greater Bay City was created, but it took two more years of haggling to eventually work out a compromise city charter. As it had shown earlier in its slow pursuit of industrial diversification, Bay City continued to follow behind its lumbertown competitors.[33]

The struggle to achieve consolidation, like the 1885 lumber strike, revealed community attitudes about the lumbertowns' determination to restructure themselves in the postlumber era. Muskegon accomplished consolidation early, but had fewer cross-town rivalries obstructing political unification. A cooperative disposition in the community was evidenced by 1889 and encouraged prompt action to combat the precipitous economic downturn. In the Saginaws, entrepreneurs, realizing that intense rivalries were no longer wise or feasible during a time of retrenchment, overcame historical community antipathy and determinedly effected consolidation by 1889. Both Muskegon and Saginaw had put aside internecine opposition by 1889 and manifested a semblance of community spirit necessary to create a diversified industrial base.

Bay City and West Bay City, in contrast, did not consolidate until sixteen years later. Both cities made sporadic attempts, but for several reasons, serious efforts toward consolidation failed. An unfortunate result of the ethnic neighborhoods, the strike, and cross-river economics was that several of Bay City's political wards developed strong personal leadership and identities. Individualistic neighborhoods could not envision the benefits of consolidation. Bay City remained, as the Tribune chastised, a city of "huddled homes separated into several communities."[34] Perhaps the main reason, though, Bay City failed to unify was because there was no intense, pressing demand in the 1890s to change the community's economic base. Imported logs from Canada kept some of the city's mills going and extended the lumber era, and several mills switched over to hardwood manufacturing; although this prolonged the lumber industry, it merely postponed the inevitable collapse. More important, many absentee lumbermen had little reason to exert the leadership or expend the capital needed to maintain Bay City's prosperity.

THE TRANSITION TO INDUSTRIAL DIVERSIFICATION, 1888–1905

The 1890s witnessed several varied efforts to combat the postlumber era depression. First efforts centered on diversification, the construction of new industries, and civic improvements. After ten years of sincere and determined reindustrialization, the economic climate still was not markedly improved in any of the three communities at the turn of the century. Nevertheless, the lumbertowns were able to begin—especially Saginaw and Muskegon—to redirect their economies and establish new and different industrial bases. The foundations were laid for a twentieth-century economy.

Muskegon and Saginaw undertook early and vigorous efforts toward industrial diversification. In 1889 the Muskegon Board of Trade was reorganized to attract new industries. Hackley became the president of this second Board of Trade—the organization growing out of the Lumberman's Exchange during the ten-hour strike—and began a Midwestern advertising campaign to attract new industries. The board stressed Muskegon's harbor facilities, docking, railroads, schools, churches, and climate. Several firms were located and supplied with capital from lumbermen to relocate at Muskegon: the Alaska Refrigerator Company, the Muskegon Chemical Fire Company, Muskegon Cracker, Sargent Manufacturing Company, the Chase Brothers Piano Company, and the Muskegon Rolling Mill. Hackley, Hume, and McGraft, John W. Moon, and other lumbermen served on the board of directors of all these industries.

In 1892 a second project undertaken by the board planned to raise $200,000 to be used in developing vacant sawmill land along the lakefront. Muskegon lumbermen, principally Hackley, Hume, Moon, Charles T. Hills, and Alexander V. Mann, took the initiative in this drive and pledged $50,000. After a public meeting another $50,000 brought the total to one-half of their goal. The first effort languished though, and little happened until January 1893 when the Board of Trade was reorganized as Muskegon's first Chamber of Commerce. Businessmen were resentful of the lumbermen's dominance on the old board, and as a result, the new chamber was a more broadly based agency, although its president and vice-president were lumbermen.

The chamber's new president, Newcomb McGraft, conspired with the city to raise the other $100,000 to create the $200,000 bonus fund. McGraft deeded a large portion of land, eighty acres, to the city for $100,000. To circumvent a law prohibiting city taxes for the benefit of companies, McGraft took payment from a $100,000 park bond issue that the citizens approved and then turned over the proceeds to the Chamber of Commerce, which administered the industry bonus fund. The money was administered by Hackley, Hume, and John Torrent, all three lumbermen. The McGraft fund attracted fifteen new firms to Muskegon within the next ten years.[35]

Further industrial revitalization efforts were undertaken by the Muskegon Improvement Company organized in 1890 as a private corporation to attract people and industry to the area. The project originated when Cornelius C. Howell, a promoter from Ohio, enlisted the support of Hackley, Louis Kanitz, H. N. Hovey, A. V. Mann, and D. D. Erwin (all were lumbermen except for Erwin, a lawyer), who together purchased six hundred acres just beyond the city limits and about two miles south of downtown Muskegon. The Muskegon Heights project was really an industrial and residential suburb. Free building sites, the presence of the Pere Marquette railroad, and low tax rates were offered as inducements to new industries.[36]

The success of the Muskegon Heights development demonstrates the entrepreneurial skills exhibited by Muskegon lumbermen. Despite a decreasing population and vacant homes in the city, the developers, through shrewd boosterism, created a real estate boom in Muskegon Heights. The Improvement Company's acreage was subdivided: 10 acres were reserved for parks, 110 for factory sites, and the rest of the land surveyed into 2,800 residential lots. In May 1890 a lottery was held and for $139 a person could purchase a lot at random. To stimulate sales the company built finished houses on several lots. On the day of the drawing the purchaser discovered the location and whether his lot had a house.[37] Meanwhile, the Improvement Company contracted with seven industrial plants to locate in the Heights. Although the promoters were somewhat dubious of success and had secretly sold seven hundred choice sites to a Toledo syndicate, within a week of their first offering all the lots were taken. So profitable was the sale that another was held sixteen months later.[38]

The growth of Muskegon Heights was rapid. A year after the first sale there were three hundred persons in the settlement and by 1893 more than thirteen hundred people. Four hundred houses were built during the first two years, and the factories paid $25,000 in wages a month. Although only one of the first contracted factories was ever built in the Heights, others were brought in and by 1892 there were six industrial concerns. In 1903 Muskegon Heights was incorporated as a city.[39]

Several manufacturers located their new industries in Muskegon because the community reputedly had a compatible and efficient work force. Laborers in Muskegon were familiar with mass production because of experiences gained in sawmills and early factories. Moreover, the lumbertown's Scandinavian and Dutch laborers were seen as "superior to Slavs, Hungarians, Poles, and Italians as artisans." These workers were not only skilled but also perceived as docile and permanent residents, factors "explained partly by the temperament of the laborers, most of whom represent northwest European stock."[40] Consequently, Muskegon's Dutch and Scandinavian workmen did not often join union organizations. According to Glasgow, two factors helped maintain open-shop conditions in Muskegon. One was the "reluctance of the Dutch and Scandinavians to affiliate with binding associations," and the other an employers association that reputedly kept blacklists of employees who identified with trade associations.[41] The open shop prevailed, wages were kept low, and no labor unrest took place after the lumber strikes. Between 1885 and 1905, according to the Bureau of Labor and Industrial Statistics, Muskegon experienced only five minor strikes.[42]

Besides industrial diversification, Muskegon also undertook many civic, educational, and cultural improvements to create a cultural milieu attractive to investors. Most of these improvements were directly attributable to the philanthropy of lumbermen, especially Hackley, Hume, and McGraft. In 1888 Hackley donated $100,000 for a public library. Two years later another $50,000 was contributed for a public park, an in 1897 another $27,000 was given to erect four Civil War commemorative statues in Hackley Park. In 1892 Hackley donated more than $200,000 for a manual training school. He later added two wings, a gymnasium, and a football field to the training school. Hackley's last gift was a community hospital completed in 1903. In all, Hackley donated nearly $6 million in the postlumber era to Muskegon, and almost single-handedly transformed the city from a lumbertown to a city of diversified industry.[43]

Few one-industry communities could replicate the enterprise exemplified in Muskegon during the difficult days of transition from lumbering to diversified industry; however, Saginaw exhibited recuperative energies like those of her cross-state rival. The change from lumbering to diversified industry, though, was more gradual in Saginaw than in Muskegon. Rafting logs across Lake Huron extended the lumber business until the 1894 tariff law. However, when the logging era ended Saginaw was already engaged in diversified industry. By 1892 almost fifty percent of the employees in Saginaw worked in nonlumbering manufactures.[44] Diversification and recovery was not quite the challenge in Saginaw as it was in Muskegon.

The first planned attempts to diversify focused on use of the hardwood timber neglected during the pine era. In 1890 the Saginaw Improvement Company was organized by several leading businessmen to provide free lots to prospective industries. Of the eight factories that located in Saginaw because of the offer, six were involved in diversified wood products. Like the Muskegon venture, the Improvement Company purchased residential lots in Saginaw, including some fine homes vacated by lumbermen moving west, and abandoned factory lands along the Saginaw River. A lottery was held for the residential lots at a cost of $150 apiece. Twenty-five hundred lots were sold quickly, and those who drew lots close to the river and downtown found appreciative owners. Others, who received land outside the city or industrial areas, simply let their lots go for taxes. Prime industrial sites near rail lines were given free of cost to prospective industries. In two years eight factories that took free land were employing 640 workers.

Although the investors in the Saginaw Improvement Company did not do well financially, they did benefit the city by fostering several new industries. These new concerns, several of which failed to survive the mid-nineties depression were, nevertheless, important. They kept Saginaw an industrial city and empolyed workers who remained in the city after the sawmills closed. More important, the employees in the new industries were not transients but worked year round, were skilled, and generally received better wages. Consequently, they were eager to purchase homes and contribute to the commercial growth of the city. As one Saginaw historian saw it:

> [T]he employees of the sawmills, like the woodsmen were a shifting element of the population, and occupied cheap rented houses, living a "hand to mouth" sort of way. The employees of a furniture factory, a carriage works, or plate glass company . . . received better wages and employment the year round; and consequently secured homes of their own and became settled residents. Such an institution employs thirty men paid as much in wages in a year as a sawmill employing one hundred men and was of much greater benefit to the city.[45]

Although total wages still fell by fourteen percent between 1890 and 1900 in Saginaw, they did not fall as dramatically as the twenty-six percent loss suffered in Muskegon.[46]

It is more difficult to evaluate the importance of the lumbermen in Saginaw's efforts to industrialize. In 1918 James Cooke Mills, who wrote a well-researched account of Saginaw's industries, bemoaned the failure of the city's lumbermen to reinvest in the community:

> The rebuilding of Saginaw's industries might have been hastened, it is believed, had our wealthy lumbermen been willing to invest heavily in enterprises to develop the natural resources of the valley. But discouraged at the ill success that attended some of the earlier ventures, and believing that the greatest source of wealth lay in the pine forest, they invested their idle capital in timber lands in Minnesota and the State of Wisconsin, and some moved their place of residence to that scene of their new activities.

Mills concluded by noting that "this policy of our moneyed men left the actual 'boosting' of the city and securing of new industries to younger men of moderate means."[47] There is little doubt that much of the eventual success for Saginaw's industrial renaissance was because of the efforts of young entrepreneurs and nonlumber investors; however, Mills's condemnation of the lumber barons is too sweeping. During the postlumber era, once prominent lumbermen continued to be involved financially in the city. The Improvement Company's board of directors included C. W. Wells as president and J. J. Rupp, A. T. Bliss, W. S. Linton, Levi Tilloston, and Clark L. Ring, all lumbermen who sat on the twelve-member board.[48]

If the lumber barons of Saginaw can be faulted, it may be that many invested too conservatively during the first years of diversification. The capital they put back into Saginaw was too often confined to industries familiar to them. Thus, woodworking plants attracted capital as did the new extractive industries of coal, oil, and sugar beets. But none of these industries ever returned the profits of lumbering. At most they were short-lived and supplied some employment during the transition period.[49]

Yet, a small core of lumbermen in Saginaw, to adopt Joseph Schumpeter's definition, effected a "creative response" to economic change. Schumpeter defines the creative entrepreneur-investor as one who responds to economic change by doing "something else, something that is outside of the range of existing practice." Like several of the lumbermen in Muskegon, Saginaw had many speculative capitalists who ventured outside wood-related industries. For example, Arthur Eddy financed the Saginaw Milling Company and Saginaw Plate Glass Company. Edward Mershon invested in iron foundries; Aaron Bliss and William Van Auken bought the National Engineering Company; and Ami Wright and Thomas Merrill purchased the Saginaw Manufacturing Company. The key to the creative entrepreneurial response is that it eventually "shaped the whole course of subsequent events and their 'long-run' outcomes." Moreover, Schumpeter sees it as creating social and economic situations for the good. There were enough creative lumbermen in Saginaw who, through industrial decision making and political activities, established new patterns of economic behavior in these postlumber years that the city was redirected and reestablished industrially in the twentieth century.[50]

The labor situation along the Saginaw River, though not as advantageous as Muskegon's, nevertheless remained attractive to new manufacturers. Skilled hands who had developed a knowledge of the factory in several Saginaw foundries and sawmills remained in town. They organized into several trade unions (thirty-two in 1902) but seldom engaged in strike activity. Of the nineteen work stoppages in Saginaw between 1885 and 1905, one-half were among the Saginaw cigar makers. Skilled manufacturing hands, as they had in the 1885 ten-hour movement, remained uninvolved in protracted strikes. The only labor unrest came in the early twentieth century when outlying coal mine workers formed a "socialist" union and coal company. Minor and isolated labor disturbances in Saginaw did not seriously detract from new investments there.[51]

Saginaw also tried to revitalize its appearance in the postlumber period, and as in Muskegon, the lumbermen carried their share in financing civic improvements. Several of the lumbermen involved with the Improvement Company were instrumental in hiring C. W. Manahan, a prominent real estate dealer from Toledo, to manage the Improvement Company's properties and to promote the Saginaw region. Manahan supervised the platting of factory sites, parks, streets, and residential lots in the property purchased by the company. He traveled throughout the state and the Midwest trying to attract new industry and printed promotional literature boasting of Saginaw's virtues. His promotional efforts physically expanded the city, and new industrial-residential sites were built along the river, south of west Saginaw. Street railway lines were extended, electric lights installed, water and sewer systems and paved roads were built. Manahan also developed nearby Merrill Park as a center of neighborhood activity. As in the Muskegon Heights project, industrial planning in Saginaw began to rearrange lumber-era residential patterns.[52]

Public parks were another improvement popular around the turn of the century, and Saginaw was endowed with lands by Jesse Hoyt, ex-Governor Aaron T. Bliss, Ezra Rust, and Thomas Merrill, all lumbermen. Hoyt also donated $100,000 for a downtown library. Lumberman Wellington Burt built a manual training school on Saginaw's east side in 1905, and not to be outdone, fellow lumber baron Arthur Hill established several educational scholarships and donated $200,000 to build a trade school on Saginaw's west side. These civic improvements not only memorialized the name of their donors but added amenities to Saginaw used to attract new residents and industries.

Twelve miles downriver from Saginaw, the cities of Bay City and West Bay City failed to respond perceptively to the economic downturn. The first response to the slump in the Bay communities was to diversify into woodworking industries. In the early 1890s, as Muskegon and Saginaw experimented with impermanent manufacturing, Bay City rafted logs from Canada and cut nearby hardwoods to feed planing mills and woodworking plants. For a few years several firms made Bay City an important center for the manufacture of hardwood flooring, plywood, woodenware, boxes, and wooden boats.

But of the three lumbertowns, Bay City was least able to afford the diversification into woodworking manufactures. Its industrial base was never as broad as Saginaw's or Muskegon's, and to continue reliance on the forests in an age before reforestation was to construct an emphemeral manufacturing foundation. Wood manufacturing was an expedient move, but it would have been worthwhile only if it was transitory and preparatory to large-scale industrial diversification. Yet as late as 1905 the Bay City Board of Trade and a prominent historian in the community continued to see the city's future in wood products.[53] To continue wood manufactures well into the twentieth century was the fateful decision that permanently arrested Bay City's economic development.

Bay City's conservative economic decision making reflected the socioeconomic construct of the community. Foremost, the lumbermen of Bay City failed to exert the leadership or will to expend capital needed to industrially restructure the town. Absentee ownership manifested the lumber barons' failure to reinvest in Bay City. The mills in Bay City, although numerous, were divided into several relatively large and many small-to-moderate producers of milled lumber. When the two largest mills owned by Sage and McGraw closed, the owners invested their profits in Western and Southern timberlands. No capital was expended to diversify the economy of Bay City. Successful lumbermen who did live in town followed the leadership of the absentee barons and invested their capital in Canadian and Western timberlands.[54]

Younger entrepreneurs and those engaged in wood manufactures also failed to reinvest in Bay City. A conservative investment philosophy trickled down throughout the Bay City business community. Because of the towns' dominance by the lumber industry, few new industries sprang up to create readily available capital for reinvestment. When indigenous capital was available, it was usually spent in new wood manufactures and timber transport companies.

The approach of the Bay City lumbermen, both resident and absentee, to the economic readjustment fits Schumpeter's description of an "adaptive response." "Whenever an economy or industry reacts . . . by expansion within its existing practice, we may speak of development as adaptive."[55] Bay City's absentee owners' movement to new timberlands set a pattern that was emulated by resident lumbermen. Those that remained adapted conservatively to the new economic order. E. B. Foss, for example, built planing mills to finish imported pine from Canada and then reship it throughout the Great Lakes. Thomas Cranage, the Eddys, and D. W. Young opened hardwood plants and organized shipping companies to raft logs to Bay City. The adaptive response, however, was only a temporary solution. By the turn of the century the planing and woodworking mills were closing. Pine and hardwood were scarce, and manufacturers of shingles, woodenware, and wooden boxes soon found their products being replaced by composition shingles, cartons, and metal containers. The lumbermen-entrepreneurs in Bay City failed to adjust "creatively" to the new industrial age.

The Bay City labor situation also dampened investors' enthusiasm. They large number of Polish, French, and German residents, who had been actively involved in past strikes, were perceived as clannish, troublesome, and uncooperative. A Depression-era historian in Bay City noted "in the twentieth century a good deal of ill feeling rose up between these types of people." The Poles, because they "shoved the average [wage] down to an almost unlivable scale," were seen as largely responsible for these antagonisms. Although they were "good workers, and blessed with the European heritage of thrift," their contribution to the valley had always "been a debatable one."[56]

Sporadic labor unrest plagued the industries in Bay City well into the twentieth century. Moreover, these strikes, unlike those in Saginaw or Muskegon, involved large companies—usually absentee-owned—and affected hundreds of employees. In 1896 six hundred men were discharged at the Wheeler Shipyard when the union tried to organize all workers. Afterward, "the firm refused to employ Union men," was sold to outstate interests, and soon shut down. Another seven hundred men were put out of work at Davidson's West Bay City shipyard because of a strike for a nine-hour workday in 1904.[57] Bay City businessmen were concerned and tried to allay these fears. In 1905 a Board of Trade pamphlet boosting the amenities of the community envisioned "the hearty cooperation of employer and employee" in a city where "common interests are strongly cemented and prevent labor disturbances, the curse of America today."[58]

As witnessed in the 1903–5 struggle to achieve government consolidation between Bay City and West Bay City, the city was not only a physically divided entity but also socially, culturally, politically, and economically separated. Absentee ownership created an economy that completely separated the monied interest from the community. Lumber barons who lived in the city felt no commitment to a work force that was perceived as transient, hostile, and uncooperative. Ethnic and religious groups isolated themselves geographically from one another and from the community as a whole. However, despite these cleavages, until 1905 the community managed to endure on the remnants of its logging heritage. Only after the wood manufacturers began to discontinue operations did the city experience the inevitable results of the absence of economic foresight.

In 1903 the economic past and future of Bay City was envisioned in a letter in the *Bay City Tribune*, signed "His Majesty, B. F. J.":

> Think back for twenty years and see how many men you can remember who made their fortunes in Bay City and when they had made themselves independent, shook the dust off their feet and departed for some larger city. Were they of any benefit to Bay City? They made all they could and then looked up new fields and quietly departed.
>
> What Bay City wants today is a blast furnace . . . a rolling mill, the nail mill, the wire works, the tubing mill, tinplate mill, and many small iron industries.

The experiences of an economy based on a few large lumber mills and absentee ownership discouraged future reliance on new and large manufacturers. Small, dependable "*internal operators* [my italics] with enterprise and a little hustle" were what was needed in Bay City.[59]

Modest prosperity from 1900 to 1905 coupled with the conservative entrepreneurial philosophy and a questionable labor supply also prevented Bay City from starting industrial booster drives. No private individuals, consortiums, local units of government, or the community Board of Trade undertook promotional campaigns to attract diversified industry. A milieu of acceptable durability developed in the community. Such an attitude was reflected in Board of Trade promotional literature. "Executive bodies" of Bay City would allow "no uncertain stone [business] to enter the foundation [Bay City]. All that was speculative or uncertain was discouraged, all that promised permanence was given substantial support."[60] But the "support" was only verbal, not financial, and the unwillingness to encourage experimental economic ventures arrested Bay City's industrial future.

Likewise, absentee ownership and the dearth of progressive leaders kept Bay City from acquiring the civic improvements undertaken in Muskegon and Saginaw. Outside Sage's donation of $60,000 in 1884 for a library in West Bay City, the lumbermen of Bay City left few legacies to benefit the community. The main public library was financed not by lumbermen but by the Carnegie Corporation. Unlike its logging town competitors during the postlumber era, Bay City did not envision a "city beautiful" movement or cultural amenities as necessary to attract diversified industry.

DIVERSIFIED MANUFACTURING, 1905–20

The lumbertowns successfully reoriented toward manufacturing between 1905 and 1920. The new direction was effected in two ways: first, by a continuation of the community boosterism practiced in Muskegon and Saginaw; and second, the phenomenal rise of the automotive industry, which resembled in many ways the rapid growth of lumbering a half-century earlier. Muskegon and Saginaw experienced growth through the continuation of diversified manufacturers begun in the postlumber era and the further dissolution of lumber and wood products industries as the automotive industry established decentralized plants in these communities. Bay City manufacturers scarcely changed from those of the postlumber era, and the city eventually was relegated to a tertiary position behind its sister lumbertowns.

In 1910, during industrial evolution, the U.S. Census reviewed the manufacturing production of each community:

> Saginaw, though reporting an increase in value of manufactured products from $8,625,978 in 1899 to $18,833,047 in 1909, dropped from third place in importance in this respect in 1899 to fifth place in 1904 and 1909. The principal industries of the city are the manufacture of beet-sugar, lumber and timber products, foundry and machine-shop products, cooperage and wooden goods, and furniture.
>
> The manufactured products of Bay City increased only 14.2 percent in value during the decade, while those of Muskegon more than doubled. In the former, the lumber industry predominates, followed by foundries and machine shops. . . .
>
> [I]n Muskegon, the industries are more diversified and include the manufacture of billiard tables, foundry and machine-shop products, furniture, hosiery and knit goods, and paper and wood pulp. Muskegon was at one time a lumber town exclusively, and affords an illustration of the successful development of other manufacturing industries to supplant the disappearing sawmills.[61]

Between 1910 and 1919, the industrial structure of the three communities followed the form they had already assumed. During this time, Saginaw's population increased by 11,000 and the value of its manufactures more than tripled. Muskegon added more than 20,000 people—almost doubling its population in a single decade—and the value of its manufactures increased five times. Bay City added only 2,388 people; and although its manufactures tripled, it remained well behind its one-time rivals, never regaining the momentum lost during postlumber-era intransigence.

The three cities continued to follow separate paths in their industrial development during the early decades of the twentieth century. Muskegon's phenomenal growth and industrial success resulted from the growth of small diversified plants into larger ones and new, large-scale industries attracted by the continuation of the city's bonus funds. Additional monies were placed into the McGraft fund by lumbermen to bring new industries into Muskegon. In 1899 the Central Paper Company moved to Muskegon upon receiving a $10,000 bonus and making a pledge to build a plant and hire eighty-five men and fourteen women. It located in an abandoned mill site and continued to expand. By the 1920s the paper mill employed more than four hundred people. The Alaska Refrigerator Company, started by lumbermen Hume and Moon in Muskegon Heights, used wood to manufacture iceboxes. It soon became the Norge Company and began producing metal refrigerators besides cabinets and stoves. Later purchased by Borg-Warner, it grew to employ 3,000 persons by the 1920s. Other small concerns started in the 1890s likewise expanded: the Shaw-Walker Office Equipment Company grew to a staff of 750; and the Stewart-Hartshorn plant, manufacturers of wood and metal curtain rollers, employed 350 persons by the end of World War I.

The year 1905 was a "banner" year for new industries in Muskegon.[62] The Wharf Fund, administered by the Chamber of Commerce, received another $100,000 through a bonding issue to build a public dock; however, the money was used instead to swell the McGraft bonus fund. Later that year a $12,500 bonus was offered to Continental Motors of Chicago if it would move its gasoline-engine-manufacturing business to Muskegon and employ 125 men within six years. By 1924 Continental Motors employed seven thousand workers. The real significance of attracting Continental Motors was its fostering of several other automobile and foundry industries in the city. Included were Campbell, Wyant, and Cannon Foundry, which came to employ about two thousand persons; the Piston Ring Company (Sealed Power); Anaconda Wire and Cable Company; and the Motor Specialties Company. By 1920 about one-fourth of Muskegon's work force was employed in the production of automotive materials.[63]

It is difficult to overemphasize the significance of Muskegon's bonus funds. The determination of the Chamber of Commerce to acquire new industries is seen in the bidding war to acquire Brunswick-Balke-Collander, a concern producing billiard tables and bowling supplies. Several Midwest cities competed for this plant. Muskegon, through inducements, triumphed over its chief rival, Grand Rapids. Brunswick became so successful that in 1911 another bonus was given to convince the firm to move its piano business to Muskegon. By the twenties Brunswick was the fourth largest employer in the city. In 1912 the Chamber of Commerce also purchased for $7,000 an abandoned plant and offered it to E. H. Sheldon, who then located his laboratory equipment plant in Muskegon. In all, the bonus funds attracted forty-six industries to Muskegon. Sixteen failed but the rest remained in one form or another until at least the Depression years.[64]

Many of the industries grew directly out of the bonus funds largely sponsored by Muskegon lumbermen. Moreover, many of the new firms were also partly capitalized by lumbermen. After Hackley's death in 1902 persons like Hume (Amazon Knitting Company), John Torrent (Sealed Power), and Moon (E. H. Sheldon Company) continued to support fledgling industries. Just before his death, Hackley reaffirmed the direction of Muskegon's economic growth. Unlike the conservative investors in Bay City who hesitated at the idea of bringing in new, large manufacturers, Hackley pointedly answered a newspaper reporter's inquiry that large firms must be the key and would move to Muskegon only if induced with bonuses from the Chamber of Commerce.[65] The results of Hackley's and other lumbermen's efforts were dramatically reaffirmed by the economic success of Muskegon.

In many ways Saginaw emulated the successful methods used in Muskegon to attract industries. Although already diversified into metal manufactures, Saginaw continued lumber manufactures and further diversified into automobile bodies and parts. The automobile industries, though, employed less than five percent of the city's work force in 1919.[66] Foundry and machine-shop products dominated, along with lumbering and bakery goods; however, many of the foundry and machine manufacturers supplied the burgeoning down-state auto plants. Saginaw resumed aggressive recruitment of industries in 1905 after several earlier enterprises began to fall on hard times. The beet-sugar industry collapsed, wood products declined further, and coal production tapered off. Consequently, in 1906 more efforts were made to revive manufacturing. The Merchant and Manufacturers Association was formed "to secure the location of new and outside industries and business enterprise" in Saginaw. The association was made up of several ex-lumbermen and manufacturers. They undertook a "spirited campaign" among the businesses and manufacturers of Saginaw and raised $212,000. The money was used to purchase land and give inducements to new enterprises or those relocating to Saginaw.[67]

By 1910 thirty-six corporations were supported in one manner or another by bonus funds of the Merchants and Manufacturers Association. Many of these were short-lived, but a few, at first unimportant concerns came to contribute to Saginaw's industrial prosperity. Two that came to be the largest employers in the Saginaw Valley were Jackson-Church and Wilcox (General Motors, Saginaw Steering Gear) and Valley Grey Iron (Chevrolet Grey Iron Foundry). By the late twenties Saginaw Steering Gear employed nearly ten thousand workers and Grey Iron and Nodular Iron nearly half as many.

Throughout the successful inauguration of many of these diversified industries, Saginaw lumbermen like the Eddys, Mershons, Hill, and Burt contributed to the association and invested in new industries.[68] As in Muskegon, Saginaw's revitalization reflected the commitment that several dedicated pioneers had to the community.

Muskegon and Saginaw became thriving industrial communities by 1920; Bay City continued to endure relying on wood products, coal, sugar beets, and some manufacturing. These industries except manufacturing were sporadic, seasonal, and offered insecure employment. Bay City's population grew slowly and its work force even declined during the immediate prewar years. Despite the inauspicious economic picture no efforts were made, even after 1905, to stimulate new industrial development.

Nevertheless, some firms did locate in Bay City between 1905 and 1920 and managed to sustain the city. The North American Chemical Company purchased the old McGraw mill and became one of the city's largest employers until it ceased operations in 1927. James Clements's Industrial Works, the largest employer in the city, prospered during the period and employed more than one thousand. The Bay City Dredge Works, manufacturers of heavy equipment, became the city's fourth largest employer in 1913. Shipbuilding enjoyed a partial revival when the Defoe Shipyard was opened in 1905. However, beyond these, few diversified concerns came to the community. Woodworking manufacturers continued to employ most of the work force, and the automobile industry, represented by Union and Natco Trucks, employed only a handful.

Two extractive industries that provided employment were the sugar beet and coal industries. Bay City, taking advantage of a state bounty on the production of sugar beets, built two processing factories in the early twentieth century. The processing of sugar beets required several thousand hands each fall, but it did not supply steady employment. When the bounty was lost and the tariff lowered to bring in Cuban sugar, the beet-sugar business collapsed in 1905–6. Coal mining became important between 1900 and 1914. Yet, like sugar beets, employment was not steady and frequently went to experienced outsiders recruited from Ohio and Pennsylvania. By the late teens most of the mines, which could not compete with West Virginia coal in price or quality, shut down. Bay City's inability to grasp at some permanent industry to replace lumbering caused its economy to languish far behind its one-time rivals.

Conclusion

By 1920 the former logging centers had plotted their future economic courses. Muskegon continued to grow as a diversified manufacturing community reaching a peak population of 67,257 in 1950. Saginaw, likewise, flourished and attained 96,992 persons in midcentury. Bay City eventually secured several diversified, auto-related industries in the 1930s; however, by 1950 its population had reached only 57,504, a mere thirty-seven percent growth in fifty years. That these once booming logging centers were able to weather the loss of their sole source of livelihood in the nineteenth century and sustain in some cases remarkable recoveries reveals the importance of aggressive and dedicated entrepreneurial leadership. Each city was equipped by geography or location with similar natural advantages; all three communities are remarkable in their physical similarities. During the postlumber era and the transition period each had efficient transport networks, suitable factory sites, favorable tax rates, water supply, and available housing. Adequate rail, water, and land transport facilitated the evolution to diversified manufacturing. All three communities had a ready work force, although the ethnic makeup was different.

The factor that separated these lumbertowns from one another was an intrinsic, unquantifiable resource: the foresight and community commitment of the lumber elite. Where there was a commitment and a determined willingness to overcome the demise of lumbering as in Muskegon and Saginaw, economic speculation and reinvestments were rewarded with growth and reasonable prosperity. In contrast the seeds of disinterest, distrust, and divisiveness sown by Bay City's lumbermen continued to germinate community discord, contentiousness, and alienation.

Comparing the lumbertowns helps clarify the role of the entrepreneur-lumberman in the evolution of American industry. The quality of the entrepreneur explains urban growth and development more convincingly than place theory or environmental determinism. Despite geographical advantages, cities like Bay City often could not effect drastic economic change in the postlumber era. In contrast Muskegon and Saginaw experienced economic revival despite the depletion of the major resource. Aggressive, though limited, entrepreneurship overcame the drawbacks of being a one-industry, natural resource settlement.

The study of the lumbermen and community redevelopment before the automobile age raises other questions. Although for Muskegon and Saginaw the lumber barons invested in some diversified industries, most of their capital went West, and the money that stayed behind was often placed conservatively into woodworking manufacturing. The observer must wonder, as one did in 1935, what would have happened to the reindustrialized lumber settlements if the lumber barons had spent more money in lumbertown manufacturing.[69] And the conception among some Michigan historians that the lumbermen were "speculators by nature" and readily put surplus capital into a highly uncertain auto industry needs reexamination.[70] From evidence, lumbermen, who at first were chance-takers, later became conservative with their accumulated wealth. As the lumber era in Michigan ended they invested primarily in Western lands. If they did commit moneys to new community industries, they were often woodworking manufacturers or extractive industries and not necessarily the machine and foundry industries or embryonic plants that gave birth to the auto industry. Hackley would commit only fifteen percent of his money to speculative ventures, although often that amount was enough to generate the success of an industrial undertaking. So the intimate relationship between lumbering and the automobile industry may be less than until now supposed.

Lastly, it should be emphasized that despite the efforts of lumbermen and entrepreneurs to create diversified economies in the declining lumbertowns, in the end the auto industry enabled the towns to experience recovery. True, diversification prepared the way for auto manufacturers; however, in the long run, the lumbertown again came to be dominated by one industry. By midcentury Saginaw and Muskegon had nearly one half of their manufacturing employees in the automobile industry. Bay City, perhaps because of the distance from the Motor City and its resistance to new industries, had only thirty-five percent of its industrial work force in auto-related businesses. Consequently, reliance solely on the auto industry has created a contemporary employment picture that reflects the days when lumbering ceased to be important in Saginaw, Bay City, and Muskegon.

CHAPTER NINE

Conclusion

> The casual observer of the political landscape in America's middle sized cities will initially receive the impression of sameness and monotony. However, an intimate look by an interested observer does reveal variations in accomplishments; while these are not of great scope, they do indicate that distinct sets of values appear to guide the individual civic spirits.
>
> —OLIVER P. WILLIAMS AND CHARLES R. ADRIAN, *Four Cities: A Study in Comparative Policymaking*

Published in 1963, Williams and Adrian's *Four Cities* is a comparative case study of the relationships in medium-size cities between public policy and community characteristics. The four Michigan cities studied between 1948 and 1957, although unidentified in the book, were Kalamazoo (Alpha), Jackson (Beta), Muskegon (Gamma), and Bay City (Delta).[1] What is remarkable about the study is that it vividly reaffirms the idea of the past as prologue. The characteristics observed between 1948 and 1957 reflect the cultural and economic milieu that emerged in the lumbertowns in the nineteenth-century.

Williams and Adrian focused on the role of leadership as well as citizen participation in local governmental activities. Citizen participation was also identified with the ethnic construct of each community. The authors' observations of Muskegon and Bay City, although written sixty years later, could have been descriptive of the characteristics of the lumbertowns at the turn of the century. Muskegon's leadership and political involvement is described as "informal," where "personalities, not issues, have the greater force in politics." It was seen as a democratic city that "consistently rated higher with respect to amenities and did not display . . . intransigence on tax referendums." The leadership remained involved, and businessmen, through the Chamber of Commerce and manufacturers' associations, often were successful in electing their candidates to local office.[2]

In contrast, Bay City was the only one of the four cities to maintain the traditional ward system of local government. Williams and Adrian noted that "in Delta [Bay City], this can be traced to a specific incident: in the 1920s when the Poles, in conjunction with the French Canadian and German neighborhood blocs, successfully worked for the reinstatement of a ward system after a brief trial with at-large elections." Consequently, this sytem continued the practice of the lumber era where economic leaders were almost totally absent from organized political activity. Bay City's politics came to be dominated by men of "modest education, neither very articulate nor capable of conducting public deliberations in an effective fashion, leadership was collective in character." Above all, "union organizations, entrenched by personnel patronage and equipped with campaign funds," controlled Bay City politically.[3]

The willingness to compromise politically in Muskegon, born in the poststrike era when DeLong and Cook along with several lumbermen informally agreed to focus on growth, reindustrialization, and urban amenities, continued well into the twentieth century. Resident economic leaders continued to influence and be involved in urban government. But in Bay City ethnic consciousness—reinforced by threatened economic and social isolation as a result of the 1885 ten-hour strike—structured a town that remained politically and socially segmented and parochial. In many ways Bay City never adjusted to the twentieth century. Saginaw, although not included in Williams and Adrian's study, would most likely parallel the developments in Muskegon. Local leadership remained strong and Saginaw's economic growth into the twentieth century outdistanced even Muskegon's.

Interestingly, Williams and Adrian also postulate that different ethnic groups and their histories in communities may contribute "in a small way" to an explanation of why Muskegon and Bay City were different.

Delta [Bay City] historically and contemporarily possessed large ethnic blocs, internally more cohesive than those in Gamma [Muskegon]. The most important of these groups was the Poles, a block which has been credited with retaining a certain separateness by Thomas and Znaniecki. . . . The Polish population was largely working class and lower-middle class. None of its members had penetrated the economic elites of the city. One found no Polish bank officers, editors, industrial executives, or prominent professional men. . . . The Polish neighborhoods gave a constant negative vote on proposals for civic improvements. Thus, there is some evidence that these ethnic blocs, especially the Polish ones, were still concerned with politics of status. They represented a public difficult to mobilize for the "broader" community aims implicit in policies directed toward economic growth and expanded amenities.

In contrast to Bay City, the authors noted of Muskegon:

> The most conspicuous ethnic group in Alpha [Kalamazoo] and Gamma [Muskegon] were the Dutch. The initial arrival of the Hollanders preceded that of the Poles in Delta . . . by about a generation. Either as a result of this earlier arrival or because of a different cultural outlook, the Dutch entered into the civic life more as individuals than as ethnic spokesmen.[4]

Still, Williams and Adrian offer an opinion of the Polish voter that reflects an elitist bias born of twentieth century progressive reformism. In the 1890s and early twentieth century, Polish voters frequently supported proposals for civic improvements, and at the turn of the century Poles were achieving some positions of leadership and recognition in Bay City. They were not, historically at least, a segment of the public "difficult to mobilize for the 'broader' community." They truly may have become a part of the problem that prevented city-building in Bay City, but the Poles in reality can only share the burden of responsibility. The absentee lumbermen, other ethnic blocs, and most important, a resident economic elite that never envisioned great things or exerted a semblance of political-economic leadership in Bay City kept that community from achieving economic growth and expanded amenities.

Despite its bias, the Williams and Adrian study can be used as historical hindsight to validate the supposition that cities develop a character or culture that often persists for generations. An urban area is often a product of its beginnings and urban character changes come sometimes slowly, if at all. Thus, throughout, especially in the latter parts, the major goal of my study has been to determine why the lumbertowns of Saginaw City, Bay City, and Muskegon differed in their responses to similar issues and problems. Variations in the answer have focused on entrepreneurial activity and ethnic consciousness. However, entrepreneurship and ethnicity are too simplistic in themselves to explain a community culturally or economically. The complexity of entrepreneurship and ethnicity as sources for depicting a community profile may be seen in the typological profile (Chart 2). The typology is intended to provide a framework for depicting the process and character of urban growth, development, and decision making. It is also a reference tool to use in summation.

All three lumbertowns were located strategically and had locational advantages to assume urban growth. They were placed at natural "transportation breaks" where travelers and commerce stopped to change conveyance and later logs were halted to be cut into boards. Moreover, in the era in which each town developed, the second quarter of the nineteenth century, technological innovations did not give one city or another the decisive edge in the competition for industry or population. All evolved into becoming lumber settlements gradually and struggled through a slow developmental period of logging technology. Environmental determinism was important, but it does not necessarily explain the eventual industrial triumph of some lumbertowns.

Although no single cause can explain all the complexities of successful urban beginnings, the performance of the urban entrepreneur may be a starting point. Saginaw, for example, was at first a paper town and then two cities competing vigorously with each other for local economic success. It was born amid the clang of competition. Persons like Norman Little and the Hoyts created an open environment for investing in both towns, especially East Saginaw, by attracting and accepting newcomers from other towns and regions. Lower Saginaw (Bay City) at its early stage was started by outside investors, and half of it, West Bay City, was originally a company-owned lumbertown. Rivalries with nearby towns did not exist, and absentee ownership crippled the migration of talent and capital. Muskegon, likewise had no real nearby economic competition. The performance of the early entrepreneurs in Muskegon was mixed; they operated in a closed environment and only moved slowly into the lumber business.

As the towns matured in the post-Civil War era, they slowly developed distinct characteristics while wrestling with almost identical economic and social problems. Their differing responses to the challenges of growth and development revealed the different character of the towns. Violence became a segment of early life in lumbertown environs. Shanty boys and mill hands took to the saloons, brothels, and streets every weekend and especially in the spring after winter logging. Throughout the 1870s and early 1880s little official effort was made to weed out vice. Economic needs encouraged the towns

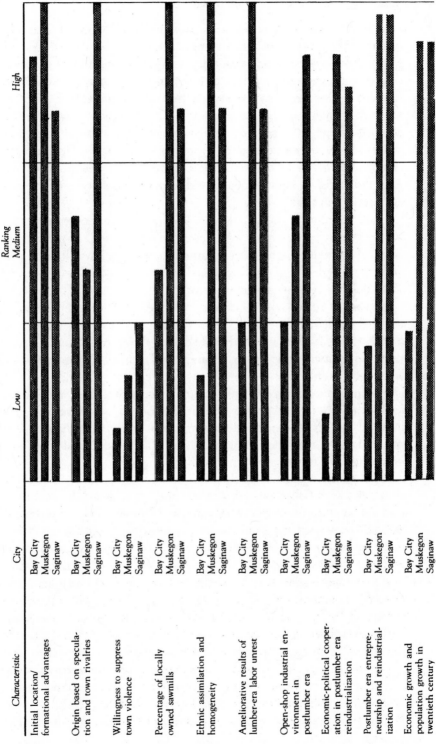

CHART 2.
A Typological Profile of the Lumbertowns

to adjust to a degree of fighting, brawling, and whoring. Saginaw made some efforts to rid itself of prostitution in the late 1870s, and Muskegon debated moral reform. Bay City's sheriff, in contrast, owned a brothel and collected taxes from the competition. The Catacombs in Bay City developed the reputation as the worst of all lumbertown vice zones. An unsavory reputation may have discouraged some from settling in Bay City, but it probably attracted others, both transient and entrepreneurial. Not one lumbertown could really claim to be holier than the rest. The toleration of logging violence, though, probably did little to negatively affect later economic practices.

However, during the boom years the local lumber economy came to be gradually dominated by fewer investors and larger lumber firms. Absentee ownership maintained its grip on Bay City and prevented the growth of a diversified local economy. When the pine was depleted, the absentee investor moved westward. These large operators set social and economic examples that were replicated by the few resident lumbermen. From the viewpoint of any natural resource town, its leaders can hardly do anything worse than to pack their equipment, take their money, and leave. In Saginaw and Muskegon, lumbermen-entrepreneurs both collectively and individually were decisive in creating economic growth. They maintained local control of their primary export, attracted new investors, and later pushed for planned industrial growth. They subordinated ethnic, religious, and labor tensions as much as possible and some mobilized for the future when the lumber era ended.

The ethnic construct of the communities differed. It is doubtful that Bay City's Polish sawmill workers alone restrained the economic and political future of that lumbertown. However, their importation as scab laborers by the lumbermen, the low wages, and some ethnic isolation led to the creation of a divided city. Economic exploitation and geographical isolation of immigrant groups established ethnic and religious enclaves that persist to this day in Bay City. The French Canadians, the Germans, and especially the Poles remained unskilled laborers and failed to experience the success associated with upward social, political, or economic mobility. Ethnic groups developed a group consciousness that caused them to distrust one another and especially the absentee owners. They established separate churches, schools, and social groups and passed on their parochial values to future generations. Their limited financial resources, lavished on their own institutions, were seldom used for the greater community good.

In contrast, at Muskegon, and to a lesser extent in Saginaw, a degree of ethnic homogeneity created work forces that were perceived for decades as being docile and compliant. The large German population in Saginaw and Dutch in Muskegon experienced upward mobility as resident lumbermen identified and worked with foreigners economically and socially. The immigrants entered civic life as individuals rather than as representatives of ethnic enclaves. These more ethnically homogeneous lumbertowns saw group consciousness dissipate early, and the towns became more centralized in their efforts to succeed at the end of the lumber era.

Ethnic groups and lumbermen-entrepreneurs influenced the directions that the ten-hour strikes took in the mid-1880s. The movements in Muskegon led to the election of laborers' leaders to several local and state offices. Here they used their powers not to carry on labor-capital conflict but to ameliorate conditions of the sawmill men and to better the physical environment of their lumbertown. Local lumbermen, at first intransigent, later, after successfully weathering the strike, voluntarily established the ten-hour day in Muskegon's sawmills. Workingmen and lumbermen would soon come to struggle together for Muskegon's economic future. The labor movement remained inactive for decades. In Bay City the Great Strike was met by lumbermen with much less finesse than in Muskegon. Absentee owner Sage threatened to close his mills for good in Bay City. Repeatedly, Bay City lumbermen fired employees and hired scab laborers. Some of this labor conflict carried over into Saginaw, and subsequently the entire valley developed a strong labor movement. The open-shop industrial environment of Muskegon did not apply to these Lake Huron shore lumbertowns.

Despite a labor movement in Saginaw, it, along with Muskegon, reindustrialized and both cities became major industrial areas. Both lumbertowns benefited from remarkably able lumbermen-entrepreneurs who guided these cities into a second—postnatural resource—stage of industrialization. Political readjustments that took place after the ten-hour strikes often aided reindustrialization. In Muskegon and Saginaw a balance and serenity evolved as citizens were willing to let the lumber oligarchy dominate politics to protect their investments and guide reconstruction. In Bay City, neither economic elites nor political factions envisioned city-building policies after the lumber era.

Likewise, from 1890 to 1910 individual lumbermen and associated organizations in Muskegon and Saginaw spearheaded bonus drives to ensure reindustrialization. They recruited other businessmen to

Muskegon and Saginaw and plowed some of their own profits into new industries and growth. When the new entrepreneurs prospered, so did the former lumbermen and sawmill workers. These economic leaders also physically revitalized their communities. They built schools, hospitals, libraries, parks, and industrial suburbs. They pushed for political consolidation to head off duplication and costly intercity competition in the postlumber period. By 1920 both Muskegon and Saginaw experienced population growth and economic recovery. They were mobilized for the twentieth century and the age of the automobile.

At the negative side of the scale of entrepreneurship was Bay City. Absentee ownership was the main reason that lumbermen showed little commitment to reindustrialization and local growth. Bay City developed a conservative business elite largely emulating the conservatism of those regional absentee lumber traders from New York. Outside control of its largest sawmills discouraged the emergence of new lumbermen-entrepreneurs in Bay City; those that did emerge eventually migrated to new forests at the end of the era. The few lumbermen who stayed invested cautiously in wood-related industries. This may have served Bay City adequately during the immediate postlumber era, but it was not a wise step considering that this stage was one of transition. Bay City's economic leaders avoided manufacturing, especially manufacturing that was speculative and controlled by nonresident corporations. The two cities, West Bay City and Bay City, consolidated only in 1905, sixteen years after both Muskegon and Saginaw. When the new industrial age emerged by World War I, Bay City remained a modest city; it had little hope of ever become a leading industrial center.

The experiences of Muskegon, Saginaw, and Bay City demonstrate that the quality of economic leaders and, at times, the cultural makeup of the town may well determine which cities grow and which stagnate. From the evidence of the lumbertowns, entrepreneurial leadership is important in determining industrial success. Ethnic factors are important, but perceptions of ethnicity perhaps are more important than reality. Demonstrable evidence makes it clear that there was little difference between the Dutch sawmill worker in Muskegon, the German laborer in Saginaw, or the Polish mill man in Bay City. However, evidence is often irrelevant in a society influenced by social Darwinist prejudices and antipathy to organized labor movements. The Poles experienced prejudice for both reasons and were perceived as less desirable citizens. It is not clear whether these perceptions retarded industrial growth in Bay City in the postlumber era, but hostility did create an ethnically divided town that prevented social and political progess well into the latter part of the twentieth century.

A study of the lumbertowns is another way to discover how cities survive the first stage—or in this case the natural resource stage—of urbanization. It also makes clear that despite common origins and economies, institutions, habits, and values are not to be found in the same combinations in fairly similar cities. Many other cities need to be studied to provide a further basis for comparative analysis. However, it is evident that a researcher simply cannot study towns quantitatively to arrive at theories of urban growth. The examples within clearly indicate that the human elements—the unmeasurable—are most important in determining urban success. The story of urban progression must be concerned with the imponderables: the aspects of change that derive from social values and attitudes. The force of entrepreneurial commitment, the sense of community identity, the fabric of the ethnic neighborhood, and the function of culture and class are the aspects that give understanding and purpose to the animated city.

Notes

INTRODUCTION

1. An interesting discussion on the neglect of forest history is found in Charles Twining, "The Lumbering Frontier," in Susan L. Flader, ed., *The Great Lakes Forest* (Santa Cruz, Calif.: Forest History Society, 1983), pp. 121–36. The Michigan lumbertowns' experiences in particular—the most important in size, output, technology, and economics of lumbering in the Great Lakes states—are not represented by a single volume that narrates the complex history of an industrial lumbertown. Scholars have offered a smattering of journal articles about experiences in individual lumbertowns, but no one has expanded these efforts into a major work of community history.

See George M. Blackburn and Sherman L. Richards, Jr., "A Demographic History of the West: Manistee County, Michigan, 1860," *Journal of American History* 57 (December 1970): pp. 600–618; Jeremy W. Kilar, "Community and Authority Responses to the Saginaw Valley Lumber Strike, 1885," *Journal of Forest History* 20 (April 1976): pp. 67–79; Jeremy W. Kilar, "Black Pioneers in the Michigan Lumber Industry," *Journal of Forest History* 24 (July 1980): pp. 142–51; George M. Blackburn, "The Timber Industry in Manistee County, Michigan," *Journal of Forest History* 18 (April 1974): pp. 14–21; Anita Shafer Goodstein, "Labor Relations in the Saginaw Valley Lumber Industry, 1865–1885," *Bulletin of the Business History Society* 27 (1953): pp. 193–221; Carl Addison Leech, "Deward: A Lumberman's Ghost Town," *Michigan History* 28 (1944): pp. 5–19. Only Daniel T. Yakes and Hugh A. Hornstein in *The Many Lives of Muskegon* (Muskegon: Muskegon Community College, 1979), a collection of chapters on different aspects of Muskegon's past, is an effort at a "community" history of a Michigan lumbertown.

2. David J. Russo, *Families and Communities: A New View of American History* (Nashville, Tenn.: American Association for State and Local History, 1974), pp. 60, 233–36.

3. Adna F. Weber, *The Growth of the City in the Nineteenth Century: A Study in Statistics* (New York: Macmillan, 1899; Ithaca, N.Y.: Cornell University Press, 1963), pp. 172–73.

4. Kenneth T. Jackson and Stanley K. Schultz, *Cities in American History* (New York: Alfred A. Knopf, 1972), pp. 2–4.

5. Ellis Lucia, "Review of *The Loggers*, by Time Life Books with text by Richard L. Williams," *Journal of Forest History* 20 (July 1976): p. 159.

6. See Robert R. Dykstra, *The Cattle Towns* (New York: Alfred A. Knopf, 1968), chap. 3.

CHAPTER 1. LUMBERING AND LUMBERTOWNS

1. George Wilson Pierson, *Tocqueville and Beaumont in America* (New York: Oxford University Press, 1938), pp. 230, 250.

2. Ibid., p. 271. For a comparative account of Tocqueville's and Beaumont's observations of the Saginaw Valley see Jeremy W. Kilar, "Tocqueville's Companion Traveler: Gustave de Beaumont and the Journey into Michigan Wilderness, 1831," *Michigan History* 68 (January/February 1984): pp. 34–39.

3. Pierson, *Tocqueville and Beaumont in America*, pp. 262–77. The pine tree they measured was twenty feet in circumference.

4. General required readings of the Great Lakes lumber frontier may begin with the recent publication of *The Great Lakes Forest: An Environmental and Social History*, ed. Susan L. Flader; William G. Rector's important *Log Transportation in the Lake States Lumber Industry, 1840–1916* (Glendale, Calif.: Arthur H. Clark Company, 1953) is mandatory reading, as is James Willard Hurst's *Lumber Industry in Wisconsin, 1836–1915* (Cambridge: Harvard University Press, 1920); and Vernon Jenson's account of labor and lumbering, *Lumber and Labor* (New York: Farrar and Rinehart, 1945); also see Hurst's, *Law and Economic Growth: The Legal History of the Lumber Industry in Wisconsin, 1830–1900* (Madison; State Historical Society of Wisconsin, 1951).

5. Milo M. Quaife and Sidney Glazer, *Michigan: From Primitive Wilderness to Industrial Commonwealth* (New York: Prentice-Hall, 1948), p. 150; and U.S. Department of Interior, Bureau of the Census, *A Compendium of the Ninth Census, 1870* (Washington: GPO, 1872), p. 58.

6. James Cooke Mills, *History of Saginaw County, Michigan* (Saginaw: Seeman & Peters, 1918), 1: 402; and Harold M. Foehl and Irene M. Hargreaves, *The Story of Logging the White Pine in the Saginaw Valley* (Bay City, MI: Red Keg Press, 1964), pp. 4–7.

7. R. V. Reynolds and Albert H. Pierson, "Tracing the Sawmill Westward," *American Forests*, XXXI, (November 1925), pp. 643–648.

8. Foehl and Hargreaves, *Logging the White Pine in the Saginaw Valley*, p. 11.

9. Bruce Catton, *Michigan: A Bicentennial History* (New York: W. W. Norton & Co., 1976), p. 102.

10. Edgar M. Hoover, *The Location of Economic Activity* (New York: McGraw-Hill, 1948), p. 7. See also Walter Isard, *Location and Space Economy: A General Theory Relating to Industrial Location, Market Areas, Land Use, Trade, and Urban Structure* (Cambridge: MIT Press, 1956), pp. 93–95. The major economic consideration was the considerable amount of waste resulting in transforming a log into dried lumber. In the nineteenth century, finished lumber represented less than forty percent of the original log's weight. Milling operations—sawing, planing, and drying—reduced the final product. Early, primitive saws cut a kerf up to 1/2 inch wide. Planing a board further reduced its thickness and drying lessened the log's weight by about five percent. Thus, because costs for hauling logs were based on weight, it made sense to convert logs into wood as close to the timber supply as possible. See Leo K. Cummins, "Disposal of Wood Wastes," in *Forest Land Use and the Environment* (Missoula: University of Montana, School of Forestry, 1971), pp. 125–31.

11. A. Koroleff, ed., *River Drive of Pulpwood* (Ottawa: Canadian Pulp and Paper Association, 1946), pp. 120–24. Michigan lumbermen never really changed to railroad logging from river logging. Charles H. Hackley noted in 1878 correspondence

that Muskegon was a lake port and that the custom was to "put lumber on the dock—not the rails." Hackley to B. F. Demming, August 14, 1878, Hackley-Hume Papers, Michigan State University Archives.

12. Rector, *Log Transportation in the Great Lakes States' Lumber Industry*, p. 128; and Roland Maybee, *Michigan's White Pine Era, 1840–1900* (Lansing: Michigan Historical Commission, 1960), p. 36; also Minutes of the Tittabawassee Boom Company, 1864–1889, 2 vols. (in files at Hoyt Public Library, Saginaw, Mich.).

13. Norman Schmaltz, "The Land Nobody Wanted: The Dilemma of Michigan's Cutover Lands," *Michigan History* 67 (January-February, 1983): 32–33.

14. Fred Dustin, *Saginaw History* (manuscript at Hoyt Public Library, Saginaw, Mich., 1949), pp. 86–90.

15. Burt Garner, "A Notable United States Military Road," *Michigan History* 20 (1936): 177–84.

16. An examination of the decennial census, 1850–1860, indicates that unimproved, taxable land was the most frequent form of land ownership. U.S. Census Office, *Seventh Census of the United States: 1850* (Washington: R. Armstrong, 1853), pp. 903–7; Michigan Department of State, *Statistics of the State of Michigan, 1860* (Lansing: John A. Kerr and Co., 1861), pp. 21, 77, 109, 237. Also George N. Fuller, *Economic and Social Beginnings of Michigan: A Study of the Settlement of the Lower Peninsula during the Territorial Period, 1805–1837* (Lansing, 1916), p. 66; and Douglas H. Gordon and George S. May, "The Michigan Land Rush in 1836," *Michigan History* 43 (March 1959): 7.

17. U.S. Department of Interior, Bureau of Land Management, Eastern Division, *Tract Books, Michigan N and E and Michigan N and W*, vols. 1–17; and Dustin, *Saginaw History*, p. 87.

18. Quoted in Dustin, *Saginaw History*, p. 42.

19. John T. Blois, *Gazetteer of the State of Michigan* (Detroit: Sydney L. Rood and Co., 1840), p. 355.

20. Mills, *History of Saginaw County, Michigan*, 2: 30.

21. For an analysis of the Saginaw County Economy in 1837 see James H. Lanman, *History of Michigan* (New York: E. French, 1839), pp. 293–94 and 300–6.

22. Ironically, this land had originally been purchased by Little's father in 1822 following his trip to Saginaw. He later sold the property to several other speculators.

23. Dustin, *Saginaw History*, pp. 96–98.

24. Ibid., pp. 97–98; a similar account may be found in Mills, *History of Saginaw County*, p. 182.

25. Michigan Department of State, *Census and Statistics of the State of Michigan, 1864* (Lansing: John A. Kerr and Co., 1865), pp. 32, 144, 200.

26. Alfred Hoyt, Jesse's brother, returned to New York after his father died in 1854. Jesse Hoyt also returned to New York shortly afterward, and although a frequent visitor to Saginaw, he managed his investments in Michigan from New York City. See Mills, *History of Saginaw County*, pp. 244–47.

27. See Dustin, *Saginaw History*, p. 120; and Stuart D. Gross, *Saginaw: A History of the Land and the City* (Woodland Hills, Calif.: Windsor Publications, 1980), p. 15.

28. *Bay City, City Directory*, 1868–69, p. 3.

29. The Center House still stands in Bay City as the oldest residence in the Saginaw Valley. It has recently been moved to become part of a historical redevelopment district on Bay City's west side.

30. Miller wrote extensively of the many difficulties, including the deception of friends, deceit from hired hands, and the weather in describing the conditions that hindered his efforts to build the sawmill. See *History of Bay County* (Chicago: H. R. Paige & Co., 1883), p. 40.

31. James G. Birney MSS, several files in Clements Library, The University of Michigan, Ann Arbor.

32. W. R. Bates, *The History, Commercial Advantages, and Future Prospects of Saginaw* (E. Saginaw, 1874), p. 40.

33. *History of Bay County*, p. 71.

34. Ibid., p. 82.

35. In 1837 the state's first geologist, Douglas Houghton, examined the Saginaw River tributaries for salt. He insisted that it was of enough quantity and quality to sink salt wells. In 1838 the legislature gave Houghton $3,000 to carry on this work. He sank a well on the Tittabawassee River near Sanford, but the project was abandoned because of cost and transport difficulties in the wilderness. See George N. Fuller, *Geological Reports of Douglas Houghton, First State Geologist of Michigan, 1835–1843* (Lansing: Historical Commission, 1928), pp. 31–34, 170.

36. Quoted in George E. Butterfield, *Bay County Past and Present, Centennial Edition* (Bay City: Board of Education, 1957), p. 162.

37. John Denis Haeger, *The Investment Frontier: New York Businessmen and the Economic Development of the Old Northwest* (Albany: State University of New York Press, 1981), p. 85. Haeger notes that Arthur Bronson, New York developer of Midwestern lands, sold his interests in several settlements near Grand Rapids because he believed they were not close enough to population concentrations in southern Michigan.

38. *Muskegon Chronicle, Romance of Muskegon, Michigan 1937, Centennial Year* (Muskegon: The Muskegon Chronicle, 1937), p. xxiii.

39. James Glasgow, *Muskegon, Michigan: The Evolution of a Lake Port* (Chicago: University of Chicago Libraries, 1939), pp. 11–12.

40. H. L. Wheeler, "Stage Coach and Iron Horse in Muskegon," typewritten manuscript in Hackley Public Library, Muskegon, p. 3.

41. Ambrosia Sanford, "Extracts from Letters Written by Mrs. Samuel R. Sanford, 1858–1867," typewritten manuscript, Hackley Public Library, Muskegon, p. 4.

42. Anita Shafer Goodstein, *Biography of a Businessman: Henry W. Sage, 1814–1897* (Ithaca, N.Y.: Cornell University Press, 1962), p. 77.

Chapter 2. Lumbertown Enterprise

1. Goodstein, *Biography of a Businessman*, pp. 112–34.

2. Wilson R. Cronenwett, "Charles Hackley: Muskegon Lumber Baron Benefactor," *Chronicle, Magazine of the Historical Society of Michigan* 15 (spring 1979): 17.

3. G. W. Hotchkiss, *History of the Lumber and Forest Industry of the Northwest* (Chicago: G. W. Hotchkiss, 1898), p. 290; and Barbara Ellen Benson, "Logs and Lumber: The Development of the Lumber Industry in Michigan's Lower Peninsula,

1837–1870" (Ph.D. diss. Indiana University, 1976), p. 143. See also *Lumberman's Gazette*, November 5, 1879; and Mills, *History of Saginaw County*, 1:396.

4. Rector, *Log Transportation in the Lake States*, p. 38; and Wilson Compton, *The Organization of the Lumber Industry: With Special Reference to the Influences Determining the Prices of Lumber in the United States* (Chicago: American Lumberman, 1916) pp. 88, 112. See also *Lumberman's Gazette*, January, February, and March 1873.

5. A sash saw consisted of a thin blade placed in a small, rectangular, wooden frame and held rigidly at the top and bottom. Like a window sash, the frame with the attached blade would be driven by water or steam power up and down, and the log would be repeatedly passed through the blade to produce boards. See Rolland H. Maybee, *Michigan's White Pine Era*, pp. 44–46.

6. Ibid., p. 47; and George F. Lewis and C. B. Headley, *Annual Statement of the Business of Saginaw Valley and "The Shore" for 1868* (East Saginaw, 1869), pp. 652–55. See also George B. Engberg, "Labor in the Lake States Lumber Industry, 1830–1930," (Ph.D. diss. University of Minnesota, 1949), pp. 205–213.

7. Mills, *History of Saginaw County*, 1: 415–16; Silas Farmer, *The History of Detroit and Michigan*, 2d ed. (Detroit: Silas Farmer & Co., 1889), 2: 1219–25; and L. H. Conger, "Pioneer Days in Muskegon" (MSS, Hackley Public Library, Muskegon, 1925), p. 10.

8. *Lumberman's Gazette*, November 3, 1877.

9. *Census of Michigan, 1874*, pp. 270–384.

10. Five bushels of salt filled one barrel. Thus the bounty was fifty cents a barrel. The average price in 1865 was $1.80 per barrel.

11. Dustin, *Saginaw History*, pp. 144–54, and *Saginaw Courier*, February 7, 1860.

12. J. W. Jenks, "The Michigan Salt Association," *Political Science Quarterly*, 3 (1941): 81.

13. See Dustin, *Saginaw History*, pp. 983–95; Butterfield, *Bay County Past and Present*, pp. 83–86; Goodstein, *Biography of a Businessman*, pp. 93–95; and Mills, *History of Saginaw County*, 1: 56.

14. H. W. Sage to H. W. Sage & Co., West Bay City, May 10, 1880, Henry W. Sage MSS, as cited in Goodstein, *Biography of a Businessman*, p. 99.

15. Ibid.

16. U.S. Census, *Tenth Census of the United States: 1880*, vol. 2, *Manufacturers*, pp. 265–71; quote cited in Butterfield, *Bay County*, p. 86.

17. Rector, *Log Transportation in Lake States*, pp. 173–74; and Clifford Allen and Harold Titus, eds., *Michigan Log Marks* (n.p., WPA and Michigan Agricultural Experiment Stations, 1941), pp. 9–11.

18. Allen and Titus, *Michigan Log Marks*, p. 13. Sage held only twenty-eight of the one thousand shares first issued. Goodstein, *Biography of a Businessman*, p. 100.

19. Minutes of Tittabawassee Boom Company, "Annual Report, January 9, 1869," typed manuscript in Hoyt Public Library, Saginaw, 1: 144. Boom company operations along the rivers were perhaps the first significant, far-reaching efforts by man to markedly alter his riverine environment. Booming operations, damming, and rearranging the very shape of the river affected aquatic habitat by adding sediment and increasing water temperatures. Species of fresh-water fish quickly disappeared and the lower reaches of the lumbertown rivers, especially, soon came to resemble modern-day industrial waterways.

20. Estimates were based on five logs being equal to a thousand board feet. See Allen and Titus, *Michigan Log Marks*, p. 32.

21. Rector notes that the association with the name Weyerhaeuser probably greatly exaggerated the reputation of the Beef Slough boom. See Rector, *Log Transportation in Lake States*, p. 32.

22. Minutes of Tittabawassee Boom Company, 1 and 2: 50–406.

23. In 1885 the state legislature did establish a twelve percent limit to boom company dividends. Large owners, like Sage and McGraw in Bay City, pressured the boom company to include them in on the rebates. The pressure and criticism directed at the Tittabawassee operators helped create the image that a Saginaw "boom ring" controlled booming operations and profited exorbitantly at the expense of Bay City lumbermen. However, despite the rate discrimination by the Tittabawassee Boom Company, Sage did not join those who pushed for a law to regulate dividends. He had controlling interest in two boom companies to the north of Bay City, along the Rifle and Au Gres rivers, and carried on similar discriminatory practices toward other loggers that he complained were being used against him on the Tittabawassee. See Goodstein, *Biography of a Businessman*, pp. 102–6.

24. *Tenth Census of the United States, 1880*, 2: 265–71.

25. Butterfield, *Bay County Past and Present*, p. 83.

26. "The Wickes Corporation," special supplement to *Saginaw News* on Wickes 125th anniversary, *Saginaw News*, May 24, 1979.

27. Michigan State Agricultural Society, *Annual Report for 1855* (Lansing: Hosmer and Fitch, 1856), pp. 828–29; also Maurice E. McGaugh, "The Settlement of the Saginaw Basin," (Ph.D. diss. University of Chicago, 1950), p. 158; *Tenth Census, 1880*, vol. 2, *Manufactures*, pp. 265–71.

28. Glasgow, *Muskegon, Michigan*, p. 39.

29. Gross, *Saginaw*, p. 175; and *Muskegon Chronicle, Romance of Muskegon*, p. lxvi.

30. John Cumming, "Little Jake: Saginaw's Merchandising Giant," *Chronicle: Magazine of the Historical Society of Michigan* 14 (summer 1978): 19–24; see also Gross, *Saginaw*, pp. 46–48.

31. Seligman is best remembered in East Saginaw for his gift of a clock tower and statue. In 1890 he purchased the Music Block, a triangular piece of land bound by Genesee, Jefferson, and Lapeer streets. Here he renovated the buildings and installed an imposing clock tower where it was visible from most of the downtown area. To crown his achievement he placed a statue on top of the clock tower that was supposed to be a replica of himself. The contrast between the statue and Seligman was apparent to contemporaries. The statue looked more like that of a Civil War soldier. Most people in 1890 accepted Seligman's eccentricities and congratulated him for his community spirit. However, later generations forgot his sense of humor and unusual braggadocio. When the statue was blown down in a fierce windstorm in 1940, some townspeople denounced Little Jake as a huckster and fraud. See Cumming, "Little Jake," pp. 22–24.

32. Kilar, "Black Pioneers in the Michigan Lumber Industry," 143–49.

33. *Muskegon Chronicle, Romance of Muskegon*, p. lxxiii.

34. Engberg, "Labor in the Lake States Lumber Industry, 1830–1930," pp. 213–16; also see Goodstein, *Biography of a Businessman*, pp. 114–15.

35. John Fitzmaurice, *The Shanty Boy or Life in a Lumber Camp*, facsimile reprint of 1889 ed. (Historical Society of Michigan, Ann Arbor, 1978), p. 174; see also Frank P. Bohn, "This Was the Forest Primeval," *Michigan History Magazine* 21 (winter-spring 1937): 23–31.

36. Fitzmaurice, *The Shanty Boy*, pp. 114–15.

37. Although the Reverend James Ballard, leading a temperance crusade in Muskegon at the time, was challenged in this assessment and a count was taken indicating eighty-four saloons, this would seem an exaggeration considering that the number of residents in the city was only fifteen hundred. See *Romance of Muskegon*, pp. cxxv, lxxviii.

38. Freeman Coats, *Diary of a Department: A History of the Saginaw Police Department* (Saginaw: Saginaw Public Libraries, 1965), p. 14; and Fitzmaurice, *The Shanty Boy*, pp. 176–77.

39. Fitzmaurice, *The Shanty Boy*, p. 174.

40. Fitzmaurice was a wanderer who worked in the woods, journeyed into the forest as a reporter for several East Saginaw newspapers, and became a "drunkard." He took the pledge in 1876, left journalism, and became a full-time temperance lecturer. Later he became a hospital agent selling accident insurance policies to woodsmen. His rhetorical style is reflective of his temperance involvement. Fitzmaurice, *The Shanty Boy*, p. 175.

41. *The Muskegon Chronicle*, September 23, 1875, reported an affair that may have taken place at the Canterbury: "Another innovation upon Muskegon morals occurred at a dance house across the lake Saturday evening, at which forty men and women stripped off their clothes and danced in as nude a condition as the aborigines of the forest."

42. *Muskegon Chronicle*, *Romance of Muskegon*, p. cxxv.

43. *Annual Report of the Bay City Board of Police Commissioners, 1883–89; 1891–93*. The only remaining copies were retrieved from materials to be discarded upon renovation of Bay City's city hall in 1978. The author has access to these reports, which now are in the collection of a private library in Bay City. These statistics confirm the observations made by Engberg, "Labor in the Lake States Lumber Industry," pp. 163–90.

44. Fitzmaurice, *The Shanty Boy*, p. 177.

45. For comparisons, see Lynn I. Perrigo, "Law and Order in Early Colorado Mining Camps," *Mississippi Valley Historical Review*, 38 (June 1941): 56–57; Frederick H. Wines, *Report on the Defective, Dependent, and Delinquent Cases, Returned to Tenth Census of the U.S., June 1, 1880* (Washington, GPO, 1880), pp. 566–76. Wines lists one hundred houses in Leadville in 1880; however, newspaper accounts claimed only thirty-eight. See David Lavender, "This Wondrous Town, This Instant City," *The American West* (August 1967), pp. 1–14; also Cy Martin, *Whiskey and Wild Women* (New York: Doubleday & Co., 1958), pp. 156–60; and also Dykstra, *The Cattle Towns*, p. 140, n. 9. Dykstra cautions that reports on the number of prostitutes often must be discounted. Adventure books and popular accounts of the Wild West invariably exaggerate these numbers beyond reason. Also, Phillip D. Jordan, *Frontier Law and Order: Ten Essays* (Lincoln: University of Nebraska Press, 1965), p. 138; and Jeremy W. Kilar, "Law and Order in Lumber Camps and Towns," *Encyclopedia of Forest and Conservation History* (New York: Macmillan, 1983), 1:334–36.

46. Fitzmaurice estimated that in Bay City the forty saloons in the Catacombs area had "from three to five 'pretty waiter girls' in each." *The Shanty Boy*, pp. 176–77. The houses in Muskegon were mentioned in newspaper accounts and police arrest reports in the *Muskegon Chronicle* and *Muskegon Journal* between 1867 and 1875. See also Wines, *Report on the Defective*, pp. 566–76. The 1880 census, according to Wines, asked for the number of houses of ill fame in 494 towns with populations of 5,000 or more. Returns were so incomplete and so many communities failed to reply accurately that the resultant published survey must be read with skepticism.

47. Fitzmaurice, *The Shanty Boy*, pp. 178–79; and *Romance of Muskegon*, p. cxxv.

CHAPTER 3. SAWDUST CITIES

1. Alexis de Tocqueville, *Democracy in America*, trans. Henry Reeve (New York: G. Dearborn & Company, 1838), 2: 106.

2. A "common" Midwestern pattern is described by Bayrd Still, "Patterns of Mid-Nineteenth Century Urbanization in the Middle West," *The Mississippi Valley Historical Review* 28 (September 1941): 187–206. Still sees a predominant concern for trade and commerce giving way in time to the needs of creating manufacturing cities.

3. Mills, *History of Saginaw County*, p. 238.

4. See *History of Bay County, 1883*, pp. 178, 182, 170; also Goodstein, *Biography of a Businessman*, pp. 20–25.

5. The original settlements incuded Port Sherman, Bluffton, Lakeside, and Pickettown. These, along with the small enclaves of Pinchtown and Brewery Hill, were annexed by Muskegon in the late 1880s or early 1890s. North Muskegon and Reedsville were on the opposite side of the lake some distance from Muskegon proper.

6. Rivers served as winter roads. The ice often offered a clearer roadway than the partly cleared land trails. Moreover, because farming was practically nonexistent in the early lumber era, agriculture exerted little pressure for improved roads.

7. This conclusion is emphasized repeatedly in early studies of the lumbertowns' basins. See Glasgow, *Muskegon, Michigan* pp. 26–28, 43; McGaugh, "The Settlement of the Saginaw Basin," pp. 77–79; and Butterfield, *Bay County Past and Present* pp. 118–19.

8. In 1856 and 1857 Congress gave Michigan 3,775,000 acres of land to distribute to railroads. Lumbermen's reservations about early railroad building are found in Glasgow, *Muskegon, Michigan*, p. 47; and Dustin, *Saginaw History*, pp. 160–61.

9. Dustin, *Saginaw History*, p. 162.

10. Bullock was also an owner and director of the Jackson and Lansing Railroad and probably wanted this line to be the first to come into Saginaw City rather than the cross-river rival line.

11. *Bay City Journal*, November 30, 1865.

12. *Bay City Journal,* March 2, 1867.

13. Sage's offer to support additional construction was accepted by the Jackson, Lansing and Saginaw Company. He advanced the railroad more money in return for a $47,000 mortgage on railroad lands. See Goodstein, *Biography of a Businessman,* p. 122.

14. *Muskegon Chronicle, Romance of Muskegon,* p. lxxi; and also Yakes, *Many Lives of Muskegon,* chap. 9, pp. 5–7.

15. City Common Council records for East Saginaw and Saginaw City, 1865–1875 in Hoyt Public Library, Saginaw. See also Mills, *History of Saginaw County,* pp. 108–212.

16. Cited in *Muskegon Chronicle, Romance of Muskegon* p. lviii.

17. Coats, *Diary of a Department,* pp. 5–6; *Bay City Journal,* March 16, 1865; also *Bay City Tribune,* November 5, 1887 (special section); and *Muskegon Weekly Enterprise,* September 9, 1870. Richard Maxwell Brown in his history of American vigilante movements fails to list any such extra-legal initiatives in Michigan. See Richard M. Brown, *Strain of Violence* (New York: Oxford University Press, 1975), appendix 3, pp. 305–19.

18. See *Muskegon Chronicle,* June 14, 1871; see also minutes of East Saginaw Common Council, 1860–1890, Hoyt Library, Saginaw.

19. See Coats, *Diary of a Department,* p. 16.

20. In 1879, for example, the *Northwestern Lumberman* mentioned the casualities usually on p. 5; and *The Muskegon News and Reporter* on April 22, 1882. A detailed enumeration of deaths especially in Wisconsin and Minnesota can be found in Engberg, "Labor in the Lake States Lumber Industry, 1830–1930," pp. 228ff.

21. Fitzmaurice, *The Shanty Boy,* pp. 105–6.

22. See *Bay City, City Directory* 1863–1885; also Engberg, "Labor in the Lake States," p. 250. In 1893 several businessmen led the way in reorganizing the subscription hospital in Muskegon and turning it into a public facility. Charles Hackley donated almost one million dollars for the land, building, and equipment for a new hospital in 1902; see Richard H. Harms, "Life after Lumbering: Charles H. Hackley and the Emergence of Muskegon, Michigan," (Ph.D. diss. Michigan State University, 1984) pp. 275–78.

23. *Saginaw Weekly Enterprise,* May 30, 1872.

24. Although, as Birney noted, the lumbertowns were not known for their pursuit of knowledge, it is ironic that in Bay City, despite the accumulated wealth, no lumber baron built that city a public library facility. Even more noteworthy is that Bay City resident William L. Clements spent a fortune collecting a personal library that was later donated along with a building to house his collection to the University of Michigan.

25. See Les Arndt, *By These Waters* (Bay City: Bay City Times, 1976), pp. 141–43; Yakes, *Many Lives of Muskegon,* chap. 10, pp. 6–9; and Gross, *Saginaw,* p. 42.

26. Still, "Patterns in Mid-Nineteenth Century Urbanization," pp. 199–200.

27. *Saginaw Enterprise,* March 21, 1872, and the *Muskegon Chronicle,* September 5, 1875. Other public-spirit efforts can be seen in the *Saginaw Daily Courier* (East Saginaw), May 21, 1875, and August 4, 1877; *Saginaw Weekly Enterprise,* February 15, 1872; and *Muskegon Chronicle,* February 14, 1872.

28. See, for example, *Saginaw Daily Courier,* May 5, May 8, and July 25, 1875.

29. See *Saginaw Daily Courier,* July 27, May 28, and August 20, 1875. Also refer to *Saginaw Weekly Enterprise,* February 15, 1872, and *Bay City Tribune,* May 27, 1885.

30. For accounts of early immigration into the state see William L. Jenks, "Michigan Immigration," *Michigan History Magazine,* vol. 28 (spring 1944): 67–110; also McGaugh, "Settlement of the Saginaw Basin," pp. 216–19.

An excellent summation of nineteenth-century efforts to sell worthless, cutover lands in Michigan can be found in Norman J. Schmaltz, "The Land Nobody Wanted: The Dilemma of Michigan's Cutover Lands," *Michigan History Magazine,* vol. 67 (January/February 1983): 32–40. See also Harold Titus, "The Land Nobody Wanted: The Story of Michigan's Public Domain," *Michigan Agricultural Experimental Station Bulletin,* no. 332 (April 1945): 10–11. Publications printed to induce immigration during the lumber era include: Jackson, Lansing, and Saginaw R.R. Co., *Guide to the Lands of the State of Michigan* (Lansing: W. S. George and Co., 1881); and S. B. McCracken, *The State of Michigan 1875* (Lansing: W. S. George & Co., 1876).

31. Quoted in C. Warren Vanderhill, *Settling the Great Lakes Frontier: Immigration to Michigan, 1837–1924* (Lansing: Michigan Historical Commission, 1970), pp. 18–22.

32. Henry W. Sage, "Speech of H. W. Sage, January 16, 1884," *Michigan Pioneer and Historical Society, 1885* (Lansing: MPHS, 1886), 7: 19. Litchfield was also from New York and a fellow investor with Sage in the Brooklyn Transit System. He also built a sawmill in West Bay City. Sage's efforts to direct city politics is seen in letters to H. W. Sage & Co., July 1 and 8, 1871, in H. W. Sage papers, quoted in Goodstein, *Biography of a Businessman,* p. 125.

33. Charles W. Jay, *My New Home in Northern Michigan and Other Tales* (Trenton, N.J.: W. S. and E. W. Sharp, 1874), p. 22.

34. An early resident of Muskegon estimated that an average pile of drying lumber contained 30,000 board feet. If the figure is correct, the lumber cut in any one of the peak years would form 20,000 piles of such size, or an average of 540 piles for each of the 37 mills in Muskegon. See Glasgow, *Muskegon, Michigan: Evolution of a Lake Port,* p. 35.

35. Five business blocks were built in 1875 in Wenona. Of these, three borrowed money from Sage: Charles Babo, $6,000; Henry Alpin, $2,400; and Henry Allard, $100. See Goodstein, *Biography of a Businessman,* p. 120.

36. Stewart H. Holbrook, *Holy Old Mackinaw* (New York: Macmillan and Co., 1938), pp. 103–4; and Fitzmaurice, *The Shanty Boy,* pp. 173–75. Examples of continued debate over the notoriety of the Catacombs may be found in Holbrook, *Holy Old Mackinaw,* p. 108; Reymond J. Herek, "Bay City's Catacombs Lured Shanty Boys," *Bay City Times,* February 24, 1974; and Coates, *Diary of a Department,* pp. 17–18. *Bay City, City Directory,* 1884, 1885, 1886.

37. Pere Marquette Park on Lake Michigan near Muskegon was owned by the Muskegon Traction and Lighting Company, "which hoped to improve business for the streetcar railway by providing an attractive park as a terminus." See *Muskegon Chronicle, Romance of Muskegon,* p. cliii. Similar parks, Wenona Beach and Riverside Park, were built in Bay City and Saginaw in the 1890s.

38. Minutes of Bay City Common Council, September 2, 1865. Bay County Historical Society, Bay City, Michigan.

39. Herbert Nolan, *In Memory of the Camp Sixteeners*, reprint of 1939 ed. (Sanford Historical Society, Sanford, Mich. 1970), p. 20.

40. Caroline Bartlett Crane, *A Sanitary Survey of Saginaw Michigan* (Saginaw: n.p., 1911), pp. 6–7.

CHAPTER 4. ADJUSTING TO VIOLENCE

1. Fitzmaurice, *The Shanty Boy*, p. 176; Dykstra, *The Cattle Towns*, p. 116. This chapter previously appeared, in different form, in the *Journal of Forest History* and is reprinted here with the permission of the publisher. See Kilar, "Great Lakes Lumber Towns and Frontier Violence: A Comparative Study," *Journal of Forest History* 32 (April 1987): 71–85.

2. See Holbrook, *Holy Old Mackinaw* p. 108; Coats, *Diary of a Department*, pp. 17–18. Herek, "Bay City's Catacombs Lured Shanty Boys," *Bay City Times*, February 24, 1974; Robert Wells, *Daylight in the Swamp* (Garden City, N.J.: Doubleday, 1978), pp. 146–51.

3. Although the seasonal nature of the work created similar boom and bust times in the Western cattle towns and mining villages, the populations of the most representative Western towns never rivaled those of the lumber settlement. At the height of the cattle era, in the 1870s and early 1880s, the Kansas boomtowns of Dodge City and Abilene had only about 3,000 and 2,000 people, respectively. Only Wichita, which grew from 4,911 people in 1880 to 23,833 in 1890, reflected a growth rate comparable to the lumbertowns. In the mining towns of Gilpin County, Colorado, site of that territory's first important gold strike in the early 1860s, fewer than 5,500 people populated several settlements. Denver, though, which became a cosmopolitan mining supply center, reflected growth patterns like the lumbertowns. Between 1870 and 1880 its population grew from 4,759 to 35,629. Leadville and Cripple Creek, Colorado, experienced rapid and sizeable growth later in the century. See U.S. Census Office, *The Tenth Census of the United States, 1880* (Washington GPO, 1883); Dykstra, *The Cattle Towns*, p. 358; and Rodman W. Paul, *Mining Frontiers of the Far West, 1848–1888* (New York: Holt, Rinehart & Winston, 1963), p. 116.

Besides Dykstra's and Paul's books, studies compared that examine frontier violence include Eugene Hollon, *Frontier Violence: Another Look* (New York: Oxford University Press, 1974); Lynn I. Perrigo, "Law and Order in Early Colorado Mining Camps," *Mississippi Valley Historical Review* 25 (1919–20): 420–40; Phillip D. Jordan, *Frontier Law and Order: Ten Essays* (Lincoln: University of Nebraska Press, 1970); Frank R. Prassel, *The Western Peace Officer: A Legacy of Law and Order* (Norman: University of Oklahoma Press, 1972); and Roger D. McGrath, *Gunfighters, Highwaymen, and Vigilantes: Violence on the Frontier* (Berkeley: University of California Press, 1984).

4. Ten- and twenty-dollar payments were made yearly to Chippewa Indians under the 1819 Treaty of Saginaw. "Payment day" and several days afterward were days of "rioting and carousing" by the Indians. Unscrupulous traders, trappers, and saloon keepers offered the Indians "river water slightly tinctured with poor whiskey."

The "horrid din" of the payment days prompted incorporation and the passage of ordinances that closed saloons on payment days and outlawed the sale of liquor to the Indians. See Coats, *Diary of a Department*, pp. 5–6, for the complete text of this undocumented quotation.

5. Butterfield, *Bay County Past and Present*, pp. 169, 177–180.

6. *Muskegon Chronicle, Romance of Muskegon*, pp. lx, lxxxiv.

7. Ibid., p. cxivii.

8. Ibid.; Coats, *Diary of a Department*, pp. 4–5; and *Bay City Tribune* (special edition), November 4, 1887.

9. Dykstra, *The Cattle Towns*, pp. 124–25; *Muskegon Chronicle*, February 11, 1876. The "total annual costs of police" is also listed in Frederick H. Wines, *Report on the Defective, Dependent, and Delinquent Classes*, pp. 566–76. See above, pp. 92–93.

10. In 1880 Muskegon (population 11,262) had a force of five men, East Saginaw (19,016) had a force of sixteen men, and Bay City (20,693) only nine men on the force. See Wines, *Report on the Defective, Dependent, and Delinquent Classes*, pp. 566–76. Despite their claim to five members on the police force, Muskegon's city officials in the early years seldom hired a policeman for a full year. Yearly salaries indicate that few policemen were paid a living wage and several had to carry on part-time or family businesses on the side. See *Muskegon Chronicle*, June 12, 1867.

11. See *Muskegon Chronicle*, June 9, 1876, and April 20, 1870. For reports of drunken officers on duty see *Muskegon Chronicle*, April 20, 1870; April 30, 1874; May 7, 1878. See also *Muskegon Chronicle*, July 13, 1883. Police court judges reflected their environment as much as the local police. Not only was A. H. Giddings an alcoholic, but in 1880 Judge A. Beardsley, a member of a funeral entourage that got drunk on the way to the cemetery, entered a respectable boardinghouse and insulted several women guests. See *Muskegon Journal*, December 1, 1880.

12. Coats, *Diary of a Department*, p. 11; *Saginaw Morning Herald*, East Saginaw, November 22, 1882; and Raymond Herek, "Hell's Half Mile," an unpublished paper, Clark Historical Collections, Central Michigan University Library, Mount Pleasant, Mich., 1978; Michigan Attorney General, *Report of the Attorney General of Michigan 1877 and 1879* (Lansing: Office of Attorney General, 1877 and 1879); Reports of Bay County for 1877 and 1879.

13. *Muskegon Chronicle*, November 1, 24, 1876; and Fitzmaurice, *The Shanty Boy*, p. 171.

14. Coats, *Diary of a Department*, p. 15.

15. Ibid., pp. 17–18.

16. *Muskegon Chronicle*, December 7, 1883. After the establishment of its metropolitan police system in 1881, Bay City had just three police chiefs in the next seventy years. See Butterfield, *Bay City Past and Present*, pp. 168–69.

17. *Muskegon Chronicle*, December 10, 1880.

18. Ibid., January 4, 1878. The usual penalty for "resorting" or "visiting a house of ill repute" was a $2 to $5 fine and court costs. Prostitutes were assessed larger fines of from $20 to $50. Shanty boys who engaged in free fights that required the attention of the police were frequently lodged in jail or given token fines. Of the 219 arrested in Bay City in 1879 on assault and battery charges, only 45 received jail sentences that averaged seven days. As in the cattle towns, an adjustment to violence was conveniently made and toleration was the norm. Michigan Attorney General, *Report*, 1879.

19. *Muskegon Journal*, August 31, 1880; *Muskegon Chronicle*, December 10, 1880.

20. Michigan Attorney General, *Report, 1868–1888*.

21. Dykstra, *The Cattle Towns* pp. 129, 142–45.

22. Dodge City was an exception. See Dykstra, *The Cattle Towns*, pp. 126–27; also Jordan, *Frontier Law and Order*, chap. 8.

23. *Muskegon Chronicle*, January 7, 1879, and April 23, 1880.

24. One or two brothels were sometimes tolerated outside the city limits. See Lynn Perrigo, "Law and Order in Early Colorado Camps," pp. 56–57.

25. Leadville and Denver reported in the 1880 census thirty-eight and seven houses of ill repute, respectively; although another, perhaps exaggerated account, reports that Denver housed a thousand prostitutes. See Wines, *Report on the Defective*; and David Lavender, "This Wondrous Town, This Instant City," *The American West* 4 (August 1967): 4–14; also Cy Martin, *Whiskey and Wild Women* (New York: Doubleday & Co., 1958), p. 168. A Dodge City editor in 1878 estimated the number of local prostitutes at forty and the dance halls at three. Abilene is reported to have housed twenty-one women in three brothels. Caldwell's police court docket, which listed all resident prostitutes in the summer of 1880, displayed the names of only twenty-five women. Wichita, whose population growth matched Muskegon's, had four brothels and fourteen women at the height of the shipping season in 1872. See Dykstra, *The Cattle Towns* p. 140, n. 9. Cy Martin reported Wichita had a score of brothels in 1872 and several hundred harlots, and Abilene between two hundred and three hundred "Chippies"; see *Whiskey and Wild Women*, pp. 156–160. Yet another source says Wichita had fifty prostitutes in 1874, its last big shipping year; see Jordan, *Frontier Law and Order* p. 138.

26. Generalizations about occupational appellations used by prostitutes can be read in Jordan, *Frontier Law and Order*, p. 115, n. 1; and Myle H. Miller and Joseph W. Snell, *Great Gunfighters of the Kansas Cowtown, 1867–1886* (Lincoln: University of Nebraska Press, 1963), pp. 112–13. Census figures enumerated from 1880, *Tenth Census, Bay County*; amd Wines, *Report on the Defective*, pp. 566–76. See also *Annual Report to the Bay City Board of Police Commissioners, 1884–1889*.

27. The eastward migration was evidenced in Jordan, *Frontier Law and Order*, p. 132, n. 41. Jordan conducted an interview with Tiovo Bena in 1967, who recalled that prostitutes came to Marquette and Ishpeming, Michigan, after working Kansas and Colorado. In the many popular lumbertown accounts and newspaper articles, there are, appearing consistently, names of prostitutes who lived to old age in one or an other lumbertown. For example, read Fitzmaurice, *The Shanty Boy*; Herek, "Bay City Times, August 3, 1980. Permanence was also reflected in an oral interview I cocnducted in March 1980 at Bay City with Mrs. Elizabeth Konifer (fictitious name), whose mother's two older sisters came to Bay City in 1879 and became prostitutes. They lived comfortably, and in the 1930s one was given an extravagant burial by a local insurance agent.

28. See *Muskegon Chronicle*, March 10, 1976; July 7, 1883; August 23, 1870; and *Muskegon Journal*, August 13, 1880.

29. See *Muskegon Chronicle*, August 23, 1875; January 12, 1877; November 23, 1879; and July 17, 1884. *Muskegon Journal*, August 13, 1880. Similar accounts of suicide among prostitutes are in *Bay City Morning Chronicle*, February 14, 1874; March 5, 1874; and April 4, 1874.

30. An excellent comparison can be had from Roger D. McGarth, "Frontier Violence in the Trans-Sierra West (Ph.D. diss. University of California at Los An-

geles, 1978), p. 300. See also McGarth's book, *Gunfighters, Highwaymen, and Vigilantes*, p. 149; and Marion S. Goldman, *Gold Diggers and Silver Miners: Prostitution and Social Life on the Comstock Lode* (Ann Arbor: University of Michigan Press, 1980), pp. 114–18.

31. Fitzmaurice, *The Shanty Boy*, p. 178.

32. *Muskegon Chronicle*, June 5, 1878; September 1, 1882.

33. *Michigan Compiled Laws, 1948* and *The Charter of the City of East Saginaw, Compiled by Order of the Common Council* (East Saginaw, 1869–1885), p. 116, title 11, chap. 3 and title 11, section 9–10 (1885). For an overview of gambling in the Midwestern cities during the nineteenth century, see Jordan, *Frontier Law and Order*, chap. 4.

34. *Muskegon Chronicle*, April 18, 1869; October 21, 1870; and Dykstra, *The Cattle Towns*, p. 127.

35. *Muskegon Chronicle*, August 7, 1872; see also *Michigan Chronicle*, July 30, 1874.

36. Michigan Attorney General, *Reports, 1869–1889*.

37. *Muskegon Chronicle*, July 30, 1876.

38. Roy L. Dodge, *Ticket to Hell: A Saga of Michigan's Bad Men* (Tawas City, Mich.: Northeastern Printers, 1975), pp. 15–16.

39. Coats, *Diary of a Department*, p. 17.

40. Invariably, every interior logging camp had its champion and every other camp was sure its champion could "put the boots" to its opponent.

41. *Muskegon Chronicle*, March 30, 1875. Accounts of persons challenging another to combat can be read in *The Daily Republican*, East Saginaw, January 22, 1875; *Bay City Tribune*, April 22, 1875; and *Muskegon Chronicle*, December 6, 1873.

42. See Dodge, *Ticket to Hell*, pp. 64–70; Herek, "Bay City's Catacombs," in *Bay City Times*, February 24, 1974.

43. In Muskegon, for example, the fights that ended tragically included: a laborer killed after being kicked and stoned in a fight (*Muskegon Chronicle*, November 20, 1873); a stone thrown fatally injuring another man during a fight (*Muskegon Chronicle*, July 26, 1878); a combatant shot in the face after a drunken argument (*Muskegon Chronicle*, December 21, 1880); a drunken companion stabbed and robbed by his comrade (*Muskegon Journal*, May 7, 1881); a shanty boy stabbed in the head at a dance by a "hook" after an argument over a female companion (*Muskegon Chronicle*, July 17, 1881); one laborer clubbing another fatally over the head (*Muskegon Chronicle*, October 28, 1885); and two other deaths resulting from fights (*Muskegon Chronicle*, April 21, 1871). Coats, *Diary of a Department*, p. 19.

44. Coats, *Diary of a Department*, p. 19. Evidence that policemen often suffered the wrath or were the object of a drunken lumberjacks' pugilistic ambitions can be found in *Bay City Tribune*, May 14, 1873; *Muskegon Chronicle*, March 30, 1873; and *Muskegon Enterprise*, June 21, 1872.

45. Police activity was often undone by the light sentences handed out by the courts. The sheer number of detainees doubtlessly dictated leniency. Between 1875 and 1889 Saginaw County averaged 311 assault and battery cases each year; Bay City, 229; and Muskegon, where the city police force was small and enforcement lacking, 73 cases per year. Upon appearance before police courts, fully 75 percent of the cases in Saginaw; 73 percent in Bay City, and 85 percent in Muskegon received

small fines, were acquitted, or not prosecuted. Considering that so many violators were quickly returned to the streets, it is not surprising that mayhem and rowdyism plagued the towns throughout the lumber period. See Michigan Attorney General, *Reports, 1869–1888.*

46. See Perrigo, "Law and Order in Early Colorado Camps," pp. 48–52; McGarth, "Frontier Violence in Trans-Sierra West," pp. 349–54; and Stanley Vestal, *Queen of the Cowtowns,* (New York: Harper & Brothers, 1952), pp. 167–69.

47. See Dykstra, *The Cattle Towns,* pp. 142–48; and Hollen, *Frontier Violence,* pp. 197–202.

48. Michigan Attorney General, *Reports, 1868–88.* The *Reports to the Attorney General* may be seen as fairly accurate of the number of homicides. In some Western towns where legal paraphernalia was lacking, murderers often escaped arrest and thus avoided enumeration. However, in the lumbertowns almost all perpetrators were at least brought before the police courts and inquests held. After preliminary judgments were made, many were not prosecuted.

Muskegon failed to file reports for the years 1882 to 1884. Newspaper accounts are relied on for the number of homicides in these years.

49. The reports of the Michigan Attorney General list persons arrested. Deaths at the hands of unknown assailants remain unaccounted for.

50. An account of labor violence can be found in Kilar, "Community and Authority Responses to the Saginaw Valley Lumber Strike of 1885," 67–79.

51. *Muskegon Chronicle,* July 31, 1884.

52. The average number of homicides per lumbertown was 1.9 per year. This compares with 1.5 per year in the five Kansas cattletowns examined by Dykstra, 3 per year in the mining town of Aurora, Nevada; and 5 per year in infamous Bodie, California. Three mining towns in Gilpin County, Colorado, reported approximately 1.6 violent deaths between 1862 and 1872. Converted into contemporary uniform crime reporting measurements, the lumbertowns experienced about 5 instances of murder or nonnegligent manslaughter per 100,000 inhabitants per year between 1868 and 1888. Aurora and Bodie, much smaller and short-lived boomtowns, experienced a phenomenal rate of 116 and 64 murders per 100,000 each year. Using Dykstra's numbers for Wichita, Ellsworth, and Abilene, the ratio would run from 20 to 40 murders per 100,000. Even between 1880 and 1888 when three-quarters of the lumbertown homicides occurred, the rate in Saginaw, Muskegon, and Bay City would only be 7.4 per 100,000. Although these statistics are misleading because of populations, the lumbertowns were apparently no match for the homicidal mayhem characteristic of many Western frontier communities. See Dykstra, *The Cattle Towns,* p. 146; McGrath, *Gunfighters, Highwaymen, and Vigilantes,* pp. 252–54; and Perrigo, "Law and Order in Early Colorado Mining Camps," pp. 46–47. The 1890 census, which related homicides by states for both 1880 and 1890, reported that Michigan experienced 6.5 murders per 100,000 in 1880; Kansas, 8.8; Colorado, 23.7; and Nevada, 73.9. See *Census Bulletin no. 182; Homicide in 1890* (Washington: U.S. Bureau of the Census, 1892.) In contrast, the FBI reported the following rates per 100,000 inhabitants in 1980: 2.4 homocides or nonnegligent manslaughters in Bay City, 14.8 in Muskegon, and 21.9 in Saginaw (Department of Justice, Federal Bureau of Investigation, *Uniform Crime Reports, 1980* (Washington: GPO, 1981).

53. Dykstra notes that few celebrated personalities in the cattle towns were involved in homicides, although McGarth sees bad men playing significant roles in deaths occurring in Bodie. Dykstra, *The Cattle Towns*, pp. 142–43; and McGarth, "Violence in the Trans-Sierra West," pp. 409–14; and McGarth, *Gunfighters, Highwaymen, and Vigilantes*, pp. 199–224; and *Muskegon Chronicle*, December 18, 1873.

54. The violent nature of the lumbertown was also evident in the suicide rate. Suicides reached such epidemic proportions in 1884 in Muskegon that local ministers in their sermons prescribed remedies for the "current melancholy." Though Muskegon's suicide rate was only slightly above the national average, newspapers reported the grisly details often enough that they reinforced the violent image of lumbertown society. See *Muskegon Chronicle*, February 29, 1884.

55. Jordan, *Frontier Law and Order*, p. 114.

56. It is precisely this complexity in lumbertown life that best explains why loggers and lumbermen have been ignored as part of the American frontier saga. Easterners who read the dime novels, newspaper accounts, and literature about the Wild West visualized a society vastly different from their own. Even lumbertown newspapers regularly carried dramatic stories about outlaws, lynchings, and Indian uprisings happening in the West. In short, to contemporaries, logging town society—and its concommitant violence—was not different from the brutality, mayhem, and murder occurring in the country's eastern municipalities. Familiar forms of violence were not attractive to readers desiring tales of rugged individuals in an imagined, adventure-filled, primitive, and lawless society.

Moreover, lumbertown violence itself was enough at variance with Western violence that it was excluded from frontier lore. There were no six-shooters on the hip or Main Street shootouts in the lumbertowns. Instead, logging town violence suggested a brutality that negated the nobility of masculine confrontations. "Putting the caulked boots" to a fallen foe and imparting "lumberjack's pox" conjured up images very different from those of the noble frontiersman. Death was all too frequently brought on by knives, clubs, or the shooting of an unarmed opponent. Violence was rampant but it was not the type of violence that ingratiated the lumberjack to those who romanticized the frontier life. For a more complete analysis of lumbertown violence and its place in the frontier tradition, see Kilar, "The Lumbertowns: A Socioeconomic History of Michigan's Leading Lumber Center: Saginaw, Bay City and Muskegon, 1870–1905" (Ph.D. diss. University of Michigan, 1987), pp. 183–86.

CHAPTER 5. LUMBERTOWN BARONS

1. Charles E. Twining, "The Lumber Frontier," in *The Great Lakes Forest*, p. 184.

2. Alexis de Tocqueville, *Democracy in America* (New York: Harper & Brothers, 1966), p. 607; Hotchkiss, History of Lumber and Forest Industry, p. 30.

3. Twining notes that in the 1950s Paul Gates observed this oversight when examining sketches in the *Dictionary of American Biography*; he found only eight lumbermen among the thousands of entries. Only four biographies of Michigan lumbermen have been published.

Several reasons for this lack of historical awareness of the lumbermen's role are offered by Twining in his essay. Perhaps lumbering was too commonplace and the cutting of the forest was done too quickly to establish the lumberman as a noticeable part of the frontier epoch. Many were too busy to put their thoughts in print. In building communities and industries the lumber barons also destroyed the wilderness. This was often perceived as plunder. Thus the lumber barons became defensive and unwilling to preserve the written or verbal records of an exploitative industry. Even more so than other businessmen of their generation, lumbermen were reluctant to grant interviews or say anything in public. Last, lumbering firms were especially subject to floods and fires that destroyed papers and business records. Although these losses are tragic to the historian, they were often easy and sometimes deliberate methods of archival decision-making. See Twining, "The Lumber Frontier," in *The Great Lakes Forest*, pp. 133–36.

4. E. Digby Baltzell, *Puritan Boston and Quaker Philadelphia* (New York: The Free Press, 1959). Baltzell presents a provocative view of two contrasting upper classes in Boston and Philadelphia. The Puritan founders of Boston and the Quaker founders of Philadelphia created, according to Baltzell, two communities very much different in life-styles, public achievements, and cultural activities.

5. See Frederick W. Kohlmeyer, "Northern Pine Lumbermen: A Study in Origins and Migrations," *Journal of Economic History* 16 (December 1956): 529–38, and Benson, "Logs and Lumber," pp. 283–92.

6. For a summary of the "island community" thesis and leadership continuity, see Robert H. Wiebe, *The Search for Order, 1877–1920* New York: Hill & Wang, 1967); Richard S. Alcorn, "Leadership and Stability in Mid-Nineteenth Century America: A Case Study of an Illinois Town," *Journal of American History* 61 (December 1974): 685-762. For the thesis of social disorder and its effect on ruling elites, see Herbert Gutman, "The Reality of Rags to Riches 'Myth': The Case of Paterson, New Jersey," in *Nineteenth Century Cities*, ed. Stephen Thernstrom and Richard Sennett (New Haven: Yale University Press, 1969), pp. 98–124; Roland Berthoff, "The American Social Order: A Conservative Hypothesis," *American Historical Review* 65 (April, 1960): 95–514. A review of this earlier literature can be found in Edward Pessen, "The Social Configuration of the Antebellum City: An Historical and Theoretical Inquiry," *Journal of Urban History* 2 (spring, 1976): 267–306.

7. Edward J. Davies II, "Regional Networks and Social Change: The Evolution of Urban Leadership in the Northern Anthracite Coal Region, 1840–1880," *Journal of Social History* 16 (fall, 1982): 47. Davies argues that regional networks were the key to the evolution of urban leadership in the anthracite region around Wilkes-Barre. Despite rapid growth and industrialization a remarkable continuity in leadership persisted because new leaders came from the same broad regional base. See also Edward J. Davies II, "Large Scale Systems and Regional Leadership: Wilkes-Barre's Upper Class and Urban Elite in the Northern Anthracite Region, 1920–1930," *The Public Historian* 4 (fall, 1982): 39–68. See also Stuart Blumin, *The Urban Threshold: Growth and Change in a Nineteenth Century American Community* (Chicago: University of Chicago Press, 1976), pp. 50–74. For a comparison between regional leadership development in the anthracite region, see Burton W. Folsom, Jr., *Urban Capitalists: Entrepreneurs and City Growth in Pennsylvania's Lackawana and Lehigh Regions, 1800–1920* (Baltimore: Johns Hopkins University Press, 1981), chap. 5.

8. This method of identifying leadership is adapted in part from Davies, "Regional Networks and Social Change," p. 49, and Ronald D. Eller, *Miners, Mill-*

hands, and Mountaineers: Industrialization of the Appalachian South, 1880–1930 (Knoxville: University of Tennessee Press, 1982), pp. 200–202.

9. An excellent discussion of these migration patterns along the Erie Canal can be found in Ronald Shaw, "Michigan Influences upon the Formative Years of the Erie Canal," *Michigan History* 38 (winter 1953): 1–18.

10. Benson, "Logs and Lumber," p. 285; Kohlmeyer, "Northern Pine Lumbermen," p. 531. Although the writers' conclusions differ, the statistical representation is similar. Kohlmeyer's interpretation of his study tends to be in language that conveys the success story he is trying to relate.

11. Kohlmeyer, "Northern Pine Lumbermen," pp. 536–37.

12. The information and generalizations, including the tables, were gathered from listings of lumber and wood manufacturing concerns appearing in city directories, newspapers, and county histories of Saginaw, Bay City, and Muskegon for the period between 1880 and 1892. A total of 161 firms, with some longevity (three-plus years) were found. Subsequently, biographical sketches were made of 223 lumbermen. Some sketches were very thorough and with others little beyond residence could be discovered. Biographical material was compiled from the following sources, listed in the order of usefulness: Hotchkiss, *History of the Lumber and Forest Industry of the Northwest*; G. W. Hotchkiss, *American Lumbermen* (Chicago: G. W. Hotchkiss, 1905–6), 3 vols.; Mills, *History of Saginaw County*, esp. vol. 2; Paige, *History of Bay County*; George N. Fuller, *Historic Michigan: Land of the Great Lakes*, 3 vols., (n.p., The American Historical Association, 1925); *Muskegon & Ottawa Counties: Portrait and Biographical Record* (Chicago: Biographic Publishing, 1893). Also some obituaries from the *Muskegon Chronicle*, *Saginaw Courier*, and *Bay City Journal*, *Morning Chronicle*, and *Tribune* were used. See also Ed Miller, *The Saginaw Hall of Fame: Biographical Sketches* (n.p., Saginaw County Bicentennial Commission, 1976).

13. Lumbermen remained residents more often in towns along the western edge of the Great Lakes lumber frontier. This persistence was more common in Wisconsin than in Michigan lumbertowns. See James B. Smith, "Movements for Diversified Industry in Eau Claire, Wisconsin 1879–1907" (M. A. thesis, University of Wisconsin, 1967); and J. Rogers Hollingsworth and Ellen Jane Hollingsworth, *Dimensions in Urban History* (Madison: The University of Wisconsin Press, 1979), pp. 60–119.

14. Kohlmeyer's lumbermen were selected from biographical works, many of which appeared around the turn of the century. Kohlmeyer emphasized the humble origins of his lumbermen and relied on sketches that were often supplied by the lumbermen themselves. Moreover, his sources would have a definite bias toward recording the biographies of those lumbermen of economic or political prominence. A simple listing of all lumbermen in a region or locality creates a much more accurate image of the nature of the nineteenth-century lumbermen. See Kohlmeyer, "Northern Pine Lumbermen," p. 529, n. 1.

15. Benson noted that seventy-two percent of her survey formed partnerships between 1855 and 1870. See Benson, "Logs and Lumber," p. 290. See, for example, R. G. Dun & Co. Credit Reports for the State of Michigan, Baker Library, Harvard University Graduate School of Business Administration, Boston: vols. 63–68, Saginaw County; vols. 60–61, Muskegon; vol. 66, Bay County. Hereafter cited as R. G. Dun & Co.

16. See Hotchkiss, *History of the Lumber and Forest Industry*, pp. 227–28; Charles Moore, *History of Michigan*, 4 vols. (Chicago: Lewis Publishing Co., 1915), vol. 3, 1938. See also C. H. Hackley & Co., Journal, 1881, Hackley & Hume papers, Michigan State University Archives and Historical Collections, East Lansing.

17. R. G. Dun & Co., Reports for Saginaw, Bay, and Muskegon countries, vols. 60, 61, 63, 64, 66.

18. Similarly, H. W. Sage aided William C. McClure in Bay City. See Mitchell and McClure Lumber Company papers, Historical Collections, Bentley Library, University of Michigan; and Hotchkiss, *History of the Lumber and Forest Industry*, p. 141.

19. Kilar, "Black Pioneers in the Michigan Lumber Industry," p. 148.

20. For a comparison with the anthracite regions of Pennsylvania, see Davies, "Regional Networks and Social Change," pp. 47–73. An equally open society that supports the findings of Kohlmeyer is found in Michigan's Manistee County. See George M. Blackburn and Sherman L. Ricards, "A Case History in Local Control: The Timber Industry in Manistee County, Michigan," *Journal of Forest History* 18 (April 1974): 21.

21. The Hollingsworths offer a brief analysis of the effects absentee-owned firms have on extractive industry towns in *Dimensions in Urban History*, pp. 21, 72–73. Also see M. N. Goldstein, "Absentee Ownership and Monolithic Power Structures: Two Questions for Community Studies," in B. E. Swanson, ed., *Current Trends in Comparative Studies* (Kansas City, Mo.: Community Studies, 1962), pp. 49–59. Herman Lantz in his study of "Coal Town" offers the views of several citizens who were interviewed about the effects of absentee ownership on the community. However, the reader is unable to learn the frequency or extent of absentee ownership in the coal town. See Herman Lantz, *People of Coal Town* (New York: Columbia University Press, 1958), pp. 61, 122–23. Folsom comments on the value of resident ownership, but does not evaluate the negative aspect of absentee ownership in the anthracite regions. Folsom, *Urban Capitalist*, pp. 63–65. In the lumbertowns Goodstein characterizes Sage's absenteeism, but fails to go beyond the activities of one, though prominent, absentee owner. Goodstein, *Biography of a Businessman*, pp. 122–34. Blackburn and Ricards in their study of Manistee conclude, without statistical support though, that until 1900 ownership of sawmills in Manistee was under local control. Blackburn and Ricards, "A Case History in Local Control," p. 21. See also C. Daniel Dillman, "Absentee Landlords and Farm Management in Brazil during the 1960s," *The American Journal of Economics and Sociology* 37 (January 1978): 1–8.

22. "A Report on Lumber Production, 1881–1882," in Paige, *A History of Bay County*, p. 44; see also Kilar, "The Lumbertowns," p. 207, for a tabulated analysis of residency and mill capacity.

23. William B. Mershon Papers, Letterbooks no. 1, 13, 35, Michigan Historical Collections, Bentley Library, University of Michigan, Ann Arbor.

24. Diary of W. C. McClure, October 5–December 1, 1886; March 15, 1887; in Mitchell and McClure Lumber Company Papers, Michigan Historical Collections, Bentley Library, University of Michigan, Ann Arbor.

25. Sage in Bay City was not inclined to condone the sport of horse racing. In 1873 he wrote indignantly to his manager in West Bay City that the mill boss, who

evidently was neglecting his responsibilities because of his prize racehorse, must choose between his job or horse racing. Later he also warned that his "jobber" must not race "fast horses on a race course. The time and thought it costs, the expense, the associations and habits—are not in line with principles which control success in business or elevation of character." To the absentee owner, any amusements that might infringe on the "industry, capacity, or convictions of moral character" of his employees and his business were out of place and should be prohibited. See Henry W. Sage to E. T. Carrington, December 12, 1873; and Henry W. Sage to Henry W. Sage & Co., June 28, 1878, quoted in Goodstein, *Biography of a Businessman*, pp. 73–74.

26. Hackley, who was childless, offered Lee $10,000 if he would drop the "Lee" from his name. The son never did. See Charles H. Hackley Journal in Hackley and Hume Papers, Michigan State University Archives, East Lansing.

27. *Muskegon Chronicle*, February 20, 1890; Harms, "Life after Lumbering," p. 278; and Miller, *The Saginaw Hall of Fame*, pp. 30–32; 66–69.

28. Reinhard Bendix, *Work and Authority in Industry: Ideologies of Management in the Course of Industrialization* (Berkeley: University of California Press, 1974), p. 435. See also Richard Hofstadter, *Social Darwinism in American Thought* (Boston: Beacon Press, 1955), pp. 31–66.

29. *American Lumberman*, August 18, 1900, pp. 1, 24.

30. Henry W. Sage to William C. DeWitt, February 17, 20, 1894, Henry W. Sage papers, quoted in Goodstein, *Biography of a Businessman*, p. 256.

31. Ibid., p. 260. Charles Merrill of Saginaw, June 30, 1903, also expressed some social Darwinist sentiments in letters written to his Aunt Minerva. See Merrill papers, Michigan Historical Collection, Bentley Library, Ann Arbor.

32. The idea that the ideological beliefs of community leaders influenced the economic, social, and cultural practices in that community is seen in Baltzell, *Puritan Boston and Quaker Philadelphia*. Also see Folsom, *Urban Capitalist*, chap. 5, in which the "venturesome" leadership in Scranton is contrasted with the "close conservative" leadership of Wilkes-Barre; and Eller, *Miners, Millhands, and Mountaineers*, chap. 6, in which the coal owners of the Appalachian South are seen as social Darwinist or paternalistic in their attitudes. Eller, though, largely ignores the effect of the absentee owner.

33. See an interview with Henry Sage, "Sage Sayings," in *Lumberman's Gazette*, July 26, 1877.

34. Michigan Bureau of Labor and Industrial Statistics, *Third Annual Report, 1885* (Lansing, Robert Smith Printers, 1886), pp. 102–3.

35. Norman Clark, *Mill Town: A Social History of Everett, Washington*, (Seattle: University of Washington Press, 1970), p. 65; and Rex Dye, *Lumber Camp Life in Michigan* (n.p., 1975), pp. 33–35.

36. *Lumberman's Gazette*, July 11, 1883, and August 1872; the *Gazette* came out monthly until the mid-1870s.

37. Quoted in *Lumberman's Gazette*, August 1873.

38. See Gerald Vanwoerkom, "They 'Dared to do Right': Prohibition in Muskegon," *Michigan History* 55 (spring 1971): 41–60.

39. *Muskegon Chronicle*, March 16, 1877; and H. W. Sage & Co., Wenona, April 11, 1876; quoted in Goodstein, *Biography of a Businessman*, p. 131.

40. See *Muskegon Chronicle, Romance of Muskegon*, pp. lxxvii, lxxix; Fitzmaurice, *The Shanty Boy*, pp. 179–80; and Norman Clark, *Deliver Us from Evil: An*

Interpretation of American Prohibition (New York, 1976), pp. 53, 12. See also Roy Rosenzweig, *Eight Hours for What We Will: Workers and Leisure in an Industrial City, 1870–1920* (Cambridge: Cambridge University Press, 1983), pp. 93–102.

41. Fitzmaurice, *The Shanty Boy*, pp. 178–81.

42. H. W. Sage to H. W. Sage & Co., Wenona, April 11, 1876; Sage to J. H. Plum, October 19, 1871, quoted in Goodstein, *Biography of a Businessman*, pp. 119, 131; and H. W. Sage to H. W. Sage & Co., Wenona, March 30, 1874, quoted in Goodstein, "Labor Relations in the Saginaw Valley Lumber Industry," *Bulletin of the Business Historical Society* 27 (December 1953): 204–05.

43. See George Y. Allen, "Speech Given to Bay City Exchange Club, 1950," Bay County Historical Society, Bay City, Michigan; and *Saginaw Daily Courier*, April 29, 1877.

44. Hackley & Hume papers, 1872–92; also Hackley Journal, August–December, 1872, Michigan State University Archives, East Lansing.

45. Mills, *History of Saginaw County*, p. 410; and Dustin, *Saginaw History*, p. 118.

46. Henry S. Dow, *The History and Commercial Advantages and Future Prospects of Bay City* (Bay City, 1875), p. 50; and *Bay City Daily Journal*, July 17, 1872.

47. H. W. Sage to H. W. Sage & Co., Wenona, July 9, 13, 1872; quoted in Goodstein, *Biography of a Businessman*, p. 85.

48. John O'Neill, "History of the Lumber Industry in the Valley of Saginaw: Social Effect of Cheap Labor" (manuscript in Bay City Historical Society, Bay City, Michigan, 1932), p. 19.

49. Ibid., p. 21. Bousefield was the owner of a large woodenware manufacturing concern in Bay City. O'Neill mentions, in another sentence, that Bousefield's accomplices included John Thomas McGraw and David Ward, absentee lumbermen.

50. In defense of the lumberman, immigrant workers in America were often seen as more reliable and hard-working employees. Many of these, including the Poles, worked hard and were extremely frugal to save enough to bring relatives and family to America or to build and own a farm or home. See Eller, *Miners, Millhands, and Mountaineers*, pp. 207–8.

51. The Davidson shipyard, which employed at times more than five hundred men, was owned by James Davidson, originally an absentee owner from Buffalo. See *Lumberman's Gazette*, October 11, 1877.

52. Quoted in Arndt, *By these Waters*, p. 153.

53. *Muskegon Chronicle*, February 12, 1884; March 16, 1886.

54. U.S. Bureau of the Census, *Tenth Census of the United States, 1880, Manufactures*, 2: 265–71.

55. See Goodstein, *Biography of a Businessman*, p. 141; Miller, *Saginaw Hall of Fame*, pp. 10–13; and James E. Defebaugh, *History of the Lumber Industry of America*, (Chicago: American Lumberman, 1906), 1: 446–63, for a discussion of the lumber trade tariff policies.

56. Mills, *History of Saginaw County*, 2: 238. Hill and Bliss each served three terms as mayor of Saginaw City in the 1880s.

57. H. W. Sage to J. H. Plum, July 8, 1871. Quoted in Goodstein, *Biography of a Businessman*, p. 124. See also *Bay City Daily Journal*, April 16, 1867.

58. H. W. Sage to J. H. Plum, July 1 and 8, 1871. Quoted in Goodstein, *Biography of a Businessman*, p. 125.

59. H. W. Sage to John McGraw, April 9, 1875, quoted in Goodstein, *Biography of a Businessman*, p. 129; also p. 126.

60. H. W. Sage to H. W. Sage & Co., Wenona, December 8, 1875; Sage to T. F. Shepard, October 30, 1876; and to H. H. Alpin, November 1, 1876, quoted in Goodstein, *Biography of a Businessman*, pp. 128–29.

61. Ibid., p. 129.

62. Veblen's definition of absentee ownership applies to corporations and not individuals. See Thornstein Veblen, *Absentee Ownership and Business Enterprise in Recent Times* (New York: Viking Press, 1923), p. 66; and Rosalind Schulman, "Absentee Ownership Reread," *American Journal of Economics and Sociology*, 21 (July 1962): 319–30.

63. The Hollingsworths characterize lumbering as an "immobile" extractive industry, which in turn lends itself to more local political involvement by ownership and management. This tends to simplify their definitions of the "autocratic" and "oligarchic" town. My experience with lumbertown industrial mobility in Michigan indicates that mobility among lumbermen was a state of mind, residency, and geographic location. New York lumbermen who moved into eastern Michigan often planned to move on once the timber was gone. There apparently was little difficulty transferring heavy equipment to Wisconsin or Minnesota. However, the Hollingsworths' study relies primarily on the experiences of Eau Claire, Wisconsin. Here at the western edge of the Great Lakes lumber frontier there was probably less mobility. The lumbermen who came here would have to make the longer move to the West Coast. Perhaps more lumbermen were reluctant to undertake this step and consequently more willing to commit themselves to permanent residence in a Wisconsin city. A community like Bay City, with high absentee ownership yet eventually achieving some economic diversity, does not comfortably fit the Hollingsworth typology. See J. Rogers and E. J. Hollingsworth, *The Dimension in Urban History*, pp. 14–24; 59–78. The lumbermen in Saginaw and Muskegon, though, reflect more accurately the Hollingsworths' typology as well as the patrician classes in Robert Dahl's *Who Governs? Democracy and Power in an American City* (New Haven: Conn.: Yale University Press, 1961), chap. 4.

CHAPTER 6. WORKERS IN THE MILL TOWNS

1. Populations of Saginaw City and East Saginaw and Bay City and West Bay City are combined through the period. See *Tenth Census of the U.S.* (Washington: GPO, 1883), pp. 65–219; *Census of the State of Michigan, 1884* (Lansing: Thorp & Godfrey, 1886), pp. clxxxiv and 110–13; *Census of the State of Michigan, 1894*, vol. 1 (Lansing: Robert Smith & Co., 1896), pp. liii–lxi and 2–54.

2. For an account of recruitment efforts by lumbermen, see Engberg, "Labor in the Lake States Lumber Industry," pp. 66–67; and *Northwestern Lumberman*, November 19, 1892.

3. George B. Engberg, "Who Were the Lumberjacks?" *Michigan History Magazine* 22 (1948): 241–43; Andrew J. Perjuda, "Sources and Dispersal of Michigan's Population," *Michigan History Magazine* 32 (1948): 364; and Engberg, "Labor in the Lake States," 46–55.

4. These figures were taken from a random sample of twenty percent of workers in the sawmills listed in the 1870 manuscript census for Muskegon, Saginaw, and Bay City. The figures are confirmed by Yakes's sample of Muskegon for 1870 and closely parallel the 1885 report of the Bureau of Labor investigating the ten-hour strike in Saginaw and Bay City. See Yakes and Hornstein, *The Many Lives of Muskegon*, p. vii–4; and Michigan Bureau of Labor and Industrial Statistics, *Third Annual Report* (Lansing: Thorp & Godfrey, 1886), p. 125.

5. For accounts of post-Civil War industrial adjustment, see Dawley, *Class and Community: The Industrial Revolution in Lynn*, (Cambridge: Harvard University Press, 1976), pp. 129–48; Herbert G. Gutman, *Work, Class, and Society in Industrializing America: Essays in American Working Class History* (New York: Vintage Press, 1977), pp. 1–78; and Eller, *Miners, Millhands, and Mountaineers*, pp. 165–75. For pre-Civil War adjustment difficulties, see Sean Wilentz, *Chants Democratic: New York City and the Rise of the American Working Class, 1788–1850* (New York: Oxford University Press, 1984), pp. 24–30.

6. H. H. Crapo to W. Crapo, November 27, 1860, in Crapo Papers, Michigan Historical Collection, Bentley Library, the University of Michigan, Ann Arbor.

7. Muskegon, the most recently settled lumbertown, had the least stable population. Saginaw, as the oldest town, reflected a slightly more stable population core. Rough persistent rates were computed from a sample population of adult laborers found in the 1860 and located again in the 1870 manuscript census records for Bay City, Saginaw, and Muskegon. For comparisons see Peter R. Knights, *The Plain People of Boston, 1830–1860: A Study in City Growth* (New York, 1971), pp. 48–77; and Paul E. Johnson, *A Shopkeeper's Millennium: Society and Revivalism in Rochester, New York, 1815–1877* (New York: Hill and Wang, 1978), pp. 37, 170; and Wilentz, *Chants Democratic*, p.25, n. 29.

8. George M. Blackburn and Sherman L. Ricards, "A Demographic History of the West: Manistee County, Michigan, 1860," *Journal of American History* 57 (December 1970): 618.

9. Crapo, *Journals*, June 29, 1864, in Crapo papers; and George W. Hotchkiss, "Autobiography" (unpublished, partial manuscript, 1900), Michigan Historical Collections, Bentley Library, The University of Michigan, Ann Arbor. Hotchkiss came to Bay City, started a lumberyard in the 1860s, and became the editor of the Saginaw *Courier* and later *The Lumberman's Gazette*. Sage to H. W. Sage & Co., Wenona, July 11, 1872, HWS Papers, quoted in Goodstein, *Biography of a Businessman*, p. 81.

10. Theodore Hersburg, Michael Katz, Stuart Blumin, Laurence Glasco, and Clyde Griffen, "Occupation and Ethnicity in Five Nineteenth Century Cities: A Collaborative Inquiry," *Historical Methods Newsletter* 7 (1974): 195. It should be noted that these figures represent only foreign-born. The 1894 Michigan census, which allows for determination of nativity based on heads of households, is a more accurate reflection of the numerical importance of the lumbertown ethnic populations. Foreign-born heads of households in Bay City represented 69%; Saginaw, 70%; and Muskegon, 65% of the towns' populations. *Census of the State of Michigan, 1894*, 1: 2–54. Also, *Tenth Census of U.S., 1880*, part 2; and *Eleventh Census of U.S.*, 4: 464–65.

11. See Bay City *Evening Press*, July 11, 1885; and *Detroit Labor Leaf*, July 15, 1885.

12. Bay City *Daily Journal*, July 13, 15, 17, 1872.

13. These observations are based on statements made in O'Neill, "The History of the Lumber Industry in the Valley of the Saginaw," pp. 19–21; Glasgow, *Muskegon, Michigan*, pp. 36, 59.

14. Glasgow, *Muskegon, Michigan*, p. 76.

15. A review of residential segregation studies is found in Kathleen Neils Conzen, "Immigrants, Immigrant Neighborhoods, and Ethnic Identity: Historical Issues," *Journal of American History* 16 (December 1979): 603–15. For observations of ghetto formation, see Sam Bass Warner, Jr., and Colin B. Burke, "Cultural Change and the Ghetto," *Journal of Contemporary History* 4 (October 1969): 182; and Howard P. Chudacoff, *Mobile Americans: Residential and Social Mobility in Omaha, 1880–1920* (New York: Oxford University Press, 1972), pp. 61–69.

16. See David Ward, "The Emergence of Central Immigrant Ghettoes in American Cities: 1840–1920," *Annals of the Association of American Geographers* 38 (1968): 343–59; and Warner and Burke, "Cultural Change and the Ghetto," pp. 173–87; Conzen, "Immigrants, Immigrant Neighborhoods," pp. 605–15; and David G. Vanderstel, "Dutch Immigrant Neighborhood Development in Grand Rapids, 1850–1900," in Robert P. Swierenga, *Dutch in America: Immigration, Settlement, and Cultural Change* (New Brunswick, N.J.: Rutgers University Press, 1985), pp. 125–255.

17. Precinct and other small-area data were not available in the 1880 U.S. census to permit precise indexing. The concept of dominance is adapted in part from its use by Olivier Zunz in *The Changing Face of Inequality: Urbanization, Industrial Development, and Immigrants in Detroit, 1880–1920* (Chicago: The University of Chicago Press, 1982), pp. 46–47. Though Zunz goes beyond the scope of this study and uses 127 clusters to determine dominance locations of several ethnic groups in several varied zones in Detroit, my purpose is merely to establish a basis on which ethnic dominance can be compared in one lumbertown with another. In doing so, clusters were formed by searching out foreign-born heads of households who lived on blocks facing each other and, where possible, backing up to each other. Thus four blocks formed one cluster. The clusters sampled indicate ethnic concentration in the heart of a well-known ghetto residential area. Unlike Zunz, I do not try to analyze the total proportion of an ethnic group in a given area or even in the city examined.

18. The Canadians were not distinguished from the French *Canadiens* in the U.S. census until 1890. Even though the distinction was based on English-speaking versus French-speaking Canadian immigrants, precise differences are difficult to arrive at because so many Canadian immigrants were bilingual. Although census figures are probably suspect, doubtless, "Canadian" settlers in the lumbertowns represented a high percentage of French *Canadiens* and Irish emigrants from Canada.

19. Glasgow, *Muskegon, Michigan*, pp. 80–82; see also Lowell B. Dana, "E. Pluribus Unum—The Unification of Muskegon" (manuscript, Hackley Public Library, Muskegon, Mich., 1936), pp. 2–3.

20. C. Warren Vanderhill, *Settling the Great Lakes Frontier: Immigration to Michigan, 1837–1924* (Lansing: Michigan Historical Commission, 1970), p. 18. Max Allardt, the only "Commissioner of Emigration" for Michigan, was from East Saginaw. He set up an office in Hamburg where, between 1869 and 1874, he was successful in

attracting several thousand German immigrants to Michigan. Because of his famil-
iarity with and personal land holdings in and around Saginaw, it is not surprising
that many immigrants were directed toward the Saginaw Valley.

21. Josias Meulen Dyke, "Dutch Settlements North of Muskegon: 1867–1897,"
Michigan History 31 (December 1947): 392–98; and George D. Graff, *The People of
Michigan* (Lansing: Michigan Department of Education, 1974), pp. 63–66.

22. Fred Read, *A Long Look at Muskegon* (Benton Harbor, 1976), p. 161.

23. Carlton Qualey, "Pioneer Scandinavian Settlement in Michigan," *Michigan
History* 24 (autumn 1940): 437. Generalizations about the Swedish community and
occupational structure of Swedish workers are borne out in Ferdinand Nelson, "My
Journey from Sweden to America, 1903," (unpublished manuscript in three vol-
umes) in Michigan Historical Collections, Bentley Library, the University of Michigan, Ann Arbor.

24. Stuart Blumin uses church membership in several affiliations to demonstrate
ethnic diversity. See Blumin, *The Urban Threshold*, pp. 82–83. An examination of
the lumbertowns' churches indicates that in Muskegon the wide variety and number
of Dutch and German churches encouraged heterogeneity among immigrant cultures. It would be difficult to argue from a religious viewpoint that common culture
and historical experience kept the Dutch and German immigrant neighborhoods
together. In contrast, almost every aspect of Polish community life revolved around
the Catholic Church of Stanislaus Kosta in Bay City. Ethnic consciousness and
group loyalty among the Poles was reinforced by the church, parish, and neighborhood. See Kilar, "The Lumbertowns," pp. 252–55.

25. Quoted in Graff, *The People of Michigan*, p. 40. Graff's observations were
based on an analysis of farms and soil conditions in areas of German settlement in
Michigan.

26. Ibid., pp. 43–44; and Yakes and Hornstein, *Many Lives of Muskegon*,
pp. vii–9.

27. Henry Ryskamp, "The Dutch in West Michigan" (Ph.D. diss., University
of Michigan, 1935), p. 84; and Vanderstel, "Dutch Immigrant Neighborhoods,"
pp. 125–55.

28. Ryskamp, "The Dutch in West Michigan," p. 84.

29. Peter A. Ostafin, "Polish Peasants in Transition" (Ph.D. diss., University of
Michigan, 1954), pp. 20–24; William I. Thomas and Florian Znaniecki, *The Polish
Peasant in Europe and America*, ed. and abr. by Eli. Zaretsky (Urbana: University of
Illinois Press, 1984), pp. 191–293; and John J. Bukowczyk, *And My People Did Not
Know Me: A History of the Polish Americans* (Bloomington: Indiana University Press,
1987), chap. 1.

30. *Bay City Evening Press*, July 11, 1885.

31. The stereotype that Polish laborers were usually docile and willing workers is
refuted in John J. Bukowczyk, "Polish Rural Culture and Immigrant Working Class
Formation, 1880–1914," *Polish American Studies* 41 (autumn 1984): 24–44. See also
John Bodnar, Michael Weber, and Roger Simon, "Migration, Kinship, and Urban
Adjustments: Blacks and Poles in Pittsburgh, 1900–1930," *The Journal of American
History* 66 (December 1979): 554.

32. O'Neill, "History of the Lumber Industry in the Valley of the Saginaw,"
p. 19; and Bukowczyk, *And My People*, p. 13.

33. Ryskamp, "The Dutch in West Michigan," p. 84.

34. Available data do not distinguish between movers within cities. The table reflects those who could be found in the data in the interval years. Also the data only infrequently distinguished between those who left and those who died. However, because the proportion who died probably remained relatively stable in the lumbertowns, the migration patterns noted here remain valid. Also, the mobility patterns in other American cities during this time were like those found in the lumbertowns, except for Bay City, which is at the lower end of the percentages of persistence. See Stephen Thernstrom, *The Other Bostonians: Poverty and Progress in the American Metropolis, 1880–1970* (Cambridge: Harvard University Press, 1973), pp. 221–32. Also for discussion of persistence and methodology employed, see Chudacoff, *Mobile Americans*, pp. 35–37; Stephen Thernstrom and Peter R. Knights, "Men in Motion: Some Data and Speculations about Urban Population Mobility in Nineteenth-Century America," in Tamara K. Harevan, ed., *Anonymous Americans* (Englewood Cliffs, N.J.: Prentice-Hall, 1971), pp. 17–47; Michael P. Weber, *Social Change in an Industrial Town: Patterns of Progress in Warren, Pennsylvania, from the Civil War to World War I* (University Park: University of Pennsylvania Press, 1976); Anthony E. Boardman and Michael Weber, "Economic Growth and Occupational Mobility in Nineteenth-Century Urban America: A Reappraisal," *Journal of Social History* 11 (fall 1977): 53–56; and Alan Burstein, "Immigrant and Residential Mobility: The Irish and Germans in Philadelphia, 1850–1880," in Theodore Hershberg, ed., *Philadelphia: Work, Space, and Family, and Group Experience in the Nineteenth Century* (New York: Oxford University Press, 1981), 174–203.

35. Thernstrom, *The Other Bostonians*, pp. 221–32.

36. In this study attempts were made to anticipate the problems inherent in the use of city directories as a primary source for migration studies. The best studies on proper use of city directories are Knights, *The Plain People of Boston 1830–1860*, pp. 127–39; and Knights, "City Directories as Aids to Ante-Bellum Urban Studies: A Research Note," *Historical Methods Newsletter* 2 (September 1969): 1–10; and Sidney Goldstein, *Patterns of Mobility, 1910–1950: The Norristown Study* (Philadelphia: University of Pennsylvania Press, 1958), pp. 58–123; and *The Norristown Study: An Experiment in Interdisciplinary Research Training* (Philadelphia: University of Pennsylvania Press, 1961), pp. 86–88; 96–97. Tracing through the halcyon and declining years of the lumbertowns would have been impossible through census manuscript data. There were fewer immigrants in 1870. To begin tracing in that year of the decennial census would have been too early. One could begin in 1880, but the missing 1890 census allows no reasonable intervening trace year, and by 1900 the economy of the lumbertowns had changed so dramatically that a sampling at that late date would be highly unreliable. The only reliable source for tracing at five-year intervals between 1875 and 1895 was the city directories.

37. Thernstrom, *The Other Bostonians*, pp. 289, 292.

38. *Third Annual Report*, pp. 92–125.

39. One teacher in 1875 later became a bookkeeper thus descending from HWC to LWC.

40. See Bukowczyk, "Polish Rural Culture," pp. 34–37.

41. Census data for 1900 may be misleading about young, Polish workers and schoolchildren. The census recorder making inquiries in Bay City's Fifth Ward listed an inordinate number of children as "at home." These numbers appear high and indicate an unreal depiction of the number who may have been working or at

school. For a detailed analysis of children's schooling in lumbertowns, see Kilar, "The Lumbertowns," pp. 277–79.

42. For discussion of girls and early work patterns, see Bodnar, Weber, and Simon, "Migration, Kinship, and Urban Adjustment," pp. 560–63.

43. Olivier Zunz, "Neighborhoods, Homes, and the Dual Housing Market," *Michigan History* 66 (November/December 1982): 33–41; see also *The Changing Face of Inequality*, pp. 152–61.

44. See Thernstrom, *Poverty and Progress: Social Mobility in a Nineteenth Century City* (Cambridge: Harvard University Press, 1964), p. 201. See also Kilar, "The Lumbertowns," pp. 281–82.

45. Bodnar, Weber and Simon, "Migration, Kinship, and Urban Adjustment," pp. 561–63.

CHAPTER 7. "TEN HOURS OR NO SAWDUST"

1. *Bay City Daily Tribune*, June 13, 1882.

2. Alan Dawley, writing of Lynn, Massachusetts, described several aspects of social control in the urban workplace. Dawley's main argument was that the legitimization of the local political system was such that city politics was a means of transforming conflicts that were destructive to capital into less harmful political disputes. See Dawley, *Class and Community*, p. 235. Harvey Boulay, however, believes that Dawley overstates his case and that his evidence does not support his sweeping conclusions. See *The Twilight Cities: Political Conflict, Development, and Decay in Five Communities* (Port Washington, N.Y.: Associate Faculty Press, 1983), pp. 41–42. See also Paul G. Faler, *Mechanics and Manufactures in the Early Industrial Revolution: Lynn, Massachusetts, 1780–1860* (Albany: State University of New York Press, 1981); Alan Dawley and Paul Faler, "Working Class Culture and Politics in the Industrial Revolution: Sources of Loyalty and Rebellion," *Journal of Social History* 9 (June 1876): 466–80; and Leon Fink, *Workingmen's Democracy: The Knights of Labor and American Politics* (Urbana: University of Illinois Press, 1983).

3. Doris B. McLaughlin, *Michigan Labor: A Brief History from 1818 to the Present* (Ann Arbor: Institute of Labor and Industrial Relations, 1970), p. 30. Chapter 2 of this work contains a narrative account of the strike. Michigan history texts devote only brief paragraphs to the strike; see F. Clever Bald, *Michigan in Four Centuries* (New York: Harper, 1954), p. 297; and Willis F. Dunbar and George S. May, *Michigan: History of the Wolverine State* (rev. ed. Grand Rapids: Wm. B. Erdmans Publishing Company, 1980), p. 608. A good description of labor relations in the Saginaw Valley as viewed through the letters of Henry W. Sage is Goodstein, "Labor Relations in the Saginaw Valley Lumber Industry, 1865–1885," pp. 193–221. Much of the same material is repeated in greater detail in Goodstein, *Biography of a Businessman*. A most important source for valuable statistical data and instructive interviews with participants in the strike is the Michigan Bureau of Labor and Industrial Statistics, *Third Annual Report*, pp. 92–125. Two sources that touch on the Saginaw Valley strike but are characterized by some inaccuracy are Vernon H. Jenson, *Lumber and Labor* (New York: Farrar & Rinehart, 1945) and Sidney Glazer,

"Labor and Agrarian Movements in Michigan, 1876–1896" (Ph.D. diss., The University of Michigan, 1932).

See also Kilar, "Community and Authority Response to the Saginaw Valley Lumber Strike of 1885," *Journal of Forest History* 20 (April 1976): 67–79. Inclusive material for coverage of the Saginaw Valley strike is taken from this previously published article and reprinted here in part by permission of the editors. For an account of the ten-hour strike in Muskegon, see Daniel J. Yakes, "Ten Hours or No Sawdust: A Study of Strikes in the Michigan Lumber Industry, 1881–88" (master's diss. Western Michigan University, 1971), pp. 24–68.

4. Rector, *Log Transportation in the Lake States Lumber Industry, 1840–1914*, p. 22; and *Lumbermen's Gazette* (Bay City), November 29, 1877.

5. Thomas McGraw, John McGraw's son and former partner of Sage, explained the decline in the quality and effects of prices on the wood cut in the eighties. See *Bay City Evening Press*, July 21, 1885. Events outside Michigan also determined lumbermen's prices. By the 1880s the lumber distribution was largely controlled by a cartel of leading producers and dealers in Chicago, Detroit, Toledo, and Albany. The cartel could limit demand and control prices. Cutthroat competition, particularly by the small sawmill owners, further lowered the price of lumber. Moreover, in 1882–83 Western railroad construction overexpanded. A slowdown in railroad building further cut demand for rough-sawn lumber. See Martin L. Primack and James F. Willis, *An Economic History of the United States* (Menlo Park, Calif.: Benjamin/Cummings Publishing Co., 1980), p. 277.

6. *Lumbermen's Gazette* (Bay City), July 26, 1877.

7. See *Lumbermen's Gazette*, August 16, 1877; also *Bay City Evening Press*, July 1, 1885. For a comparison with Detroit's wages, see Zunz, *The Changing Face of Inequality*, pp. 230–31.

8. Louis P. Haight, *The Life of Charles Henry Hackley* (Muskegon: Dana Printing Co., 1948), p. 39.

9. See Herbert G. Gutman, "Work, Culture and Society in Industrializing America, 1815–1919," *American Historical Review* (June 1973): 556–57; also *Detroit Labor Leaf*, July 22, 1885; and *Lumbermen's Gazette*, July 11, 1883.

10. *The Lumbermen's Gazette* gave an account of speed-up practices in John McGraw's mill; see issue of November 3, 1877.

11. *Third Annual Report*, table 29, p. 264; and Jensen, *Lumber and Labor*, p. 51.

12. Conclusions about immigrant cultures are drawn from several sources. For comments on the Poles see Thomas and Znaniecki, *The Polish Peasant in Europe and America*, chap. 2; Bukowczyk, "Polish Rural Culture and Immigrant Working Class Formation, 1880–1914," pp. 23–44; John Bodnar, "Immigration, Kinship, and the Rise of Working Class Realism in Industrial America," *Journal of Social History* 14 (fall 1980): 56; and Ostafin, "Polish Peasants in Transition," pp. 22–24. On the French, see C. Warren Vanderhill, *Settling the Great Lakes Frontier*, p. 18; Tamara K. Hareven and Randolph Lagenback, *Amoskeag: Life and Work in an American Factory City* (New York: Partheon Books, 1978), pp. 19–27; Edith Worley Ash, *Lingering Shadows of the Fleur de Lis: Michigan's French Heritage* (Grand Marais, Mich.: Voyager Press, 1975), pp. 5–20.

For the Dutch in Michigan see Josias Mevlen Dyke, "Dutch Settlements North of Muskegon: 1867–1897," *Michigan History* 31 (December 1947): 392–98; Henry Ryskamp, "The Dutch in West Michigan," Gordon W. Kirk, Jr., *The Promise of*

American Life: Social Mobility in a Nineteenth Century Immigrant Community: Holland, Michigan, 1847–1894 (Philadelphia: American Philosophical Society, 1978); and Robert P. Swierenga, ed., *The Dutch in American Immigration*, pp. 105–24. On the Germans see John Andrew Russell, *The Germanic Influence in the Making of Michigan* (Detroit: University of Detroit, 1927), pp. 336–47; Pete Marschlack, "German Emigration to the United States," *Perspective in American History* 7 (1973): 499–559; and Kathleen Neils Conzen, *Immigrant Milwaukee, 1836–1860* (Cambridge, Mass.: Harvard University Press, 1976).

See also Gerald Rosenbloom, *Immigrant Workers: Their Impact on the American Labor Radicalism* (New York: Basic Books, 1973), pp. 30–39. Rosenblum argues that immigrant workers accepted their employee status because of their European cultural frame of reference. See also John Bodnar, *Workers' World: Kinship, Community, and Protest in an Industrial Society, 1900–1940, Studies in Industry and Society*, no. 2 (Baltimore: Johns Hopkins University Press, 1982) and Bodnar, *The Transplanted: History of Immigrants in Urban America* (Bloomington, Ind.: Indiana University Press, 1985).

13. On the transient character of the immigrant worker see Bodnar, "Immigration and Modernization: The Case of Slavic Peasants in Industrial America," *Journal of Social History* 10 (1976): 54–56; and Detroit *Labor Leaf*, July 22, 1885.

14. H. W. Sage to H. W. Sage and Co., Wenona, July 9 and 13, 1872, in Goodstein, "Labor Relation in the Saginaw Valley," p. 209. *Bay City Daily Journal*, July 19, 1872, and *Lumbermen's Gazette*, July 1982; and *Saginaw Courier*, October 2–17, 1873.

15. See *Unionist* (Detroit), April 21, July 24, and September 18, 1882; and January 8 and March 5, 1883. See also Glazer, "Labor and Agrarian Movements in Michigan," p. 42, where he cites the *Knights of Labor National Proceedings, 1886* listing the membership of various Michigan cities, pp. 326–28; and Jonathan Garlock, *Guide to Local Assemblies of the Knights of Labor* (Westport, Conn.: Greenwood Press, 1982), pp. 208–28.

16. Francis W. Cook came to Michigan from Cheming, New York, in 1855, as a young boy. He studied law with John Q. Patterson in Ovid, Michigan, and after passing the bar moved to Muskegon in 1870. He entered politics and was elected justice of the peace on the Greenback-Democratic ticket in 1872. He tried unsuccessfully for a circuit court judgeship and prosecuting attorney. In 1877 he was appointed city attorney, a post he resigned during the labor troubles of 1881. Cook was an accomplished speaker, who managed to acquire the attention of courtrooms and crowds. See Michigan Historical Commission, *Michigan Biographies*, vol. 1 (Lansing, 1924), p. 34.

17. Workers were susceptible to strike activity because a recent plague of bad weather in the three weeks before their next payday led to a loss of wages and bleak prospects for fall income. See *Muskegon News and Reporter*, October 1, 1881.

18. Nelson DeLong was born in Essex, Michigan, in 1848. He graduated with a law degree from the University of Michigan in 1871 and arrived in Muskegon in 1873. He ran and won the job of prosecuting attorney in 1876 and was reelected every year until 1882. In his early days he was a Republican but later allied himself with the Greenback-Democrats. DeLong was reputedly an able orator and was once called the "ablest jury lawyer in Central and Western Michigan." He supposedly won more cases than any other prosecuting attorney in that part of Michigan. See

Portrait and Biographical Record of Muskegon and Ottawa Counties, Michigan (Chicago: Chicago Biographical Publishing Co., 1893), pp. 141–42.

19. *Muskegon Daily Chronicle*, October 3, 1881; see also Leon Fink, *Workingman's Democracy*, pp. 10–14, for a discussion of the nature of the Knight's political and social objectives.

20. See *Muskegon News and Reporter*, March 20, 1882.

21. Quoted in commemorative edition of the *Muskegon Observer*, February 19, 1928, p. 67. These observations confirm Leon Fink's characterization of the Knights as an organization that crossed class lines and looked to "labor as a source of order in a disorderly age." See Fink, *Workingmen's Democracy*, pp. 12–13.

22. Fink, *Workingmen's Democracy*, p. 223.

23. The immediate impetus may have been the reluctance of sixty newly recruited German contract laborers to work longer than ten-hour days. They refused to work, broke their contracts, were arrested, and sued by the lumbermen. Although the lumbermen received no legal satisfaction, the militancy of the new workers may have given Cook, DeLong, and other mill hands the incentive they needed to pursue the ten-hour day.

24. *Muskegon Journal*, October 11, 1881.

25. See *Muskegon Daily Chronicle*, October 12 and 10, 1881.

26. Ibid., October 10, 1881; and Fink, *Workingmen's Democracy*, pp. 14, 221–22. This alliance can be seen in the different representative assemblies in Muskegon. Between 1882 and 1886 there were thirteen LAs, including skilled, "Sawmill Operators," "Boom men," "Lumber Inspectors," "Longshoremen," and one "German" LA. In the lumber occupations, Muskegon had more skilled Local Assemblies than either Bay City or Saginaw. See Garlock, *Guide to Local Assemblies*, pp. 208–23.

27. *Muskegon Daily Chronicle*, October 13, 1881.

28. Ibid.

29. Ibid., October 17, 1881.

30. Of the thirty-five sawmills in Muskegon, twenty-three reopened, sixteen on ten-hour schedule and seven working eleven hours. The remaining mills closed for the season. *Muskegon Daily Chronicle*, October 25, 1881.

31. *Muskegon Reporter*, March 11 and 15, 1882.

32. The *Muskegon News and Reporter* came out foresquare for the "Citizen's Ticket" (April 1, 1882). The *Muskegon Daily Chronicle* remained neutral during the campaign (April 1–4, 1882).

33. *Muskegon Daily Chronicle*, April 7, 1882.

34. See *Muskegon Daily Chronicle*, April 12, 1882. The *Chronicle* emphasized that most boom men were young men who "did not really come to Muskegon to work."

35. Hackley to A. R. Colburn & Co., Michigan City, Indiana, April 7, 1882. Hackley Papers, Michigan State University, East Lansing.

36. The workers' wrath focused on Newcomb McGraft, owner of the McGraft and Montgomery mill at Lakeside. On April 11 two strikers entered McGraft's mill and tried to persuade the few workers still employed to join the strike. After a violent exchange, during which both McGraft and one of the strikers rolled down a flight of stairs fighting, McGraft drew his pistol and chased the men from the pre-

mises by firing in the air. The strikers returned to town and incited a large rally where McGraft was threatened and hanged in effigy. The strikers' next petition to the boom company demanded McGraft's resignation as president of the boom and blamed him personally for the intransigence of the lumbermen. The company refused to accept McGraft's resignation.

37. *Muskegon Chronicle, Romance of Muskegon*, p. xcvii.

38. *Muskegon Daily Chronicle*, April 27, 1882.

39. *Muskegon News and Reporter*, May 24, 1882. Governor David Jerome was a Saginaw lumberman.

40. See *Muskegon Daily Chronicle*, May 18; May 7; and May 10, 1882.

41. In 1883 DeLong won a close election by a twenty-six-vote margin.

42. See *Muskegon Daily Chronicle*, April 16, 1884.

43. Ibid., May 29, 1882; and February 19, 1928.

44. Ibid., April 20, 1883.

45. Paternalism is an important but much neglected subject in nineteenth-century urban history. Anthony Wallace showed a more intimate paternalism in *Rockdale: The Growth of an American Village in the Early Industrial Revolution* (New York: Knopf, 1975), and Eller's *Miners and Millhands* comments extensively on paternalism in the Appalachian South, pp. 204–37. The view of paternalism and entrepreneurial democracy expressed herein is taken in part from Helena Flam's "Democracy in Debt: Credit and Politics in Paterson, N.J., 1890–1930," *Journal of Social History* 18 (spring 1985): 445–48.

46. Characteristics of cross-class community may be found in Fink, *Workingmen's Democracy*, p. 223; and Flam, "Democracy in Debt," p. 45. The rise of the working class into civic government is documented in Dawley, *Class and Community*, pp. 216–19; and Harvey Boulay's study of five New England industrial cities, *The Twilight Cities*, pp. 40–45.

47. The 1885 strike in the Saginaw Valley was the longest strike to date in Michigan and is considered by one labor historian to have been "the most important strike in nineteenth century Michigan history." See McLaughlin, *Michigan Labor*, p. 30.

48. Ninety-four saw and shingle mills in Bay City–Saginaw employed 6,675 mill hands; eighteen planing mills employed 701 laborers. See *Third Annual Report*, p. 220; and tables 3 and 5, pp. 120, 121, 123.

49. Ibid., pp. 103 and 125. The nationwide depression that began in 1884 affected the price and production of Saginaw Valley lumber. Production in 1884 by July 1 was 281 million board feet; in 1885, during the same period before the strike, the figure had fallen to 248 million. The decline in production sent wages and prices downward. See *Bay City Evening Press*, July 1, 1885.

50. The petition is reprinted in *Third Annual Report*, p. 106.

51. Goodstein, "Labor Relations in the Saginaw Valley," p. 213.

52. Thomas Barry, the leader of the strike in the Saginaw Valley, was a state representative who authored the original ten-hour bill. Barry was born in Cohoes, New York, in 1852, where he started work at the age of eight. He later moved to Cleveland and worked as an ax maker. He was fired in 1882 for taking part in a strike and moved to East Saginaw. Barry worked there as an ax maker until his labor activities were discovered, and he was fired in 1884. In that same year he ran

for, and was elected to, the state house. See Detroit *Labor Leaf*, August 12, 1885. The entire ten-hour law is reprinted in the *Journal of United Labor* (Pittsburgh, Penn.), September 25, 1885.

53. *Third Annual Report*, p. 93.

54. The three men arrested were Jacob Frenski for assaulting a drayman and Godfrey Schultz and Joseph Genoski for assaulting a policeman. See *Bay City Evening Press*, July 8, 1885.

55. *Saginaw Courier*, July 7, 1885.

56. *Bay City Evening Press*, July 15, 1885.

57. Considering the fragments of his speeches and writings presented in other newspapers, Blinn displayed some socialist tendencies; however, a definitive conclusion cannot be made for no copies of the *Labor Vindicator* are available.

58. *Third Annual Report*, p. 95; *Saginaw Evening News*, July 14, 1885; and *Alpena Labor Journal*, July 18, 1883.

59. *Bay City Evening Press*, July 11, 1885; *Third Annual Report*, p. 94; and Detroit *Labor Leaf*, July 15, 1885.

60. These conclusions are drawn from names appearing on arrest records and representative committees of workers. See *Saginaw Evening News*, August 13, 1885; *Bay City Evening Press*, July 11, 12, 15, 1885.

61. *Third Annual Report*, p. 105; and Detroit *Labor Leaf*, July 8, 1885.

62. *Third Annual Report*, p. 102.

63. Garlock, *Guide to Local Assemblies*, pp. 208–9, 222–23.

64. Glazer, "Labor and Agrarian Movements in Michigan, 1876–1896," p. 96. This assumption can also be found in Goodstein, "Labor Relations in the Saginaw Valley," p. 212.

65. *Bay City Evening Press*, July 12; *Saginaw Evening News*, July 16, 1885.

66. *Third Annual Report*, p. 103; and *Bay City Evening Press*, July 11, 1885.

67. Sage to H. W. Sage and Co., July 9 and 10, 1885, quoted in Goodstein, *Biography of a Businessman*, p. 88.

68. *Bay City Evening Press*, July 13, 1885. There is some disagreement about the date of the Pinkertons' arrival. The Bay City sheriff reported it as Sunday morning.

69. Ibid., July 12 and 13, 1885. Later the Knights admitted a willingness to guard only those mills working ten hours and paying old wages.

70. Sage to H. W. Sage and Co., July 11, 1885, quoted in Goodstein, *Biography of a Businessman*, , p. 89.

71. *Third Annual Report*, p. 101; and *Bay City Evening Press*, July 12, 1885.

72. *Third Annual Report*, pp. 100–101.

73. Alger to J. R. Mulliken, January 4, 1886, Russell Alger Papers, Clements Library, University of Michigan, Ann Arbor.

74. Blinn and Barry were arrested under Michigan's Baker Conspiracy Law, which prohibited conspiring to interfere in the regular operations of business. Francis Cook of Muskegon represented Barry at the latter's trial. See Detroit *Labor Leaf*, August 26, 1885; also *Saginaw Daily News*, October 30, 1949.

75. *Bay City Evening Press*, July 15, 1885; and *Alpena Labor Journal*, July 25, 1885.

76. *Bay City Evening Press*, July 26, 1885.

77. Catton, *Michigan*, p. 155; and Robert Warner and C. Warren Vanderhill, eds., *Michigan Reader, 1865 to the Present* (Grand Rapids: Eerdmans Publishing Co., 1974), pp. 65–66; and *Saginaw Daily News*, October 30, 1949.

78. *Bay City Evening Press*, July 25, 1885.

79. *Saginaw Evening News*, July 16, 1885.

80. Alger's activities presaged practices that Helena Flam indicated became widespread during and immediately after World War I in Eastern industrial cities as business and political leaders began to use extra-legal means to suppress dissent and unions. See Flam, "Democracy in Debt," pp. 445–47.

81. *Saginaw Evening News*, July 23, 1885.

82. At a general meeting of the Knights on July 25, Barry warned that logs were piling up at the Tittabawasse booming grounds and beginning to dam the river. Water was overflowing onto valuable agricultural lands south of the Saginaws. This threatened crops, incensed farmers, and turned many otherwise sympathetic citizens against the strike. See *Saginaw Evening News*, July 25, 1885.

83. See *Third Annual Report*, p. 108; McLaughlin, *Michigan Labor*, p. 47, and *Saginaw Evening News*, July 30, 1885. Powderly's advice may also have undermined Barry's leadership and inaugurated the fierce dislike Barry was soon to have of the Grand Master. In 1889 Barry wrote, "I have learned to actively hate this man Powderly, and I have sworn to drive him out of the labor movement." Barry to Joseph Labadie, East Saginaw, February 5, 1889, Labadie Collection, Hatcher Graduate Library, University of Michigan, Ann Arbor.

84. *Bay City Evening Press*, July 15, 1885; and Detroit *Labor Leaf*, July 29, 1885.

85. *Saginaw Evening News*, August 6, 1885; *Bay City Evening Press*, August 12, 1885.

86. Detroit *Labor Leaf*, October 7, 1885.

87. *Saginaw Evening News*, August 7, 1885; and Detroit *Labor Leaf*, October 14, 1885.

88. Sage to H. W. Sage and Co., August 15, 1885, quoted in Goodstein, "Labor Relations in the Saginaw Valley," p. 218.

89. See Fink, *Workingmen's Democracy*, pp. 221–24; and Rosenzweig, *Eight Hours for What We Will*, pp. 30–31.

90. See Dawley, *Class and Community*, pp. 235, 216–18; Boulay, *Twilight Cities*, pp. 29–55; and David Montgomery, "Gutman's Nineteenth Century America," *Labor History* 19 (summer 1979): 416–29.

91. See Hollingsworth and Hollingsworth, *Dimensions in Urban History*, pp. 22–23.

CHAPTER 8. END OF THE WHITE PINE ERA

1. See Joseph A. Schumpeter, "The Creative Response in Economic History," *The Journal of Economic History* 7 (November 1947): 150.

2. Catton, *Michigan: A Bicentennial History*, p. 102.

3. *Muskegon Chronicle*, "Romance of Muskegon," p. cxxix. See *Bay City Tribune*, August 29, 1903; and *The Timberman* (Chicago), April 11, 1891; also *Muskegon Daily Chronicle*, November 1, 6, 1890; and January 12, 1891.

4. In 1894 the Wilson-Gorman Tariff put a $2.00 duty on lumber imported from Canada. This was primarily legislated in the interest of the lumbermen in Wisconsin and Minnesota and the far West who did not want Michigan competi-

tion to continue based on imported Canadian logs. The Canadian government soon rang the death knell for Michigan logging by prohibiting the export of boom sticks and logs unless they were first processed in Canada. Thus, many Saginaw Bay lumbermen moved their operations to Canada. See Robert C. Johnson, "Logs for Saginaw: An Episode in Canadian American Tariff Relations," *Michigan History* 34 (September 1950): 213–23.

5. U.S. Census Office, *Twelfth Census of the United States, 1900, Population,* vol. 1 (Washington: U.S. Census Office, 1901), pp. 850–904.

6. These conclusions were arrived at using *City Directories* for the 1890s in Saginaw and Bay City and tracing shifts in housing patterns. Many Germans in Saginaw's old Germania section began to move to Saginaw's west side and into new housing tracts.

7. W. Carpenter, "The Story of a Log" (manuscript, Hackley Public Library, Muskegon), p. 7. U.S. Census, *Twelfth Census of U.S., 1900,* pp. 850–904; U.S. Census Office, *Thirteenth Census of U.S., Population,* vol. 2 (Washington GPO, 1913), pp. 932–43; and Kilar, "Black Pioneers in the Michigan Lumber Industry," pp. 143–49.

8. Similar changes taking place in a declining one-industry town are seen in Lantz, *People of Coal Town.*

9. *Bay City Tribune,* April 3, 1888. Although many of the saloons closed, prostitution and associated vice remained common in Bay City, at least until federal pressure by the Council of Hygiene prompted cleanup; see Julie Rinehart, "The Belles of Bay City Beckoned" (student paper, Delta College Library, University Center, Michigan), pp. 14–15.

10. Accounts of the fires can be read in *Muskegon Chronicle,* "Romance of Muskegon," p. cxxxvi; Butterfield, *Bay County Past and Present,* pp. 178–79; and Gross, *Saginaw: History of the Land and the City,* p. 55.

11. See *Muskegon Weekly Chronicle,* April 7, 1887; April 4, 1889; April 7, 1892; and April 10, 1884.

12. For comparison see Smith, "Movements for Diversified Industry in Eau Claire," chap. 4; and Hollingsworth and Hollingsworth, *Dimensions in Urban History,* p. 72.

13. *Muskegon Weekly Chronicle,* April 7, 1887, and April 9, 1891.

14. Ibid., April 6, 1893.

15. Ibid. This pattern in Muskegon reflects the Hollingsworths' description of the small "autocratic" community where, when political and economic elites overlap, official decisions are often reflective of the private interests of public officials. See Hollingsworth and Hollingsworth, *Dimensions in Urban History,* p. 15.

16. *Muskegon Chronicle,* "Romance of Muskegon," p. cxxxviii.

17. Dawley, *Class and Community,* pp. 219, 235. In 1887, though, the labor movement could not muster enough support to elect Nelson DeLong circuit judge on a fusion ticket. See *Muskegon Weekly Chronicle,* April 7, 1887.

18. Glasgow, *Muskegon,* pp. 78–79. See also Daniel J. Walkowitz, *Worker City, Company Town: Iron and Cotton Protest in Troy and Cohoes, New York, 1855–84* (Urbana: University of Illinois Press, 1978), p. 170.

19. See Paul Kleppner, *The Cross of Culture* (New York: The Free Press, 1970), pp. 69–91, for a more detailed discussion of religious and ethnic values affecting political participation. *Muskegon Weekly Chronicle,* April 10, 1884; April 7, 1887.

20. Lumberman Lyman Bliss was mayor of Saginaw City in 1888–90.

21. See *Saginaw Evening News*, April 3, 1894.

22. Ibid., March 24, 1894.

23. Ibid., April 4–9, 1902.

24. Ibid., April 5, 1887; April 8, 1891; April 7, 1896.

25. Ibid., April 3, 1894.

26. *Bay City Tribune,* April 7, 1887.

27. Ibid., April 2, 1895.

28. See Catherine Baker, "Mayors of Bay City" (list of mayors in Bay City Public Library).

29. See *Bay City Tribune,* April 3, 1888; April 2, 1889; April 6, 1897; April 5, 1903; and April 2, 1889.

30. In contrast, the Third and First wards voted 153–117 and 115–101 against the city hall project. These wards, where the elite and business interests lived, were the only two to vote against the project. See *Bay City Tribune,* April 2, 1889. Voting tabulations are found in the *Tribune,* April 3, 1888; April 2, 1889; April 6, 1897.

31. *Bay City Tribune,* April 6, 1897.

32. Ibid., special edition, February 25, 1887; and March 25, 1903.

33. Augustus A. Gansser, ed., *History of Bay County, Michigan and Representative Citizens* (Chicago: Richmond and Arnold, 1905), pp. 167–68. This is an excellent "booster" account of consolidation in Bay City.

34. *Bay City Tribune,* March 14, 1903.

35. It was clear to the voters that the money would be used for new industrial development. See *Muskegon Daily Chronicle,* March 16, 1893. Much of the correspondence between the Chamber of Commerce and new industries is collected in the Hackley-Hume Papers, Boxes 56–57, Michigan State University Archives; and John Beukama Papers, Michigan State University Archives, East Lansing.

36. See *Muskegon Morning News,* September 18, 1890.

37. The purchase price was not due until all lots were sold and factories under construction.

38. The Muskegon Heights project not only involved salesmanship and industrial growth but also good planning. Building restrictions as to costs and location of each house were enforced. Paved streets, sidewalks, a belt line railroad, and a connecting streetcar line to Muskegon were also planned before settlement.

39. Of the six industrial concerns, three developed into important manufacturing concerns and remained in operation through the Great Depression; they are the Alaska Refrigerator, Shaw-Walker Co., and Morton Manufacturing Co.

40. Glasgow, *Muskegon,* p. 78.

41. Ibid., p. 79.

42. Ibid., pp. 78–79. Hackley wrote D. A. Blodgett of Grand Rapids on October 6, 1891, requesting that one R. Carson be replaced as a scaler at one of Blodgett's camps. Hackley and Hume Papers, Michigan State University, East Lansing.

Bureau of Labor and Industrial Statistics, *Seventh to Twenty-Second Annual Reports,* 1890–1905. Specifically, see *Fifth Annual Report, 1888,* pp. 398–421; *Thirteenth Annual Report, 1896,* pp. 248–69; *Eighteenth Annual Report, 1901,* pp. 242–51; *Nineteenth Annual Report, 1902,* pp. 341–59; *Twentieth Annual Report, 1903,* pp. 331–51; and *Twenty-First Annual Report, 1904,* pp. 158–59.

43. Hackley's contributions are related in two memorial publications: The Hackley Memorial Association, *Charles Henry Hackley: An Appreciation* (Muskegon, 1929); and Haight, *The Life of Charles Henry Hackley.*

44. See Mills, *History of Saginaw,* p. 493. Approximately twenty-five percent of those employed in nonlumbering manufactures were involved in wood manufacturing of some sort.

45. Ibid., p. 494.

46. U.S. Census Office, *Twelfth Census of the United States, 1900,* vol. 2, *Manufactures* (Washington GPO, 1902), p. 413.

47. Mills, *History of Saginaw,* p. 496.

48. *Eleventh Annual Report Issued by the Saginaw Board of Trade and Saginaw Improvement Co.*, 1891, p. 9.

49. Sugar beets were not necessarily a commodity lumbermen were acquainted with, but a state bounty at first guaranteed a profit. Soon, however, so many processing plants were built in the valley that there was no market for Saginaw beet sugar and most factories closed.

The coal industry declined rapidly after 1915 because of an inferior product, and oil was a short-lived speculative venture that failed in 1913.

50. Schumpeter, "The Creative Response in Economic History," pp. 150–51.

51. See n. 42 above.

52. *Eleventh Annual Report,* p. 81. Manahan's success was also envied in Bay City; see *Bay City Tribune,* March 19, 1903.

53. Gansser, *History of Bay County,* pp. 195–220; and Bay City Board of Trade, *Bay City of Today: A City of Industrial Progress* (Bay City: Board of Trade, 1905), pp. 3–4.

54. Several of the largest mills that trailed Sage and McGraw in production but were owned by Bay City residents (G. B. Foss, Eddy Bros., Thomas Cranage, and Eddy, Avery and Eddy) invested outside the city at the end of the lumber era.

55. Schumpeter, "The Creative Response in Economic History," p. 150. It is not difficult to explain Bay City's adaptive response. Schumpeter postulates that entrepreneurial activity has much to do with the quality of personnel available in a society and decisions, actions, and patterns of behavior undertaken by entrepreneurs. According to sociological casting, the Bay City lumbermen were conservative, social Darwinists who operated their lumber interest from distant outposts. They were accustomed to packing up and moving west whenever the logs ran out. There was no reason to continue in Bay City as diversified industrialists. The entrepreneurs were qualified as lumbermen, and as adaptive managers they saw little reason to adjust to new industrial needs.

56. O'Neill, "The History of the Lumber Industry in the Valley of the Saginaw," pp. 19–21.

57. Bureau of Labor and Industrial Statistics, *Fourteenth Annual Report* (Lansing, Mich.: Robert Smith Printing Co.,1897), pp. 380–81.

58. Bay City Board of Trade, *Bay City,* p. 4. A popular belief existed among many businessmen that the unskilled labor of southeastern Europe was not trainable or adaptable to manufacturing. Glasgow in his dissertation on Muskegon (1939) gives credit to the presence of Scandinavian and Dutch immigrants for the city's ability to successfully begin diversified manufacturing. See Glasgow, *Muskegon,* pp. 78–79.

59. *Bay City Tribune*, April 1, 1903.

60. Bay City Board of Trade, *Bay City*, p. 4.

61. U.S. Bureau of Census, *Thirteenth Census of U.S.*, *1910. Abstract of the Census, with Supplement for Michigan* (Washington GPO, 1913), pp. 681–82.

62. *Muskegon Chronicle, Romance of Muskegon*, p. clvi.

63. Glasgow, *Muskegon*, p. 74.

64. *Muskegon Chronicle, Romance of Muskegon*, p. clvi.

65. Muskegon *Morning News*, March 12, 1903.

66. In Mills's thorough discussion of new industries in Saginaw in 1918, he gave only scant attention to the auto industry and said nothing, in comparison, to other industries about the potential for its success. Mills, *History of Saginaw*, pp. 460–510.

67. Ibid., p. 498.

68. Jackson & Church began as a small company producing steam engines to run gang saws. One of the co-founders of Valley Grey Iron was Edward Mershon, a lumber manufacturer.

69. Haight, *Hackley*, p. 84.

70. Catton, *Michigan*, p. 178.

CHAPTER 9. CONCLUSION

1. Oliver P. Williams and Charles R. Adrian, *Four Cities: A Study in Comparative Policy Making* (Philadelphia: University of Pennsylvania Press, 1963), p. 11. My attention was drawn to Williams and Adrian's book during an oral interview late in my research (May 14, 1986) with Ira Butterfield, a retired probate judge in Bay City. Judge Butterfield, after considerable discussion about Bay City, casually mentioned the book and identified the four cities. The Williams-Adrian study was an exciting discovery. It was a modern-day reaffirmation of the lumbertowns' historic characteristics described throughout my study. Because the four cities are never identified in the Williams-Adrian book, traditional bibliographical references do not mention it. I later confirmed these observations and the identity of the four cities in a long telephone conversation with Charles Adrian at Riverside, California, February 12, 1988.

2. Williams and Adrian, *Four Cities*, pp. 314, 276, and 73.

3. Ibid., pp. 277, 294, and 75.

4. Ibid., pp. 277–78.

Selected Bibliography

PRIMARY SOURCES

Public Documents

Annual Report to the Bay City Board of Police Commissioners: 1883–89; 1891–93.

Bay City Board of Trade. *Bay City Today: A City of Commercial and Industrial Progress.* Bay City: Board of Trade, 1905.

Bay City Directory: 1870–1895. Yearly editions. Detroit: R. L. Polk & Co., 1870–95.

Charter of the City of East Saginaw, Compiled by Order of the Common Council. East Saginaw: n.p., 1869, 1885.

East Saginaw City Directory, 1870–1889. Yearly editions.

Michigan. *Census and Statistics of the State of Michigan: 1864.* Lansing: John A. Kerr & Co., 1865.

Michigan. *Census of the State of Michigan: 1874.* Lansing: W. S. George and Co., 1875.

Michigan. *Census of the State of Michigan: 1884.* 2 vols. Lansing: Thorp and Godfrey, 1886.

Michigan. *Census of the State of Michigan: 1894.* 2 vols. Lansing: Robert Smith and Co., 1896.

Michigan. *Census of the State of Michigan: 1904.* 2 vols. Lansing: Wynkopp Hallenbeck Crawford Co., 1906.

Michigan Compiled Laws: 1884. Vol. 4. St. Paul, Minn.: West Publishing, 1885.

Michigan, Department of Labor. *First Annual Report of the Bureau of Labor and Industrial Statistics: 1883.* Lansing: W. S. George & Co., 1884.

Michigan. *Third Annual Report of the Bureau of Labor and Industrial Statistics: 1885.* Lansing: Thorp & Godfrey, 1886.

Michigan. *Fifth Annual Report of the Bureau of Labor and Industrial Statistics: 1887.* Lansing: Thorp & Godfrey, 1888.

Michigan. *Seventh Annual Report of the Bureau of Labor and Industrial Statistics: 1889.* Lansing: David D. Thorp, 1890.

Michigan. *Thirteenth Annual Report of the Bureau of Labor and Industrial Statistics: 1896.* Lansing: Robert Smith Printing Co., 1897.

Michigan. *Fourteenth Annual Report of the Bureau of Labor and Industrial Statistics: 1897.* Lansing: Robert Smith Printing Co., 1898.

Michigan, State Agricultural Society. *Annual Report for 1855.* Lansing: Hasmer and Fitch, 1856.

Muskegon County Directory, 1875–76. Muskegon: R. L. Polk, 1875.

Muskegon City and County Directory, 1880–1900. Detroit: R. L. Polk & Co., 1880–1900.

Saginaw Board of Trade. Saginaw, Michigan. Saginaw: Board of Trade: n.d.

Saginaw City Directory, 1889–1900. Yearly editions. Detroit: R. L. Polk & Co., 1889–1900.

U.S. Census Office. Eighth Census of the United States: 1860. Populations and Manufactures. Washington: Government Printing Office, 1865.

U.S. Census Office. Ninth Census of the United States: 1870. Vols. I and II. Washington: Government Printing Office, 1872.

U.S. Census Office. Tenth Census of the United States: 1880. Population, vol. 1; Manufactures, vol. 2. Washington: Government Printing Office, 1886.

U.S. Census Office. Eleventh Census of the United States: 1890. Compendium on Population, vol. 1; Manufacturing Industries, vol. 2. Washington: Government Printing Office, 1895.

U.S. Census Office. Twelfth Census of the United States: 1900. Population, vols. 1 and 2; Manufactures, vol. 8. Washington: Government Printing Office, 1901, 1902.

U.S. Census Office. Manuscript Census for Bay, Muskegon, and Saginaw counties, 1880, 1890, 1900. Microfilmed copies.

U.S. Department of Interior, Bureau of Land Management, Eastern Division. Tract Books, Michigan N and E and Michigan N and W. Vols. 1–17.

Wines, Frederick H. Report on the Defective, Dependent, and Delinquent Classes . . . Returned to the Tenth Census of the U.S., 1880. Washington: Government Printing Office, 1888.

Newspapers and Trade Journals

Bay City Chronicle, 1871–87, weekly.
Bay City Daily Journal, 1865.
Bay City Daily Tribune, 1873–1916.
Bay City Evening Press, 1879–1891.
Bay City Times, 1884–1900.
Lumberman's Gazette, 1873–1886 (Bay City).
The Muskegon Chronicle, 1869–1900, weekly.
The Muskegon Daily Chronicle, 1880–1906.
Muskegon Enterprise, 1870–1873.
The Muskegon Journal, 1877–1881.
Muskegon Reporter, 1859–1864.
The Muskegon News and Reporter, 1870–1887.
The Saginaw Evening News, 1881–1910.
The Saginaw Courier, 1868–1889.
Saginaw Weekly Courier, 1879–1889.

Manuscript Collections

Alger, Russell A. Papers. Clements Library, University of Michigan, Ann Arbor. Provided some material on the governor's involvement in 1885 lumber strikes through newspaper accounts and clippings.

Birney, James G. Collection. Clements Library, University of Michigan, Ann Arbor. Some notes on early life in Bay City.

Boyce, Jonathan, Lumber Company. Collection. Clarke Historical Collection, Central Michigan University, Mt. Pleasant. Notes on Boyce's operations in Muskegon and Bay City.

Clements, William C. Papers. Clements Library, University of Michigan, Ann Arbor. Some insight into Clements's activities in Bay City at the end of the white pine era, but most material is relating to founding of the library.

Crapo, Henry H. Papers. Michigan Historical Collections, Bentley Library, University of Michigan, Ann Arbor. Extensive personal correspondence, but most is before the heyday of the lumber era. Crapo was a lumberman from Flint.

Dun & Bradstreet Credit Reports for Michigan. Baker Library, Harvard University, Cambridge, Massachusetts. Information on financial status of sawmills and ownership, but best material is before period of research.

Estabrook, John S. Papers. Michigan Historical Collections, Bentley Library, University of Michigan, Ann Arbor. Sketchy material on Saginaw lumberman's operations.

Hotchkiss, Everitt S. Reminiscences. Michigan Historical Collections, Bentley Library, University of Michigan, Ann Arbor. Memories of early Bay City.

Hotchkiss, George W. Autobiography. Michigan Historical Collections, Bentley Library, University of Michigan, Ann Arbor. Thirty-nine-page account experiences in Bay City-Saginaw of the founder of the Lumberman's Gazette.

Immigration Sources Project. Michigan Historical Collections, Bentley Library, University of Michigan, Ann Arbor. Letters, especially those of Dutch settlers, describing life in Michigan.

Labadie, Charles Joseph A. Collection. H. Hatcher Graduate Library, University of Michigan, Ann Arbor. Material on Labadie and the Knights of Labor.

Leech, Carl A. Papers. Michigan Historical Collections, Bentley Library, University of Michigan, Ann Arbor. Leech's research folders contain some materials on Michigan, especially Muskegon, lumbering.

Merrill Lumber Company. Papers. Michigan Historical Collections, Bentley Library, University of Michigan, Ann Arbor. Mostly business records of the large Saginaw operation.

Mershon, William B. Papers. Michigan Historical Collections, Bentley Library, University of Michigan, Ann Arbor. Mostly business records, but letter books provide some evidence of Mershon's personal activities. Valuable for idea of leisure pursuits of lumberman-entrepreneur.

Michigan-California Lumber Company. Records. Michigan Historical Collections, Bentley Library, University of Michigan, Ann Arbor. Business records of Blodgett family who had mills in Muskegon and Saginaw.

Mitchell and McClure Lumber Company. Records. Michigan Historical Collections, Bentley Library, University of Michigan, Ann Arbor. Mostly business records, but W. C. McClure's diary provides some insight into cultural life of lumbermen.

Nelson, Ferdinand. Papers. Michigan Historical Collections, Bentley Library, University of Michigan, Ann Arbor. Three manuscripts on the life of a Swedish immigrant settled in Muskegon.

Torrent, John. Records. Michigan Historical Collections, Bentley Library, University of Michigan, Ann Arbor. Muskegon Lumberman's business records.

Interviews

Butterfield, Ira. May 14, 1986. Bay City, Michigan.
Conifer, Elizabeth. March 1980. Bay City, Michigan. The interviewee did not want her real name used.
Drury, Patricia. November 3, 1983, and subsequent correspondence. University Center, Michigan.

UNPUBLISHED SOURCES

Benson, Barbara S. "Logs and Lumber: The Development of the Lumber Industry in Michigan's Lower Peninsula, 1837–1870." Ph.D. diss., Indiana University, 1976.
Conger, Louis H. "Pioneer Days in Muskegon (covering to 1850)." Manuscript in Hackley Public Library, Muskegon.
Dana, Lowell B. " 'E Pluribus Unum': The Unification of the Muskegon." Manuscript in Hackley Public Library, Muskegon, 1926.
Dustin, Fred. "Saginaw History." Manuscript in Hoyt Public Library, Saginaw, 1949.
Engberg, George Barker. "Labor in the Lake States Lumber Industry, 1830–1930." Ph.D. diss., University of Minnesota, 1949.
Glasgow, James. "Muskegon, Michigan: The Evolution of a Lake Port." Ph.D. diss., University of Chicago, 1939.
Glazer, Sidney. "Labor and Agrarian Movements in Michigan, 1876–1896." Ph.D. diss., University of Michigan, 1932.
Harms, Richard Henry. "Life after Lumbering: Charles Henry Hackley and the Emergence of Muskegon, Michigan." Ph.D. diss., Michigan State University, 1984.
Kilar, Jeremy W. "The Lumbertowns: A Socioeconomic History of Michigan's Leading Lumber Centers: Saginaw, Bay City, and Muskegon, 1870–1905." Ph.D. diss., University of Michigan, 1987.
Krog, Carl. "Marinette: Biography of a Nineteenth-Century Lumbering Town." Ph.D. diss., University of Wisconsin, 1971.
McGaugh, Maurice E. "The Settlement of the Saginaw Basin." Ph.D. diss., University of Chicago, 1950.
McGrath, Roger. "Frontier Violence in the Trans-Sierra West." Ph.D. diss., University of California at Los Angeles, 1978.
O'Neill, John. "History of the Lumber Industry in the Valley of Saginaw: Social Effect of Cheap Labor." Manuscript, Bay City Historical Society, 1932.
Ostafin, Peter A. "Polish Peasants in Transition." Ph.D. diss., University of Michigan, 1954.
Rogers, David L. "The Lumberman's Gazette, America's First Lumber Journal." M.A. thesis, Michigan State University, 1973.
Ryskamp, Henry. "The Dutch in West Michigan." Ph.D. diss., University of Michigan, 1935.

Sanford, Ambroasia. "Extracts from Letters Written by Mrs. Samuel R. Sanford, 1858–1862." Manuscript, Hackley Public Library, Muskegon.

Smith, James Bruce. "The Movements for Diversified Industry in Eau Clare, Wisconsin, 1879–1907: Boosterism and Urban Development Strategy in a Declining Lumber Town." M.A. thesis, University of Wisconsin, 1967.

———. "Lumbertowns in the Cutover: A Comparative Study of the Stage Hypothesis of Urban Growth." Ph.D. diss., University of Wisconsin, 1973.

Wheeler, Harold L. "Stage Coach and Iron Horse in Muskegon." Manuscript, Hackley Public Library, Muskegon, n.d.

Yakes, Daniel J. "Ten Hours or No Sawdust: A Study of Strikes in the Michigan Lumber Industry, 1881–1885." M.A. thesis, Western Michigan University, 1969.

SECONDARY SOURCES

General Works

Allen, Clifford, and Titus, Harold. Michigan Log Marks. East Lansing: Works Progress Administration, 1942.

Blackburn, George M., and Ricards, Sherman L. "A Demographic History of the West: Manistee County, Michigan, 1860." Journal of American History 57 (December 1970): 600–618.

Blois, John T. Gazetteer of the State of Michigan. Detroit: Sydney L. Rood and Co., 1840.

Bodnar, John. The Transplanted: A History of Immigrants in Urban America. Bloomington: Indiana University Press, 1985.

Bohn, Frank, P. "This Was the Forest Primeval." Michigan History 21 (Winter-Spring 1937), 23–31.

Boulay, Harvey. The Twilight Cities: Political Conflict, Development, and Decay in Five Communities. Port Washington, N.Y.: Associated Faculty Press, Inc., 1983.

Brinkes, Herbert. "The Effects of the Civil War in 1861 on Michigan Lumbering and Mining Industries." Michigan History 44 (1940): 102–6.

Catton, Bruce. Michigan: A History. New York: Norton Company, 1976.

Chudacoff, Howard P. Mobile Americans: Residential and Social Mobility in Omaha, 1880–1920. New York: Oxford University Press, 1972.

Clark, Norman. Mill Town: A Social History of Everett, Washington. Seattle, University of Washington Press, 1970.

Compton, Wilson. The Organization of the Lumber Industry: With Special Reference to the Influences Determining the Prices of Lumber in the United States. Chicago: American Lumberman, 1916.

Conlin, Joseph R. "Food in Logging Camps." Encyclopedia of Forest and Conservation History, vol. 1. New York: Macmillan Company, 1983.

———. "Oh Boy, Did You Get Enough of Pie?" Journal of Forest History 23 (October 1979): 164–85.

Dawley, Alan. Class and Community: The Industrial Revolution in Lynn. Cambridge: Harvard University Press, 1976.

de Beaumont, Gustave. *Marie; or Slavery in the United States: A Novel of Jacksonian America.* Trans. Barbara Chapman. Stanford, Calif.: Stanford University Press, 1958.

Defebaugh, James E. *History of Lumber Industry of America.* Chicago: American Lumberman, 1906.

Dodge, Roy L. *Ticket to Hell: A Saga of Michigan's Bad Men.* Tawas City, Mich.: Northeastern Printers Inc., 1975.

Doyle, Don Harrison. *The Social Order of a Frontier Community: Jacksonville, Illinois, 1827-1870.* Urbana: University of Illinois Press, 1978.

Dykstra, Robert. *The Cattle Towns.* New York: Knopf, 1968.

Farmer, Silas. *The History of Detroit and Michigan.* 2 vols. Detroit: Silas Farmer & Co., 1889.

Fink, Leon. *Workingmen's Democracy: The Knights of Labor and American Politics.* Urbana: University of Illinois Press, 1983.

Fitzmaurice, John. *The Shanty Boy or Life in a Lumber Camp.* Reprint of 1889 edition. Ann Arbor: Historical Society of Michigan, 1978.

Flader, Susan L., ed. *The Great Lakes Forest.* Santa Cruz, Calif.: Forest History Society, 1983.

Flam, Helena. "Democracy in Debt: Credit and Politics in Paterson, N.J., 1890–1930." *Journal of Social History* 18 (Spring 1985): 439–62.

Folsom, Burton W., Jr. *Urban Capitalists, Entrepreneurs, and City Growth in Pennsylvania's Lackawanna and Lehigh Regions, 1800–1920.* Baltimore: Johns Hopkins Press, 1981.

Fuller, George N. *Economic and Social Beginnings of Michigan.* Lansing: 1916.

——— . *Geological Reports of Douglas Houghton, First State Geologist of Michigan, 1835–1843.* Lansing: Michigan Historical Commission, 1928.

——— . *Historic Michigan.* Chicago: Lewis Publishing Co., 1939.

——— . *Michigan: A Centennial History of the State and its People.* 2 vols. Chicago: Lewis Publishing Co., 1939.

Gordon, Douglas H., and May, George S. "The Michigan Land Rush in 1836." *Michigan History* 43 (March 1959): 7–14.

Haeger, John D. *The Investment Frontier: New York Businessmen and the Economic Development of the Old Northwest.* Albany: State University of New York Press, 1981.

Hershberg, Theodore, ed. *Philadelphia Work, Space, Family, and Group Experiences in the Nineteenth Century.* Oxford: Oxford University Press, 1981.

Holbrook, Stewart H. *Holy Old Mackinaw.* New York: Macmillan and Co., 1938.

Hollen, Eugene. *Frontier Violence: Another Look.* New York: Oxford, 1974.

Hollingsworth, J. Rogers, and Hollingsworth, Ellen Jane. *Dimensions in Urban History: Historical and Social Science Perspectives in Middle-Size American Cities.* Madison: University of Wisconsin Press, 1979.

Hotchkiss, George W. *History of the Lumber and Forest Industry of the Northwest.* Chicago: G. W. Hotchkiss & Co., 1898.

Jackson, Kenneth T., and Schultz, Stanley K. *Cities in American History.* New York: Alfred A. Knopf, 1972.

Jay, Charles W. *My New Home in Northern Michigan and Other Tales.* Trenton, N.J.: W. S. and E. W. Sharp, 1874.

Jenks, William L. "Michigan Immigration." *Michigan History* 28 (1944): 67–110.

Jensen, Vernon H. *Lumber and Labor.* New York: Farrar and Rinehart, Inc., 1945.

Jordan, Phillip D. *Frontier Law and Order: Ten Essays.* Lincoln: University of Nebraska Press, 1965.

Kilar, Jeremy W. "Black Pioneers in the Michigan Lumber Industry." *Journal of Forest History* 24 (July 1980): 143–49.

————. "Community and Authority Response to the Saginaw Valley Lumber Strike, 1885." *Journal of Forest History* 20 (April 1976): 67–79.

————. "Law and Order in Lumber Camps and Towns." *Encyclopedia of Forest and Conservation History,* vol. 1. New York: Macmillan Company, 1983.

Kirk, Gordon W., Jr. *The Promise of American Life: Social Mobility in a Nineteenth Century Immigrant Community, Holland, Michigan, 1847–1894.* Philadelphia: American Philosophical Society, 1978.

Kuhn, Madison. "Tiffin, Morse, and the Reluctant Pioneer." *Michigan History* 50 (June 1966): 111–38.

Lantz, Herman R. *People of Coal Town.* New York: Columbia University Press, 1958.

Lavender, David. "This Wondrous Town, This Instant City." *The American West* 4 (August 1967): 4–14.

Lucia, Ellis. "Review of *The Loggers,* by Time-Life Books with text by Richard L. Williams." *Journal of Forest History* 20 (July 1976): 159.

Martin, C. *Whiskey and Wild Women.* New York: Doubleday & Co., 1958.

Maybee, Rolland H. *Michigan's White Pine Era, 1940–1900.* Lansing: Michigan Historical Commission, 1960.

Miller, Nyle H., and Snell, Joseph W. *The Great Gunfighters of the Kansas Cowtowns, 1867–1886.* Lincoln: University of Nebraska Press, 1963.

Nolan, Herbert. *In Memory of the Camp Sixteeners.* Reprint of 1934 ed. Sanford Mich.: Sanford Historical Society, 1970.

Paul, Rodman W. *Mining Frontiers of the Far West, 1848–1888.* New York: Holt, Rinehart & Winston, 1963.

Perrigo, Lynn I. "Law and Order in Early Colorado Camps." *Mississippi Valley Historical Review* 28 (June 1941): 56–61.

Peters, Bernard C. "The Remaking of an Image: The Propaganda Campaign to Attract Settlers to Michigan, 1815–1840." *The Geographic Survey* 3 (January 1974): 25–52.

Pierson, George Wilson. *Tocqueville and Beaumont in America.* New York: Oxford University Press, 1938.

Rector, William G. *Log Transportation in the Lake States Lumber Industry, 1840–1918.* Glendale, Calif.: The Arthur H. Clark Co., 1953.

Rosenzweig, Roy. *Eight Hours for What We Will: Workers and Leisure in an Industrial City, 1870–1920.* Cambridge: Cambridge University Press, 1983.

Russo, David J. *Families and Communities: A New View of American History.* Nashville, Tenn.: American Association for State and Local History, 1974.

Schmaltz, Norman J. "The Land Nobody Wanted: The Dilemma of Michigan's Cutover Lands." *Michigan History* 67 (January–February 1983), 32–40.

Titus, Harold. "The Land Nobody Wanted: The Story of Michigan's Public Domain." *Michigan Agricultural Experimental Station Bulletin,* no. 332 (April 1945): 10–11.

Vanderhill, Warren C. *Settling the Great Lakes Frontier: Immigration to Michigan, 1837–1924.* Lansing: Michigan Historical Commission, 1970.

Weber, Adna F. *The Growth of the City in the Nineteenth Century: A Study in Statistics.* New York: The Macmillan Co., 1899.

Wells, Robert. *Daylight in the Swamp.* Garden City, N.J.: Doubleday, 1978.

Wilentz, Sean. *Chants Democratic: New York City and the Rise of the American Working Class, 1788–1850.* New York: Oxford University Press, 1984.

Woodford, Frank B. *Lewis Cass: The Last Jeffersonian.* New Brunswick, N.J.: Rutgers University Press, 1950.

Zunz, Olivier. *The Changing Face of Inequality: Urbanization, Industrial Development, and Immigrants in Detroit, 1880–1920.* Chicago: University of Chicago Press, 1982.

Bay City

Arndt, Les. *By These Waters.* Bay City: Bay City Times, 1976.

Butterfield, George M. *Bay County Past and Present.* Centennial Edition. Bay City: Board of Education, 1957.

Dow, H. S. *The History, Commercial Advantages, and Future Prospects of Bay City, Michigan.* Bay City: n.p., 1875.

Gansser, Augustus A., ed. *History of Bay County, Michigan, and Representative Citizens.* Chicago: Richmond and Arnold, 1905.

Goodstein, Anita Shafer. *Biography of a Businessman: Henry W. Sage, 1814–1897.* Ithaca, N.Y.: Cornell University Press, 1962.

Hargreaves, Irene M., and Foehl, Harold M. *The Story of Logging the White Pine in the Saginaw Valley.* Bay City: Red Keg Press, 1964.

History of Bay County, Michigan. Chicago: H. R. Page & Co., 1883.

Muskegon

Anatomy of a Community: Characteristics of the People of Muskegon County Area. Muskegon: Civic Affairs Research, Inc., 1968.

Cronenwett, Wilson R. "Charles Hackley: Muskegon Lumber Baron Benefactor." *Chronicle, Magazine of the Historical Society of Michigan* 15 (Spring 1979): 16–19.

Dana, Edward B. "Muskegon 50 Years Ago." *Michigan History* 16 (Autumn 1932): 413–21.

Hackley Memorial Association. *Charles Henry Hackley: An Appreciation.* Muskegon: Hackley Memorial Association, 1929.

Haight, Louis P. *The Life of Charles Henry Hackley.* Muskegon: Dana Printing Co., 1948.

Harford, W. M. *Muskegon and Its Resources.* Muskegon: Harford & Latimer, 1884.

Hauser, H. L., ed. *Headlight Flashes along the Grand Trunk Railway System, Muskegon, Michigan.* Chicago: Chicago Railroad Publishing Co., 1897.

History of Muskegon County, Michigan. Chicago: H. R. Page & Co., 1882.

Holt, Henry. "The Centennial History of Muskegon." In *Muskegon County Pioneer and Historical Society Annual for 1887.* Muskegon: Chronicle Printing and Binding House, 1887.

Lewis, Albert Walker. *Greater Muskegon: Its Importance as a Manufacturing Center.* n.p., 1911.

Muskegon Chamber of Commerce. *Muskegon, Michigan: A Booklet Descriptive of the City as an Industrial Center.* Muskegon: Chamber of Commerce, 1916.

Muskegon Chronicle. Romance of Muskegon, Michigan, 1937 Centennial Edition. Muskegon: *Muskegon Chronicle,* 1937.

Portrait and Biographical Record of Muskegon and Ottawa Counties, Michigan. Chicago: Biographical Publishing Co., 1893.

Read, Frederick. *A Long Look at Muskegon: The First Two Hundred Years in Muskegon.* Benton Harbor, Mich.: Patterson College Publications, 1976.

Steketee, Cornelius. "Hollanders in Muskegon, 1850–1897." *Michigan History* 31 (December 1847).

Yakes, Daniel J., and Hornstein, Hugh A. *The Many Lives of Muskegon.* Muskegon: Muskegon Community College, 1979.

Saginaw

Bates, W. R. *The History, Commercial Advantages, and Future Prospects of Saginaw.* East Saginaw: n.p., 1874.

Bush, George. *Wide World of Wickes.* New York: McGraw-Hill, 1976.

Coats, Freeman. *Diary of a Department: A History of the Saginaw Police Department.* Saginaw Public Libraries, 1965.

Crane, Caroline Bartlett. *A Sanitary Survey of Saginaw Michigan.* Saginaw: n.p., 1911.

Cummings, John. "Little Jake: Saginaw's Merchandising Giant." *Chronicle: Magazine of the History Society of Michigan* 14 (Summer 1978): 19–22.

Dustin, Fred. "The Treaty of Saginaw, 1819." *Michigan History* 4 (1920): 265–80.

Emery, Frank. "Fort Saginaw." *Michigan History* 30 (July–September 1946): 476–503.

Garner, Burt. "A Notable United States Military Road." *Michigan History* 20 (1936): 177–84.

Gross, Stuart D. *Saginaw: A History of the Land and the City.* Woodland Hills, Calif.: Windsor Publications, 1980.

Kilar, Jeremy W. "Tocqueville's Companion Traveler, Gustave de Beaumont and the Journey into the Michigan Wilderness in 1831." *Michigan History* 68 (January–February 1984): 34–39.

Lewis, George F., and Headley, C. B. *Annual Statement of the Business of Saginaw Valley and "The Shore" for 1868.* East Saginaw: n.p., 1869.

Mills, James Cooke. *History of Saginaw County, Michigan.* Saginaw: Seeman & Peters, 1918.

Mitchell, W. K. *Bicentennial History of Saginaw County.* Saginaw: n.p., 1976.

Stroebel, Ralph W. *Saginaw Treaty Sesquicentennial.* Saginaw: Saginaw Treaty Sesquicentennial, Inc., 1965.

Williams, E. S. "Personal Reminiscences of Ephraim S. Williams." *Michigan Pioneer and Historical Society Historical Collections* 8 (1884): 244–61.

Index

Absentee owners and ownership, 100, 161–63, 324 n. 13; in Bay City, 42, 209, 287–88, 302; and city loyalty, 156; and lumbermen, 84–85, 137–38, 144–45, 159; and politics, 267; in postlumber era, 288–90; residence of, Table 7, 144–45; in Saginaw-Bay City (1885), 243–45
Adrian, Charles R., 297–300
Alaska Refrigerator Company (Norge), 281
Alger, Governor Russell A., 237–40, 243
Allardt, Max H., 99, 179
Allen, Andrew B., 225
American Fur Company (Muskegon), 43
Andre, Peter C., 88
Astor House (Bay City), 70
Atwood, William Q., 141, 143
Automobile industry, 292, 294

Baker, James H., 69
Baltzell, E. Digby, 136
Bancroft House Hotel (East Saginaw), 32, 70, 212
Banks (West Bay City), 39, 180, 183
Barry, Thomas: biography of, 337 n. 52; and dislike for Powderly, 339 n. 83; and Saginaw Valley strike (1885), 232–34, 238–46; and ten-hour law, 227
Bay City: absentee ownership in, 42, 209, 287, 302; decline of lumber industry in, 262–65; demographics of, 262; early description of, 39; early development of, 34–39; early sawmills in, 38; ethnic residential patterns in, 179–83; geographical location of, 35; immigrant settlers in, 177, 209–10; investments in,

35–36; labor force in, 189–94; physical development of, 84, 264–65; population of (1860), 39, 208–10; postlumber era politics in, 275–78
Bay City Dredge Works, 294
Bay County, 38–39
Beardsley, Levi, 221
Beecher, Henry Ward, 150
Benson, Barbara, 138, 141
Birney, James G., 36, 38, 39, 57, 95
Birney, James G., Jr., 89
Blacklists, 178, 283
Blacks, 69, 264
Blinn, D. C.: and *Labor Vindicator*, 338 n. 57; and strike in Saginaw Valley (1885), 231–32, 233–35, 238, 244
Bliss, Aaron T., 141, 150, 158, 275, 285–287
Bliss, Lyman, 158–59
Blodgett, D. A., 141
Bluffton, 44, 181, 264. *See also* Muskegon
Boardinghouses, 70–71, 121, 264
Boards of Trade: in Bay City, 287, 289–90; in Muskegon, 281–82, 292; in Saginaw, 274–75
Booming and booming companies: costs of, 60; labor in, 60; legal establishment of, 59–60; log marks, 59; Muskegon Booming Company, 59, 181, 218–19; Tittabawassee Booming Company, 60, 217, 240–41
Boosterism, 97–100
Bousfield Woodenware Company (Bay City), 61, 179, 264
Bradley, H. M., 91
Bradley, Nathan, 159
Brennan, Martin, 212
Brewery Hill (Muskegon), 181
British Fur Company (Muskegon), 43

Populations (*cont.*)
84; in Michigan (1830–37), 20; and
persistence, 329 n. 7; and population pyramids for Muskegon,
Saginaw, and Bay City, 191–94;
in postlumber era, 187–88;
and sources of immigrants,
Table 8, 177
Portsmouth (Bay City), 35–36
Powderly, Terence, 219–21, 241
Prostitution and prostitutes, 73–75,
120–23, 314 n. 46, 319 nn. 25, 27,
340 n. 9

Reindustrialization (in postlumber era),
280–96
Reinmann, Lewis Charles, 135
Reynolds, Dr. Henry A., 152
Riley, John, 36
Ring, Clark L., 285
Rivers, 23–24. *See also specific rivers;*
Waterways and river systems
Roads, 27, 30, 61
Robinson, Jim, 114, 117
Rodgers, Alexander, 63, 90
Rotterdam (Muskegon), 179, 182
Rouse, W. B., 212, 230
Ruddiman, George and John, 48
Rupp, J. J., 285
Russo, David, 14
Rust, Amasa, 60
Rust, Ezra, 287
Ryan, Patrick, 118
Ryerson, Martin, 44, 46, 86; and early
road building, 46–48; as merchant,
68; and salt processing, 57

Sage, Henry W., 38, 40–42, 51, 287;
as absentee owner, 100, 160–62;
and boom companies, 312 n. 23;
closes West Bay City sawmill
(1892), 263; and community
relations, 160–62; and company
housing, 153–54, 257; and early
visit to Bay City (1847), 37–38;
and labor, 213–14; and local taxation, 159–61; and mill in West Bay
City, 42; and politics in West Bay
City, 316 n. 32; and public
improvements, 159–60; and railroads, 89, 315 n. 13; and salt pro-

cessing, 58; as social Darwinist,
150; and strikes, 217–18, 235–36
Saginaw: Board of Trade, 274–75; decline of lumber industry in, 263;
demographics of, 262; ethnic residential patterns in, 178–87; labor
force in, 191–94, 208–11; politics
and city consolidation of (1889),
279; postlumber era politics in,
271–75; visited by Tocqueville
(1831), 19–20. *See also* East Saginaw; Saginaw City
Saginaw and Bay City Salt Company,
58
Saginaw and Grand River canal
(1837), 28–29
Saginaw Bay Company, 36
Saginaw City, 27–30. *See also* East Sag-
inaw; Saginaw
Saginaw County, 27
Saginaw Improvement Company, 284
Saginaw River, 22, 86, 101, 109–10
St. Mary's Hospital (East Saginaw),
94–95
Saloons, 71–75, 120, 122
Salt processing: and Douglas Hough-
ton, 310 n. 35; fails in Muskegon,
57–58; labor and costs of, 57–58;
Michigan Salt Association, 58; as
subsidiary to lumber trade, 39–40,
57–59, 311 n. 10
Salzburg, 39–40, 181
Sanford, Ambrosia, 48
Sawdust Flats, 50, 115, 265
Schultz, Stanley, 15
Schumpeter, Joseph, 285–86, 288
Seligman, Jacob, 68–69, 312 n. 31
Shearer, Mayor George A. (Bay City),
231, 234, 276
Sheldon, E. H., 292
Shipbuilding, 62, 279, 289
Slade, Lewis C., 142
Still, Bayrd, 96
Strikes: and class awareness, 228–29,
245–49; and class awareness in
Muskegon, 224–25, 227; and class
awareness in Saginaw Valley, 231–
32; and local newspapers, 244; and
lumbermen, 227–28; in Muskegon,
218–29; and Pinkertons, 236; and
Poles in Bay City, 239, 241; in
postlumber era Bay City, 288–89; in
Saginaw Valley, 217–18, 229–45;

Jeremy W. Kilar is Professor of American History at Delta College in Michigan. He received the B.A. degree from the University of Detroit, the M.A. degree from Central Michigan University, and the Ph.D. degree from the University of Michigan. He is co-author, with Bradley F. Smith, of *Tobico Marsh: A Story of the Land and the People*; a co-editor of *Poems for the Bicentennial*; and a contributor to Michigan's sesquicentennial history, *Michigan: Visions of Our Past*. His articles on lumbering, violence, and labor unrest in nineteenth-century Michigan have appeared in the *Encyclopedia of Forest and Conservation History*, *Michigan History*, *Journal of Forest History*, *Nebraska History*, and other journals.

The manuscript was edited for publication by Thomas B. Seller. The book was designed by Jim Billingsley. The typeface for the text and the display is Goudy Old Style. The book is printed on 50-lb. Spring Forge paper and is bound in Joanna Arrestox cloth.

Manufactured in the United States of America.